D1458911

LD 39572404

END TO END STUFF

LES SCOTT
END TO END STUFF
THE ESSENTIAL FOOTBALL BOOK

BANTAM PRESS

LONDON • TORONTO • SYDNEY • AUCKLAND • JOHANNESBURG

TRANSWORLD PUBLISHERS
61–63 Uxbridge Road, London W5 5SA
A Random House Group Company
www.rbooks.co.uk

First published in Great Britain
in 2008 by Bantam Press
an imprint of Transworld Publishers

A CIP catalogue record for this book
is available from the British Library.

ISBN 9780593060681

Addresses for Random House Group Ltd companies outside the UK
can be found at: www.randomhouse.co.uk
The Random House Group Ltd Reg. No. 954009

The Random House Group Limited supports The Forest Stewardship
Council (FSC), the leading international forest-certification organization. All our
titles that are printed on Greenpeace-approved FSC-certified paper carry the FSC logo.
Our paper procurement policy can be found at www.rbooks.co.uk/environment

Typeset in 9.75/13pt Scala Sans by
Falcon Oast Graphic Art Ltd.
Printed and bound in Great Britain by
Clays Ltd, Bungay, Suffolk

2 4 6 8 10 9 7 5 3 1

End-to-End Stuff is dedicated to Ken Bolam, Dave Scott and John Turnock who, over the years, have indulged and nurtured my love of the beautiful game – far more than I had any right to expect.

For Jane, Lauren, Ruby and Charley – for everything.

Why do you continue supporting them? They only cause you pain and grief. There is no love that does not pierce the feet.

All the records in *End-to-End Stuff* apply, unless otherwise stated, to British football, and are correct to the end of the 2007–8 season.

Owing to the multiple changes in names of divisions over the past few decades, where possible the name of the division at the time has been used. The Premiership, however, refers to the division, and the Premier League to the governing body.

Contents

Acknowledgements

Very special thanks are due to the following for making this book far better than it might have been: Julian Alexander and all at literary agents Lucas Alexander Whitley; Phillip Dann and Dean Staham; Tommy Docherty; Giles Elliott, Doug Young, Dan Balado and all at Transworld Publishers; Don Mackay, Arthur Montford, Ian Rush, and all players, managers, supporters and officials past and present without whose achievements and antics this would be a very slim volume indeed.

Author's Note

As I have been at pains to stress within these pages, this is not a book of football records and statistics – heaven forbid. *End-to-End Stuff* is, hopefully, an entertaining, informative and fun read whose subject matter is, to my mind, the greatest entertainment of all – football.

While I would like to believe this is the essential football book for genuine lovers of the game, it is by no means intended as a definitive account of stories, facts, anecdotes and the like. Should you, my friend, have a curious tale or fact to tell about your favourite club or player, then I would love to hear of it. Should you contact me via the publishers, I will get back to you. Despite what certain people are attempting to do to our beautiful game, let us continue to celebrate the irreverence and fun of football. Here's hoping you enjoy this book and that you do have fun dipping in and out of its pages. In essence, that was the idea behind its creation.

Les Scott, 2008

All-Rounders

1

 Denis Compton was **the** all-round sportsman. The hero worship I felt then for him cannot be described in fewer than three volumes with footnotes and full index . . . Denis Compton once addressed two words to me, and if you have a long evening to spare I'll give you the full story.

MELVYN BRAGG

Arsenal boast the record as the club with the most players (12) who also played county cricket: Brian Close, Denis and Leslie Compton, George Cox, Ted Drake, Andy Ducat, Joe Hulme, Arthur Milton, Don Roper, Jim Standen, Harry Storer and Ray Swallow. Arsenal chairmen Samuel and Denis Hill-Wood played county cricket too, for Derbyshire. Denis Compton was a dual international in both football and cricket, his brother Leslie played football for England (one cap), and Close, Ducat and Milton represented England at cricket.

Six players who played in the same position, at outside-left, and all for London clubs, also played Test match cricket for England: Les Ames (Clapton Orient), John Arnold (Fulham), Denis Compton (Arsenal), Bill Edrich (Tottenham Hotspur), Laurie Fishlock (Millwall) and Patsy Hendren (Brentford).

In the 1880s, Albert Hornby played football for Blackburn Rovers, cricket for Lancashire, and rugby for Preston Grasshoppers, and captained England at both cricket and rugby.

Alfred Lyttelton played football for Cambridge University and was capped by England against Scotland in 1877. He also represented England at cricket. When his playing days were over he entered politics and became a Cabinet minister in the government of Arthur Balfour (1902–05).

C. B. Fry represented England at football and cricket and, as an athlete, once equalled the world long jump record. He played for Southampton in the 1902 FA Cup Final against Sheffield United. United won the replay 2-1, the winning goal coming from Ernest 'Nudger' Needham who was also a county cricketer, with Derbyshire. Following the FA Cup Final, Fry played cricket for England in the Test series against the touring Australians.

Patsy Hendren played football for Brentford and appeared as full-back for England against Wales in the 'Victory' international at Ninian Park in 1919. Hendren was an outstanding cricketer for Essex and England, scoring 3,525 runs in Test matches at an average of 47.

In the late 1940s, Rochdale's Wally Jones also played a number of matches for Rochdale's rugby league team and, in the summer, turned out for Rochdale Cricket Club.

In addition to being on the books of Arsenal, Leeds United and Bradford City, Brian Close also played football for England Youth. When playing cricket for Yorkshire and England, Close gained a reputation for fielding only a matter of feet from the opposition batsmen. As Fred Trueman said in his autobiography *As It Was*, 'Those folk living around Headingley didn't have to read a newspaper to know the cricket season had started, they used to listen out for the sound of Brian Close being hit with the ball.'

In 1946–47, Eric Houghton was in his 20th season with Aston Villa when, in August, he was called upon to make his first-class debut for Warwickshire against India at Edgbaston.

Nothing doing. In the 1940s, Yorkshireman and inside-forward George Dews was once pressed into action as a goalkeeper when playing for Middlesbrough and kept a clean sheet. He also played county cricket, and in his first three innings for Worcestershire was out for a duck each time.

In the early 1950s, Yorkshire and England cricketer Fred Trueman played for Lincoln City reserves and was good enough to be offered full-time professional terms, but decided to concentrate on a career in cricket.

Joe Payne, who set a Football League record by scoring ten goals for Luton Town in a match against Bristol Rovers, played Minor Counties cricket for Bedfordshire. In 1952 he scored a century for his county in only 90 minutes.

Willie Watson (Huddersfield and Sunderland) also played cricket for Yorkshire and Leicestershire and was a 'dual' cap, representing England at both football (four caps) and cricket. Watson, who once scored 257 for England in the West Indies, played in 25 Tests for England. He began his football career as a wing-half at Huddersfield Town but after his transfer to Roker Park often played at outside-right. Len Shackleton once said of Watson, 'The Sunderland players returned from a pre-season tour and played a charity cricket match against Whitburn. Willie hit the ball further than we'd been on tour.'

While doing his National Service, Bobby Charlton won the high jump, javelin and 1,000 yards in the Army Sports Championship.

David Oliphant (Wolves, 1959–61) represented Cumberland Schools at football, rugby, swimming, athletics, cricket and cross-country. He also had trials for England Schoolboys at rugby.

Not content with being one of the greatest footballers of all time, Sir Stanley Matthews was also a decent cricketer and played in many a game in aid of a good cause. He once scored 64 not out for Soweto Lions in a charity match in South Africa.

In September 1956, Bill Etheridge signed for Bristol City, and on the same day also signed a contract with Gloucestershire County Cricket Club.

In 1956–57, Charlton Athletic boasted four players who also played first-class county cricket: Stuart Leary, Sid O'Linn and Derek Ufton for Kent, and Mickey Stewart for Surrey.

In 1959–60, the Derby County team included three players – Ian Buxton, Ian Hall and Ray Swallow – who also played first-class cricket for Derbyshire.

In 1960 top British tennis player (not a misprint) Mike Sangster signed for Torquay United and on his debut for United reserves scored a hat-trick in an 11-0 victory over Barnstaple. Which was quite something, as a top tennis player: if anyone knew how to avoid the net it was Sangster.

The West Ham United goalkeeper in the 1964 FA Cup Final against Preston North End, Jim Standen, went on to achieve a unique double. Having won an FA Cup winners medal with West Ham, later that summer Standen won a County Championship medal with Worcestershire as their wicket-keeper.

England 1966 World Cup hero Sir Geoff Hurst (West Ham United, Stoke City and West Bromwich Albion) played county cricket for Essex.

Aston Villa goalkeeper of the 1970s Jim Cumbes played cricket for Worcestershire and is now chief executive at Lancashire CCC.

Ted Hemsley played football for Sheffield United and Shrewsbury Town and was an accomplished batsman with Worcestershire. He was a member of the Sheffield United team that won promotion to Division One in 1971.

The only post-war players to have played in an FA Cup Final and a cricket Test match for England are Denis Compton (Arsenal v. Liverpool, 1950, and 78 Tests for England) and Mick Lambert (Ipswich Town and Middlesex). Lambert was a member of the Ipswich team that defeated Arsenal at Wembley in 1978, and as a youngster on the Middlesex groundstaff was called upon to field for England in a Test at Lord's when England were reduced to ten men, the twelfth man having been recalled by his county.

He gave football a try. Welsh international rugby legend Gareth Edwards signed for Swansea City in 1980–81 and played a number of matches for the club's reserves.

Liverpool legend Alan Hansen represented Scotland at four different sports: football for the full national team, and at Under-18 level at squash, volleyball and golf (though curiously, not football!).

Tim Buzaglo, who sensationally scored a hat-trick for non-league Woking against West Bromwich Albion in the third round of the FA Cup in 1991, was also an international cricketer with Gibraltar.

He was an all-rounder, someone who was average at more things than the average person.
FREDDIE TRUEMAN

Steve Gatting (brother of England cricketer Mike and Joe of Brighton and Hove Albion and Sussex CCC Academy) enjoyed a successful career with Brighton and Hove Albion and also played cricket for Middlesex.

West Indies and Somerset legend Viv Richards played football for Antigua in the qualifying rounds of the 1978 World Cup.

Chris Balderstone is the only man to have played first-class football and first-class cricket on the same day. On 15 September 1970, Balderstone played for Leicestershire against Derbyshire at Chesterfield, and in the evening played in midfield for Doncaster Rovers against Brentford in Division Four. Following the match he then played for the Doncaster Players darts team against a team of fans in the Rovers supporters club. And today's players complain about busy playing schedules . . .

England cricket legend Ian Botham played for Scunthorpe United (1980–85), albeit intermittently due to cricket winter tours with England.

Gary Lineker played for Leicestershire Second XI and once scored a crisp century for them.

Christopher Columbus went around the world in 1492, which was above par but not a bad score when you consider the distance.
TOMMY DOCHERTY

2

The strict definition of an amateur footballer is one who receives no payment or expenses whatsoever for playing the game.

The oldest football club in the world is Sheffield FC (now in the Northern Counties East League), which was founded as an amateur club on 24 October 1857. The minutes book of that first season is still in existence. Given that Sheffield FC was the first football club in the world, it invites the question, who did they play against?

Hallam FC (Sheffield) of the Northern Counties East League and formerly of the Yorkshire League has the oldest football club ground in the world. Sandygate dates back to 1860. Hallam is also the second-oldest football club in the world (at last, Sheffield had someone to play against). The first fixture between the two clubs took place on Boxing Day 1860 and ended in a 2-0 win for Hallam.

Corinthian Casuals shirts of chocolate and pink were the racing colours of their first captain, Frank Bickley (1883), and later those of Sir Winston Churchill. Initially Casuals players were gleaned only from Charterhouse, Eton and Westminster schools.

The FA Amateur Cup was introduced in 1894. The first winners of the trophy were Old Carthusians who beat Casuals 2-1 at Richmond. Prior to the final a debate took place as to whether or not penalties should be allowed. An official of Old Carthusians told *The Times*, 'Penalties are an unpleasant indication that our conduct and honesty is not all it should be.'

The first official England Amateur match took place on 1 November 1906 (England beat France 15-0 in Paris). The first England Amateur match took place on home soil on 7 December 1907, at White Hart Lane (England beat Ireland 6-1).

A Great Britain Amateur XI won a gold medal at the first Olympic Games, staged in 1908 in London; Great Britain beat Denmark 2-0 in the football final. Four years later, when the Olympics were held in Stockholm, Great Britain repeated their gold medal success and against the same opposition, on this occasion beating Denmark 4-2. Great Britain have never won an Olympic gold for football since.

In Enfield's early days as a club, their Bailey's Field ground was situated in London's Baker Street where a stable was used for getting changed. When the club moved to a new ground at Cherry Orchard Lane in Enfield it was some three years before a pavilion with dressing rooms was erected. Teams changed about 500 yards away in the George Hotel and players ran through the streets to the ground. Enfield now ground-share with landlords Borehamwood.

One of the finest amateur clubs of the first half of the twentieth century were Northern Nomads who, prior to joining the Manchester League in the 1950s, operated as a 'touring side'. They played all their matches away from home and boasted an unbeaten record abroad. They defeated the Austro-Hungarian international team, Belgium and Holland, and went on to win both the English and Welsh Amateur Cups. Consisting of mainly schoolteachers, Nomads never had a player cautioned or sent off in the first 63 years of their existence.

The captain of Liverpool Schoolboys and England Schoolboys in 1920–21 was Bobby Fairfoul.

In 1935–36, Southall became the first amateur club to play through the qualifying rounds of the FA Cup to the third round proper.

In 1938, Eton School (which enjoyed representation on the FA Council) played St Helen's Auckland Social Services XI, a team comprising young unemployed miners from the north-east. The match was staged as a means of raising funds for the families of unemployed miners in that part of England. The game ended 2-2.

In 1941–42, Erith and Belvedere, then of the South Eastern Combination League, created a goalscoring record in senior amateur football by netting 253 goals in 44 games – an average of just under six per match.

Walthamstow Avenue, once a force in amateur football, possessed the world's only wooden cup. The club won the cup outright during World War Two in a competition involving London-based amateur clubs. The cup was made from the mast of one of the small boats that ferried survivors from Dunkirk in 1940, as metal was scarce during the war.

The first FA Amateur Cup Final to be staged at Wembley took place in 1949 when Bromley defeated Romford 1-0.

In 1949, Dagenham (now Dagenham and Redbridge of the Football League) failed in their application to join the Corinthian, Delphian and Isthmian Leagues, so the club decided to form its own league, the Metropolitan League, which attracted junior sides from all the major professional clubs in London including Arsenal, Chelsea and Spurs.

One of the most prolific goalscorers in post-war senior amateur football was George Brown, who played for Bromley. In 1948–49, Brown's goals helped Bromley win the Athenian League, the Kent Cup and the FA Amateur Cup. He amassed 129 of them, including a seven, a double hat-trick, two fives, three fours and six hat-tricks.

Charlie Mortimore completed the 1949–50 season as Aldershot Town's leading goalscorer in Division Three (South) with 15 goals. He became only the second amateur player to head the goalscoring for a Football League club since World War One.

Northern League side Billingham Synthonia completed the 1950–51 season without conceding a single goal at home.

Maidenhead hold the proud record of having competed in every FA Cup competition since 1871.

England cricketer Trevor Bailey (Essex) was a member of the Walthamstow Avenue team that beat Leyton 2-1 in the 1952 FA Amateur Cup Final at Wembley.

In 1953, an FA Amateur Cup tie between Brigg Sports (now Ford United) of the Spartan League and Bishop Auckland (Northern League) attracted a crowd of 58,121 to Newcastle United's St James' Park.

The longest FA Amateur Cup Final lasted five hours and thirty minutes and involved three matches. In 1954, Crook Town drew 2-2 with Bishop Auckland at Wembley. The replay at St James's Park also ended 2-2 before Crook finally triumphed 1-0 at Ayresome Park, Middlesbrough. The three games registered record receipts and attendances for the competition: a total of 196,727 spectators watched the three matches, paying £46,787. As amateur players were involved, the three games were exempt from entertainment tax, and each club received £11,000 (almost twice as much as the finalists in the FA Cup). As amateurs, the players, of course, received nothing.

In 1954–55, Chelsea gave a Football League debut to an amateur player, Seamus O'Connell. It proved a memorable and remarkable day for O'Connell: he scored a hat-trick, against Manchester United, but United won 6-5.

The first team to win the Amateur Cup in three successive seasons was Bishop Auckland (1955–57). The captain on each occasion was Bob Hardisty.

Bishop Auckland hold the record for the most Amateur Cup wins (ten).

In 1955, the game between 415 Coast Regiment and 46 AA Regiment at Gravesend had a first-half which lasted for 70 minutes because the referee's watch had stopped.

In April 1956, Mickey Stewart (father of Alec), who had been playing cricket for England in the West Indies, flew in to Teesside airport to play for Corinthian Casuals in the Amateur Cup Final replay against Bishop Auckland. Unfortunately, Stewart arrived at Middlesbrough's Ayresome Park five minutes after kick-off. Despite his non-appearance, after the game he was offered a professional contract with Charlton Athletic.

In the 1950s, the Kettering Amateur League boasted a club called Mrs Morris's Football Club. The reserves were called Mrs Morris's Reserves.

In 1956–57, Tooting and Mitcham recorded an attendance of 17,500 for an FA Cup tie against Queens Park Rangers.

In 1957, the vice-president of Wood Green Town was comic actor Peter Sellers.

In the late 1950s, the main stand at Wimbledon's Plough Lane ground boasted a self-contained flat. It was, for a time, home to Jimmy Greaves (Chelsea) and his new bride Irene. In return for a reduction in rent, Jimmy agreed to keep the Plough Lane terraces free of litter and weeds.

Isthmian League club Bromley enjoyed better attendances than several lower division Football League clubs in 1960–61. A crowd of 6,987 watched an Isthmian League XI play Japan, and four days later 5,876 spectators watched Bromley against Dulwich Hamlet in the league.

In the 1950s and early 1960s, clubs in the top London-based amateur leagues often boasted average attendances well in excess of 3,000. The names of these leagues – Isthmian, Athenian, Spartan, Delphian and Corinthian – derived from classical history as it was thought the founders were Old Etonians and Harrovians who had studied the classics. Members included current Football League clubs Wycombe Wanderers, Dagenham (now Dagenham and Redbridge) and Barnet, as well as Wimbledon.

In 1961, West Auckland Town celebrated their centenary by winning the Northern League and reaching the final of the Amateur Cup. In 1909, West Auckland beat Juventus to win the Sir Thomas Lipton (of tea fame) Trophy, the 'unofficial' European Cup of its day (also known as 'the first World Cup'), and retained the trophy in 1911.

Although rules in the 1960s prohibited Football League clubs from signing foreign players, in 1961, Finchley of the Athenian League signed three players who had played at international level for Hungary 'B': Istvan Kovac, Endere Elias and Florian Pallsay.

In 1961, Delphian League side Edmonton blamed falling attendances at their Barrass Stadium on the fact that the ground was so close to White Hart Lane. People preferred to watch Spurs in their double-winning season.

In 1962, Bishop's Stortford of the Athenian League had a supporters club with a membership of 6,000.

There are not many people who would turn down an opportunity to sign for Manchester United, but actor Sean Connery did, in 1962. Connery, who had played for Scottish junior club Bonnyrigg Rose and had also turned out for Corinthian Casuals reserves, was appearing in a production of *South Pacific* in Manchester when Matt Busby, having received a scout's report on the Scot, asked him to join United. The young Connery, however, decided to pursue his career as an actor, and only a matter of months later received his big break when cast as James Bond in *Dr No*. Connery continued to play football, regularly turning out for the Show Biz XI in games to raise money for charities and worthy causes. The team also featured comic actor Ronnie Corbett, comedian Dave King, singer Tommy Steele and all-round entertainer Des O'Connor.

Goalkeeper Alex Stepney, who won a European Cup winners medal with Manchester United in 1968 and was a member of England's 1970 World Cup squad, began his career as an amateur with Tooting and Mitcham in 1962.

Wimbledon is the only club to have won both the Amateur Cup (4-2 v. Sutton United, 1963) and the FA Cup (1-0 v. Liverpool, 1988). In the win against Sutton United all four goals were scored by centre-forward Eddie Reynolds, and they were all headers. What's more, all six goals were scored in the second-half of the game.

The last amateur footballer to play top-flight football in England was Mike Pinner, who kept goal for Leyton Orient in Division One in 1962–63. Pinner was a solicitor.

By the 1970s, Middlesex Wanderers had played in more countries since World War Two than any other football club in the world. Yet they had never played a home game. Wanderers did not have a single signed player, yet all their players were amateur internationals. The Wanderers were a side chosen from the cream of amateur players from England, Scotland, Wales and Ireland which every close season formed a touring party to play matches all over the world.

Foreign managers are nothing new in English football. In 1967, Athenian League club Southall appointed Italian Vince Siccardi as their manager. During his football career in Italy, Siccardi had played for several clubs in Serie B.

In 1967, Britain's first all-Sikh team, Sikh Hunters, gained admission to the Bloxwich Combination League. Players were allowed to wear turbans as it was considered intrinsic to their religious beliefs. The club still thrives today.

Whitburn were members of the Wearside League in the 1950s and 1960s. In 1969, their team included players by the name of Day and Knight, and Welsh and Scott; there was also a Pratt, a Walley and a Burke.

Writer and author Tony Pawson played amateur football for Pegasus and England Amateur, and cricket for Kent; and in 1984 he became world fly-fishing champion.

Leeds United chairman Ken Bates played amateur football for Chase FC of Chertsey when the club was the nursery team of Arsenal.

North Shields's winning goal against Sutton United in the Amateur Cup Final of 1969 was scored by Brian Joicey, who went on to enjoy a successful career as a professional with Sheffield Wednesday and Coventry City. Shields might be said to have 'stolen the match': their nickname is 'The Robins' but they were erroneously referred to in the Wembley final programme as 'The Robbers'.

In 1973, a representative side from the Wolverhampton Sunday Morning League toured West Germany. Their fixtures included a game against Mainz of the Bundesliga who agreed to the fixture in the mistaken belief that the touring team was Wolverhampton Wanderers. Mainz won the match 21-0.

The FA Amateur Cup ended as a competition in 1974. The last winners of the trophy were Bishop's Stortford, who beat Ilford 4-1.

The fastest goal in any match at Wembley (20 seconds) was scored by Maurice Cox for Cambridge University against Oxford University on 5 December 1979.

Throughout the 1950s, 1960s and early 1970s amateur football in England was increasingly subjected to what was termed 'shamamateurism' – that is, players receiving money either in the form of 'extravagant expenses' or by way of illegal payment, often referred to as 'boot money', as players would return from showering after a match to find money in their boots. In 1974, the FA abolished the status of the amateur, declaring that all footballers should be referred to simply as 'players' irrespective of whether they received money for playing the game or not.

The only amateur club currently in senior British football is Queen's Park, founded 1867, whose home ground is Hampden Park. The Spiders were twice beaten finalists in the English FA Cup (1884 and 1885), but they have won the Scottish Cup ten times, though the last occasion was in 1893!

In 1981, Ledbury Town banned supporter Sam Phillips from attending matches after he attacked a referee following a game. Undaunted, Mr Phillips continued to watch his favourite team through a gap in the hedge surrounding Ledbury's ground. Mr Phillips was 82 years old.

The sixth-round FA Cup tie between Manchester City and Stoke City at Maine Road on 3 March 1934 attracted an attendance of 84,569 – a record for an English club match other than an FA Cup Final.

A total of 149,547 spectators attended the Scotland–England international match at Hampden Park on 17 April 1937, at the time a world record attendance for a football match. It was the first all-ticket match in Scottish football, but it is estimated that another 10,000 fans entered the ground for free when an exit gate was forced open. Official receipts for the game, which Scotland won 3-1, were a record £24,303. Each England player received a match fee of £10 plus second-class rail travel; Scotland players received a match fee of £9. The game also marked the first time numbered shirts were worn by both teams in an international match.

Seven days later, Hampden set another attendance high when 144,433 spectators saw Celtic beat Aberdeen 2-1 in the Scottish FA Cup Final – a record for the competition. On this day it was estimated some 20,000 fans were locked out when the Hampden turnstiles were closed.

A total of 202,343 spectators watched the thrice-played fifth-round FA Cup tie between Aston Villa and Charlton Athletic in 1938: 76,031 attended the original tie at the Valley, 61,530 the replay at Villa Park, and 64,782 the second replay at 'neutral' Highbury. Villa won 4-1 after scores of 1-1 and 2-2.

The meeting between Rangers and Celtic at Ibrox on 2 January 1939 attracted a crowd of 118,567 – a British record for a domestic League match.

The highest aggregate cup tie attendance is 265,199 for the Scottish FA Cup Final original tie and replay between Rangers and Morton, 1947–48.

A record attendance for a Football League match was set when 83,260 spectators watched Manchester United play Arsenal at Maine Road in January 1948. The game was held at the home of Manchester City, as United's Old Trafford was out of action due to bomb damage sustained during World War Two.

The record aggregate attendance for a single day's matches in English League football is 1,272,185 on 27 December 1949 (44 matches producing an average attendance of 28,913).

The record attendance for a Second Division (now Championship) match is 70,302 (Tottenham Hotspur v. Southampton, 25 February 1950).

For a Third Division (South) match, it's 51,621 (Cardiff City v. Bristol City, 7 April 1947).

For a Third Division (North) match, it's 49,655 (Hull City v. Rotherham United, Christmas Day 1948).

For a Third Division (now League One) match, it's 49,655 (Sheffield Wednesday v. Sheffield United, Boxing Day 1979).

For a Fourth Division (now League Two) match, it's 37,774 (Crystal Palace v. Millwall, 31 March 1961).

The record attendance for a friendly match in the United Kingdom is 104,493, who saw Rangers lose 3-2 to Eintracht Frankfurt at Hampden Park on 17 October 1961.

On 4 March 1964, the official attendance for the Sunderland–Manchester United FA Cup sixth-round replay (2-2 aet) at Roker Park was 46,727. It is estimated, however, that the attendance was nearer 65,000, up to 20,000 additional spectators having gained entry when an exit gate at the Roker End collapsed allowing fans free entry to the ground. Thousands more were left outside: the *Sunderland Echo* estimated that '90,000 supporters descended on Roker Park'. Reports tell of the experience of a Mr Jacques, who lived in a street adjoining Roker Park. Mr Jacques left his home to buy a packet of cigarettes from a corner shop. When the exit gate at the Roker End collapsed, Mr Jacques was carried into the ground by the momentum of the surge and ended up on the Roker End terracing, in his carpet slippers. He eventually managed to return home at 10.25 p.m., minus cigarettes and carpet slippers. It was following the mayhem at this game that the FA decided 'all high-profile FA Cup ties' should be made all-ticket.

On 5 May 1966, the attendance for Arsenal's First Division match against Leeds United at Highbury was an all-time club record low of 4,554; it was also a post-war record low for the First Division. The miserable total was in part attributable to the fact that the match clashed with 'live' TV coverage of the European Cup Winners' Cup Final between Liverpool and Borussia Dortmund. Or so Arsenal maintained.

The lowest post-war attendance for an English League match is 450, for Rochdale v. Cambridge United, Division Three, 5 February 1974. The match was played on a Wednesday afternoon as clubs were not allowed to use floodlights due to a national power crisis. As one Rochdale supporter put it, 'It was like watching a game on the moon – no atmosphere.' (That's a good one, a football joke that will still be loved and enjoyed when it is a hundred years old – a week on Monday.)

The lowest attendance for a Premiership match is 3,039 (Wimbledon v. Everton, 26 January 1993) – also the lowest post-war attendance for a top-flight English game. One Everton fan remarked, 'I arrived in Wimbledon, asked for directions to Plough Lane, was told to "follow the crowds", and ended up in Argos.'

Not to rest on their laurels, Wimbledon also recorded the lowest post-war attendance in the top two divisions of English football – 849, v. Rotherham United (Division One) at Selhurst Park, 29 October 2002. (Editor's note: the move to Milton Keynes had controversially been endorsed by the autumn of 2002 and supporters stayed away in protest. Author's note: the editor is a Wimbledon fan.)

On 9 September 1995, the attendance for England's international against Colombia at Wembley (0-0) was 20,038. In the same week, Birmingham City's Anglo-Italian Cup tie against Genoa at St Andrews drew a crowd of 20,430 – 392 more than attended Wembley.

In 1998-99, the match between Sunderland reserves and Liverpool reserves at the Stadium of Light was watched by a crowd of 34,217.

On 31 July 1999, the League Cup tie between Clydebank and East Stirling attracted an official attendance of only 29 – the lowest ever recorded for a Scottish senior football fixture. At the time Clydebank were homeless and the match was switched to Cappielow Park, home of Morton FC.

The official world record attendance for a football match is 199,850, at the 1950 World Cup Final between Brazil and Uruguay held in the Maracana Stadium. And there were still supporters who moaned that they couldn't get a ticket.

The lowest attendance for an England match at Wembley is 15,628, against Chile on 23 May 1989. Amazing, really, considering that John Fashanu and Tony Cottee were playing for England.

In 2006-07, the fourth best-attended league in the world was the Championship (11,066,189, including play-offs), behind the Premiership, the Bundesliga (Germany) and La Liga (Spain).

Given that there are more clubs in the Football League, more spectators watch Football League matches (16.4 million in 2007) than the Premiership (12.8 million in 2007).

The aggregate attendance in 2006-07 in English football's second tier, the Championship, topped ten million for the first time since 1951-52, when its equivalent was known as the Second Division. Twelve clubs enjoyed an average attendance in excess of 20,000 whereas only two clubs, Luton Town and Colchester United, had an average attendance of less than 10,000.

In 2006-07 the attendance at the Stadium of Light for Sunderland's Championship home match against Burnley (44,448) was higher than that at Stamford Bridge for the Chelsea–Liverpool Champions League semi-final in the same week.

On 24 March 2007, the new Wembley opened its doors. The attendance for the Under-21 international that day against Italy was restricted to 55,700, but was still a record for an England Under-21 home game.

The record aggregate attendance for a single season in English football is 41,271,414, in 1948-49. In 2006-07 it was 29.2 million.

The lowest aggregate attendance in a Football League season is 16,488,577, in 1985-86 – some 14 million less than for the Premiership and Football League combined in 2006-07.

It is often written that the Premiership came along and saved English football from descending into oblivion. In fact, prior to the formation of the Premiership in 1992-93, aggregate attendances at Football League matches had enjoyed a year-on-year rise for six consecutive seasons. So, rather than 'saving' English football, one could say that the Premiership, attendance-wise, exploited a growth trend.

 How do you make God laugh? When you pray, tell Him you're going to attend a game at Fulham.

BRYON BUTLER, football journalist

Football League Aggregate Attendances in Seasons Leading to Formation of Premiership

1986–87	17,379,218	1989–90	19,445,442
1987–88	17,959,732	1990–91	19,508,202
1988–89	18,464,192	1991–92	20,487,273

First Season of Premiership and Football League

1992–93	20,657,327

Whereas aggregate attendances have since 1987 experienced a year-on-year rise to date, the first season of the Premiership actually saw a slight fall compared to the previous season – that is, the last of the old-format Division One (1991–92, 9,989,160; 1992–93, 9,759,809).

Aggregate attendances at Premiership matches rose annually from 1992–93 to 1994–95, decreased in the following two seasons, but from 1997–98 (11,092,106) increased season by season to 13,303,136 in 2003–04. There was a slight downturn in 2004–05. Attendances rose again in 2005–06, then experienced another modest drop in 2006–07.

Some three million more spectators watched Premiership matches in 2006–07 than did in the first season of the Premier League in 1992–93.

Attendances in the Championship have almost doubled since 1992–93. In 1992–93, the aggregate attendance for what was then termed Division One was 5.8 million; in 2006–07 the figure exceeded ten million.

Aggregate attendances for the other two divisions of the Football League are also significantly up. In 1992–93, 3.4 million spectators watched matches in Division Two; in 2006–07, the figure for what is now called League One was 4.3 million. In 1992–93, the figure for Division Three was 1.5 million; in 2006–07 (now League Two) it was 2.5 million.

The best-supported club in English football is Manchester United, whose average attendance in 2007–08 exceeded 75,000.

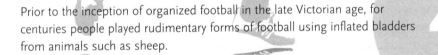

Prior to the inception of organized football in the late Victorian age, for centuries people played rudimentary forms of football using inflated bladders from animals such as sheep.

The oldest football in existence is the one displayed in Stirling Smith Museum (Scotland). It is 450 years old and made from an outer casing of deer skin containing a pig's bladder. It is claimed it was once the property of Mary Queen of Scots.

The mid-19th century saw the first footballs as we know them today, a circular shell comprising leather panels sewn together. The early leather footballs contained pig's bladders.

Rules governing the size, shape and weight of a football were not initially laid down by the Football Association, formed in 1863. This resulted in balls of varying sizes and weights being used throughout the 1860s.

In 1872, the FA decided that footballs used in FA Cup matches should be of a regulation size and weight. All footballs, it was decreed, should be made of an outer casing consisting of leather panels and should contain a bladder suitable for inflation and maintaining air. The size of match balls was to be 27–28 inches (68–70cm) in circumference, and at the commencement of a match each had to weigh 16 ounces or one pound (450 grams) with an internal pressure of 0.6–1.1 atmospheres, that is 8.5–15.6lb/square inch at sea level.

Pig's bladders continued to be used in footballs until the mid-1880s, when they were replaced by synthetic materials, usually rubber.

In 1888, the FA and Football League agreed that all match balls had to be inspected and approved by the referee. The ball could not be changed during a match unless authorized by the referee. Rules also stipulated that should a ball burst during a free-kick, penalty, throw-in, goal-kick or corner-kick, then the kick or throw-in had to be retaken; if the ball burst during open play, a new ball had to be summoned and the game restarted with a drop-ball at the approximate point where the original match ball was considered to have burst.

After World War One the FA and Football League stipulated that every match should have a new match ball. Prior to 1914 this had not always been the case.

It is believed that the tradition of presenting the match ball autographed by both teams to a player who scored a hat-trick in a match began in the 1920s. Charles Buchan was presented with the match ball as a souvenir following his hat-trick in Sunderland's 5-1 victory over Blackburn Rovers on 17 November 1923, though in all probability there were earlier instances.

The 1930s and 1940s saw footballs of various sizes used in international matches as FIFA had yet to stipulate the regulation size and weight of match balls.

In the 1930 World Cup, the match between Argentina and Uruguay was delayed because neither side could agree on which type of football should be used (Argentinian and Uruguayan footballs differed in size and weight). A compromise was eventually reached. The first-half of the match was played with the Argentinian regulation football, and at half-time Argentina led 2-1. In the second-half Uruguay fought back to win 4-2 using the Uruguayan regulation ball.

In the 1930s, two types of match ball were used in English football: the 'Tugite', which cost 24s 6d (£1.22), and the Thomlinson 'T' ball, costing 18s 6d (92p). The Tugite was considered the superior ball, which is why it cost more. The advantage of the Tugite over the Thomlinson 'T' was that it did not gather mud on heavy grounds. This resulted in the Thomlinson 'T' being favoured mainly when ground conditions were dry and firm.

 At Stoke we used an old Tugite leather ball in practice games that was so old and lacerated, if you were playing in skins, every time you jumped to head it, it gave you twenty lashes.
STANLEY MATTHEWS

The problem with using either ball on dry, firm pitches was that they appeared overly light and were prone to a higher and more erratic bounce, which made them difficult to judge and control. To counteract this, and thus to make the balls easier to judge and control, during the 1930s many trainers took to soaking the match ball overnight in a bucket of water, and often inserted an additional bladder, which increased the weight of the ball (Sir Stanley Matthews reckoned the weight could increase by half). This, and the varying quality of the cow hide used, often resulted in footballs losing their shape during the course of a match, or 'bloating', which is why many photographs of players of that era in training show them kicking practice footballs the size of large balloons.

 Whenever I see a bald man walk down the street I never think, 'There's a man who has done a lot of worrying,' I think, 'There's a man who looks like he was a good header of a ball.'
STANLEY MATTHEWS

Neither the Tugite nor the Thomlinson 'T' benefited from a laminate coating on the leather panels. In inclement weather this resulted in the leather of the ball soaking up moisture, and during the course of a match the ball increased in weight. From the regulation weight of 16 ounces at the start of a match, during wet weather match balls could reach 20 ounces or even more. To offset the absorption of moisture the leather panels were smeared with dubbin.

During a Second Division match in 1936 between Chesterfield and Burnley, Chesterfield centre-forward Walter Ponting fired a shot which beat the opposing goalkeeper only for the ball to burst and fail to cross the goal-line.

 Have you ever seen those large concrete balls on pillars either side of a gate leading to a country estate? Imagine kicking one of those and you'll have some idea what it was like to kick the old leather caseball on a muddy pitch.

RAY KING, Newcastle United, Port Vale and England 'B'

The 1946 final tie between Derby County and Charlton Athletic was the first occasion when the ball burst in an FA Cup Final. Oddly, it happened again the following season, in the final between Charlton and Burnley.

On 25 May 1947, England notched up their record away win in Lisbon. The match was delayed when officials from the Portuguese FA protested about the type of ball to be used in the game, the FIFA-designated match ball, of the size and weight used in English football, larger than the match balls used in Portugal. Eventually the game commenced using the larger, English-type football. With England having established an early lead, the ball went out of play for a throw-in. The Portugal bench swapped the ball for their preferred smaller version. But if they thought the smaller ball would offer an advantage to their players they were sadly mistaken: England won the game 10-0.

The 1950s saw a distinct improvement in the quality of match balls, in the main due to new technology and FIFA increasingly asserting its authority as the governing body of world football. Match balls in international matches now had to be 'FIFA Approved' or 'FIFA Inspected'.

When I played in goal, our manager used to put a bell in the ball so I could hear it coming.

BOB 'THE CAT' BEVAN

In the 1950s, English football used three types of FA-approved football: the Webber 'Premier', the 'Super Straight' manufactured by Stuart Surridge, and an improved version of the 'T' ball. Surridge later introduced the 'Double Crown', the first laceless ball used in British football. Seven sewn leather panels, rather than the traditional three, now enabled footballs to maintain their shape and weight irrespective of the weather. Initially, all four types of football had to be 'dubbined' to make them water resistant, but in the late 1950s technology allowed for the leather panels to be laminated. The Thomlinson 'Golden T' even boasted a 'Peblex Suregrip Surface' which the manufacturers claimed 'prevents miskicks and fumbles'!

White footballs were first introduced to English football in 1951, though rarely used until 1954, when a white ball featured in a prestigious floodlit friendly match between Wolverhampton Wanderers and a Honved side containing several of the Hungary team that had beaten England 6-3 at Wembley the previous year. The second-half of the match was televised by the BBC, which brought the white ball to prominence. Following the Wolves–Honved game, more and more clubs opted for a white ball for use in matches.

The first all-synthetic balls were manufactured in the early 1960s. Among the first of this type of ball was the Mitre 'Matchplay'. One of the advantages of the Matchplay was that its trajectory held true – that is, it did not swerve and dip when travelling through the air as contemporary footballs do, making it easier for players to judge and control.

Ron Tindall's shot had so much power it's a wonder the Doncaster goalkeeper didn't catch pneumonia from the draught the ball created as it flew past him.

JIMMY GREAVES

The first 32-panel football was devised and used in Denmark in 1954.

For many years Shrewsbury Town, whose ground at Gay Meadow backed on to the River Severn, employed Fred Davies and his coracle to paddle out into the river and retrieve match balls that had been kicked over the top of the Riverside Stand.

In the 1960s, Adidas introduced the first black and white panelled footballs to West German league matches. This design, it was thought, would be more easily seen by both players and spectators alike.

The first World Cup tournament to use an all-synthetic ball was the 1986 Finals in Mexico. The ball was manufactured by Adidas and went under the name of the 'Adidas Mexico'.

Four different match balls were used in less than a minute of Leicester City's Second Division match against Fulham on 4 December 1982. The chosen match ball was kicked over a stand at Filbert Street and not recovered. The game restarted with a second ball, but it was rejected after complaints from Leicester players that it was under-inflated. A third ball appeared, but it did not meet with the satisfaction of the referee, who then called for a fourth ball. Leicester won the game 2-0. Their second goal was scored by Gary Lineker.

In 1998–99, the Football League experimented for the first time with a high-visibility yellow ball.

The 1998 World Cup Finals saw the introduction of the Adidas 'Tricolore', an all-synthetic football which also contained a syntactic foam layer under the panelling.

The ball used in Premiership matches in recent years, the Nike 'Total 90 Aerow' is lighter by some three to four ounces than the former regulation weight of 16 ounces. These new footballs dip and swerve through the air making the trajectory difficult to judge for goalkeepers.

The design of many of the match balls used in official matches today is based on the 'Buckminster Soccer Ball', devised by American architect Richard Buckminster-Fuller. The Buckminster ball comprises a series of synthetic leather hexagons, pentagons and triangles. Today's match balls are designed to be waterproof and faster in flight, and not to absorb energy so that all of the kicking force is translated into forward motion – which is why, on the pristine pitches of today, players find it easier to make long crosses and passes than players of yesteryear.

B

5 Mistakes are part and parcel of football. As former manager Bob Stokoe once said, 'If players didn't make mistakes, there wouldn't be any goals.' To err is human, but occasionally in football, making a simple mistake is seemingly not enough.

Prior to playing Wales in March 1902, England had scored in 52 consecutive internationals, dating back to 1884 when they were defeated 1-0 by Scotland in Glasgow. With the score goalless against Wales, England were awarded a penalty which Sheffield United's Ernest Needham insisted on taking, only for him to drive the spot-kick wide. The game ended 0-0, and thereafter England scored in each of their following 32 internationals. Had it not been for Needham's failure from the penalty spot, England would boast a world record of having scored in 85 consecutive international matches.

Sheffield Wednesday did not compete in the FA Cup of 1886-87, nor Birmingham City in 1921-22 or Queens Park Rangers in 1926-27, and all for the same reason: having completed the application forms for the Cup, office staff forgot to post them to the FA.

During a match in the 1930 World Cup between the USA and Italy, the USA trainer ran on to the pitch to administer treatment to an injured player, took a bottle of chloroform from his bag and, in testing it, inhaled so much he passed out and had to be stretchered from the field.

In August 1938, Arsenal paid Wolves a world record transfer fee of £14,500 for Welsh international Bryn Jones. A shy, retiring type, Jones was never comfortable in the limelight and within months his form was such that he was a regular in the Arsenal reserves. Then war put an end to competitive football in England. To place Jones's colossal transfer fee in perspective, it was to be nigh on ten years before the amount Arsenal paid for him was eclipsed.

The meeting between a Great Britain XI and the Rest of Europe at Hampden Park in 1948 was billed as 'The Match of the Century'. Prior to the game, the Rest of Europe's French goalkeeper, Julien Darui, was advised by a 'health expert' to drink three glasses of red wine laced with sugar to improve his 'agility, alertness and stamina'. Despite cautionary words from team-mates, Darui adhered to the advice. Final score: Great Britain 6 Rest of Europe 1.

In 1950–51, Carlisle United, then of the Third Division North and managed by Bill Shankly, drew 1-1 against Arsenal at Highbury in the FA Cup. So confident were locals of victory over Arsenal in the replay that magistrates ordered an extension to the licensing hours in the city's pubs (at the time government-owned) so that the community could celebrate 'a famous victory'. Arsenal won the replay 4-1.

In the 1950s, Neil Franklin of Stoke City and England was widely regarded as the best centre-half in Europe. Players were then subject to a maximum wage of £17. Keen to provide long-term security for his family, Franklin accepted an offer to join Los Millionarios of Bogotá in Colombia, a country whose football association was not then a member of FIFA. Franklin was promised £160 per week, a signing-on fee of £1,500, a villa with servants, a car and a generous win bonus system. The money never materialized, and after a few months a disconsolate Franklin returned home only to find himself shunned by Stoke City and England. He eventually signed for Hull City but failed to replicate the form he'd shown with Stoke and soon dropped into non-league football.

Five months after the 6-3 watershed defeat at the hands of Hungary in 1953 – England's first defeat against foreign opposition on home soil – England travelled to Budapest for the return. When asked by the press for his thoughts on the outcome of the game, FA secretary Stanley Rous said, 'I assure you, gentlemen, the result last November was an aberration. This time England will win.' Final score: Hungary 7 England 1.

On the morning of his FA Cup Final appearance against Wolves in 1960, Blackburn Rovers centre-forward Derek Dougan handed in a transfer request to manager Jack Marshall. Dougan retained his place in the Rovers side but it is said his request had an unsettling effect on his team-mates: Rovers were beaten 3-0.

Fulham conceded a goal to Sheffield Wednesday at Craven Cottage in 1961 without the opposition having touched the ball. Fulham kicked off the match and worked the ball back into their own penalty area where it was played across goal, hit defender Alan Mullery and rebounded past goalkeeper Tony Macedo. The unique own-goal was timed at 33 seconds and Wednesday took it as their cue to go on and win the game 6-1.

Tony Macedo was once winded in a match against Leeds United by a shot from one of his own players. The second-half was a minute old when Macedo raced from his goal to field a long through-ball which was being shepherded by Fulham forward 'Tosh' Chamberlain, who suddenly had a rush of blood to the head and fired a cannonball shot at goal which floored the advancing Macedo. In offering his apologies, Chamberlain excused his faux pas by saying he'd momentarily forgotten the teams had changed ends at half-time.

In 1961, Scotland's first-choice goalkeeper, Lawrie Leslie, sustained an injury prior to the game against England at Wembley. The press called for Bill Brown of Spurs to be called up as Leslie's replacement, but the Scottish selectors opted for Celtic's Frank Haffey. England won 9-3 (they scored a tenth, but it was controversially deemed offside). It remains Scotland's heaviest ever defeat, and Haffey was never chosen to play for Scotland again. He returned to play for Celtic, but the cruel tag of 'Hapless Haffey' continued to dog him and he soon emigrated to Australia. Such was the ill feeling borne against Haffey by

Scotland fans that in the 1980s when former Manchester United and Scotland inside-forward Denis Law met Haffey in Australia and was asked, 'Is it safe for me to come back to Scotland?', Law replied, 'Not yet, I'd give it another few years.'

As a 15-year-old, Alan Ball wrote to every club in the north-west asking for a trial. He received only two offers, one from hometown club Bolton who, following a trial, told him he was too small to make it as a professional footballer, and one from Blackpool, who signed him as an amateur and later as a professional. Ball went on to join Everton from Blackpool for a British record transfer fee of £110,000 and, of course, was a World Cup winner with England in 1966.

Malcolm Macdonald (Luton, Newcastle United, Arsenal and England) was playing for non-league Tonbridge in 1967; his goals helped the club reach the final of the Kent FA Cup. For the final it was arranged that Macdonald would join the Tonbridge coach in the centre of Folkestone. When Macdonald arrived he found the coach to be empty and sat on the back seat. The coach driver arrived and, not seeing Macdonald, set off, with the Tonbridge centre-forward thinking that the driver was on his way to pick up the rest of the team. Macdonald was thrown into a panic when 30 women subsequently boarded for a day trip. By the time 'Super Mac' had made his own way to the ground, the cup final was well underway.

Even the great Sir Stanley Matthews was not immune from making a blunder. In 1967, as general manager of Port Vale, Stan gave a trial to a young lad from the north-east, Ray Kennedy, who failed to impress the maestro. Stan informed Kennedy he didn't think he possessed what was required to make the grade as a professional footballer. Kennedy joined Arsenal, was a member of their double-winning team in 1971, and went on to enjoy an illustrious career with Liverpool and to win 17 caps for England.

In the 86th minute of the 1968 FA Cup Final, Everton's Johnny Morrisey's cross found Jimmy Husband unmarked on the edge of the six-yard box with the goal at his mercy. Husband, however, contrived to head the ball over the bar. Opponents West Bromwich Albion heaved a sigh of relief and went on to win the cup in extra-time with a goal from Jeff Astle.

In 1971, Chelsea and Manchester City met in the semi-finals of the European Cup Winners' Cup. Chelsea won the first leg 1-0 but City were very much in the ascendancy in the second leg when Chelsea were awarded an indirect free-kick. Keith Weller opted to take it and drove the ball towards the City goal. No player made contact, but just as the ball was about to enter the net, City keeper Ron Healey decided to make a save when there was no need. The luckless Healey failed to hold the ball, which squirmed from his grasp and rolled into the net to give Chelsea a 2-0 aggregate win.

Prior to their 1970 World Cup quarter-final against West Germany in Mexico, England's regular goalkeeper Gordon Banks succumbed to a mystery stomach bug. His replacement was Chelsea's Peter Bonetti. With England leading 2-0, manager Alf Ramsey decided to substitute Bobby Charlton, who had quelled the threat of Franz Beckenbauer, with a view to keeping Charlton's ageing legs 'fresh for the semi-final'. No longer shackled by Charlton, Beckenbauer began to assert his authority on the game and Bonetti proceeded to produce a nightmare performance. First he allowed a Beckenbauer shot to creep under his body to give West Germany hope. After that, Bonetti was caught in no-man's land when an Uwe Seeler header looped over him and into the net for the equalizer. Then Gerd Müller scored what proved to be the decisive goal. The game, or rather England's performance, was later committed to the ranks of infamy by an episode of the BBC's successful comedy series *What Ever Happened To The Likely Lads?* Referring to England having conceded their two-goal lead, Bob (Rodney Bewes) says, 'I had to go and lie down in a darkened room. I felt so bad, I was off my beer for a week.'

In 1972, Derby County and Manchester United were locked in a battle to sign Ian Storey-Moore from Nottingham Forest. Derby appeared to have won the race when they paraded the Forest winger before their supporters prior to a home game at the Baseball Ground; a crowd of some 36,000 then watched Storey-Moore sit at a small desk and put pen to paper for the Rams. But in their haste to sign Storey-Moore, Derby had failed to complete every section of the transfer forms, in addition to which the forms had not been 'signed off' by the club secretary, as was the requirement. United seized their opportunity and Storey-Moore subsequently went to Old Trafford for a fee of £200,000. To compound Derby's woes, they were fined £5,000 by the Football League for parading Storey-Moore in front of their supporters when he was still registered to Forest as a player.

England's World Cup angst did not begin and end in 1970 – far from it. In October 1973 England needed to beat Poland at home to qualify for the World Cup Finals in West Germany. England had lost 2-0 to Poland in Chorzow, a blunder by Bobby Moore presenting the Poles with their second goal; as a consequence Moore was replaced in the England team by Norman Hunter (Leeds). England totally dominated proceedings at Wembley but failed to find a way past Polish keeper Jan Tomaszewski. In the second-half Hunter went to intercept an innocuous-looking ball by the halfway line on England's right, but hesitated too long on the ball. Poland's Gregorz Lato arrived on the scene, toe-poked the ball through Hunter's legs and raced clear before finding Robert Gadocha bearing down on the England goal. Gadocha's shot from the right appeared to be meat and drink to a goalkeeper of the calibre of England's Peter Shilton but, uncharacteristically, Shilton allowed the Polish striker's weak effort to pass under his body. England did equalize from the penalty spot, but it proved too little too late. The double blunder contributed in no small way to England failing to qualify for the World Cup Finals, and to all intents and purposes signalled the end of the international careers of Sir Alf Ramsey, Bobby Moore and Norman Hunter.

Acting as a summarizer for ITV on the above game, during the half-time interval Brian Clough said it would be only a matter of time before England scored the goals needed to take them to the World Cup Finals as the Poland keeper was 'a clown'. Tomaszewski's efforts in goal for Poland that night subsequently earned him the Man of the Match award.

No wonder they went bust! In 1974, the year of the World Cup Finals in West Germany, sportswear manufacturers Bukta designed a strip for use by Manchester United which they called 'Munich'.

German efficiency was questioned at the start of the 1974 World Cup Final between West Germany and Holland when the English match referee, Jack Taylor from Wolverhampton, delayed kick-off having noticed that there were no corner flags on the pitch.

British football was astounded in 1974 when Manchester City manager Malcolm Allison paid a record fee of £1,437,500 to Wolves for Steve Daly. The fee remains Daly's only real claim to football fame: in just over two years at City he failed to make any real impression and after only 48 League appearances he moved to the USA.

Upset at not being able to command a regular first-team place at Nottingham Forest, and chagrined at having not been included in the team for a testimonial match, prior to the 1980 European Cup Final Stan Bowles informed Forest's assistant manager Peter Taylor that he wished to leave the club. Taylor suggested to Bowles that he should 'think again' as there was every possibility of his getting a shirt for the final. Bowles failed to turn up for the trip to Munich and never returned to Forest, who went on to beat Malmö 1-0 to win the European Cup for a second successive season. Bowles subsequently joined Orient.

When it comes to signing British players, AC Milan have not been the shrewdest of judges. In 1961, the Italian club signed Jimmy Greaves from Chelsea. There was no doubting Greaves' pedigree as a goalscorer, it's just that he had never wanted to join Milan, and he left after a few months. In 1981 Milan went British again, signing Joe Jordan from Manchester United – another move that did not work out. Two years later Milan bemused both British press and football fans alike by paying Watford £1.2 million for Luther Blissett. Blissett struggled with life in Serie A, prompting reports in the Italian press that Milan scouts must have mistaken him for John Barnes. Blissett did, however, become a 'cult' figure with Milan fans and, dubious as this sounds, his name was adopted by an Italian anarchist collective.

Brian Clough applied for the vacant manager's job at Sunderland on two separate occasions, the second of them prior to being appointed manager of Nottingham Forest (in 1975). On both occasions Clough's application was rejected by the Sunderland board. Having enjoyed success with Derby County between 1967 and 1973, during which time he guided the club to promotion to Division One and the Football League Championship, he was appointed manager of Leeds United in 1974, but the club dispensed with his services after only 40 days in the job. Clough went on to be the catalyst to a renaissance at Forest, winning the League Championship, League Cup (four times) and European Cup (twice).

In the early 1970s, Stoke City were one of the top teams in England; they won the League Cup in 1972. In 1977, a storm badly damaged the club's Butler Street Stand. The club was inadequately insured, could not afford the cost of the replacement stand, and consequently were forced to sell Alan Hudson, Jimmy Greenhoff, Geoff Salmons and Peter Shilton. Bereft of their star players, Stoke went into decline and were relegated to Division Two.

An FA Cup Final can often determine how a player will be perceived by people for all time. His performances and goals may have been instrumental in his team reaching Wembley, but should he make a blunder on the day, that is what he will be remembered for. Such is the case of Gordon Smith. In the 1983 final between Brighton and Manchester United, Smith gave Albion the lead. Then, with the score at 2-2 and the game deep into the second period of extra-time, he was presented with a golden opportunity to win the cup for Brighton. He found himself in front of goal with only Gary Bailey to beat, but shot tamely into the midriff of the United keeper. United comfortably won the replay 4-0, and Brighton also suffered the ignominy of being relegated from Division One. When Smith found himself with only Bailey to beat, ITV match commentator Brian Moore uttered the ill-conceived words, 'And Smith must score!' In a touch of bitter irony, this was later adopted as the title of the Brighton supporters' fanzine.

For a time during 1977–78, the Northern Ireland FA believed Derek Spence was snubbing the national team. Spence was playing in Greece for Olympiakos, but the telegrams informing him of his selection for the Northern Ireland squad were sent to AEK Athens by mistake.

Wolves defeated Nottingham Forest 1-0 in the 1980 League Cup Final at Wembley courtesy of an uncharacteristic blunder by Forest goalkeeper Peter Shilton. Forest defender David Needham went to clear a high ball from Wolves' Peter Daniel only for Shilton to come off his line and clatter into his centre-back. The impact of the collision sent both players staggering either side of each other. Andy Gray ran through the gap and tapped the ball over the line for the only goal of the game.

Sunderland fans believed a golden age of success lay ahead when chairman Tom Cowie and his fellow directors persuaded Lawrie McMenemy to leave Southampton and become the club's new manager in the summer of 1985. McMenemy's salary at Sunderland was such that Margaret Thatcher once used it as evidence that English football was in no need of financial assistance from central government. In his first season in charge, Sunderland narrowly escaped relegation to Division Three; the following year McMenemy left some weeks before the end of the season with Sunderland occupying one of the relegation places. They didn't survive, losing to Gillingham in a play-off system that at the time required the team third from bottom of the Second Division to play the team that finished third in Division Three.

For the want of a nail . . . In 1981, Sunderland manager Ken Knighton needed a striker and bid £70,000 for Newport County's leading goalscorer. Oxford United were also keen on the same player and offered County £75,000 for his services. Newport got back to Knighton informing him of the Oxford bid and told him, should Sunderland equal it, the player would be theirs. Sunderland chairman Tom Cowie refused to pay the extra £5,000, so Sunderland missed out on John Aldridge.

It was only on completion of Grimsby Town's new Findus Stand in 1982 that the club discovered the sheer height of the stand interfered with the reception of television sets in the homes surrounding Blundell Park. As a consequence the club had to pay for cable TV to be installed at every home in the vicinity of the ground.

Tottenham Hotspur took to the field in the 1987 FA Cup Final against Coventry City wearing a mismatch of shirts. Spurs' new strip, designated for use the following season, was delivered for use in the Cup Final only for some players to request short-sleeved shirts for their big day at Wembley. The short-sleeved shirts were duly delivered in time but no one noticed that they did not bear the logo of the club's sponsors. Consequently Spurs played at Wembley with some players in long-sleeved shirts that carried the logo of sponsors Holstein, while others wore short-sleeved shirts bearing no sponsorship logo. The advertising agency of a rival brewer were quick to react. Days later, national newspapers carried an advertisement featuring Glenn Hoddle at Wembley wearing one of the 'sponsor-free' shirts with the caption 'I bet he drinks Carling Black Label'.

For the first three months of 1989–90 no one noticed that the goalposts at Portsmouth's Fratton Park were seven inches lower than the regulation height.

Leeds United won the League Championship in 1992 (the last year of the Football League in its old format). On the books at the time was Eric Cantona who, due to a personality clash with manager Howard Wilkinson, was unable to command a regular first-team place and often found himself on the substitutes bench. Though later to be a regular in the team, when Alex Ferguson made an offer for Cantona, Leeds manager Howard Wilkinson had no hesitation in selling him to Manchester United.

England's match against Germany in Munich in 1994 was cancelled when it was discovered the German FA had unwittingly scheduled the match for 20 April – the date of Adolf Hitler's birthday.

In 1994–95, the draw for the second round of the Auto Windscreens Cup included 'Exeter City or Cardiff City will play . . . Exeter City or Cardiff City'. Rather than one ball specifying the number of the unresolved tie between the teams being entered into the drum, both clubs had had numbered balls entered.

In 1995, the Pro-Line Pools Company in Canada issued 1,940 football pools coupons of which 1,690 shared the winning jackpot, resulting in the company having to pay out some $800,000. The matches featured on the coupon in question were from the English Football League, all of which had ended earlier that day.

Dia by name . . . In 1996, Southampton manager Graeme Souness announced to the media that he had signed the Senegal international Ali Dia. The new signing was scheduled to play in a midweek reserve match, but it was postponed. Souness named Dia as a substitute for Southampton's Premiership match against Leeds United on 23 November and introduced him into the game after 24 minutes following an injury to Matthew Le Tissier. After only minutes on the field it became obvious to Souness and everyone present that Dia was not the player he was supposed to be. Such was his 'performance', Souness substituted Dia after 53 minutes. It transpired that Souness and Southampton had been misled by the player's representatives; rather than being a Senegal international, Dia had only played for an amateur club in Senegal. His contract was terminated and Dia left the club to return to Senegal.

Playing for England in a 2006 World Cup qualifier against Croatia, goalkeeper Paul Robinson (Spurs) received a harmless-looking back-pass from Gary Neville. Robinson decided to kick the ball upfield, missed it completely, and the ball travelled under his boot and into the net to give Croatia what proved to be an unassailable 2-0 lead.

In 2007, David Beckham left Real Madrid for LA Galaxy. Financially, a great move for Beckham. Career-wise . . .

During the 2006 World Cup Finals, English referee Graham Poll booked Josip Šimunić of Croatia twice before sending him off for a third offence.

In 2006–07, Bury became the first club to win in the second round of the FA Cup but not to appear in the third. In round two Bury defeated Chester City, only for the FA to discover that Bury had fielded an ineligible player. Bury were expelled from the competition and Chester reinstated.

On 31 January 2008, Brechin City were expelled from the Scottish FA Cup for fielding two ineligible players in their fourth-round tie against Hamilton Academical. Initially the SFA had fined Brechin £10,000 for playing loanee Michael Paton as a substitute. When it subsequently came to light that Willie Dyer was also ineligible, the decision was overruled, expulsion was the new punishment, and Hamilton were reinstated.

 Prior to the saturation coverage of football by television and radio and the growth of the internet and mobile phones, other than results and match reports in newspapers, football magazines and annuals were the prime source of information for supporters. Many have long since disappeared, but a number continue to enjoy success . . .

Charles Buchan's Football Monthly

This iconic football magazine was founded by Charles Buchan (Sunderland, Arsenal and England). Buchan was also one of the founders of the Football Writers Association.

The first edition appeared in September 1951 and featured on its cover Stanley Matthews (Blackpool) – another first for Stan. It was edited by Charles Buchan and John Thompson, who wrote, 'Our object is to provide a publication that will be worthy of our National game and the grand sportsmen who play and watch it.' (Target market males, then.)

The magazine had three different titles: *Charles Buchan's Football Monthly* (editions 1–240); *Football Monthly* (editions 241–264); and *Football Monthly Digest* (editions 265–274). The final edition, number 274, was published in January 1974.

Following the death of Charles Buchan in 1960, the magazine was edited by John Thompson until April 1970, and from May 1970 to the final edition in 1974 by Pat Collins.

In its first year of existence the magazine sold 60,000 copies per month. In 1959, monthly sales were 120,000, peaking to some 150,000 in 1961-62.

The price of the first edition was 1s 6d (7.5p). It remained at that price for eleven years. In August 1962 it increased to two shillings (10p), but to compensate, content was also increased, to 64 pages. In April 1966 the price rose again, to 2s 6d (12.5p); in April 1968 (200th issue) to three shillings (15p); in January 1971 to 17p; and in August 1972 to 20p, which remained the price until the magazine's demise in January 1974.

CBFM broke new ground by having a colour picture on its cover. From the first edition to 1957, colour pictures of players and teams were hand-tinted on to original black and white photographs. This was also the case for the magazine's annual, *Charles Buchan's Soccer Gift Book*, a mainstay of Christmas stockings in the 1950s and 1960s. For many readers the pictures of players in *CBFM* were the only way supporters could see what a player from another team looked like, should he not actually have appeared at their home football ground.

The first original colour photographs appeared in the November 1957 edition, at which time *CBFM* was the only football magazine to carry original colour pictures of players and teams. In the 1960s, the vast majority of these photographs were the work of Peter Stuart.

Popular photographic features were action shots from matches, a collection of shots of a famous footballer at home (almost always featuring the player and his car), team shots, and posed photographs of individual players. Invariably the latter involved a player having just kicked a ball posing like a Tiller girl, or arms behind head with ball in hands as if about to take a throw-in.

The magazine devoted a page to the Charles Buchan's Boys Club, which in 1967 had 100,000 members.

A page was also devoted to a feature on an amateur club. This was compiled and written by Norman Ackland, whose surname, for many readers, was suggestive of an amateur football club, such as Bishop Auckland or West Auckland. Ackland was London-based and obviously on limited expenses as just about every club featured was situated in London or the home counties.

'Lead' time – the time between submission of copy and actual publication – was lengthy. *CBFM* carried reports of major matches such as England internationals that had taken place up to three months earlier, but, curiously, they still managed to convey immediacy. The first black and white pictures of England's World Cup success in July 1966 did not appear until the September edition; the first colour photographs of the tournament featured in the October edition.

Unlike newspapers, *CBFM* carried every transfer that took place under the heading 'Transfer Market Moves'. Again, this information could be up to three months old, but as it detailed transfers of players between lower division and also non-league clubs, for many readers it was 'news'. Such information was not available from any other source.

Other popular *CBFM* features: interviews with players, which usually carried a startling and revealing headline such as 'The Army MADE Me Play Right-half' (by Johnny Newman); 'Soccer Sideshow' by Leslie Yates, a compendium of curious stories from clubs; 'Swap Your Programmes – Here!'; 'The Things They Say' –a digest of opinions from the press; 'Dear Sir' – readers' letters, invariably featuring a letter suggesting look-alike players (the magazine would print photographs of the two players concerned but never adopted the cliché of swapping names under the pics). In the days before Sunday football was given official blessing, 'Fixtures Wanted' expanded into a double-page spread of small ads from teams all over the country asking for friendly games within a certain radius. Many of the teams boasted elaborate names such as Real Bexhill or Internazionale Celtic (from Hampshire).

In the early 1970s, as coverage of football on television increased, and in response to this newspapers began to devote more column space to the game and change the way they reported football, circulation of *CBFM* decreased rapidly until the magazine finally folded in January 1974.

It is well over 30 years since *Charles Buchan's Football Monthly* last hit the news stands, but the magazine still enjoys considerable popularity with football fans of a certain age and is widely collected. In 2006, *The Best of Charles Buchan's Football Monthly* was published. As the title suggests, it was a compilation of articles, photographs and features from past editions of the magazine.

Soccer Star

Began life on 8 November 1952 as *Raich Carter's Soccer Star*, though whether the former Sunderland, Derby, Hull City and England player was as involved in the editing of this magazine as Buchan was with *CBFM* is doubtful. The name was shortened to *Soccer Star* in the mid-1950s.

Unlike *CBFM*, *Soccer Star* was a weekly football magazine.

Its unique selling point was that it featured different team photographs every week, on the front and back cover.

Though the cover was glossy paper, the inside pages were matt and did not carry colour photographs until the late 1960s.

A regular contributor to *Soccer Star* was the football writer and historian Jack Rollin, who later launched and edited *Rothmans Football Yearbook*.

Every week *Soccer Star* carried results, teams and attendances for every game in England and Scotland. Though this information was two, some-times three weeks old, it still suggested immediacy as at the time no other newspaper or magazine conveyed such statistics.

In addition to news of clubs and players in England and Scotland, *Soccer Star* also carried news of world football and numerous semi-professional and amateur leagues. In these days of Premiership-dominated football news, a football magazine that devoted almost half of its coverage to the lower divisions of the Football League and non-league football is almost unthinkable; but part of the success of *Soccer Star* was, as editor Graham Payne once wrote, that 'We recognize that the majority of football fans do not support First Division clubs.' Laudable as this was, *Soccer Star*'s policy of heavily featuring lower division and non-league football contributed to its downfall in the late 1960s when the requirements of the majority of readers/supporters were primarily geared towards top-flight and international football. Like *CBFM*, *Soccer Star* suffered from poor sales in the late 1960s and folded in 1970.

World Soccer

World Soccer was launched in September 1960 and, as the name suggests, brought its readers news from the international football scene. The magazine featured league results and tables from all continents, and for almost two decades was the only source of this type of information for UK football fans.

In the early days of publication, unlike *CBFM* and *Soccer Star*, there was little, if any, room for levity, which engendered in many readers a notion that the magazine took itself very seriously.

World Soccer has always featured authoritative articles on the world football scene by writers such as Brian Glanville and John Ballard.

In 1982, *World Soccer* launched a series of awards: Player, Manager and Team of the Year. In 2005, the annual awards were expanded to include Young Player of the Year and Referee of the Year.

World Soccer remains the periodical authority on world football. It is now a part of IPC Media, and a member of an umbrella group of similar titles published in other countries, such as *Kicker* (Germany), *A Bola* (Spain), and *La Gazzetta dello Sport* (Italy).

Television coverage of major European and international competitions and the influx of overseas players into British football has broadened the horizons of football fans in the UK and has helped *World Soccer* maintain healthy sales in the UK.

FourFourTwo

FourFourTwo is the UK's best-selling monthly football magazine, with monthly sales figures in excess of 100,000.

In February 2007, the magazine celebrated its 150th edition.

The magazine features a mixture of authoritative and serious-minded articles together with irreverent humour and nostalgia pieces. Another reason for its success is its ability to relate to the needs and feelings of the regular supporter.

Current contributors include Henry Winter and James Richardson; past contributors include Brian Clough, Stan Bowles, David Platt and Robbie Savage.

Since its launch over 20 years ago, *FourFourTwo* has seen off opposition from all manner of monthly football magazines, including *Total Football* and BBC's *Match of the Day* magazine.

Popular features include 'Magic Moment'; 'Upfront' – an interview with a leading football figure; 'They Said What?' – quotes; 'Insider' – football rumours; and 'My Perfect XI', in which a player chooses his dream team of players from the club he is most associated with. The 'Reviews' section offers comprehensive coverage of the latest books, DVDs and games, though for some readers such reviews can occasionally border on the precious and pretentious.

The magazine also prints versions in Norway and Australia.

Shoot

Shoot was launched as a weekly football magazine in 1968, aimed at the teenage market.

The cornerstone of its success was articles and interviews with leading figures in English and Scottish football, colour photographs of players and teams, and columns written by star players. Past contributors include Kevin Keegan, Charlie Nicholas and Bryan Robson; contemporary contributors include Joe Cole and David James.

One popular feature of the magazine was Paul Trevillion's comic strip 'You Are the Ref' which has since been afforded cult status and now appears in the *Observer* sport supplement.

Shoot often presented its readers with free gifts. 'League Ladders' were the most popular, and were often given free before the start of every season. The gift comprised a thin sheet of card on which were printed blank tables, one for every division in the Football League, with a slit in the card for each position. Over the weeks readers received T-shaped card tabs on each of which was printed the name of a club in team colours; readers could then insert each tab into the relevant slit according to the club's position in the division. Having begun this exercise with great gusto, the enthusiasm of readers to keep their League Ladders up to date, however, invariably waned on a weekly basis; often the League Ladders were cast aside after a few weeks. Did anyone regularly update them from season start to finish?

Shoot quickly established itself as the UK's top-selling weekly football magazine, a position it held until the early 1990s.

In the late 1990s, *Shoot* became a monthly magazine. It was still aimed at the teenage market, so was not in 'direct' competition with *FourFourTwo*. It continues to flourish.

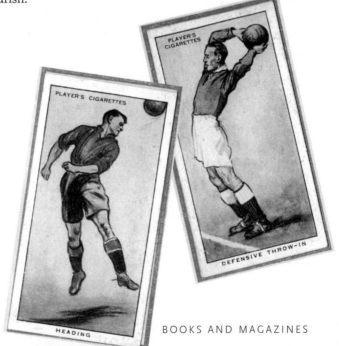

Match

Match was launched in 1979 as a weekly football magazine aimed at the teenage and pre-teen market, and it has since then enjoyed considerable success.

The cover price in 1979 was 25p.

The magazine specializes in big-name interviews, quizzes and features on star players and major clubs. Colour photographs of leading players and folded picture pull-outs are also a popular feature of the magazine.

In the 1990s, *Match* overtook *Shoot* as the UK's top-selling weekly football magazine with sales of 200,000 per week. In 2006, weekly sales stood at 130,000.

Match has been a monthly since 2007. Its target market remains teenage and pre-teen football fans, primarily of the major Premiership clubs.

When Saturday Comes

The 'thinking' supporters' favourite football magazine, *WSC* first appeared in March 1986 as the football organ of the music fanzine *Snipe*.

WSC was created by Mike Ticher, a 'multi-tasker' who wrote, edited and produced the artwork and layout for issue one virtually by himself. As *WSC* grew in popularity, Ticher assumed the role of editor before eventually emigrating to Australia.

When Saturday Comes took its name from the Undertones song of the same title.

Self-billed as a 'half decent football magazine' – but that's being characteristically modest. Over the years it has developed into a football magazine out of the 'left field' containing authoritative, revealing and objective articles, humour and informed comment aimed at the more 'intelligent' supporter while continuing to convey the impression that it is written by the ordinary football fan – which it is.

WSC remains true to the policy adopted when it first appeared: no platitudes, no clichéd football writing, no sycophantic interviews, no forelock tugging to club PR departments, no adherence to moronic tribal rivalries, and against the carpet-bagging individuals and groups who take control of clubs purely as money-making ventures.

One of WSC's strengths is that it has always been an organ for the voice of the true supporter, welcoming contact and contributions.

One of its distinguishing features is the 'joke' that forms the front cover of every edition. This is a photograph of personalities in the game (usually players or managers), the gag, always topical, taking the form of a speech bubble emanating from the mouths of the subjects.

In December 2007, WSC celebrated its 250th issue.

Regular features include 'Newswatch' and 'Webwatch'; 'Shot! Archive' – a poignant football-related photograph from times gone by; 'As Good As It Got' – for a team or player; a letters page; reviews of books, DVDs, games, etc.; and 'Season in Brief' – a thumbnail look at the events of a past season, or a single division in a particular season.

WSC also sells a variety of football-related products, such as T-shirts, which invariably carry a 'left field' message, profound statement or funny line. It also has its own publishing arm for books.

Sky Sports Football Yearbook

Considered the 'bible' of British football, the yearbook has always had a sponsor. From its launch at the start of the 1970–71 season to 2002–03 it was known as the *Rothmans Football Yearbook*. From 2003–04 it became the *Sky Sports Football Yearbook*.

It contains a comprehensive guide to every club and its teams, results, goalscorers and attendances for the previous season. There is also a Players Directory, an historic and annual guide to English and Scottish club statistics and all cup competitions, and a complete records section. Other major sections feature comprehensive and historic coverage of European, international and non-league football, obituaries, and a day-by-day diary of events for the previous season.

The book runs to some 1,100 pages and is packed with facts and information. It is widely used by managers, football writers, broadcasters and supporters alike – an indispensable guide to football which improves every year.

Originally the book was compiled and edited by Jack Rollin and Leslie Vernon; today, Jack's daughter Glenda is the senior editor.

The only downside to the yearbook is that the paperback versions are so voluminous and weighty that over time the binding on the spine gives up the ghost and you are left with loose leaves.

News of the World Football Annual

A 'pocket battleship' of a football encyclopaedia which was first published in 1887. The annual has its origins in the 1940s and early 1950s when it was known as the *Sunday Chronicle Football Annual*. In 1956 the *Empire News* purchased the *Sunday Chronicle* and the 1956–57 annual changed its name accordingly to *Empire News and Sunday Chronicle Football Annual*. In 1961–62, following the acquisition of the *Empire News* by the *News of the World*, it went out under the title *News of the World and Empire News Football Annual*. In 1956–66 the association with the *Empire News* was dropped and the annual became known simply as the *News of the World Football Annual*.

Like the *Sky Sports Football Yearbook*, the *NOW Annual* contains a comprehensive guide to English, Scottish, European and international football, including detailed current and historic records and statistics. The current edition also contains a wealth of information not to be found in other annuals, such as every FA Cup Final team since 1900, 'Famous Club Feats' and a glossary of 'unusual' football records and achievements – again, an indispensable guide for the football fan.

In addition to a comprehensive coverage of all aspects of football, up until the mid-1980s the annual also covered rugby league and rugby union.

In the 1960s, the annual was edited by Frank Butler and Malcolm Gunn, in the 1970s by Frank Butler and Patrick Collins.

Playfair Football Annual

Playfair, launched in 1948–49, also offered a comprehensive guide to clubs, players, records and statistics (particularly relating to the previous season), but what gave it an advantage over its rivals was that it contained numerous photographs of teams, players and major matches of the previous campaign. From its launch through the 1950s, *Playfair* also included a review of how each English and Scottish club had fared the previous season.

Among the first editors were Gordon Ross and Albert Sewell.

In keeping with rival publications, each edition contained articles by leading figures in football: managers, administrators and players. The 1951–52 edition, for instance, featured pieces by Jackie Milburn (Newcastle United), Arthur Rowe (Tottenham manager) and W. R. Wall (assistant secretary of Arsenal).

Indicative of the status given to amateur football at the time, in particular leagues comprising teams of former public schoolboys, such information was often given preference over major non-league football and even results and summaries of a World Cup.

Originally, *Playfair* was not a pocket-sized annual, measuring seven inches by five inches (18cm by 12cm). It changed to pocket size in the late 1950s.

In 1947, *Playfair* also launched a cricket version of its annual. For a number of years this was also edited by Gordon Ross.

In the late 1960s, *Playfair* launched a non-league version of the annual.

Despite stiff competition, from other annuals, the internet and elsewhere, the *Playfair Football* (and *Cricket*) *Annual* is still going strong.

They Enjoyed Their Moment in the Sun . . .

Goal, launched in August 1968, a weekly that prided itself on 'big colour pictures and big interviews with the biggest names in the game' – but not, over time, big sales. One regular *Goal* feature was 'The Girl Behind the Man', a photograph and profile of a footballer's wife – the original WAG feature.

Football Weekly News (early 1970s); *Northern Football* (early to mid-1960s); *Football League Review* (see 'Programmes'); *Inside Soccer* (newspaper of the early 1970s.

Foul – fanzine of the 1970s and a forerunner of and inspiration for *When Saturday Comes*. Radical views on the game as espoused by fine young writers of the time such as Steve Tongue and Stan Hey.

The Park Drive Book of Football (annual of the 1960s), which carried the disclaimer 'It is not suggested in any way that mention of any individual implies that he is a smoker or in favour of any brand of cigarette'.

The Big Book of Football Champions – annual with hand-tinted photographs, not of the quality of Charles Buchan's, which made players' faces sport an inscrutable look and an unnerving pinky-orange complexion.

News Chronicle and Daily Dispatch Football Annual, the 1957–58 edition of which began with the startling sentence 'How many people realize there's a revolution going on? Yes, a revolution. What else can you call it when thousands of football fans are switching to Fixed Odds betting?' Che sera sera.

Arguably the most esoteric and, judging by the title, dullest football book ever published? *The Parallel Growth and Development of Telecommunications and Soccer* by Bruno Amatucci and Luciano Ragno, which hit the bookshelves in the mid-1990s. (Now why didn't I think of that for the Ph.D.?).

Caps

Caps are awarded to players making international appearances for England, Scotland, Wales and Northern Ireland. It is a tradition dating back to the origins of the Football League in the Victorian age when, during games, players routinely wore caps denoting club colours. When the first ever international match took place between England and Scotland in 1872, players wore caps, as was the norm. When outfield players ceased to wear caps some years later, representing one's country at football continued to be marked by the symbolic presentation of a cap. The first caps were awarded to the players who participated in the Scotland v. England international on 31 March 1886 in Glasgow.

Between 1953 and 1984 the four British Football Associations decided to award players who participated in the Home International Championship with one cap for the series (three matches) rather than for each individual match. England skipper Billy Wright (Wolves) appeared in 18 home internationals between 1953 and 1959 for which he was awarded six caps. Thus Wright's career total of 105 England 'caps' is, in reality, 93.

Peter Shilton holds the record for the most caps (international appearances) for England – 125 between 1970 and 1990.

England cap centurions: Peter Shilton 125, Bobby Moore 108, Bobby Charlton 106, Billy Wright 105, David Beckham 102.

The following players hold the record for caps awarded by the other home nations and the Republic of Ireland: Kenny Dalglish (Scotland, 102, 1971–86); Pat Jennings (Northern Ireland, 119, 1964–86); Neville Southall (Wales, 92, 1982–97); Steve Staunton (Republic of Ireland, 102, 1988-2002).

On 30 May 2006, Theo Walcott became the youngest player to make his debut for England when he appeared against Hungary at the age of 17 years and 75 days.

The youngest British player ever to be awarded a full cap is Norman Whiteside (Manchester United) who was 17 years and 41 days old when he made his full international debut for Northern Ireland against Yugoslavia (World Cup) on 17 June 1982. Consequently Whiteside is also the youngest British player to make his debut in the finals of a World Cup.

The youngest player to be capped by Scotland is John Lambie, at 17 years and 92 days, v. Ireland, 20 March 1886.

The youngest player to be awarded a cap by Wales is Gareth Bale (then of Southampton), who on 27 May 2006, aged 16 years and 315 days, appeared as a substitute against Trinidad and Tobago. On 7 October 2006, Bale also became the youngest player to score for the full Wales national team when he netted in the game against Slovakia.

The oldest player to have received a cap from England is Stanley Matthews, who was 42 years and 103 days old when he played against Denmark in Copenhagen on 15 May 1957.

In 1955, Doncaster Rovers goalkeeper Ken Hardwick was delighted to be chosen for his first cap for England Under-23s. Unfortunately Hardwick was never to represent England at that level: the FA was soon alerted to the fact that he was 30 years old.

The oldest player capped by any of the home nations is Billy Meredith (Manchester City), who was 45 years and 229 days old when he played for Wales against England at Highbury on 15 March 1920. It was Meredith's 48th cap for Wales.

The oldest player to receive his first England cap is Alexander Morten, a goal-keeper with Crystal Palace, who was 41 years and 113 days old when he kept goal against Scotland on 8 March 1873. It was Morten's only appearance for England.

Jack Cock (Huddersfield Town) was the first Cornishman to be capped for England (v. Northern Ireland, 1920). Following his transfer to Chelsea he won a further two caps (both against Scotland). At the post-match buffet for the latter game against Scotland Cock entertained the players by singing a number of songs. His talent was spotted by a theatrical agent who contracted him to sing in music halls. Cock went on to become a popular variety star and also appeared in a number of British films.

Arsenal centre-half Leslie Compton was 38 years and 64 days old when he received his first England cap in the 4-2 victory over Wales at Roker Park on 15 November 1950.

The oldest debutant cap for Scotland is Ronnie Simpson (Celtic), who was 36 years and 186 days old when he kept goal against England at Wembley on 15 April 1967. It was a memorable day for both Simpson and Scotland, who inflicted upon England their first defeat (3-2) since the World Cup win in July 1966.

Walter Winterbottom, England manager from 1947 to 1962, did not have total control over the England team, which was chosen by an FA selection committee. Though Winterbottom exerted an influence over the years, he was forever struggling to wrest selection of the England side away from the committee. He later said, 'There were occasions when the FA selection committee chose a player for England for no other reason than they thought he was a gentleman and a good sportsman, and this deserved a cap.'

The first Fourth Division player to win an international cap was Vic Rouse (Crystal Palace) for Wales v. Northern Ireland in 1959.

George Berry was born in Rostrup, West Germany. His grandfather was Scottish and his father Jamaican. George won his first international cap for Wales against West Germany in 1979. He qualified to play by virtue of the fact that his mother was Welsh.

Johnny Carey (Manchester United, 1938–53) won 29 caps for the Republic of Ireland and seven for Northern Ireland. He also appeared for a Great Britain XI.

Carey, along with Billy Gorman (Brentford), holds the distinction of having played against England for two different international teams within two days. On 28 September 1946, Carey and Gorman played for Northern Ireland in the 7-2 defeat by England at Windsor Park, and two days later (30 September), both were in the Republic of Ireland team that lost 1-0 to England at Dalymount Park. Included in the Republic side that day were brothers Dr Kevin and Michael O'Flanagan, both Bohemians and both of whom also played rugby for Ireland. Billy Walsh (Manchester City), who had been capped by England as a schoolboy, also turned out for Ireland that day.

Davy Walsh (Linfield and West Bromwich Albion) is the only player to have represented both Northern Ireland and the Republic of Ireland in World Cup matches – for Northern Ireland (1950) v. Wales, and for the Republic v. Sweden in 1949 and twice against France in 1953.

George Antonio, a winger with Stoke City, was selected for his first cap for Wales in 1937, only for the Welsh FA then to discover that his parents' house, in which he was born, was situated 75 yards over the border in Shropshire. As a result, Antonio was de-selected. He never did win a cap for Wales – or England.

Cecil Moore (Sheffield United) was capped for Northern Ireland in 1949, emigrated to America, and appeared for the USA against England in 1953.

Tom Keane (Swansea) was awarded two caps for playing a single international for Northern Ireland. Keane's only international appearance was against Scotland in 1949, but when he was presented with his cap it was noticed that the words 'British Home International Championship' had been omitted. The cap was retained by the Northern Ireland Football Association and a new one presented to Keane.

There are only two instances of players capped by England who have also played against England in an international match. During World War Two, Stan Mortensen (Blackpool) was named as reserve for a game against Wales at Wembley. During the first-half Ivor Powell sustained an injury that resulted in him taking no further part in the match. All wartime internationals were deemed 'unofficial', so during the half-time interval it was agreed Mortensen would take the place of Powell in the Wales team. Thus Mortensen made his international debut for Wales against England prior to winning his first cap for England, against Portugal in 1947. Tommy Smith (Liverpool) was capped by England against Wales in 1971, and in 1976, while spending the summer playing for Tampa Bay Rowdies, he was selected to play for the USA in an 'unofficial' international against England.

Ian Callaghan (Liverpool) won his second England cap against France during the World Cup of 1966, and his third 11 years later against Switzerland at Wembley in 1977.

Frank Rankmore (Peterborough United) won his first and only cap for Wales when he came on as a substitute for Glyn James (Blackpool) against Chile in Santiago on 22 May 1966 – only he had to wait 25 years to receive it. The Welsh FA deemed that Frank (who also played for Cardiff City) did not merit a cap for his 15-minute appearance; what's more, he was not allowed to keep his shirt as a memento. For years Frank's son campaigned on behalf of his father and he was finally rewarded for his efforts a quarter of a century later when the Welsh FA had a special cap made to mark his father's appearance against Chile.

Kevin Keegan was awarded his first England cap against Wales on 15 November 1972. His second cap was also against Wales (24 January 1973), as was his third (11 May 1974). He remains the only player to have played his first three games for England against the same opposition.

Willie Humphries gained caps for Northern Ireland (1962-65) when playing for Irish, English and Welsh clubs – Ards, Coventry City and Swansea.

Charlie George, widely considered one of the best players in Britain during the 1970s, was capped only once by England, and he didn't last the full 90 minutes. George won his only cap against the Republic of Ireland in 1977 but was substituted by manager Don Revie after only 57 minutes.

Bill Nicholson (Spurs) won his first (and only) cap for England against Portugal at Wembley on 19 May 1951. It was very much a day of 'firsts' for Nicholson: he also scored his first goal for England in the first minute of the match with his first touch of the ball.

Johnny Byrne won his first cap for England in 1962 (v. Northern Ireland) while playing for Crystal Palace in the Third Division. Tommy Lawton (Notts County), Reg Matthews (Coventry City), Peter Taylor (Crystal Palace) and Steve Bull (Wolverhampton Wanderers) also gained England caps while playing their club football in the Third Division.

On 3 April 1974, Sir Alf Ramsey set a record by including six new caps in the England team that played Portugal – his last game in charge as England manager. The debutants were Phil Parkes (QPR – his only cap), Mike Pejic (Stoke City), Martin Dobson (Burnley), Dave Watson (Sunderland), Stan Bowles (QPR) and Trevor Brooking (West Ham United). England drew 0-0.

On 12 February 2003, Sven-Göran Eriksson also gave an outing to six new caps, in England's game against Australia at Upton Park, the impact of which was somewhat diluted by the fact that five of the debutants were introduced at half-time when Eriksson made 11 changes to the side!

Gary Howlett (Brighton) travelled to the other side of the world to earn his first and only international cap, and played for only 19 minutes. On 3 June 1984, Howlett was named as a substitute for the Republic of Ireland's game against China which was taking place in Sapporo, Japan. Nineteen minutes from time Howlett replaced Pat Byrne (Hearts), but was never chosen for the Republic again.

The only player to win both semi-professional and full caps for England is Steve Guppy. Guppy was chosen for the England semi-professional team while playing for Wycombe Wanderers in the Conference in 1989–90, and in 1999, when at Leicester City, he won his first and only full cap for England against Belgium at the Stadium of Light (Sunderland).

In 1996, Sir Geoff Hurst sold the cap awarded to him for playing for England in the 1966 World Cup Final for £37,600 at an auction at Christie's.

The 'Billy Wright' collection of England caps, medals and other personal memorabilia fetched £100,000 at Christie's auction in Glasgow in 1996.

At an auction in 2002, TV personality Nick Hancock purchased an England cap awarded to Sir Stanley Matthews for £3,525. Sir Stanley Matthews won 54 England caps, the vast majority of which, over the years, he donated to charitable causes to be sold to raise funds.

Television reference to international caps, from Johnny Speight's *Till Death Us Do Part*:

Alf Garnett:	You know bloody nothing 'bout football!
Else:	I do.
Alf Garnett:	Go on then, tell me one thing you know 'bout football.
Else:	Billy Wright . . . he's won the most hats for England.

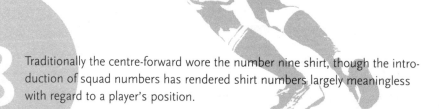

8 Traditionally the centre-forward wore the number nine shirt, though the introduction of squad numbers has rendered shirt numbers largely meaningless with regard to a player's position.

In the 1970s, the tactic of playing two men up front as a spearhead attack led to such players being referred to as 'strikers'. As a consequence, the term 'centre-forward' was used less and less.

In essence, the job of the centre-forward is to score goals. Goalscorers invariably make headlines, which resulted in the position being widely thought of as the most glamorous in a team.

The most prolific centre-forward English football has seen in terms of goals scored is Arthur Rowley (West Bromwich Albion, Fulham, Leicester City and Shrewsbury Town, 1946–64). In 619 League appearances his aggregate of 434 goals still stands as a Football League record. He also scored 32 FA Cup goals and one for England 'B'. He scored 20 League goals or more in a season 13 times.

Though an inside-forward rather than a centre-forward, Jimmy Greaves (Chelsea, AC Milan, Tottenham Hotspur and West Ham United, 1957–70) amassed a record 491 goals if cup, international and representative matches are included. Greaves holds the record for the most goals scored (357) in the top division of English football.

On 12 September 1883 Arbroath centre-forward John Petrie scored 13 in his club's historic 36-0 victory over Bon Accord in the Scottish Cup first round – a British record for a player in an individual game.

Between 1922 and 1938, Jimmy McGrory scored 397 goals for Celtic and 13 for Clydebank, a career tally of 410, which is a record in Scottish senior football. Should one include internationals and representative matches, McGrory scored 550 goals during his career.

The most League goals scored by a centre-forward for a single club is 349 by 'Dixie' Dean, for Everton (1925–37). Dean also played for Tranmere Rovers and Notts County and scored a total of 379 League goals during his career. He also holds the record for the most hat-tricks scored – 34.

Other notable one-club goalscoring centre-forwards: George Camsell (Middlesbrough, 1925–39), 326 goals; John Ayteo (Bristol City, 1951–66), 315 goals; and Vic Watson (West Ham United, 1920–35), 306 goals.

In 1919–20, Millwall's leading goalscorer was centre-forward Jimmy Broad with 32 goals. The second leading scorer netted just four.

Prior to World War Two, Sunderland's David Halliday scored 30-plus goals in four successive seasons: 38, 36, 36 and 49 (1925–26 to 1928–29).

Hughie Gallacher holds the record for the most goals (five) scored by an individual in a match for Scotland. Result: Ireland 3 Scotland 7, in Belfast on 23 February 1929.

No one has scored more goals in his first season of first-class football than Glentoran centre-forward Fred Roberts. In 1930–31, Roberts scored an astonishing 96 goals in his debut season for the Irish club – 55 in the League,

28 in the City Cup, seven in the Antrim Shield, four in the Irish Cup and two in the Belfast Charity Cup.

On 14 December 1935, Ted Drake scored all seven of Arsenal's goals in their 7-1 victory at Aston Villa. In so doing he equalled the number of goals scored by an individual player in a First Division match (the other holder is James Ross, for Preston v. Stoke City, 1888) and set a new record for the number of goals scored by an individual whose team was playing away from home. Amazingly, Drake's first six goals were the fruits of his first six shots at goal.

Twelve days after Drake's feat, Robert 'Bunny' Bell scored a triple hat-trick (nine goals) for Tranmere Rovers, who beat Oldham Athletic 13-4 (Division Three North).

On 13 April 1936, due to injuries to key players, Joe Payne, a reserve wing-half with Luton Town, was pressed into service as a centre-forward against Bristol Rovers in the Third Division South. Payne set the individual scoring record in the Football League by netting ten goals in Luton's crushing 12-0 win.

Sunderland centre-forward Bobby Gurney and inside-forward Raich Carter were the last two players from the same team to score 30-plus goals in a single season in top-flight English football. Both scored 31 League goals in 1935–36.

Between 1946 and 1955, Harold Bell played 401 consecutive matches for Tranmere Rovers.

In 1952, Don Robson was given a trial as a centre-forward by Doncaster Rovers. Robson played in a reserve team match, scored seven goals, and was immediately signed. He was at the time doing National Service in the RAF which refused him leave, and he never again played for Doncaster. When he was demobbed in 1953 he signed for Gateshead United (Division Three North).

The record number of goals in a Football League representative match is six, by Bolton Wanderers centre-forward Nat Lofthouse. Nat achieved this feat in the 7-1 win against the Irish League at Molineux (Wolverhampton Wanderers) on 24 September 1952.

In the 1950s, Manchester United tried 'A' team goalkeeper Ray Wood at centre-forward in a match and he scored four goals. Wood, however, preferred goalkeeping, and as a keeper went on to help United win the Football League Championship, and played in the 1957 FA Cup Final.

21 February 1959 was a bleak day in Dundee. Dundee United lost 8-2 at Berwick Rangers, for whom centre-forward Eric Adamson scored a double hat-trick (a record for the club), while Dundee lost 6-4 at home to Motherwell, the latter's centre-forward, Gerry Baker, scoring four.

In 1959–60, Grimsby Town centre-forward Ralph Hunt scored in ten successive League matches. The Grimsby matchday programme ventured to suggest that 'This club will, in all probability, never witness such a feat again.' Two years later, in 1961–62, Hunt's replacement at Grimsby Town, Ron Rafferty, scored in ten successive League matches. Curiously, both players had started their careers at Portsmouth.

In the 1960s, when the England team organized its own 'fun' practice matches after official training at the Bank of England Ground, Bobby Charlton usually opted to play in goal and Gordon Banks chose to play centre-forward. Just for a change!

On 17 March 1962, winger Davie Wilson switched to centre-forward for Rangers' match against Falkirk and scored six goals in a 7-1 victory.

 When Jackie [Mudie] was manager of Port Vale he couldn't attract a 20-goal-a-season centre-forward if he asked one to beat him with a shitty stick. Understandable, really, because it was a strange request.

EDDIE CLAMP, former team-mate of Mudie at Stoke City

In 1965–66, centre-forward Alan Gilzean scored 12 goals for Spurs – all at White Hart Lane.

Sir Geoff Hurst was the last player to score six goals in a League match, in West Ham United's 8-0 victory over Sunderland (Division One) on 19 October 1968. In an interview after the game, Sunderland defender Martin Harvey ironically informed the press, 'We are so gutted, we attended the post-match player's buffet and ate nothing.'

As one might expect, centre-forwards hold the divisional records for the highest number of goals scored in a single season:

PREMIERSHIP:
34 goals – Andy Cole (Newcastle United) 1993–94 and Alan Shearer (Blackburn Rovers) 1994–95.
FIRST DIVISION:
60 goals – 'Dixie' Dean (Everton) 1927–28 (39 games).
SECOND DIVISION (now Championship):
59 goals – George Camsell (Middlesbrough) 1926–27.
THIRD DIVISION (now League One):
39 goals – Derek Reeves (Southampton) 1959–60.
THIRD DIVISION NORTH (now defunct):
55 goals – Ted Harston (Mansfield Town) 1936–37.
THIRD DIVISION SOUTH (now defunct):
55 goals – Joe Payne (Luton Town) 1936–37.
DIVISION FOUR (now League Two):
52 goals – Terry Bly (Peterborough United) 1960–61.
SCOTTISH PREMIER LEAGUE:
35 goals – Henrik Larsson (Celtic) 2000–01.
SCOTTISH DIVISION ONE:
52 goals – Bill McFadyen (Motherwell) 1931–32.
SCOTTISH DIVISION TWO:
66 goals – Jim Smith (Ayr United) 1927–28 (see Clubs).
SCOTTISH DIVISION THREE:
38 goals – Kenny Deuchar (Gretna) 2004–05.

Brian Clough's career as a centre-forward was ended prematurely through injury when the Sunderland player was only 29. Clough, however, established the highest ever goals-per-game average in English football, having scored 251 goals in a career of 274 matches, 192 for Middlesbrough (1955–61) and 54 for Sunderland (1961–64). Clough sustained his injury when playing for Sunderland against Bury on Boxing Day 1962: he had up to that point of the season scored 27 goals, and though he missed Sunderland's remaining 24 League and cup matches he still ended the season as the club's leading goalscorer. In 1964–65 he attempted a comeback and played for Sunderland reserves against Halifax Town reserves, scoring five times in a 7-1 victory. He then played three matches in the First Division, scoring one goal (against Leeds United, 5 September 1964) before retiring on the advice of doctors.

Wimbledon centre-forward Alan Cork holds a record for having scored in all four divisions of the Football League and the Premiership. Cork achieved this feat between 1977 and 1995 playing for Wimbledon, Sheffield United and Fulham.

Paul Mariner (Ipswich Town) scored in five successive England matches between November 1981 and June 1982: 1-0 v. Hungary (one goal); 2-0 v. Holland (one goal); 1-0 v. Scotland (one goal); 4-1 v. Finland (two goals); and 3-1 v. France in the 1982 World Cup (one goal). Having scored six goals in five successive internationals, Mariner then failed to score in his next nine games for England.

Ian Rush scored a record 346 goals for Liverpool in all competitions (229 in the Football League). Rush also scored 28 in 73 appearances for Wales. Along with Sir Geoff Hurst he holds the record for the most number of goals scored in the League Cup (49), and the record for goals scored in Merseyside derbies (25).

John Aldridge scored a career total of 329 goals for Newport County, Oxford United, Liverpool and Tranmere Rovers. In all competitions for those clubs he scored 410 goals in 737 matches. Aldridge also scored 45 goals in 63 matches for Real Sociedad.

Since World War Two, Alan Shearer is the only player to have scored more than 30 top-division goals in three successive seasons – 31 in 1993–94, 34 in 1994–95 and 31 in 1995–96.

Ruud van Nistelrooy began his career as a central defender with Dutch club FC Den Bosch, but following a transfer to Heerenveen was converted to a centre-forward. He joined Manchester United from PSV Eindhoven. In 2002–03, van Nistelrooy scored 44 goals in all competitions for United. In 2005–06 he was the second leading goalscorer in the Premiership with 21 but was dropped to the substitutes bench for the Carling Cup Final against Wigan Athletic. On his return to the United first team he scored against West Ham, but was dropped again for the next game. He came on as a substitute and scored United's winning goal in a 2-1 victory over Bolton Wanderers, but to the surprise of many he was then made available for transfer. He joined Real Madrid, and in his first season (2006–07) scored 33 goals in 43 matches and equalled Hugo Sanchez's La Liga record of scoring in eight successive matches.

Alan Shearer was the last player (up to 2007–08) to score five goals in a single match in top-flight English football (Newcastle United 8 Sheffield Wednesday 0, 19 September 1999).

Wayne Rooney is widely considered to be the most exciting prospect in current English football. In October 2002, at the age of sixteen, he scored for Everton at Goodison Park to end Arsenal's unbeaten run of 30 matches (Everton won 2-1). Following his transfer to Manchester United he assumed a deep-lying role but is still considered by many a centre-forward. He scored 15 goals in 64 appearances for Everton and in his first 100 matches for Manchester United netted 41 times.

Archie Thompson scored 13 goals in Australia's 31-0 victory over American Samoa in a World Cup Oceania Group qualifying match in Coffs Harbour, New South Wales on 11 April 2001.

The record number of goals by an individual in an England international is five. Three players have achieved this feat: Steve Bloomer, v. Wales at Ninian Park, Cardiff, on 16 March 1896 (Wales 1 England 9); Willie Hall, v. Ireland at Old Trafford on 16 November 1938 (England 7 Ireland 0); and Malcolm Macdonald, v. Cyprus at Wembley on 16 April 1975 (England 5 Cyprus 0).

For football fans of a certain age, arguably the most famous of all centre-forwards is the fictional Roy Race. Roy played for Melchester Rovers in a football comic strip entitled 'Roy of the Rovers' which appeared in the boys' weekly *Tiger*, before his persona and popularity earned him a comic all of his own. Roy began his 'career' with Milston Youth Club FC in 1954, when he was spotted by Melchester Rovers scout Alf Leeds, who also ran the Rovers 'A' team. He made his first-team debut for Melchester in August 1955 against Elbury Wanderers (also the debut of Blackie Gray), won every honour the game has to offer, scored over 500 goals and played his final game in 1993. Given that he was 15 when he was spotted playing for Milston, this means that Roy played his last match for Melchester Rovers at the age of 54 – a career to eclipse even that of Sir Stanley Matthews.

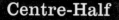

9

> Think of how gormless the average centre-half is, and it's frightening to think that half of them have to be even more gormless than that.

JACKIE BLANCHFLOWER

Over the years the role of a centre-half in a team has undergone many changes and variations, but in essence it remains the position in the centre of defence and is also often referred to as centre-back. A common alternative term for centre-half was 'a pivot', as all defensive play was deemed to revolve around the player wearing the number five shirt in the heart of defence, though one seldom hears the word today.

The idea of using a tall defender to achieve aerial dominance at the position of centre-half was first deployed by Arsenal in 1925–26. Up to this point the position of centre-half had been what today one might term midfield. It was not the Arsenal manager, Herbert Chapman, but centre-forward Charlie Buchan who suggested that the centre-half should be deployed solely as a defender and be the tallest man in defence. Chapman readily agreed.

Between 1950 and 1972, Roy Sproson played 761 League matches for Port Vale – a club appearance record, and also the record number of League matches by a centre-half. Roy's nephew, Phil Sproson, carried on the family tradition, playing 495 matches as centre-half for Vale (1978–89). Phil's father, Jess, also played for Port Vale (1940–47, 38 games), but as an inside-forward.

If there wasn't such a thing as football, we'd all be frustrated footballers.

MICK LYONS, Everton centre-half

In a playing career that spanned 20 years (1979–99), Steve Bruce played 737 League matches as a centre-half – 205 for Gillingham, 141 for Norwich City, 302 for Manchester United, 72 for Birmingham City and ten for Sheffield United. In 1990–91, he scored 13 goals for Manchester United – a record for a centre-half in a single season.

Sproson and Bruce apart, the only other regular centre-half to have played in excess of 700 League matches is John Wile. Wile began his career (1966–86) at Sunderland but never played a first-team match for the Wearsiders. He was transferred to Peterborough United, for whom he made 205 League appearances; then he moved to West Bromwich Albion, where he played exactly 500 League games.

All the team are 100 per cent behind the manager, but I can't speak for the rest of the squad.

BRIAN GREENHOFF, Manchester United centre-half, reasssuring manager Dave Sexton

Welsh football legend John Charles was equally happy playing centre-forward or centre-half. The 'Gentle Giant' maintained that playing centre-half was easier as 'you are always facing play, as opposed to when playing as a centre-forward'. Charles (whose brother, Mel, was also a centre-half and Welsh international) won the first of his 38 caps for Wales against Northern Ireland in 1950 shortly after his 18th birthday; he was, at the time, the youngest ever Welsh international. In 1957, he was transferred from Leeds United to Juventus for a then record fee for a British player of £65,000. He played mainly as a centre-forward for Juventus, scoring 93 goals in 155 appearances, only six of which were as a central defender.

1970s Manchester United centre-back Martin Buchan has a university degree in Languages. He attended university while playing for United and often studied on the team coach while travelling to away matches.

Jack Charlton was centre-half when England beat West Germany 4-2 (aet) in the 1966 World Cup Final. Jack signed for Leeds United in 1952 but did not win his first cap for England until 1965 (v. Scotland), when he was almost 30. He remained with Leeds throughout his career, scoring 95 goals in 772 matches – a more than decent strike rate for a central defender. When Charlton made his debut for Leeds, against Doncaster Rovers in 1953, manager Raich Carter didn't give the young man any instructions prior to kick-off. As the Leeds players prepared to leave the dressing room, the debutant turned to his manager and asked, 'What do you want me to do out there, boss?' Carter replied, 'See how fast their centre-forward can limp.'

Given that centre-halves are forever in the thick of it during games, no central defender has ever been sent off while playing for the full England team. The first centre-back to be red-carded while playing for an England team was Paul Elliott (Luton Town) in the Under-21 international against Denmark at Maine Road on 26 March 1986.

Charlie Hurley enjoys legendary status on Wearside and was voted by Sunderland supporters as the club's 'Player of the Century'. And Hurley's prowess and skill as a centre-half was not only appreciated on Wearside: in 1963–64, he was runner-up by virtue of a single vote to Bobby Moore as 'Footballer of the Year' at a time when Sunderland were in the Second Division. Hurley joined Sunderland from Millwall in September 1957 and had a baptism of fire in a struggling team: on his debut, Sunderland lost 7-0 at Blackpool; in his second match, they were thrashed 6-0 at Burnley. Hurley went on to play 400 matches for Sunderland (26 goals) and to win 40 caps for the Republic of Ireland. It is estimated that in all he received some 150 stitches to his head as a result of injuries sustained when challenging for the ball in the air.

> Without picking out individuals, I thought Tony Adams was excellent in the heart of defence.
>
> GRAHAM TAYLOR

When Bob Stokoe was appointed manager of Sunderland in November 1972, the Sunderland centre-forward was Dave Watson. One of Stokoe's first moves was to switch Watson to centre-half. Watson went on to win 65 caps for England in that position and to help Sunderland win the FA Cup in 1973.

> Sol Campbell appears to have got over his problems and is playing like a new man. Much more like his old self.
>
> JOHN MOTSON

Legendary Rangers and Scotland centre-half George Young was a one-club man. Equally comfortable at right-back, Young spent his entire career at Ibrox (1941–57), and in 1948–49 was a member of the Rangers side that became the first team to win all three major domestic Scottish trophies in a single season (League, FA Cup and League Cup). In 53 appearances for Scotland he captained his country on 48 occasions. His nickname among his team-mates was 'Corky' because he always carried to matches a 'lucky' champagne cork in his jacket pocket.

Paul McGrath's (Aston Villa, Manchester United) testimonial at Lansdowne Road, Dublin, on 17 May 1988 realized record receipts (at the time) of £600,000. Some 39,000 spectators paid tribute to this great Irish centre-back and watched a Jack Charlton XI beat a Republic of Ireland XI 3-2. Irish international Ronnie Whelan (Liverpool) told the story of how once, when the Republic were staying at a hotel prior to a match, manager Jack Charlton locked McGrath in his room for fear he would go to the hotel bar and drink too much. The following morning when Jack opened McGrath's door he was stupefied to find him the worse for wear. McGrath had drunk the contents of the room's mini-bar.

City lead one-nil, the goal the result of a mistake by Wigan's Titus Bramble.

FIVELIVE MATCH COMMENTATOR

Yes, but he's a good lad, Titus Bramble, he doesn't make those mistakes on purpose.

DEAN SAUNDERS, summarizer

Rio Ferdinand has twice been the world's most expensive defender. He joined Leeds United from West Ham United in November 2000 for a fee of £18 million; in July 2002, he joined Manchester United from Leeds for a fee of £28.5 million – an all-time British record fee for a player, a record fee between British clubs, and a world record fee for a defender. Just as well he didn't go shopping that day.

Former Wolves centre-half Stan Cullis remains the youngest manager of an FA Cup Final team: he was 33 when he led out Wolves in the 1949 final. As Wolves beat Leicester City 3-1, Cullis is also the youngest ever manager of an FA Cup-winning team.

The days of the tall, rugged, stopper centre-half of renowned aerial prowess came to an end in the 1970s when Bob Paisley persuaded Liverpool manager Bill Shankly to deploy centre-backs who were comfortable on the ball and who won possession through interception rather than tough tackling, in much the same mould as the imperious Bobby Moore. Paisley wanted cerebral centre-backs who could read a game well, bring the ball out of defence and pass it as well as any midfield player – which led to the emergence of players such as Alan Hansen, Phil Thompson, Mark Lawrenson and Emlyn Hughes (switched from midfield to centre-back) in Liverpool teams.

Ian Culverhouse, playing as a central defender for Swindon Town against Everton in the third round of the FA Cup on 5 January 1997 at Goodison Park, was red-carded after only 52 seconds for deliberate hand-ball – the record for the fastest sending-off in an FA Cup tie.

Appropriately for a player who gave his all when playing for England, Tony Adams was born in 1966 (albeit three months after England won the World Cup). Adams was a colossus in defence for Arsenal and England, one of the few England players who always sang the national anthem with gusto. He made his debut for Arsenal against Sunderland on 15 November 1983 and went on to make 668 appearances for the Gunners (only David O'Leary has played more), helping his club win four titles (1989, 1991, 1998 and 2002), three FA Cups (1993, 1998 and 2002), two League Cups (1987 and 1993), the European Cup Winners' Cup (1994) and three Charity Shields. He won 60 caps for England and, again somewhat appropriately, played his last game for his country on the occasion of the last international match played at the old Wembley, against Germany in October 2000.

 Jim Holton is a fine centre-half, strong, great in the air, sledge-hammer tackle, fine passer of the ball. You have to be talking good money for a stopper like him; one hundred thousand wouldn't buy him.

TOMMY DOCHERTY, looking to sell Holton to Sunderland manager Bob Stokoe

I know, and I'm one of them.

BOB STOKOE's reply

10 Preston North End were the first champions of the inaugural Football League in 1888–89. They remained unbeaten throughout a season comprising 22 matches and also won the FA Cup without conceding a goal. Preston were also the first club to retain the First Division championship, winning the title again the following season, 1889–90. Their hold on the championship was broken the following season (1890–91) when Everton won the title with 29 points (out of a maximum 44) – the lowest points tally of any championship-winning team.

In their Scottish championship season of 1897–98, Celtic remained unbeaten in the League. In winning the Scottish League title the following season Rangers emulated this feat, though they went one better by winning every one of their 18 League matches.

In 1912–13, Sunderland gained only two points from their first seven League matches but won 25 of their remaining 31 games to win the championship. This remains the record for the worst start to a season by a team which then went on to be crowned champions.

Burnley and Wolves are the only two clubs to have won all four championships of the Football League, in its old format. Wolves hold the distinction of also having won the Third Division North title, prior to the lower divisions of the Football League being de-regionalized in 1958.

2001–02 Premiership champions Arsenal became the first club since Preston North End in 1888-89 (the inaugural season of the Football League) to remain unbeaten away from home during the course of a top-division season. Arsenal bettered this in 2003–04 by remaining unbeaten in the League for the entirety of their championship season, winning 26 and drawing 12 of their 38 matches.

Four clubs have achieved championship hat-tricks – that is, three consecutive League titles: Huddersfield Town, 1923–24 to 1925–26; Arsenal, 1932–33 to 1934–35; Liverpool, 1981–82 to 1983–84; and Manchester United, 1998–99 to 2000–01.

In 1930–31, Arsenal became the first southern-based club to win the Football League Championship, setting a new record of 66 points. Runners-up Aston Villa set a new record for goals scored – 128 (42 matches). Arsenal scored 127.

Only 16 points separated 1937–38 champions Arsenal from Manchester City and West Bromwich Albion, both of whom were relegated to Division Two, – the tightest points margin in the history of the top division. Manchester City thus became the first and to date only team to win the championship (in 1937) and be relegated the following year.

Stoke City and Liverpool were in contention for the title as the 1946–47 season drew to an exciting climax. Prior to their last three matches of the season, Stoke sold prize asset Stanley Matthews to Blackpool, even though Matthews had indicated he would prefer to see the season out at Stoke. Liverpool's last four matches were all away from home but they dropped only one point. Having completed their season, Liverpool had to await the outcome of Stoke's final match at Sheffield United, Stoke needing a win to clinch the title. A Matthews-less Stoke lost, and Liverpool became the first post-war champions. Stoke goalkeeper Denis Herod later described the club's decision to sell Matthews as 'insane', adding, 'It cost us the championship.'

Prior to winning the championship in 1948–49, Portsmouth had never finished higher than fourth in Division One. In one of the tightest title races in the history of the Football League, Portsmouth secured a second successive championship in 1950 by virtue of goal average from Wolves – only the second time the title had been won in such a way. Only six points separated the top nine clubs.

After having finished runners-up in four of the five seasons since football recommenced after World War Two, Manchester United were crowned champions in 1952. It was United's third League Championship success, but their first for 41 years.

In what was the tightest race on record, Arsenal pipped Preston to the title in 1952–53 on goal average. Both teams finished on 54 points and had identical results – 21 wins, 12 draws and 9 defeats – but Arsenal's goal average of 1.51 was 0.1 better than that of Preston (1.41).

Chelsea won the championship for the first time in their history in 1954-55 with the lowest points tally (52) from a 42-match season. As champions, Chelsea entered the newly launched European Cup, but under pressure from the Football League and FA they withdrew. Chelsea had been drawn against Swedish champions Djurgården.

In 1955–56, champions Manchester United equalled the record margin of victory, finishing 11 points ahead of Blackpool and Wolves. Following their second successive League title in 1956–57, United defied the Football League and FA to become the first English champions to compete in the European Cup.

In 1957–58, Wolverhampton Wanderers were champions in every sense of the word. Every team connected with the club won its league title: Football League Division One, Central League (reserves), Birmingham League (youth team) and Worcester Combination (Colts). The Wolves youth side also won the FA Youth Cup, and apart from the first team and the FA Cup, all other Wolves teams also won their respective leagues' cup competitions.

In winning the Scottish League title in 1957–58, Hearts built up a record margin of goal difference for any British club, a record that holds to this day: in 34 League matches Hearts scored 132 goals and conceded just 29 – a goal difference of 103.

When, in their final match of 1959–60, Burnley beat Manchester City to take the First Division title, it was the first time the Turf Moor club had been at the top of the division at any stage of the season.

In 1960–61, Tottenham Hotspur became the first club in the twentieth century to win the League and cup double. In so doing Spurs created several new records. They equalled the points record (66) set by Arsenal in 1930–31, began the season with 11 consecutive victories, won 31 of their 42 games, and achieved 16 away wins (including eight in a row). In scoring 115 League goals, five players reached double figures: Bobby Smith (28), Les Allen (23), Cliff Jones (15), John White (13) and Terry Dyson (12). Spurs were also watched by a record 1,867,596 spectators in the League and 384,011 in their seven FA Cup matches – a grand total of 2,251,607.

When Liverpool clinched the championship in 1964 by beating Arsenal at Anfield, the players paraded a papier mâché reproduction of the League Championship trophy. The previous season's champions, Everton, had refused Liverpool's request to pass the trophy to Anfield in anticipation of a win over Arsenal, adhering instead to regulations stating that it should be returned to the Football League. Undaunted, following victory over Arsenal, skipper Ron Yeats was presented with the mocked-up trophy which the players took on a lap of honour around Anfield.

Kilmarnock met Hearts on the final day of 1964–65 in a match to decide the Scottish championship. To pip the Edinburgh club to the title, Kilmarnock had to beat Hearts by two clear goals, which they did. Kilmarnock secured the title from Hearts on a goal average of 0.04 – the narrowest margin for a championship victory in the history of British football.

When Liverpool won the League Championship in 1965–66 they used only 14 players, a feat equalled by Aston Villa in their title season of 1980–81. Nowadays a Premiership club will have more players on the pitch and substitutes bench for a single game.

In 1966–67 Celtic could quite literally boast an all-conquering side. In addition to winning the Scottish League Championship, Celtic also won the Scottish FA and League Cups, the European Cup and the Glasgow Cup, scoring over 200 competitive goals in the process (a record for British football). Only one member of the team, Bobby Lennox, was born outside Glasgow, and then only 24 miles away in Saltcoats, Ayrshire.

Jock Stein must be the best football manager of all time. Who else could have won the European Cup with a Glasgow District XI?

HUGH McILVANNEY, sports journalist

There has been one instance of both a father and son winning League Championship medals: Johnny Aston (Manchester United) in 1952, and John Aston (also with Manchester United) in 1967.

Scotland's First Division became the Premier League in 1975–76, 17 years before the idea was adopted in England. The first champions of the Scottish Premier League were Rangers.

The record number of points accrued in the course of a championship season of 42 matches is 68, by Liverpool in 1978–79 (when it was still only two points for a win). The club also set a new record for the fewest goals conceded (16), and their goal record at Anfield, where they remained unbeaten, read goals for 51, goals against 4.

Ryan Giggs holds the record for the most championship medals won by an individual player at ten, all with Manchester United: 1993, 1994, 1996, 1997, 1999, 2000, 2001, 2003, 2007 and 2008. Phil Neal and Alan Hansen both won eight championship medals with Liverpool, Neal in 1976, 1977, 1979, 1980, 1982, 1983, 1984 and 1986; Hansen in 1979, 1980, 1982, 1983, 1984, 1986, 1988 and 1990.

On the final day of the 1967–68 season both Manchester clubs were in contention for the title. United needed victory at home to lowly Sunderland to clinch the title, whereas City travelled to Newcastle knowing that victory there would not be enough should United win. Sunderland pulled off the shock of the season by beating United 2-1 (Sunderland's last victory at Old Trafford), while City came from behind to win 4-3 at Newcastle. United's consolation came just days later: they went on to win the European Cup.

Sunderland take on champions elect Manchester United knowing they are only here to make up the numbers today.

KENNETH WOLSTENHOLME's opening line on *Match of the Day*, 11 May 1968

In 1968–69 Leeds United set a new points record (67) for League champions. Football had changed: the emphasis was now on teams not conceding goals rather than scoring them, as evidenced by the fact that Leeds secured more points than goals scored. Leeds' tally of 66 goals was the lowest by any champion club since the offside law was changed in 1924.

Arsenal became the second club in the twentieth century to win the League and cup double in 1970–71. It was a remarkable feat as their manager, Bertie Mee, had never been a professional footballer. He was, by profession, a physiotherapist.

Derby County secured the championship in 1972 in leisurely fashion, sitting on a Spanish beach! Derby had completed their fixture programme and were holidaying when they received the news that Leeds United had failed to beat Wolves, thus handing Derby the title.

In 1975, Derby won their second League title in four seasons. The title race was the most open in the history of the Football League: the lead changed hands 21 times among ten clubs – a record.

Nine men have played in and managed League Championship-winning teams: Ted Drake played for Arsenal (1934, 1935, 1938) and managed Chelsea (1955); Bill Nicholson played for Tottenham Hotspur (1951) and also managed Spurs

(1961); Alf Ramsey played for Spurs (1951) and managed Ipswich Town (1962); Joe Mercer played for Everton (1939) and Arsenal (1948 and 1953) and managed Manchester City (1968). Dave Mackay played for Spurs (1961) and managed Derby County (1975); Bob Paisley played for Liverpool (1947) and managed the club in their title successes of 1976, 1977, 1979, 1980, 1982 and 1983; Howard Kendall played for Everton (1970) and managed them (1985 and 1987); George Graham played for Arsenal (1971) and managed them (1989 and 1991); and finally, Kenny Dalglish played for Liverpool (1979, 1980, 1982, 1983 and 1984), player-managed them (1986, 1988, 1990) and managed Blackburn Rovers (1995). He also won four Scottish championship medals while a player at Celtic (1972, 1973, 1974 and 1977).

In 1978, Nottingham Forest emulated Ipswich Town (1962) by winning the championship in the season following their promotion from Division Two.

In 1981, Villa won the League Championship, and the FA Cup for Spurs. Aston Villa were League champions, and Ricardo Villa scored Spurs' winner at Wembley in the FA Cup Final replay against Manchester City.

In 1982, Liverpool created a new record by winning their fifth championship in seven seasons; in 1990 they made it ten titles in 15 seasons.

In 1985–86 Kenny Dalglish (Liverpool) became the first player-manager to guide a team to the championship. He also won the double as Liverpool beat near neighbours Everton in the first all-Merseyside FA Cup Final.

In 1988, the year in which the Football League celebrated its centenary, Liverpool were crowned champions amid allegations by Manchester United manager Alex Ferguson that referees were intimidated when officiating at Anfield.

In the most dramatic finale to any championship, Arsenal and Liverpool met on the final day of the 1988–89 season as the only two teams left in contention for the title. Liverpool needed only a draw, whereas Arsenal had to beat Liverpool by two clear goals. Amazingly, at Anfield, Arsenal did just that. Their second and decisive goal, scored by Michael Thomas, arrived just three minutes from time.

In 1991–92, Leeds United became the last champions of the Football League in its old format. The following season the Premiership was introduced and the championship trophy was awarded to the champions of what was then referred to as Division One (later to become the Championship).

In 1993, Manchester United became the first champions of the Premiership. Manager Alex Ferguson received news of his club's triumph while golfing, on the day when nearest rivals Aston Villa were defeated by Oldham Athletic.

At the end of January 1996, Newcastle United were 13 points clear at the top of the Premiership but ended up conceding the title to Manchester United. In March 1998, Arsenal trailed Premiership leaders Manchester United by 11 points with ten matches remaining but went on to win the title.

In winning the championship in 1999–2000, Manchester United set a new record for the number of goals scored during a 38-game season – 97.

When Chelsea took the title in 2004–05 they set a new record for the number of games won in the course of a 38-match Premiership season – 29.

No English manager has ever won the Premiership.

In winning the Scottish League Championship in 1995–96, Rangers set a record for the number of victories (27) in the course of a 36-match season. Rangers also hold the record for the number of games won in the course of a 44-match championship season (33, in 1991–92 and 1992–93) and a 42-match season (35 in 1920–21).

When Arsenal won the Premiership in 1997–98 they lost more matches (six) than they did when finishing as runners-up the following season (four).

The biggest points margin achieved by any championship-winning side is 18 (Manchester United in 1999–2000). United won the title with 91 points, Arsenal were runners-up with 73, and Leeds (who also qualified for the Champions League) finished third, 25 points behind United.

Liverpool have the most championship wins (18), though to date they have not won the Premiership. Manchester United's Premiership title success of 2007–08 was the club's 17th championship – seven Football League, ten Premiership.

Eric Cantona won four consecutive championships with three different clubs: Marseille (1990–91), Leeds United (1991–92) and Manchester United (1992–93 and 1993–94).

Players who have won English championship winners medals with two different clubs: David Batty (Leeds United 1992 and Blackburn Rovers 1995); Henning Berg (Blackburn Rovers 1995 and Manchester United 1999 and 2001); Eric Cantona (Leeds United 1992 and Manchester United 1993, 1994, 1996 and 1997); Archie Gemmill (Derby County 1972 and Nottingham Forest 1978); Ray Kennedy (Arsenal 1971 and Liverpool 1979, 1980 and 1982); Francis Lee (Manchester City 1968 and Derby County 1975); Larry Lloyd (Liverpool 1973 and Nottingham Forest 1978); John Lukic (Arsenal 1989 and Leeds United 1992); John McGovern (Derby County 1972 and Nottingham Forest 1978); Bobby Mimms (Everton 1987 and Blackburn Rovers 1995); Kevin Richardson (Everton 1985 and Arsenal 1989); and Peter Withe (Nottingham Forest 1978 and Aston Villa 1981). From this you will deduce that four members of Nottingham Forest's title-winning team of 1978 had previously won the championship with other clubs – the only instance of this having happened.

Rangers hold the world record for the most domestic championship wins, in 2007 standing at 51. No team other than one of the 'Old Firm' has ever won the Scottish Premier League. The only occasion when Celtic and

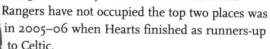

Rangers have not occupied the top two places was in 2005–06 when Hearts finished as runners-up to Celtic.

Fifteen clubs have changed their name since becoming members of the Football League (year of change of name in brackets): Arsenal, formerly Woolwich Arsenal (1913); Birmingham City, formerly Small Heath (1905) then simply Birmingham (1946); AFC Bournemouth, formerly Bournemouth and Boscombe Athletic (1971); Burton United (now no longer in Football League), formerly Burton Swifts (1901); Gateshead United (now no longer in Football League), formerly South Shields (1930); Hartlepool United, formerly Hartlepools United (1969) then simply Hartlepool (1977); Leicester City, formerly Leicester Fosse (1919); Leyton Orient, formerly Clapton Orient (1946), Leyton Orient (1967), Orient (1987, in which year the club reverted to Leyton Orient); Manchester City, formerly Ardwick (1894); Manchester United, formerly Newton Heath (1902); Milton Keynes Dons, formerly Wimbledon (2004); Rotherham United, formerly Rotherham County (1925); Sheffield Wednesday, formerly The Wednesday (1929); Stoke City, formerly Stoke (1925); and Swansea City, formerly Swansea Town (1970).

In 1980–81, Arbroath won only three league matches at home but ten away from home. Arbroath's Gayfield stadium is the nearest senior British football ground to the sea. One stand is only a matter of 30 yards from the beach.

Aldershot was the first club to win a Football League play-off final, beating Wolverhampton Wanderers over two legs to win promotion to Division Three in 1986–87. Teddy Sherringham can number Aldershot among his many clubs. He played six games for the Shots in 1985 while on loan from Millwall.

Arsenal began life not as Woolwich Arsenal but as Dial Square – the name of one of the workshops at the Royal Arsenal in Woolwich – and played their first matches on Plumstead Common. A matter of months after formation, the club changed its name to Woolwich Arsenal, and in its second year of existence moved home to the Sportsman's Ground in Woolwich.

Aston Villa's first ever match as a club was in 1874; their opponents were Aston Brook St Mary's rugby team. The game comprised a first-half of rugby and a second-half of football.

Ayr United centre-forward Jim Smith holds the record for averaging the most goals per game in the course of a season. In 1927–28, Smith scored 66 goals in 38 matches for Ayr – an average of 1.7 per match.

Barnet's game against Tooting and Mitcham (Athenian League) in 1946 was the first non-FA Cup and first amateur football match to be broadcast 'live' on television (BBC).

Barnsley had three managers in the 1980s all of whom were former Leeds United players: Allan Clarke (1978–80), Norman Hunter (1980–84), Bobby Collins (1984–85) and Allan Clarke again (1985–89).

Berwick Rangers are the only English club playing in the Scottish League, and are still 'officially' at war with Germany. In 1914, when Britain went to war, the official declaration specifically included the name of Berwick as it was still undecided whether the town was part of England or Scotland. When peace came in 1918 the official declaration named Great Britain, the USA and member countries of the Commonwealth but omitted Berwick as during the course of the war it had been determined that the town was English.

Birmingham City was the first English club to participate in a major European competition. In 1956, they were drawn against Inter Milan in the Inter-Cities Fairs Cup (later UEFA Cup).

One of the founder members of Blackburn Rovers in 1875 was John Lewis, who later was also a founder of the Lancashire FA, refereed two FA Cup Finals, and became vice-president of both the Football League and FA.

In the 1970s and 1980s, Blackpool boasted the largest car park of any football club in the world. The site adjacent to their Bloomfield Road ground was formerly a railway station terminus and sidings.

Bolton Wanderers are said to be known as The Trotters because in their formative years, when the team was run by a succession of secretaries and not a manager, training was said to consist of players simply trotting around the field. The suffix Wanderers comes from their early days as a club and reflects the distance the players were willing to travel to matches.

When Bournemouth were elected to the Football League in 1923, the draw had already been made for the preliminary round of the FA Cup. As newly elected members, Bournemouth were admitted to the first round proper and their qualifying tie, against the Portsea Island Gas Company, scratched.

Bradford City owe their formation to two other sports. In 1903, cash-strapped Manningham Rugby Club held an archery contest to raise much-needed funds. When little money was collected the club decided to give up rugby and turn to football, and continued to play at their Valley Parade ground. It proved a profitable change of sport: within eight years Bradford City had won the FA Cup.

In 1937–38, Brechin City suffered three successive 10-0 defeats, against Airdrieoneans, Albion Rovers and Cowdenbeath, but still finished mid-table in the Scottish Second Division.

Brentford's nickname The Bees has nothing to do with the insect, but the letter B. Brentford may have spent much of their existence in the lower divisions but they can lay claim to a player who went on to win 100 international caps. Brian

Turner played for Brentford in the late 1960s and early 1970s and won his 100th cap for New Zealand in a World Cup qualifying match in 1982.

Brighton's record transfer fee was paid to Manchester United over a quarter of a century ago. In 1980, the club handed over £500,000 for Andy Ritchie.

In 1962–63, Bristol City scored 100 League goals but only finished 14th in Division Three.

Prior to becoming members of the Football League, Bristol Rovers were known as The Black Arabs because they wore black shirts. When black was officially adopted as the uniform of match officials, Rovers changed to blue and white quartered shirts. Their nickname The Gasheads is derived from the fact that their former home at Eastville was adjacent to a gasworks.

In the early 1960s, Burnley had 13 players on their books whom they had signed from the north-east of England. Burnley even had a nursery team in Sunderland, Hylton Colliery Welfare. In 1965–66, when Burnley defeated Sunderland 4-0 at Roker Park, the local sportspaper, the *Sunderland Football Echo*, suggested that Burnley's away success was down to the fact that 'the majority of their team were, in fact, playing at home'.

Bury's Gigg Lane is the only League ground that backs on to a cemetery.

Cardiff City is situated in a rugby stronghold, but was formed in 1899 from Riverside Cricket Club.

From 1997 to 1999, the Carlisle United manager and chairman were one and the same – Michael Knighton.

Celtic were formed in 1888 and have never been based anywhere other than at their present home of Parkhead.

Charlton Athletic are often referred to as The Addicks. The name's origins lie in the club's formative years, when players changed in a room over a fish and chip shop in East Street. The fishmonger was a Charlton supporter and attended matches with a haddock nailed to a stick, which he waved in the air during matches. Though why he chose to do this seems lost in the mists of time.

Since 1962, Chelsea have had 18 managers, eight of whom have also played for the club: Tommy Docherty, Eddie McCreadie, Ken Shellito, John Hollins, David Webb, Glenn Hoddle, Ruud Gullit and Gianluca Vialli.

In 1994–95, the Chester City fanzine was edited by the Reverend Colin Mansley, and the Chester squad included Eddie Bishop, Chris Priest, Graham Pugh and Wayne Parsonage.

Chesterfield have long had a tradition for producing top-class goalkeepers. Among those to have graduated from the Spireites over the years are Gordon Banks (Leicester, Stoke and England), Bob Wilson (Arsenal and Scotland), John Osborne (West Bromwich Albion), Steve Hardwick (Newcastle United) and Steve Ogrizovic (Liverpool and Coventry).

After World War Two, Clyde were so strapped for cash they could not afford new shorts for the players. For a number of matches Clyde players wore khaki shorts purchased from a Glasgow Army and Navy Surplus store.

Colchester United are the only club to play in the Championship that have ever won the FA Trophy, in 1992, following relegation from the Football League to the Conference. Colchester were relegated to League One in 2008.

Coventry City were once managed by TV pundit Jimmy Hill, who introduced a series of innovative ideas to the club in the early 1960s. One idea of Jimmy's was to invite local Sunday league clubs to play home games at Highfield Road so that he and his scouts could spot emerging local talent.

In 1984, Cowdenbeath's Central Park ground was filled to its 8,000 capacity – not for a football match but for a meeting of Scottish miners. The guest speakers were Scottish NUM leader Mick McGarghy, Dennis Skinner MP and young political hopeful Gordon Brown.

Crewe Alexandra were so called because the first club meetings were held in The Alexandra pub in Crewe. The suffix was not adopted as a tribute to Queen Alexandra, as is often stated.

Crystal Palace is the only club in British senior football whose name begins with five consonants.

Crystal Palace have a track record of asking a manager to come back. Steve Coppell had four managerial stints at the club, and Malcolm Allison, Terry Venables, Steve Kember and Alan Smith have all managed Palace twice.

In 2007–08 Dagenham and Redbridge displayed a sign on a stand that read 'No Ball Games Allowed'.

Five is a number of some significance for Darlington. The highest position the club has ever achieved is fifth, which they maintained for two weeks in Division Three North in 1925–26 (final position 15th); and the furthest the club has ever gone in the FA Cup and the League Cup is round five, in 1958 and 1968 respectively.

In the 1990s Derby County boasted its own railway station. Ramsline Halt was situated 200 yards from the club's then home, the Baseball Ground. British Rail timetabled four services routed via Ramsline Halt as stopping at the station only Monday to Friday.

For many years Doncaster Rovers' former home Belle Vue was one of only two Football League grounds to have a pitch of Cumberland turf – the same turf used for Wembley. (The other was Ayresome Park, Middlesbrough.)

Dumbarton and Rangers both finished with 29 points in 1891 and boasted identical records: 13 wins, three draws, two defeats. The teams met in a play-off to decide the Scottish championship and drew 2-2. It was then decided that the title should be shared – the only instance of this ever happening in Scottish football.

Dundee and Dundee United are the closest local rivals in British football. To get to the boundary wall of United's Tannadice Park from that of Dundee's Dens Park requires only a short walk of some 89 steps. Dundee is the only club in British senior football whose name does not contain any letters that appear in the word 'football'.

In 1958–59, Dunfermline had to win their final match to avoid relegation. They beat Partick Thistle 10-1.

East Fife are the only club from outside the top division of the Scottish League to have won the Scottish FA Cup. In 1938, the Fifers, then in Division Two, beat Kilmarnock 4-2 in a replay.

In 2003–04, East Stirling recorded only two victories in the League but in so doing notched up a double: both victories came at the expense of Elgin City. Following a 3-1 victory over Elgin on 1 November, East Stirling recorded 24 consecutive defeats. Their second success against Elgin came in their final match of the season which, curiously, was watched by almost twice as many spectators (363) than had seen their first home game of the season against Montrose (182).

Elgin City's best performance in the Scottish FA Cup was as a non-league side. In 1968, the club reached the quarter-finals.

Everton's Neville Southall did not join his team-mates to celebrate victory over Manchester United in the 1989 FA Cup Final. Rather than stay in London to attend the club's post-match banquet, immediately after the game Southall drove back to his family home in North Wales.

Exeter City's nickname is The Grecians, which originates from 1908 when the club was situated in the parish of St Sidwell's. Those who resided in St Sidwell's were commonly referred to as 'Grecians' (Southey's Common-Place Book, 1669) because the parish was situated outside the city walls, the connection being made with the Greeks who laid siege to Troy in Homer's *Iliad*.

Falkirk's most capped player is Alex Parker, who won 14 caps for Scotland while he was with the club. Following a transfer to Everton in 1958 a lengthy international career was predicted for the full-back; but for all that Parker became a regular at Goodison Park he was to make only one further appearance for Scotland, against Paraguay in the 1958 World Cup.

You don't have to be mad to support Forfar Athletic, but you do have to be a loony. The club's nickname is The Loons.

Pelé played only once in London, in the 1960s for Santos in a friendly against Fulham.

On 5 September 1987, Gillingham entertained Chesterfield who had yet to concede a goal in the League. Gillingham won 10-0. In their previous match at the Priestfield Stadium, Gillingham had beaten Southend United 8-1.

Gretna, sadly, serve as a reminder of the age-old football adage that when a club whose meteoric rise has much to do with being dependent on the financial backing of one individual – 'It will all end in tears'.

Grimsby Town hold the dubious record of having been relegated more times than any other English club.

Hamilton Academical is the only senior club in British football still to bear the name of a school. When the club was formed in 1888 it was named after Hamilton Academy.

Hartlepool United's most capped player is Ambrose Fogarty – one cap for the Republic of Ireland against Spain in 1964.

Heart of Midlothian did not get their name from the Walter Scott novel. The club was formed in 1874 and named after a local dance hall, which in turn had been named after an old Edinburgh toll booth.

On 6 September 1992, Hereford United had four players sent off in a match at Northampton Town but still held out for a 1-1 draw, the Hereford scorer one Brain. This is the record for the number of dismissals from one team in a single League match.

Hibernian were the first British team to play in a major European competition. In 1955–56, Hibs entered the inaugural European Cup and reached the semi-finals.

Huddersfield Town were elected to the Football League in 1911, but the cost of upgrading their Leeds Road ground led to the club going into liquidation in 1912. In 1919, the financial position was so acute it was decided to move the club to Leeds as a replacement for the defunct Leeds City; but Town supporters protested, and rather than move to Leeds the club remained at Leeds Road.

Hull City is the only English League club whose name contains letters you can't shade in.

Inverness Caledonian Thistle were formed in 1994 by a merger between Inverness Caledonian and Inverness Thistle (both formed in 1885) at the suggestion of the Inverness and Nairn Enterprise Board, though a merger was first mooted as long ago as 1937.

The Cobbold family had a long and fine relationship with Ipswich Town. When the club was formed in 1888 its first president was local MP T. C. Cobbold. The Cobbold family maintained their connection with the club for over a hundred years. The most colourful family member was former chairman John Cobbold who in the 1960s used to drive to the local station with his fellow directors to escort the visiting team and their officials to Portman Road.

Kilmarnock goalkeeper of the early 1960s Sandy McLaughlin had a mighty deadball kick. During one match against Hearts, McLaughlin took a goal-kick that visiting keeper Gordon Marshall collected in his own six-yard box without the ball having bounced.

Leeds United's financial problems in the new millennium were well documented. Following the exit of chief executive Peter Ridsdale, former Yorkshire and England cricketer Fred Trueman (a Leeds fan) suggested that Ridsdale should write a book about his experiences at Leeds and for the title used the word 'United' printed backwards – 'Det-I-Nu' to imply 'Debt I Knew'.

Those were the days? In 1974, Leicester City provided three players – Peter Shilton, Keith Weller and Frank Worthington – for successive England matches against Northern Ireland, Scotland and Argentina. Also included in the England team was Derby full-back David Nish, recently transferred from Leicester.

Leyton Orient owe the suffix in their name to the fact that in the early days of the club many of the players were employees of the Orient Shipping Line.

Was it over the line, ref? The northern boundary of Lincoln City's Sincil Bank ground used to be formed by a railway embankment. For many years the club paid British Railways an annual fee to retrieve and return footballs found on the line.

Liverpool's Bob Paisley has the best record of any British manager in terms of European trophies won. Paisley guided Liverpool to three European Cup successes, two UEFA Cups and a European Super Cup.

Livingston were formerly known as Meadowbank Thistle, and prior to that Ferranti Thistle. On applying to join the Scottish League they were ordered to drop the word 'Ferranti' from their name because, having been formed as a works team, 'Ferranti' had commercial implications.

Luton Town had a bitter-sweet experience in 1987–88. The club reached the FA Cup semi-finals for the first time since 1959, but their tie against Wimbledon drew the lowest attendance in the twentieth century for an FA Cup semi-final – 25,963.

In 1994–95, Macclesfield Town won only two of their remaining 13 Conference fixtures but still finished as champions, winning promotion to the Football League.

Manchester City is the only League club to have scored and conceded a century of goals in a single season. In 1957–58, City scored 104 goals in Division One but conceded 100.

Manchester United have had only eight managers since 1945: Sir Matt Busby, Wilf McGuinness, Frank O'Farrell, Tommy Docherty, Dave Sexton, Ron Atkinson and Sir Alex Ferguson. Ferguson is currently English senior football's longest-serving manager at any one club (since 1986).

In 1999, Mansfield Town signed striker Michael Boulding from non-league Hallam. Boulding had swapped professional tennis for professional football. He had been a member of the Great Britain Davis Cup squad and was a room-mate of Tim Henman.

Middlesbrough were beaten 9-0 by Blackburn Rovers on 6 November 1954. They kept the same team the following week against Fulham and won 4-2.

Millwall were founded in 1885 by employees of the Morton Jam and Marmalade Company.

In 1972–73, Montrose supporters held a poll for the Player of the Year in Division Two. The player who came first was Brian Third.

Morecambe transferred Gordon Milne to Preston in 1956. Milne went on to play for Liverpool and was a member of England's 1966 World Cup squad.

On 11 August 1962, Motherwell led Falkirk 9-0 at half-time. The final score was 9-1.

Newcastle United qualified for Europe in 1967–68 despite finishing tenth in Division One. Though clubs such as Spurs, Chelsea and Arsenal finished higher, Newcastle were entered for the Fairs/UEFA Cup as UEFA rules then stated there should be only one club per city in the competition. Newcastle made the most of their good fortune: they went on to win the Fairs Cup the following season.

Stand-up comedian Alan Carr is the son of former Northampton Town manager Graham Carr, who was in charge of The Cobblers from 1985 to 1990.

With the exception of just three weeks, from 5 September 1992 to 20 February 1993 Norwich City remained top of the Premiership. They eventually finished the season in third place.

For 117 years Nottingham Forest were not run by a board of directors but by a committee. The club eventually became a limited company with directors in 1982, two years after their second (and back-to-back) success in the European Cup.

Notts County is the oldest Football League club, formed in 1862, 26 years before the League's inaugural season. Notts County and Nottingham Forest are the closest League clubs in England: from boundary wall to boundary wall their respective grounds (Meadow Lane and City Ground) are 400 yards apart, albeit separated by the River Trent.

Oldham Athletic reached their first FA Cup semi-final in 1913 and their second 77 years later, in 1990. They did not have to wait so long again for their third appearance: it occurred four years later in 1994.

Partick Thistle joint managers Bertie Auld and Pat Quinn once took a player off even though they had used all their substitutes. The pair were so under-whelmed by the performance of striker Jim Melrose that they ordered him to the bench, content to play with just ten players.

As a non-league club, Peterborough United lost only once in the Midland League between 1956 and 1960. Their record enabled the club to gain election to the Football League, and in their first season they finished champions of Division Four, scoring 134 goals in the process.

Plymouth Argyle beat Charlton Athletic 6-4 in 1959–60. The following season Plymouth beat Charlton again, 6-4.

Portsmouth won the Football League Championship in 1948–49 with a team that did not include a single international player.

In 1953–54, Port Vale won the Third Division North and in 30 of their 46 matches did not concede a goal – a record for the Football League.

Preston North End started life as North End Cricket and Rugby Club. The club also played tennis and golf and had athletics and swimming teams before forming a football section in 1879. Three years later, the club turned exclusively to football.

Queen of the South is the only football club to be mentioned in the Bible. Luke, chapter 11, verse 31: 'And the Queen of the South shall rise up in judgement with the men of this generation and condemn them.'

Queen's Park came within an ace of winning a unique double in 1884. The Spiders won the Scottish Cup and lost 2-1 to Blackburn Rovers in the final of the English FA Cup.

Queens Park Rangers took part in the first ever Charity Shield match, in 1908. Rangers, champions of the Southern League, met Football League champions Manchester United and lost 4-0 after a replay. Rangers also contested the Charity Shield in 1912, losing 2-1 to Blackburn Rovers.

Raith Rovers number among their supporters Prime Minister Gordon Brown.

Rangers' most capped player is Ally McCoist, who won 60 caps for Scotland while at Ibrox.

In 1946, Reading signed amateur player Maurice Edelston who in 1946–47 scored successive hat-tricks against Crystal Palace and Southend United, the only amateur player to have achieved this feat in English League football.

Rochdale were in Division Four when they reached the final of the League Cup in 1962. They lost 4-0 on aggregate to Norwich City.

Ross County's record victory was registered in the Scottish FA Cup, 11-0 v. St Cuthbert Wanderers, in 1993.

In 1951–52, Rotherham United finished ninth in Division Two. Of their regular team, only one, wing-half Colin Rawson, was not a Yorkshireman. Rawson was born just over the county border in Nottinghamshire.

St Johnstone is the only first-class club in Scotland or England that contains the letter J in its name.

St Mirren's Alex Miller was the first player to receive three red cards in the same match. Against Motherwell in 1986, Miller was red-carded for fighting with an opponent, a second time for dissent, and a third for further dissent when leaving the pitch. This dubious honour was later equalled by Andy McLaren of Dundee against Clyde in December 2006.

From 1900 to 1958, Scunthorpe United had only six managers. In the ensuing 18 months the club engaged four different managers: Tony McShane, Bill Lampton, Frank Soo and Dick Duckworth.

In the 1950s, Sheffield United had two forwards named Fred Smith. One was six feet one inch tall, the other five foot seven; for identification purposes they were referred to as Big Fred and Little Fred. In the 1960s, United had three players by the surname of Shaw, Bernard, Joe and Graham, and two by the name of Wagstaff, Tony and Barry.

In 1903, Sheffield Wednesday (known then as The Wednesday) fielded a first and reserve team which won five of the six competitions they entered (the exception being the FA Cup). The first team won the First Division Championship and Sheffield Challenge Cup, and Wednesday reserves won the Midland League, the Plymouth Bowl and the Wharecliffe Charity Cup.

Shrewsbury Town have never won the FA Cup, but they have won the Welsh FA Cup on three occasions, the first in 1891.

Southampton's St Mary's Stadium is aptly named. When the club was formed in 1880 most players were connected with St Mary's Church and the founding name of the club was Southampton St Mary's.

Southend United were once managed by England World Cup-winning captain Bobby Moore (1984–86).

In 1978, the tea bar at Stenhousemuir's Ochilview Park carried a handwritten sign that read 'Try Our Hot Pies, You'll Never Get Better'.

Stirling Albion lays claim to the greatest winning margin in modern senior British football. In 1984, Albion defeated Scottish non-league club Selkirk 20-0 in the first round of the FA Cup.

In 2006–07 Stockport County broke a 119-year-old Football League record by going nine consecutive matches without conceding a goal.

Stranraer was formed in 1870 but did not enjoy a major success until they were crowned champions of Division Two in 1993–94.

The first mass pitch invasion of supporters celebrating a goal took place at Sunderland's Roker Park on 4 March 1961 during a match against double-chasing Tottenham Hotspur in the sixth round of the FA Cup. An estimated 3,000 supporters from the 61,326 who attended invaded the field following Willie McPheat's second-half equalizer, causing the game to be held up for seven minutes. The invasion was featured on the BBC. Rather than being considered unruly, it was seen by commentator Alan Weekes as 'testimony to the great enthusiasm of fans in the north-east for football'.

Swansea City's record victory came in European competition. In 1982, the Swans beat Sliema Wanderers of Malta 12-0 in the first round first leg of the European Cup Winners' Cup.

Swindon Town is the only English League club whose name does not contain any letters that appear in the word 'mackerel'.

Tottenham Hotspur is the only British football club to be named after a character from Shakespeare: Tottenham's suffix comes from Harry Hotspur (*Henry IV*).

BBC football presenter Ray Stubbs was once on the books of Tranmere Rovers.

Walsall's Tony Richards, who played for the club from 1954 to 1963, once scored a penalty and saved a penalty in the same match. Having scored from the spot for Walsall against Bournemouth, Richards then took over in goal following an injury to the Saddlers' keeper and went on to save a penalty kick.

Watford celebrated their centenary in 1991. The club, however, was formed in 1881. Watford were then called Watford Rovers, who later changed their name to West Herts, who absorbed another local club, Watford St Mary's, before being known simply as Watford.

In 2004–05 West Bromwich Albion became the first Premiership side to avoid relegation after having been bottom of the table at the turn of the year. Yet West Brom won only five of their 18 Premiership matches in 2005.

West Ham United are often referred to as The Hammers or The Irons, nicknames that date back to the club's early days in the late nineteenth century, when they went by the name of Thames Iron Works FC, the works team of the famous shipbuilding company of the same name.

Wigan Athletic's most celebrated supporter may not be former owner Dave Whelan but former Russian premier Mikhail Gorbachev, who is on record as saying his favourite football team is Wigan.

From 26 October 1938 to 6 April 1963, England played 148 international matches and at least one Wolverhampton Wanderers player featured in the starting line-up of every game.

Wrexham are the oldest Welsh club still in existence. They were formed on 28 September 1872 as an off-shoot of Wrexham Cricket Club. The first match in

1872 took place against a team comprising local insurance men – so the opposition claimed.

Wycombe Wanderers are nicknamed The Chairboys because the club was formed in 1887 by workers from a local furniture-making company. In their first season in a local league they finished mid-table.

Yeovil Town players were the first to benefit from commercial sponsorship. During the club's FA Cup run of 1948–49 the Yeovil players were sponsored and booted by local footwear company Templeman's.

I had sixteen clubs, seventeen if you include Stringfellow's.

FRANK WORTHINGTON

12 No matter how good the coach, he can't put in what God left out.

STANLEY MATTHEWS

The strict definition of a coach is a club official mainly responsible for team training, tactics and development of individual skills.

The first British player officially to coach abroad was Charlie Bunyan, who accepted a coaching post in Sweden in 1891. Bunyan had indeed made progress: he was the goalkeeper for Hyde in 1887 when the Cheshire side were beaten by the record FA Cup score of 26-0 by Preston North End. So, not a specialist goalkeeping coach then.

 The result is disappointing, but you couldn't fault the effort and work rate of the players today.

MICK McCARTHY finds comfort in a Sunderland defeat

The first English League club officially to appoint a first-team coach was Arsenal who in 1959 engaged Ron Greenwood (later to manage England) from non-league football.

In the early 1950s, British, in particular English, football woke up to the fact that it had fallen behind other nations. Hungary's emphatic victories over England at Wembley and in Budapest in 1953 and 1954 proved a watershed for English football. Change was to come, albeit slowly. In the late 1950s, England manager Walter Winterbottom established his FA coaching courses at Lilleshall. In order for English football to 'catch up', Winterbottom wanted players, managers and trainers to achieve an FA-recognized coaching qualification that involved both practice and theory.

Real Madrid's outstanding victory over Eintracht Frankfurt in the 1960 European Cup Final emphasized the need for quality coaching in English football. Real demonstrated that individual skill was much more effective when harnessed to collective skill. In essence, Real's victory proved the catalyst to the success of Winterbottom's FA coaching courses; many players and would-be managers signed up as a result. The class that attended Lilleshall in 1960 and 1961 included Tommy Docherty, Bob Paisley, Don Revie, Frank O'Farrell, Peter Taylor, Jimmy Adamson, Dave Sexton, Billy Bingham, Bert Johnson, Alan A'Court, Phil Woosnam, Malcolm Musgrove, Jimmy Andrews, Syd Owen and Malcolm Allison, the majority of whom would go on to exert great influence on the English game and how it was played in the 1960s, 1970s and beyond.

On the plus side, I thought the effort and work rate of the players was first class.

GARY MEGSON finds comfort in a West Brom defeat

Chelsea's first coach was Tommy Docherty, appointed player-coach to manager Ted Drake at Stamford Bridge in February 1961. Docherty's appointment was the decision of the Chelsea board. On his first day at the club he introduced himself to Drake who replied, 'You know, I never wanted you here.' The Doc replaced Drake as manager in 1962.

I thought the effort and work rate was very good.

ARSÈNE WENGER finds comfort in an Arsenal defeat in the Champions League

During his interview for the job of player-coach at Stamford Bridge, the Chelsea vice-chairman Mr Pratt informed Tommy Docherty that the board were also considering former West Bromwich Albion player Vic Buckingham. With characteristic bravado and cheek, Doc replied, 'Appoint him and it won't be a coach this club will be in need of, it'll be a hearse.'

Steve McClaren has been offered a part in pantomime in Darlington. As if his time as England manager wasn't pantomime enough. He's been offered the part of Buttons in *Cinderella*. They should have offered him the part of the pumpkin. A least then he'd turn into a decent coach.

KEN BOLAM, TV/music producer

Danny McLennan, who played for various Scottish clubs in the 1960s, went on to coach eight different teams in the 1970s and 1980s, all of them international sides: Bahrain, Iran, Iraq, Jordan, Mauritius, Philippines, Saudi Arabia and Zimbabwe.

During the course of a match the coach is allowed to convey instructions to players as long as he or she remains within the designated technical area. Strictly speaking, only one person at a time is allowed to convey instructions to players, and once such instructions have been delivered that person must 'immediately return to the designated seating area'. As if . . .

Well, yes, disappointed. But I couldn't have asked for more in the way of effort and work rate from the players.

ALAN CURBISHLEY finds comfort in a West Ham defeat

In England, the FA has five levels of coaching qualification. The lowest level is the FA Junior Team Manager Certificate, which applies to coaching youngsters aged between seven and 16; the highest level is the FA Coaching Diploma. UEFA's 'B', 'A' and 'Pro' coaching awards (sometimes referred to in the form of colours, e.g. Gold for Pro) are the equivalent of the three higher levels of FA qualification. In order to manage an English club, UEFA stipulate that the person must be a fully qualified/approved coach. Nowadays the term 'coach' is often interchangeable with that of 'manager', as in England coach Fabio Capello.

 I once went to an FA coaching course, because there is always something you can pick up, even from the most stupid people, but I didn't stay. Will a piece of paper make me a better manager or coach? Chamberlain came back from Munich waving a piece of paper – worst piece of paper we've ever had. People ask me my qualifications for being a manager and coach. I have one answer – Bill Shankly. They're my qualifications, the way I was born, the way I am. And that's all the qualifications you need in the game I'm in. People say to me, 'Oh, but so and so at this club, he is a fully qualified coach.' And I reply, 'That's as may be, but my team are League champions.' If a boxing coach is teaching you how to hit a punch ball and Cassius Clay [Muhammad Ali] comes along and shows you the professional way, you don't look at the other fellow. It's Clay you follow.

BILL SHANKLY on coaching (interviewed by John Keith)

It was the beer. On 20 October 1979, during the Division Three match between Reading and Exeter City, Exeter manager Brian Godfrey instructed coach Alan Beer that substitute Ian Pearson should replace defender Richard Forbes (number six). Beer held up the number board upside down and leading goalscorer Keith Bowker trooped off the field. The mistake was soon rectified.

On 21 November 1981, Huddersfield Town were so depleted by injuries that they played youth team coach Steve Smith in their FA Cup first round tie at Workington Town. Smith had not played competitive football for over four years but helped Town achieve a 1-1 draw.

That said, there were positives. I thought the players' effort and work rate was terrific.

TONY PULIS finds comfort in a Stoke City defeat

12

One of the most famous and, for a time, effective and successful coaches was Helenio Herrera. The Argentinian coached Puteaux (France), Red Star '93 (Parisian club formed by Jules Rimet), Stade Français, Atlético Madrid, Malaga, Valladolid, Seville, Barcelona, Inter Milan and Roma; he was also manager/coach of both Spain and Italy. Herrera was in his pomp in the 1960s, coaching Inter Milan to European Cup success in 1964 and 1965 and the Serie A title in 1963, 1965 and 1966. He also won the Spanish League title with Atlético Madrid (1950 and 1951) and Barcelona (1959). At Inter he perfected the system of *catenaccio*, an ultra-defensive style of play which involved a sweeper playing behind a back-four formation. The system relied mainly on a break-away to score a goal, and once in the lead Herrera was content for his side to sit back and defend, which often resulted in dour football. Herrera's nemesis was the 1967 European Cup Final: after taking a 1-0 lead, his Inter Milan team were beaten 2-1 by Celtic whose cavalier approach to the game was a triumph for attacking football over defensive tactics.

And their manager and coach, Terry Neill, isn't here today, which suggests to me he is elsewhere.

BRIAN MOORE, on ITV

For much of his time as England manager, Alf Ramsey had a backroom staff of two – trainer Les Cocker (Leeds United) and trainer cum kit man Harold Shepherdson (Middlesbrough) – though a doctor was always present. During the 1966 World Cup, Ramsey employed Wilf McGuinness (Manchester United) to help him with the coaching of the England players.

In 1966, Ramsey deployed both 4-4-2 and 4-4-3 systems of play. Neither was new. The systems were used by the Swiss national team of the 1930s and subsequently by teams across Europe. Variations had been deployed by a number of English club sides since the 1950s. Stanley Matthews said that Blackpool manager Joe Smith played a version of 4-4-2 in the 1953 FA Cup Final. Following England's the success in the 1966 World Cup, Ramsey's 'wingless wonders' formation was slavishly copied by managers and coaches throughout the British game, from Division One to parks football. What better example was there to follow than that of the world champions? Ironically, a World Cup Final that produced six goals paved the way to more cautious football. Seemingly overnight, the emphasis in British football changed from scoring goals to not conceding them. Teams became better organized, but the downside was fewer goals were scored.

 I hear managers and coaches say, 'You couldn't fault the effort and work rate of the players.' You could take eleven supporters out of the crowd and put them in the team. They might not be able to play football but, by their standards, I bet you wouldn't be able to fault their effort and work rate.

JIMMY GREAVES

13 The scorer of England's first goal against Scotland in the international of 1900–01 was Blackburn of Blackburn (Fred Blackburn played for Blackburn Rovers).

Bolton Wanderers can boast two players who, on leaving the club, entered politics with the same party. In 1913, full-back Jack Slater became a Conservative Party activist and was elected Member of Parliament for Eastbourne. In the 1960s, full-back Roy Hartle became a Tory activist and was elected as a councillor for the Halliwell Ward in Bolton.

In 1920, Chelsea signed three players from Queens Park Rangers: David Cameron, Ken McKenzie and John Bell. When their playing days were over they all became doctors. The joke was, when they signed autographs no one could decipher the writing, except chemists, who told them to come back in ten minutes.

In 1922–23, Southampton finished mid-table in Division Two; their record read won 14, drawn 14, lost 14, goals for 40, goals against 40, 42 points from 42 matches. During the season Southampton were awarded four penalties and conceded four penalties.

In 1926, Tom McDonald of Newcastle United set a new record for the number of goals scored by a defender in a single game when he netted a hat-trick against Cardiff City. On 21 April 1934 his record was equalled by William Imrie, also playing for Newcastle (against Wolves).

In 1926–27 Cecil Smith and James Smith both scored in 13 successive matches for Wrexham, who finished the season in 13th place in Division Three North.

On Christmas Day 1936, not one of the 11 matches in Division One was won by the away team. The fixtures were reversed for the following day (Boxing Day) and again, not one match was won by the away team.

In 1937–38, Wolverhampton Wanderers had a professional staff of 40 players and not one was married.

Villa Park was once the home of the fastest scoring records in both football and rugby. On 3 December 1938, Bob Iverson scored after only nine seconds against Charlton Athletic – then the fastest recorded goal in the history of the Football League. On 17 September 1947, a touring Australian XV scored a try after only seven seconds of their match against a Midlands Counties XV – at the time the fastest recorded try in rugby union in England.

In 1942, Alf Ramsey and Harry Evans signed for Southampton on the same day. On 9 August 1955, Ramsey took up his first managerial role, at Ipswich Town, and on the same day Evans took his first steps in football management at Aldershot Town.

When Italy beat Hungary 3-2 on 11 May 1947, ten of their victorious team were Juventus players and several of the Hungarian team played for champions Ujpesti TE. Weeks later Juventus met Ujpesti TE in a friendly, and won 3-2.

Abe Rosenthal was transferred six times in eight seasons, and he kept returning to the same two clubs. Towards the end of 1946–47 Rosenthal was sold by Tranmere Rovers to Bradford City. In 1948–49, Bradford sold Rosenthal to Oldham Athletic, but within a matter of months Oldham transferred him back to Tranmere. Rosenthal was on the move again in

1952 when Tranmere sold him back to Bradford, who in 1954 sold him back to Tranmere. In July 1955, Tranmere decided to cash in on Rosenthal's talent and sold him – back to Bradford. After retirement, Rosenthal concentrated on his business as an ice cream manufacturer, but he continued to have an involvement in the game as a scout – first for Tranmere, then for Bradford.

It's enough to give you the Williams. In 1950–51, Rotherham United's first team, reserves, 'A' team and juniors were all captained by players whose surname was Williams, but none were related. The skippers were, respectively, Horace, Danny, Ken and Bobby. In 1961, West Bromwich Albion played Walsall in a pre-season friendly and their team contained five players by the name of Williams: Graham, Stuart, Mark, David and Geoff, none of whom, again, were related. Wrexham began 2007–08 with five unrelated players named Williams in their team: Anthony, Eifon, Danny, Mark and Mike.

13 Len Shackleton (Bradford Park Avenue, Newcastle United, Sunderland and England) is a true legend of British football. Nicknamed 'The Clown Prince of Soccer', Shackleton was of the mind that 13 was his lucky number, and not without just cause. The name Len Shackleton comprises 13 letters. He first played for England Schoolboys at the age of 13 and scored in the 13th minute. He was transferred from Bradford to Newcastle for £13,000. He made his debut for Newcastle against Newport County, a game Newcastle won 13-0 (Shackleton scored six goals). He was subsequently transferred to Sunderland, and in his third match for the Wearsiders he scored his first goal for them after 13 minutes at Sheffield United to earn his team a 1-1 draw.

During 1955–56, Stoke City signed Andy Graver from Leicester City for a fee of £11,000. On successive Saturdays Graver found himself playing for Stoke against all his previous clubs: Leicester City (FA Cup, 28 January), Lincoln City (League, 4 February), Leicester City (League, 11 February) and Newcastle United (FA Cup, 18 February).

In 1955–56 the Darlington forward line for much of the season comprised John Spuhler, Harry Bell, Ken Morton, Dickie Davis and Tom Reynolds. All five had previously been at Sunderland.

In 1956–57, all four Football League divisional champions scored in excess of 100 goals – the first time this had happened since 1931-32. The teams were Manchester United (Division One, 103 goals), Leicester City (Division Two, 109 goals), Ipswich Town (Division Three South, 101 goals) and Derby County (Division Three North, 111 goals).

On the opening day of the 1958–59 season, Vic Metcalfe played for Hull City in their 1-1 draw against Plymouth Argyle. Metcalfe had to wait until the opening match of the following season (1959-60) before being selected again for Hull – against Plymouth Argyle.

In 1958, George Stewart was transferred three times, and the deals involved six different clubs. How? Well, there were three George Stewarts. Centre-forward George Stewart was transferred from Accrington Stanley to Coventry City; his goalkeeping namesake was transferred from Stirling Albion to Bradford City; and a third George Stewart, a full-back, joined Barrow from Montrose.

Barrow goalkeeper Alan Coglan broke a leg in a reserve-team game against Sunderland in 1958–59. Coglan made his comeback for Barrow in a reserve-team fixture against Sunderland, only to break his leg again. In 1962, he broke a leg for a third time while playing for Barrow reserves – against Sunderland.

In 1958–59, the Gateshead United team (Division Four) contained two players whose name was Ken Smith. For identification purposes the Football League designated them Ken Smith 1 and Ken Smith 2. All very straightforward – until, that is, Gateshead beat Carlisle United 4-1 at Redheugh, a game in which Ken Smith 1 scored twice and Ken Smith 2 scored once, which read in the classified results as follows: K. Smith 1 (2), K. Smith 2 (1). And they say football was a simpler game back then.

On 27 September 1958, British Railways introduced a new type of football excursion, 'The Away Day Specials'. On the same day, eight Division Three teams won away from home – the most away wins in any division of the Football League on a single day.

John King scored his first three goals in the Football League with three different clubs in three different seasons in three different divisions: Everton (Division One, 1958–59), Bournemouth (Division Three, 1960–61) and Tranmere Rovers (Division Four, 1961–62).

In 1963–64, West Ham United had a first-team squad comprising 20 players, 12 of whose surnames began with the letter B: Jim Barrett, Peter Brabrook, Peter Bennett, David Bickles, John Bond, Eddie Bovington, Ronnie Boyce, Martin Britt, Ken Brown, Jack Burkett, Dennis Burnett and Johnny Byrne. The non-Bs were Jim Standen, Lawrie Leslie, Joe Kirkup, Bobby Moore, Martin Peters, John Sissons, Geoff Hurst and Brian Dear.

In 1995–96, Brighton seemingly had a liking for players whose surname began with M. At various times nine such players turned out for the Brighton first team: Craig Maskell, Paul McCarthy, Paul McDonald, Junior McDougald, Kevin McGarrigle, Jeff Minton, Stuart Munday, Denny Mundee and Stuart Myall, in addition to which trainees Kerry Mayo and Ross McNally appeared for the reserves.

During 1996–97, Blackpool fielded a team that included eight players whose surnames also began with B: Steve Banks, Phil Barnes, Junior Bent, Mark Bonner, Gary Brabin, Darren Bradshaw, Marvin Bryan and Tony Butler.

George Best's debut for Manchester United reserves was against West Bromwich Albion; the full-back given the job of marking him was Graham Williams. Best made his first-team debut for United in Division One against West Bromwich Albion, and the opposing full-back was Graham Williams. In 1964, Best made his international debut for Northern Ireland against Wales and yet again found himself up against Graham Williams.

In 1965–66, Queens Park Rangers manager Alec Stock handed his fountain pen to his new signing so that he could put pen to paper. The player's name? Brian Inkpen.

On 19 November 1966, Sunderland trailed 3-1 at home to Burnley but fought back to win the game 4-3. On 3 April 1972, Burnley again visited Roker Park and raced into a 3-1 lead only for Sunderland to come back and win 4-3.

On 1 January 1966, Chester beat Aldershot 3-2 in a Division Four match. Both Chester full-backs were called Jones (Ray and Bryn) and both sustained a broken leg.

In July 1973, John Ritchie, Stoke City's regular number nine, was given the number eight shirt for a tour match against Otago of New Zealand. Ritchie opened the scoring after eight minutes and went on to score all Stoke's goals in an 8-0 victory. His haul remains an individual club record.

In 1973–74, the Brentford manager was Mike Everitt, the first-team trainer was Jess Willard and the club's general manager was Denis Piggott. They all shared the same birthday – 16 January.

On 5 October 1974, Tottenham Hotspur were 2-0 down at half-time against Burnley: both Burnley goals were own-goals, by Spurs' John Pratt and Mike England. Spurs scored twice in the second-half to earn a 2-2 draw, their goals coming from John Pratt and Mike England – the only instance of this ever happening in the Football League.

Long-serving West Brom striker Tony Brown scored his first goal for the club against Ipswich Town, whose goalkeeper was Roy Bailey. When Brown created a post-war club record by scoring his 213th goal against Manchester United, the United keeper was Roy Bailey's son Gary.

Gary Rowell was a great favourite with Sunderland supporters in the 1970s and early 1980s. His name was often chanted by supporters at both the Roker and Fulwell Ends at Roker Park. Rowell is a portmanteau word, comprising the 'Ro' of Roker and the 'well' of Fulwell.

On 28 April 1979, Bradford City beat Crewe Alexandra 6-0 at Valley Parade. On the same day, at Gresty Road, Crewe Alexandra reserves beat Bradford City reserves 6-0.

David Grant and Brian Strutt were in the same class at school. Both were ball-boys at Sheffield United's Bramall Lane and, in addition to their school team, played for the same local youth team. They played in the same Sheffield City Schoolboys team too, and were chosen together to play for Yorkshire Boys. When they left school in 1981 (on the same day) both were subsequently offered terms by Sheffield Wednesday.

On 20 February 1983, Brighton beat Liverpool 2-1 in the fifth round of the FA Cup. Liverpool were top of Division One and Brighton were bottom. The Brighton manager was ex-Liverpool player Jimmy Melia, and their winning goal was scored by Jimmy Case, also ex-Liverpool. It was Liverpool's first home defeat for 12 months. The last side to have won at Anfield was – Brighton.

On 19 October 1985, the attendance for Torquay United's home game against Northampton Town was 1,282; the game ended as a draw. Torquay then played two successive away matches but returned to Plainmoor on 2 November to face Orient. The game ended in a draw and the attendance was 1,282.

On 24 March 1987, Wimbledon held the record for the lowest ever attendance at a First Division match for all of one minute. Their match at Plough Lane against Coventry City drew a miserly crowd of 4,370. As the record was being announced on BBC Radio's *Sports Report*, news came in that the First Division match between Charlton Athletic and Oxford United at Selhurst Park had attracted only 4,205 spectators.

On 21 March 1987, Southampton's £5,000 lottery draw was won by Guy Askham, the club's financial director. On the very same day, Sunderland's weekly £500 lottery was won by manager Lawrie McMenemy.

On 5 February 1991, Mansfield Town entertained Bury at the Field Mill. Mansfield goalkeeper Andy Beasley received a red card for a foul on Bury striker Tony Cunningham. Chris Withe, on loan to Mansfield from Bury, took over in goal and saved Cunningham's penalty. Towards the end of the game, with Bury leading 1-0, Mark Kearney, on loan to Bury from Mansfield, cleared the ball from the goal-line enabling Bury to hold on to their lead and win 1-0. Bury's goal was scored by Kevin Hulme, who once had a trial with Mansfield.

On 2 September 1995, Chester defeated Hereford United 2-0; the Chester goals were scored by Cyrille Regis (5 minutes) and Kevin Noteman (23 minutes). On 14 October, Chester won 2-0 at Leyton Orient, their goals coming from Cyrille Regis (5 minutes) and Kevin Noteman (23 minutes).

On 31 August 1996, three home nations and the Republic of Ireland were involved in World Cup qualifying matches and all four teams were captained by former Southampton players: Iain Dowie (Northern Ireland), Barry Horne (Wales), Alan Shearer (England) and Andy Townsend (Republic of Ireland).

In 1997–98, three Premiership matches were halted due to floodlight failure. This coincidence proved too much for the Premier League, who launched an inquiry into possible sabotage by betting syndicates from the Far East.

David Beckham's grandfather 'Westy' was not a professional footballer but good enough to play for the Army in the late 1940s. Westy's best pal and team-mate in the same Army team was Tommy Docherty, later to manage Manchester United. After National Service, Westy and the Doc lost contact with each other. They were reunited some 50 years later through their mutual association with David Beckham.

 Since I retired from the game I like to have the occasional bet. I was reading the paper one day when I saw the odds for Liverpool winning the Premiership the following season, in 2005, were 5-1. It was Friday the fifth of May, the fifth month, so I went down the bookie's and put a fiver on Liverpool. They finished fifth.

TOMMY SMITH

14 In 1908–09, Newcastle United dominated the early exchanges in the Tyne–Wear derby against Sunderland at St James' Park but the score at half-time was 1-1. Sunderland scored eight in the second-half to register a record away win in the Football League. Sunderland's 9-1 victory included five goals in a blistering eight-minute spell. Despite this mauling, Newcastle staged a remarkable comeback: they won ten of their next 11 League matches and went on to win the First Division Championship.

In the first round of the 1911–12 FA Cup, Wolves drew 0-0 at Watford having cleared two efforts by the home side off the line. Wolves won the replay 10-0.

In 1931–32, in an FA Cup tie at St James' Park, Newcastle United were held 1-1 by Southport (Division Three North). Newcastle were under so much pressure in the replay at Haig Avenue – Southport hit the visitors' woodwork twice in extra-time – that they were happy to settle for another 1-1 draw. Having been outplayed in two matches, in the second replay Newcastle swept Southport aside, winning 9-0.

The greatest FA Cup Final comeback of all, in what was arguably the greatest final of all, took place in May 1953. With little over 20 minutes of the match remaining, Blackpool trailed Bolton Wanderers 1-3 when Stan Mortensen scored his second goal of the match to make the scoreline 2-3. Inspired by a brilliant display from 38-year-old Stanley Matthews, Blackpool continued to attack but were thwarted by a doughty rearguard action from Bolton. With one minute of normal time remaining, Mortensen completed his hat-trick, rifling a 20-yard free-kick into the net. Extra-time appeared a certainty, but with seconds of injury-time remaining Matthews danced down the wing, beat two defenders and cut the ball back for Bill Perry to score the winner and give Blackpool the cup. A Blackpool season ticket holder who had been blind since early childhood and who relied on friends to relay 'commentary' of matches to him memorably said after this amazing final, 'I have been blind nearly all my life, but I've seen everything now!'

Stan Mortensen scored a hat-trick against Bolton – the only man to have a cup final named after him: The Matthews Final.

LAWRIE McMENEMY

In 1955–56, after 79 minutes of a Birmingham Charity Vase tie, Whitwick Colliery led Brush Sports 4-0, only for Sports to live up to their name, brush the opposition aside and score five goals in 11 minutes to win 5-4.

The most extraordinary comeback in a League match took place at the Valley on 21 December 1957. Charlton Athletic were reduced to ten men after 15 minutes and at one point were trailing Huddersfield Town 5-1. They then staged a sensational revival in the second-half to lead 6-5. Two minutes from time Huddersfield equalized, but with the last kick of the game John Ryan netted to make the final score 7-6.

An amazing turn-around: within a couple of minutes Manchester United have scored twice in a two-minute spell.

ALAN PARRY

In 1957–58, Lincoln City found themselves rooted to the bottom of Division Two with only six matches remaining. In order to be sure of escaping relegation, they had to take at least 11 points from the remaining 12 (at a time when two points were awarded for a victory). Incredibly, having endured what up to that point had been a miserable season, Lincoln won five matches on the trot and drew their final match to avoid the drop. Notts County and Doncaster Rovers were relegated instead.

On 13 September 1961, Spurs lost 4-2 to Gornik Zabrze in Katowice (European Cup preliminary round) but won the return at White Hart Lane 8-1. In the quarter-finals, Benfica lost 3-1 in Germany to Nuremberg but won the second leg 6-0 and went on to defeat Real Madrid in the final (5-3).

In 1962–63, Dunfermline staged one of the most remarkable comebacks in the history of the Fairs/UEFA Cup. They lost their second round first leg match in Valencia 4-0, but won the return at East End Park 6-2. With the tie 6-6 on aggregate a play-off was necessary. Sadly, after their Herculean effort at home, Dunfermline lost the third match in neutral Lisbon 1-0.

In the first round first leg of the 1964–65 Fairs/UEFA Cup, Kilmarnock lost 3-0 to Eintracht Frankfurt in Germany. Few gave Kilmarnock any chance of progressing in the tournament, particularly when Eintracht scored to equalize on the night in the first-half of the second leg at Rugby Park; but the never-say-die attitude of Killie would not be suppressed: they stormed back to win the match 5-1 and clinch the tie 5-4 on aggregate.

On 19 March 1966, Spurs led Aston Villa 5-1 at half-time in a League match at White Hart Lane, only for Villa to stage an amazing second-half comeback and draw 5-5.

In the 1966 World Cup quarter-final at Goodison Park, North Korea sensationally led much-fancied Portugal 3-0 (Pak Seung Jin, Li Dong Woon and Yang Sung Koek the scorers). For a time it appeared the biggest World Cup shock since England's 1-0 defeat by the USA in 1950 was on the cards. But, inspired by Eusebio, Portugal staged a remarkable fight-back to win the game 5-3. Eusebio scored four goals, two of them from the penalty spot, and the other Portugal goal came from José Augusto.

Who would have thought it, who would have believed it? Three-nil up, North Korea stormed back to lose 5-3.

HUGH JOHNS, on ITV

Even with a history of Scottish fight-backs in the Fairs/UEFA Cup, in 1967-68 few gave Hibernian any chance of progressing when they lost their Fairs Cup second round first leg 4-1 against Napoli in Italy. On what was a highly memorable night at Easter Road, Hibernian crushed Napoli 5-0 to win the tie 6-4 on aggregate.

In a Durham Minors (Under-17) Cup tie in 1967, Gus Carter FC trailed Hetton United Boys Club 6-0 after 58 minutes but stormed back to win 7-6.

On 10 March 1971, Chelsea lost 2-0 at Bruges in the European Cup Winners' Cup (quarter-final first leg) but won the return at Stamford Bridge 4-0 (aet).

The last time these two sides met, Brighton led 2-0, but Manchester United came back to draw 2-2, both United goals coming from Manchester United.

DAVID COLEMAN

In 1975–76, Real Madrid lost 4-1 to Derby County in a European Cup tie, but won the second leg in Spain 5-1 after extra-time. Derby's Charlie George scored four goals in the tie – the only British player to have scored four against Real and still end up on the losing side.

A lot of people wrote us off and some of these players never dreamed they'd be playing in a cup final at Wembley – but here they are today, fulfilling those dreams.

LAWRIE McMENEMY

The 1978 World Cup in Argentina consisted of two stages, the first involving four groups, the second just two; the two winners of those groups would progress to the World Cup Final. Brazil completed their three 'stage two' group matches with a 3-1 victory over Poland to finish on five points; their nearest rivals, Argentina, were due to play later that evening. To overhaul Brazil, Argentina had to beat Peru by four clear goals. In the event, Argentina scored six without reply to qualify for the final. Their performance was hailed by some as an incredible display of determined attacking football; others seriously questioned the commitment of Peru (already eliminated) and the fact that Peru's goalkeeper, Ramón Quiroga, was born in Argentina.

They're still only 1-0 down – if there's such a thing as being only 1-0 down against Brazil.
ALAN PARRY

In 1980–81, Watford lost 4-0 in the second round first leg of the League Cup at Southampton, but won the second leg at Vicarage Road 7-1.

In 1983–84, Spain looked doomed not to qualify for the finals of the European Championship. In order to do so they had to beat Malta by 11 clear goals in their final qualifying match. Despite missing an early penalty, Spain won 12-1 and thus qualified for the finals at the expense of Holland.

Well, it's Ipswich 0 Liverpool 2, and if that's the way the score stays then you've got to fancy Liverpool to win.
PETER JONES, BBC Radio

In 1984–85, Partizan Belgrade lost 6-2 to Queens Park Rangers in a UEFA Cup tie played at Highbury because Rangers' synthetic pitch at Loftus Road was not approved by UEFA. Partizan won the second leg 4-0 in Belgrade and progressed on away goals.

In the 1992–93 Champions League – as the European Cup had just been rebranded – Leeds United lost a first-leg tie 3-0 in Stuttgart but won the second leg 4-1 at Elland Road. The aggregate score was 4-4 but Stuttgart won the tie on the away goals rule. It was then discovered by UEFA that the German champions had played four instead of the three permitted foreign players so it was decreed that the two teams should meet in a play-off at a neutral venue. Leeds won through, beating Stuttgart 2-1 in Barcelona.

Even when you're dead you shouldn't lie down and let yourself be buried.

GORDON LEE, Everton manager (1977–81)

In the First Division play-off final at Wembley in May 1995, Bolton found themselves 2-0 down against Reading but fought back to win the game 4-3 after extra-time.

On 9 March 1996, Ipswich Town were losing 3-0 at Barnsley with only four minutes of the game remaining but staged a sensational late comeback to earn a 3-3 draw.

On 29 September 2001, Manchester United trailed Spurs 3-0 at half-time in their Premiership match at White Hart Lane, but United rallied magnificently in the second-half to win the match 5-3. Three years later Spurs were at it again, against United's rivals Manchester City. Spurs were 3-0 up at half-time in a fourth round FA Cup tie but City, reduced to ten men, stormed back in the second-half to win 4-3. As one wag put it, 'Spurs have been subjected to more comebacks than Frank Sinatra's manager.'

 Beckham, coming forward with the ball, never believing a game is over until the final whistle has blown.

JOHN MOTSON

The greatest comeback ever seen in a final in European competition was staged by Liverpool on 25 May 2005. At half-time Rafael Benitez's side were 3-0 down against AC Milan in the Champions League final. No fiction writer would have dared dream up the events of the second-half. In the 54th minute Steven Gerrard scored what appeared to be little more than a consolation goal for Liverpool, but then, within an unforgettable five-minute spell, first Vladimir Smicer then Xabi Alonso spun the final on its head. These goals, and a superb save by Liverpool keeper Jerzy Dudek to deny Andriy Shevchenko, propelled the game into a penalty shoot-out after extra-time. Serginho (Milan) missed, Hamann (Liverpool) scored, Pirlo missed, Cissé scored, Tomasson scored, Riise missed, Kaká scored, Smicer scored, Shevchenko missed, and it was all over for Milan. No other team has ever recovered such a deficit in a European final. For once the superlatives heaped on a team by the media were fully deserved.

The Conference League is the league at the top of the non-league pyramid system in England. It was formed in 1979–80 as a single division and was expanded to three divisions in 2006, the latter two regionalized as North and South. The National Conference is the premier division which enjoys promotion and relegation with League Two of the Football League (two clubs going either way). Conference North and South are feeder leagues to the National Conference. Four clubs are relegated from the National Conference to North or South, depending on their geographical position.

The first members of the Conference in 1979–80 were Altrincham, Bangor City, Barrow, Barnet, Bath City, Boston United, Gravesend and Northfleet, AP Leamington, Maidstone United, Northwich Victoria, Nuneaton, Kettering Town, Redditch United, Scarborough, Stafford Rangers, Telford United, Wealdstone, Weymouth, Worcester City and Yeovil Town.

When the league began every club was part-time professional. Today the majority of Conference clubs are full-time professional.

Initially, the champions of the Conference had to apply in the time-honoured way for election to the Football League, along with the bottom four clubs in Division Four. There was no automatic promotion.

The first club to achieve automatic promotion from the Conference to the Football League was Scarborough in 1986-87.

Only six clubs have won the Conference twice: Altrincham (1980 and 1981), Barnet (1991 and 2005), Enfield (1983 and 1986), Kidderminster Harriers (1991 and 2000), Macclesfield Town (1995 and 1997) and Maidstone United (1984 and 1989).

It was claimed that Colin Cowperthwaite scored for Barrow after only 3.5 seconds against Kettering Town on 8 December 1979, though this time was never officially verified.

In 1987–88, Mark Carter scored after five seconds of Runcorn's game against Enfield. In Runcorn's following match, against Sutton United, Carter scored after six seconds.

The fewest goals scored by a team throughout the course of a Conference season is 26 – Redditch United (1979–80).

The all-time record for goals by an individual player in a single season is 41 by Paul Culpin (Nuneaton Borough, 1983–84).

In 1987–88, attendances at Conference matches rose by 36 per cent to a record aggregate of 578,535. Such has been the success of the league, in 2005–06 aggregate attendances topped one million for the first time – 1,134,234.

Following a major sponsorship deal, in 2007–08 the league took on the name the Blue Square Conference. The deal also encompassed the North and South divisions.

The record attendance for a Conference league match is 11,065, Oxford United v. Woking at the Kassam Stadium (Boxing Day 2006). Perhaps some supporters didn't see enough to persuade them to return: the match ended goalless.

The record attendance for any game between Conference clubs is 19,126, for the 2003–04 play-off final between Aldershot Town and Shrewsbury Town at the Britannia Stadium.

In addition to Oxford United (see above), another two clubs have attracted attendances in excess of 9,000 for a league match: Lincoln City (v. Wycombe Wanderers, 9,432, on 2 May 1988) and Carlisle United (v. Barnet, 9,215, on 6 October 2004).

In 1985–86, Kim Casey scored 36 league goals for Kidderminster Harriers. The following season he scored 38.

In 1987–88, Cheltenham Town drew 20 matches – a Conference League record.

The most consecutive defeats in a single season is 12 – Dagenham (1987–88). The most matches without a win is 26 – AP Leamington (1981–82).

The record number of league goals scored by a team in a single season is 103 – Barnet (1990–91) and Hereford United (2003–04).

The most goals scored away from home in a single Conference season is 57, by Barnet (1982–83 and 1987–88) and Colchester United (1991–92).

The highest winning margin is nine – Runcorn 9 Enfield 0 (3 March 1990). On 22 September 1990, Sutton United won 9-0 at Gateshead United – the record away win for the Conference League.

In 1990–91, Altrincham enjoyed a run of 28 consecutive league matches without a defeat.

The most victories in a single league season is 30 – Wycombe Wanderers (1991–92). Wycombe's manager at the time was Martin O'Neill.

The fewest goals conceded by a team in a single season is 25 – Kettering Town (1993–94).

The most clean sheets achieved by a team in a single season is 24 – Kettering Town (1993–94).

In 1993–94, Bath City recorded 12 goalless draws – a record for the league.

In July 1997, Stevenage Borough received a transfer fee of £300,000 from Bristol Rovers for Barry Hayles. In the same year fellow Conference club Woking received £150,000 for Steve Foster – also from Bristol Rovers.

Only one club has gone an entire season unbeaten away from home in the league, Yeovil Town (1998–99), who repeated the feat in 2001–02.

In November 1999, Aldershot Town paid £20,000 to Woking for the services of Grant Payne – a club record for a transfer fee paid.

The fewest league wins in a single season is four, by AP Leamington (1981–82), Northwich Victoria (2003–04) and Leigh RMI (2004–05).

Forest Green Rovers' ground in Nailsworth, Gloucestershire, is called 'The Lawn'.

The most points achieved in a 42-match season is 95 – Yeovil Town (2002–03). Yeovil also scored exactly 100 goals in the league that season.

The record number of defeats sustained in a single season is 32 – Leigh RMI (2004–05). The fewest number of defeats in a season is four – Yeovil Town (2002–03).

The highest aggregate score in a league match is 11 goals – Altrincham 7 Nuneaton Borough 4 (9 November 1987); Altrincham 9 Merthyr Tydfil 2 (10 February 1991); and Burton Albion 4 Telford United 7 (8 February 2003). Nuneaton Borough, along with Dover Athletic (Doncaster Rovers 5 Dover Athletic 4, 19 December 1998), are the last two teams to have scored four goals away from home but still lose the match.

In 2002–03, Woking set a Conference record for the most consecutive draws – nine matches.

The last player to score 30 or more league goals in a single season was Daryl Clare (30), for Chester City in 2003–04.

In 2003–04, Hereford United enjoyed a run of 11 consecutive victories – a Conference record.

In 2004–05 Scarborough boasted an unbeaten home record in the league. Two seasons later (2006–07), Scarborough were relegated and the club went into administration.

In 2007, Gravesend and Northfleet changed their name to Ebbsfleet.

In their days as a Northern Premier League club, Northwich Victoria took part in the Anglo-Italian Tournament. England entered semi-professional clubs, Northwich competing along with the likes of Redditch and Chelmsford City; Italian opposition included Sampdoria, Lecce and Verona.

Histon enjoyed a meteoric rise. In 2000, they were playing in the Eastern Counties League and then won four promotions in seven seasons to win a place in the Blue Square Conference.

Northwich Victoria share their Wincham Park ground with another Conference club – Witton Albion of the Blue Square Conference North.

In the third round of the 2004–05 FA Cup, Exeter City achieved a goalless draw against Manchester United at Old Trafford. United, however, won the replay at St James' Park 2-0, the United goals coming from Ronaldo and Rooney.

Give us a break! As part of a major sponsorship deal for the club, York City changed the name of their ground from Bootham Crescent to Kit-Kat Crescent.

In 1965–66, the first signings Brian Clough made as a manager were Les Green (goalkeeper), Tony Parry and Stan Aston, who joined Clough at Hartlepool United from Burton Albion. Burton's current manager is Nigel Clough, son of Brian.

Clubs you might have forgotten who were once members of the Conference League: Carlisle United, Chorley, Colchester United, Darlington, Dartford, Leek Town, Lincoln City, Slough Town, Trowbridge Town, Wealdstone, Worcester City.

George Hilsdon was on fire when he made his debut for Chelsea on 1 September 1906 against Glossop in Division Two. He scored a hat-trick, and Chelsea won 9-2.

16

The youngest player to make his debut in the Football League is Albert Geldard, who played for Bradford Park Avenue against Millwall (Division Two, 16 September 1929) at the age of 15 years and 128 days.

The oldest player to make his debut in the Football League is Andy Cunningham, 38 years and two days old when he played for Newcastle United against Leicester City (Division One, 2 February 1929).

The oldest post-war player to make his debut in the Football League is David Donaldson, who was 35 years, seven months and 23 days old when he played for Wimbledon against Halifax Town on 20 August 1977. This was not Donaldson's Wimbledon debut as he played for the club in their non-league days.

The oldest player to make his debut in British senior football is John Ryan (owner of Doncaster Rovers), at 52 years, 11 months and 21 days old. With promotion to the Football League assured, Ryan came on as a last-minute substitute for Rovers against Hereford United in a Conference League match (26 April 2003).

Stan Milton had a baptism of fire when, on 3 January 1934, he made his Football League debut as a goalkeeper for Halifax Town against Stockport County (Third Division North). He conceded 13 goals and Halifax lost 13-0.

Blackpool's Stan Mortensen enjoyed a sensational international debut for England in Lisbon on 27 May 1947. Mortensen scored four times in England's 10-0 rout of Portugal – to date, England's record away win.

On 20 October 1951, Billy Foulkes scored on his debut for Wales with his first touch of the ball against England at Ninian Park, Cardiff.

On 31 March 1954, Peter McParland (Aston Villa) scored with his first touch of the ball on his debut for Northern Ireland against Wales. The Wales goalkeeper was Jack Kelsey (Arsenal), who was also making his international debut. His first touch of the ball was to pick it out of the net as McParland scored after only 40 seconds.

The fastest scoring debut is that of Bernard Evans, who in the 1954–55 season netted after only 25 seconds of his first appearance for Wrexham, against Bradford Park Avenue.

Len Shackleton scored a double hat-trick on his debut for Newcastle United, who beat Newport County 13-0 on 3 October 1946.

Dennis Evans made his debut as a goalkeeper for non-league Gorleston against Gillingham in the first round of the FA Cup in 1957 and conceded ten goals. Final score, 10-1.

Danny Hegan signed for Sunderland in September 1961 but had to wait 12 years before making his debut for the Wearsiders. Having been signed from Albion Rovers, Hegan spent two years at Sunderland without ever breaking into the first team. In July 1963 he was transferred to Ipswich Town, and after a number of successful seasons at Portman Road he moved to Wolverhampton Wanderers, from whom Sunderland re-signed him in November 1973. Hegan eventually made his first-team debut against Nottingham Forest on 24 November 1973.

Malcolm Clarke had a lovely 'first touch', though he was unable to demonstrate it when making his debut for Leicester City against Leeds United on 29 September 1965, because he never made contact with the ball at any time. Coming on as a substitute in the 88th minute, Clarke never touched the ball during his two minutes on the pitch. The *Sunday People* thought he did OK though: in the player marks at the end of their match report, Clarke was given a '6'.

Sir Stanley Matthews made his debut for Stoke City against Bury on 19 March 1932 and played his last League match for the club 33 years later, on 6 February 1965. Stan's is the longest career of any player in English senior football.

Jimmy Greaves is the only player to have scored on his debut in senior football for every team he played for: Chelsea, AC Milan, Tottenham Hotspur (hat-trick), West Ham United, Chelmsford City, Barnet, England Under-23s and the full England team.

Steve Heighway made his debut for Liverpool at Mansfield Town on 22 September 1970 (second round replay, League Cup). The following night he made his international debut for the Republic of Ireland against Poland in Dublin. Twenty-four hours is a record for the shortest timespan between a club football debut and an international debut.

Tony Ford made his Football League debut on 4 October 1975 for Grimsby Town against Walsall, and played his last game in the League 26 years later, on 3 November 2001, for Rochdale against Torquay United (Division Three). Ford played a total of 931 League games in his career – a record for an outfield player in English football.

In 1977–78, Tony Woodcock (Nottingham Forest) and Peter Ward (Brighton) both scored hat-tricks on their debuts for England Under-21s. Ward scored his in England's 6-0 victory over Norway on his home ground at Brighton on 6 September; Woodcock achieved his in England's 8-1 defeat of Finland at Boothferry Park (Hull) on 12 October.

Also in 1977–78, Colin Lee scored four goals when making his debut for Spurs against Bristol Rovers. Spurs won 9-0.

On 9 April 1988, Alan Shearer scored a hat-trick on his Southampton debut in the 4-2 victory over Arsenal. At 17, he became the youngest player to score a First Division hat-trick on his debut.

Kevin Todd had a memorable debut for Berwick Rangers against East Stirling on 22 September 1990. He scored a hat-trick, hit the East Stirling bar and post, was booked, and then got injured five minutes from time.

David Beckham made his Football League debut not for Manchester United but for Preston North End, against Doncaster Rovers (4 March 1995). Beckham was on loan from United, appeared as a second-half substitute, and scored in a 2-2 draw. He made his full League debut in Preston's following match at home to Fulham (11 March) and scored again in a 3-2 win. Beckham played a further three matches for Preston – at home to Bury (5-0) and away at Exeter City (1-0) and Lincoln City (1-1) – before returning to Old Trafford.

A week after having played for Preston at Lincoln City, on 2 April 1995, Beckham made his League debut for Manchester United in a goalless draw with Leeds United. He had, however, made his first ever appearance in the United first team earlier in the season, on 7 September, in United's 2-1 victory at Port Vale in the Coca Cola Cup. Also making their full debuts in the United team that night were Nicky Butt, Gary Neville and Paul Scholes, who scored the goals.

Steven Gerrard made his Liverpool debut as a substitute against Blackburn Rovers on 29 November 1998. He made his first start in Liverpool's following match at Tottenham Hotspur (5 December). In addition to Michael Owen and Robbie Fowler, the Liverpool team at the time included David James, Steve Staunton, Jason McAteer, Phil Babb, Paul Ince and Jamie Redknapp.

Gerrard made his debut for England against Ukraine on 31 May 2000. He soon became something of a lucky talisman for England: in his first 21 internationals England did not lose a single game – the longest unbeaten start by any player to an England career.

Wayne Rooney made his debut for Everton in the Premiership against Tottenham Hotspur (2-2) on 17 August 2002 and was substituted after 65 minutes. Of his next 19 appearances for Everton, 15 were as a substitute. In the four matches he started, he was substituted on two occasions.

It was a totally different story when Rooney made his debut for Manchester United at Old Trafford on 28 September 2004 in the Champions League against Fenerbahçe: he scored a hat-trick in a 6-2 win for United.

Rooney made his England debut at the age of 17 years and 111 days, against Australia (12 February 2003). At the time he was the youngest player ever to have appeared for England.

Prior to Rooney's international debut, England's youngest debutant was Michael Owen, who was 18 years and 59 days old when he played against Chile at Wembley (11 February 1998).

17 A meeting of two local clubs is often referred to as a 'derby' match. The term dates back to the Victorian age when working men wore cloth caps. On special occasions, however, such as weddings, anniversaries or funerals, many men would wear their 'Sunday best' hat, often a derby hat of the bowler variety. As the meeting of two local clubs was regarded as a special event in the fixture list, such games began to be referred to as 'derby' matches, the insinuation being that men should attend wearing their best derby bowler hat as opposed to their everyday working cap. The term is also accredited to the Earl of Derby.

The word 'soccer' originated in the 19th century. 'Student speak' at Oxford University often involved adding 'er' to many words, as in 'champers' (champagne), 'swotter' (a student keen on studying), 'rugger' (rugby). In the late Victorian age football was referred to as 'Association Football', after the Football Association, as a means of distinguishing the game from rugby football. Students at Oxford abbreviated the term, adopting the 'soc' from the word 'association' and adding 'er' as was the trend – hence the word 'soccer' as an alternative to the word 'football'.

The directors box is mandatory under the rules of the Football League. It must have clearly marked home and away areas, with a minimum of 16 seats for visiting directors and 24 for the home club.

Why are some stands/terracing at grounds referred to as 'The Kop', as at Anfield and Hillsborough? The term has its origins in the Boer War. On 6 January 1900 British troops, many of them from Merseyside and South Yorkshire regiments, fought the Boers at the Battle of Spion Kop, a hill in South Africa. When the war ended and the troops returned home, many resumed supporting their local football teams. Many of the Merseyside-based soldiers who had fought at Spion Kop took to congregating on a bank of terracing at Anfield; as it was hill-like and populated by so many veterans of the battle, the terracing was popularly referred to as 'The Kop'. Likewise, the bank of terracing at Hillsborough was popular with Wednesday-supporting Boer War veterans from South Yorkshire.

The English Schools Football Association was founded in 1904 and its headquarters are in Stafford.

In 1907–08, Herbert Chapman (later to enjoy legendary success as a manager with Huddersfield Town and Arsenal) had three goals disallowed when playing for Northampton Town (then of the Southern League) against Sutton Town in a qualifying round of the FA Cup. He did, however, score twice in Northampton's 10-0 victory.

There is a monument in Porto that commemorates Arsenal losing a friendly match. In the summer of 1948, Arsenal embarked upon a tour of Portugal during which they lost to Oporto. Such was the delight and excitement of the locals it was decided there must be a permanent reminder of this 'momentous' occasion. A public subscription raised the equivalent of £20,000 and a monument was erected. It still stands in the city, just off Praça de Lisboa.

The first £100,000 jackpot was won on the football pools in 1950. The first £1,000,000 win was in 1987. In the 1950s, pools companies employed an estimated 100,000 people.

The FA Youth Cup began in 1953 and in the first six years of its existence was won by Manchester United.

Aston Villa and Sunderland became the first clubs to play each other in 100 League matches when they met at Roker Park on 1 January 1953. The game ended 2-2.

Bill Spurdle of Manchester City didn't play for City in the 1956 FA Cup Final due to an outbreak of boils. (Imagine what the press would make of that today should, say, Wayne Rooney have the misfortune to suffer from a similar ailment.)

When did Charlton score for Charlton when Charlton didn't score? Answer: on Easter Saturday 1957 during Charlton Athletic's 3-1 defeat against Arsenal. The Charlton goal was an own-goal by Arsenal defender Stan Charlton.

Career on the slide? Starting from September 1957, Tony McNamara played in all four divisions of the Football League inside twelve months. Everton (First), Liverpool (Second), Bury (Third) and Crewe Alexandra (Fourth).

Today's academies not working? The Football League introduced the apprentice scheme in 1960. In its first ten years, 2,126 young players were offered apprenticeships with League clubs of which over half (1,157) went on to be offered full-time professional terms. From 1970 to 1980, 2,408 young players were offered apprenticeships of which 1,311 were offered full-time terms – again, over half. A success rate considerably better than that of the academies.

The academies aren't working. They're simply not producing the players they should be producing. I've been searching all over for a centre-forward. Years ago they used to be ten-a-penny, not now.

STEVE BRUCE, Wigan Athletic manager, January 2008

Football academies were the brainchild of the then FA technical director Howard Wilkinson, as a scheme to develop and coach young players from the age of eight to 21.

Arthur Longbottom, who played regularly for Port Vale in the early 1960s, changed his name by deed poll to Arthur Langley.

Real Madrid legend Alfredo Di Stefano was kidnapped and held for ransom in February 1964 during Real's tour of Venezuela. He was later released without the ransom having been paid.

Bobby Moore's middle name was Chelsea.

During the winter of 1962–63, known as 'The Big Freeze', to earn some degree of income Halifax Town invited local people on a Saturday to pay for and use their pitch as an ice rink.

The InterToto Cup was first launched by UEFA in 1961 and revamped in 1995 as a route into the UEFA Cup.

On several occasions in the 1970s, games between Sheffield United and Arsenal featured Currie and Rice – Tony Currie (Sheffield United) and Pat Rice (Arsenal).

In the 1970s, Sunderland had a player called Barry Wardrobe.

The Watney Cup was a pre-season knockout tournament of the early 1970s which was the first in England to feature the penalty shoot-out, which had been pioneered in the North American Soccer League. The first winners of the Watney Cup in 1971 were Derby County, who beat Manchester United 4-1 in the final. The last winners were Stoke City, who beat Hull City 2-0 in 1973.

The Football Trust was established in 1979 to help develop football in England, particularly grounds. It was initially funded by a levy placed on 'Spot the Ball' competitions run by pools companies.

The San Siro, home of both AC and Inter Milan, is still commonly referred to by that name, even though in 1979 it was renamed Stadio Giuseppe Meazza in honour of the striker who played for both clubs in the 1930s and for Italy in the 1934 and 1938 World Cups.

The most common result in League football is 2-1.

The League Managers Association, the organization that represents the interests of all managers in the Football League, was founded in 1980.

The Island Games, established in 1983, is held every two years and includes a football cup competition for islands with fewer than 125,000 inhabitants.

The Football Supporters Association was formed in 1985 in the aftermath of the Heysel Stadium disaster.

The 'Mexican Wave' first appeared during the 1986 World Cup in Mexico.

One of the top clubs in Trinidad and Tobago is called Joe Public FC.

The term 'libero' means a sweeper who instigates attacks. (Oh yeah?)

The Screen Sport Super Cup was a competition for English clubs that would have qualified for Europe had it not been for the ban imposed by UEFA following the Heysel Stadium disaster. The cup was sponsored by European satellite sports channel Screen Sport but lasted for only one season – 1985–86. In the two-legged final Liverpool beat Everton 7-2 on aggregate.

Jimmy Greaves never said, 'It's a funny old game.' It was uttered by Greaves' *Spitting Image* puppet, voiced by Harry Enfield.

On the subject of what it was like to play in Italy, Ian Rush never said, 'It's like playing in a foreign country.' The line was impishly accredited to Rush by Liverpool manager Kenny Dalglish and told to a football journalist as a wind-up.

CONCACAF stands for Confederación Norte-Centroamericana y del Caribe Fútbol (Northern and Central America and Caribbean Football Federation), and, as you would expect, encompasses clubs in those areas of the globe.

It is important for a team to be familiar with their opposition, but Burnley and Stockport took this to the extreme. On 26 January 1991, Burnley and Stockport met for the 11th time in little over a year: four times in Division Four, three Leyland DAF Cup ties, and twice in both the FA and League Cups. Burnley won four games, Stockport three, with four drawn.

In 1991–92, the FA Cup Final broke with tradition when the losing team ascended the steps of the royal box first to collect their medals, prior to the winners collecting the cup.

Chester City's Deva Stadium is derived from the Roman name for Chester, Castra Devana ('the camp on the Dee').

David Beckham's middle names are Robert and Joseph, and his mother's family are Jewish.

The only current player whose name is featured in a Monty Python sketch is Kevin Phillips, as in Kevin Phillips-Bong (Slightly Silly Party) in Python's 'Election Night Special'.

One of the top clubs in Madagascar is Mpiasa Mpianatra Mirka who once played a friendly against Turkish club Makina Kimya Endustrisi Ankaragucu Kolubu. The chanting of the names of the clubs from the terraces alone must have been worth the admission price.

Pelé was awarded an honorary knighthood in 1997.

In 1998, Manchester United reached an agreement with Belgian club Royal Antwerp for it to be United's nursery club for young talent. Other clubs have similar agreements: Arsenal with Beveren and St Etienne, West Ham with Kingsway Olympic (later called Sydney Hammers), Sheffield United with China Blades.

The Italian championship is often referred to as the 'Scudetto', which is the championship shield badge worn on the shirts of the current champions. A team that has won the Italian title ten times has the right to wear a gold star on their shirts. This was adopted on England shirts in 2004 to indicate the winning of the World Cup in 1966.

Not since 1896–97 has a senior English team gone through a complete season without drawing a single match. The last club to do so were Darwen, who won 14 and lost 16 of their 30 matches in Division Two.

The club with the longest unbroken membership of the top division in English football is Arsenal, since 1919. Next is Everton, since 1954.

The first Welsh Cup Final took place between Wrexham and Druids on 30 October 1877, though there was no actual trophy to present to the winners (Wrexham).

What did Jimmy Greaves and Dave Mackay have in common during their days together as players with Spurs? Neither wore studded boots. Even in heavy conditions, both preferred to play in boots with moulded rubber soles/studs.

Birmingham City were the first club to become a limited company.

On 27 December 1948, Bill Gray played two matches for his club and was on the winning side on each occasion. On the morning of the 27th he played for Leyton Orient reserves at West Ham United only to be called up for the Orient first team in the afternoon for the game against Port Vale.

The first South American club to tour in Europe was Peñarol (Uruguay), in the late 1950s.

The Charlton Athletic team that faced Preston North End in 1953 contained five South African players: Ken Chamberlain, Eddie Firmani, John Hewie, Stuart Leary and Sid O'Linn.

At the start of 1959–60, the longest-serving member of the Bradford Park Avenue team was right-back Gerald Baker, who, though only 20 years and four months old, had been with the club since the age of 15.

When Liverpool signed Alec Lindsey from Bury in the early seventies they'd actually got the wrong player. The Bury player who had impressed the Liverpool scout was Jimmy Kerr.

In St Johnstone's first ever match in European competition, the UEFA Cup in 1971-72, they beat Hamburg 3-0 (4-2 on aggregate).

By the time Sunderland played Liverpool in the 1992 FA Cup Final they had finished 18th in Division Two – the lowest-placed team to contest an FA Cup Final since Leicester City (19th in Division Two) in 1948–49.

The game between Exeter City and Bury on 27 April 1996 was 'interrupted' by a 'special news flash' broadcast over the public address system. The news was that the local council had agreed to purchase the club's St James' Park ground, thus saving the club from possible extinction.

Quantum leaps. It is amazing that the careers of two players who were, for a time, contemporaries spanned the eras of 'Dixie' Dean and David Beckham, but this is the case with Stanley Matthews and Peter Shilton. Matthews joined Stoke City in 1930 when Dean was still scoring for Everton and played his final League game in 1965 when Shilton was at Leicester City. Shilton played his last League game (for Leyton Orient, in 1997) when Beckham was already turning out for Manchester United.

Alan Shearer is a cousin of jazz musician and singer Louis Hoover (real name Steven Sparling), whose career is picking up nicely.

18 In 1913, the Arsenal board obtained a 21-year lease on Highbury from the Ecclesiastical Commissioners at a cost of £20,000. The deal involved Arsenal directors agreeing not to stage games on Good Friday or Christmas Day. The restriction was eventually lifted in 1925–26, but it cost the Arsenal directors a further £60,000.

Behind every successful manager there is a surprised chairman.

MANNY CUSSINS, former chairman of Leeds United

In the days of the maximum wage it was not uncommon for players to join a club and also accept a part-time job with a company owned by a club director. These part-time jobs were known as 'dolly jobs' as the player invariably never worked for the company but appeared on the pay roll so that the club could pay him more than the maximum wage. The most startling example of this was England centre-forward Tommy Lawton, who in 1947 was transferred from First Division Chelsea to Notts County of the Third Division for a fee of £20,000. In addition to playing for County, Lawton also 'worked' as an 'advisory consultant' for an engineering company owned by one of the County directors. Stanley Matthews once asked Lawton if he had actually given any advice to the directors of the engineering company. 'Yes,' said Lawton. 'I once told them to put a few bob on Bell Boy in the two thirty at Kempton Park.'

In his autobiography of the 1950s *The Clown Prince of Soccer*, Len Shackleton (Newcastle, Sunderland and England) included a chapter entitled 'What the Average Director Knows about Football', which was followed by a blank page. When his playing days were over, Shackleton became a director of Fulham.

 We're hopeful the game will go ahead. In this respect we've spared no expense. We've even hired a snow plough, if you get my drift.

SYD COLLINS, Sunderland chairman

For many years Viscount Montgomery of Alamein was president of Portsmouth. In the 1950s, the Fulham chairman, comedian and comedy actor Tommy Trinder, was appearing in a show on the south coast when he was invited to a Portsmouth home game as the guest of Viscount Montgomery. Following the game, Trinder was in the directors' room when he heard on the radio that Fulham had won 2-0, both their goals coming from young Johnny Haynes.

'Hear that, sir?' Trinder asked Monty. 'Both goals from young Haynes. He's a terrific player, a fantastic athlete. Mark my words, he'll captain England one day.'

'How old is he?' enquired Monty.

'Seventeen,' replied Trinder.

'Seventeen? What about his National Service?' asked Monty.

'Ah, that's the only sad thing about the lad,' said Trinder, thinking on his feet. 'He's a cripple.'

Tommy Trinder's wisecracking was legendary in the Fulham boardroom which, rather than being exclusive on matchdays, operated something of an 'open house' policy. After one game at Craven Cottage, against Manchester United, the wife of United chairman Louis Edwards found herself talking to the Fulham groundsman. When Mrs Edwards returned to the company of her husband

and Trinder, the Fulham chairman asked if she was enjoying her visit to his club.

'Yes,' said Mrs Edwards, 'but could you speak to your groundsman about his language? I happened to remark how well the pitch was looking. He told me the secret was barrowloads of manure. Could you ask him to use the word "fertilizer" instead? I find the other word very vulgar.'

'You gotta be joking,' replied Trinder, his considerable jaw dropping. 'It took me six months to get him to call it manure!'

On 10 April 1957, Sunderland were found guilty of making illegal payments to players. The chairman and three directors were banned from football for life, the club was fined £5,000, and 14 players were fined six months' benefit qualifications. The latter was overturned in 1962.

Following Ipswich Town's championship success in 1961–62, Frank Wilson of the *Daily Mirror* sought the reaction of Ipswich chairman John Cobbold.

'I suppose this has been a season of wine, women and song for the board,' said Wilson.

'I can't remember us doing much singing,' replied Cobbold.

In the 1960s, the Brentford chairman was Jack Dunnett MP (later chairman of the Football League). In November 1964, Dunnett signed centre-forward Ian Lawther from Scunthorpe United; the signing took place inside the House of Commons. Lawther is the only player to have signed for a Football League club in Parliament.

Traditionally, directors provided funds to buy players in the transfer market. In some clubs, one director might have provided the bulk of the funds not only for transfers but for the day-to-day running costs too. In 1964, football journalist Bryon Butler asked Burnley chairman Bob Lord, 'What would you have been if you had not been chairman of Burnley?'

'A millionaire,' replied Lord.

In October 1966, when Workington Town increased the membership of their board of directors to 13, they had more directors than full-time professional players.

> When I joined West Ham, the chairman told me it was a 'family club'. . . and it was. There was an argument going on in every room I went into.
>
> JIMMY GREAVES

When Tommy Smith retired as a player with Liverpool, he applied for the vacant position of manager at Walsall. During the interview, one Walsall director informed him that the board had the final say on which players signed for the club, not the manager.

'That's not how it was at Liverpool,' Smith informed the director.

'You'll find we do things different here to Liverpool,' replied the board member.

'Which is probably why you're still in the Third Division and Liverpool are European champions again,' replied Smith.

> Villa chairman Doug Ellis told me he was right behind me. I told him I'd rather have him in front of me where I could see him.
>
> TOMMY DOCHERTY

In 1981–82, Fulham manager Malcolm Macdonald became the first paid director of an English League club.

> I left the boardroom as I arrived, fired with enthusiasm.
>
> JOHN McGRATH, on being dismissed at Preston

The first chairman-manager of a senior British club was Jim McLean, team manager of Dundee United and appointed club chairman on 20 December 1988.

The first chairman-manager of a Football League club was Ron Noades (Brentford), July 1998 to March 2001.

Arthur Montford, one of the most respected of all football commentators, became a director of Morton in 2003. He was invited to join the board by chairman Douglas Rae. The pair had been, quite literally, long-standing supporters of Morton.

During an interview for Central TV, Wolves chairman Sir Jack Hayward was asked how much he was willing to invest in the club. Hayward replied, 'Well, I'm willing to keep throwing money at it until we get it right, or the men in the white coats take me away.'

Try to keep a straight face. Alan Sugar has become a major television personality through his involvement with *The Apprentice*, a series which, among other things, requires Sugar to assess and pass judgement on ideas would-be employees have for his company. When chairman of Tottenham Hotspur, Sugar was behind the launch of a new company product, 'The Amstrad Face-straightener' (a certain irony there?), the purpose of which was to get rid of wrinkles. The product, which initially was to be sold through Boots and promoted by Julia Carling, never took off. Well, let's face it . . .

In 1995–96, Manchester United lost 3-0 at home to York City in the second round first leg of the League Cup. Prior to the second leg at Bootham Crescent, the United chairman, Martin Edwards, informed his York counterpart Douglas Craig, 'We shall be playing our first team tonight.'
    'Really?' replied Craig. 'So will we.'

Roman Abramovich acquired control of Chelsea for a reported £150 million. In January 2007, it was said that Abramovich's investment in the club stood at £600 million.

Malcolm Glazer first acquired shares in Manchester United in 2003. In 2005, he took control of the club at an estimated cost of £800 million, £600 million of which, it was widely reported, was said to have been borrowed.

I used to tour when I didn't want to, just to buy Watford a centre-forward.
ELTON JOHN

Nowadays it is often enough to acquire some degree of celebrity status just for being a club director. The following were celebrities before joining the boards of their respective clubs:

Sir Richard Attenborough (Chelsea)
Sir Matt Busby (Manchester United)
Jasper Carrott (Birmingham City)
Frank Carson (Colchester United)
Willie Carson (Swindon Town)
Tommy Cannon (Rochdale)
Sir Bobby Charlton (Manchester United)
Jim Davidson (Bournemouth)
Derek Dooley (Sheffield United)
Arthur English (Aldershot Town)
Barry Hearn (Leyton Orient)
Elton John (Watford)
Bill Kenwright (Everton)
Robert Maxwell (Oxford United/Derby County)
Brian Moore (Gillingham)
John and Cecil Moores (Everton)
Mohammed Al Fayed (Fulham)
Eric Morecambe (Luton Town)
Sir Alf Ramsey (Birmingham City)

ALF RAMSEY

Delia Smith (Norwich City)
Alan Sugar (Tottenham Hotspur)
Tommy Trinder (Fulham)
Charlie Williams (Barnsley)
Norman Wisdom (Brighton)

The only British club currently to have a chairman who formerly played for the club is Sunderland (Niall Quinn).

In 2007–08, former Manchester City full-back Ray Ranson became chairman of Coventry City.

In 2008, ten Premiership clubs were under non-British ownership: Aston Villa, Chelsea, Derby County, Fulham, Liverpool, Manchester United, Manchester City, Portsmouth, Sunderland and West Ham United.

In 2008, only one Scottish club was under foreign ownership – Hearts.

'It is great news. This will establish Derby's brand worldwide through alliances with supporters in the USA, the Far East and Africa.'

ADAM PEARSON, Derby County chairman, commenting on the proposed takeover of the club by a US consortium in January 2008. (No comment as to whether it would be good news for supporters who actually attend Derby matches, then.)

19

In December 1920, Horace Fairhurst (Blackpool) sustained a head injury while challenging for the ball in a game against Barnsley at Oakwell and died as a result of his injury in hospital in the New Year.

Twenty-three-year-old Celtic goalkeeper John Thompson died following an incident during the Rangers v. Celtic 'Old Firm' match at Ibrox on 5 September 1931. Thompson flung himself at the feet of oncoming Rangers forward Sam English and fractured his skull in the collision; he died five hours later in Glasgow Victoria Infirmary. Nigh on 50,000 mourners assembled at Queen Street station to see his coffin off, and over 3,000 attended his funeral.

Thompson was the second Scottish goalkeeper to die following a collision during a match. In 1921–22, Dumbarton keeper James Williamson lost his life following an incident during a game against Rangers on 12 November.

Sunderland goalkeeper Jimmy Thorpe died days after having played against Chelsea on 1 February 1936. The cause of death was diabetes, which the coroner stated had been accelerated by 'rough usage of the goalkeeper' during the game against Chelsea. The coroner criticized the match referee, but an FA commission later exonerated the official, stating that he had 'acted totally in accordance with his instructions'.

On 8 September 1996, David Longhurst suffered a heart attack while playing for York City against Lincoln City and died as a result. York City named one of their stands at Bootham Crescent (now Kit-Kat Crescent) after him.

Marc Vivien Foe (formerly of West Ham United) collapsed while playing for Cameroon against Colombia on 23 January 2003 and later died in hospital. An autopsy revealed the cause of death to be a heart attack that resulted from an enlarged right ventricle.

In August 2007, 16-year-old Walsall youth team player Anton Reid collapsed on the training field and later died as a result of heart failure.

On 25 August 2007, Spanish international Antonio Puerta died after suffering a heart attack during Sevilla's opening game of the La Liga season against Getafe.

On 29 December 2007, Motherwell captain Phil O'Donnell died after suffering heart failure during his club's Scottish Premier League match against Dundee United. O'Donnell, capped by Scotland, began his career at Motherwell and returned to the club in 2004 following spells with Celtic and Sheffield Wednesday.

In January 2008, FIFA announced that it was considering introducing mandatory heart screenings for all players.

On 5 April 1902, 25 spectators were killed when part of a terracing collapsed during the Scotland v. England international at Ibrox, Glasgow. The game was held up for 20 minutes but then continued for the duration. The final score was 1-1, but the game was erased from the official records of both associations.

On 9 March 1946, 33 spectators were killed and an estimated 550 suffered injuries when crowd barriers collapsed during the sixth round FA Cup tie between Bolton Wanderers and Stoke City at Burnden Park. Following two protracted hold-ups it was decided the game should continue to its conclusion.

On 4 May 1949, 18 Torino players, many of whom were members of the Italy national squad, were killed when the aeroplane they were travelling in crashed into a hillside on the outskirts of the city. In all, 31 people lost their lives, including their English manager Les Leivesley. Torino had won four consecutive Italian League Championships. Their remaining League fixtures for 1948–49 were completed by their youth team, who played the youth teams of their opponents.

The BEA Elizabethan aircraft carrying Manchester United players and officials and a team of journalists crashed when taking off from Munich airport on 6 February 1958. United were returning from a European Cup tie against Red Star Belgrade. As a result of the crash eight Manchester United players lost their lives: Roger Byrne, Geoff Bent, Eddie Colman, Mark Jones, David Pegg, Tommy Taylor, Bill Whelan and Duncan Edwards, who died later in hospital. United coach Bert Whalley, trainer Tom Curry and secretary Walter Crickmer were also killed, along with the following football journalists: Alf Clarke, Don Davies, George Follows, Tom Jackson, Archie Ledbrooke, Henry Rose, Eric Thompson and former Manchester City and England goalkeeper Frank Swift. Among those who survied the crash were Manchester United manager Matt Busby and players Bobby Charlton, Dennis Viollet, Bill Foulkes, Ken Morgans and Harry Gregg. Johnny Berry and Jackie Blanchflower also survived but as a result of their injuries never played football again.

On 25 May 1964, 300 spectators died following a riot during Peru's match with Argentina in Lima. The trouble started when the referee disallowed a Peruvian goal.

On New Year's Day 1971, 66 spectators died, many of them trampled to death, and over 100 were injured towards the end of the game between Rangers and Celtic at Ibrox. The tragedy occurred on Stairway 13 when, with Celtic leading 1-0, hundreds of fans tried to return to the terraces following the award of a penalty to Rangers. This disaster led to the introduction of the Safety of Sports Grounds Act 1975.

Two disasters befell British football in 1984–85. On 11 May 1985, 56 spectators died and 220 were treated in hospital for burns and smoke inhalation as a result of a fire which started in the main stand at Valley Parade during the game between Bradford City and Lincoln City. An investigation revealed that beneath the flooring of the wooden stand (erected in 1909) was an accumulation of litter which ignited when, in all probability, a cigarette end was discarded. Only eighteen days later, on 29 May, prior to the start of the European Cup Final between Liverpool and Juventus at the Heysel Stadium in Brussels, 39 spectators (32 of them Italian) died and hundreds were injured when a wall and safety fence collapsed during rioting between fans of both clubs. Back in the dressing rooms the players were not initially told of the extent of the tragedy and the game went ahead, but when the death toll became apparent players simply went through the motions of a game. Juventus won 1-0, a result which bore no significance.

On 10 September 1985, the Scotland team manager, and one of the greatest managers of all time, Jock Stein collapsed and died as a result of a heart attack during his team's World Cup qualifying match against Wales at Ninian Park, Cardiff.

On 15 April 1989, 96 Liverpool supporters were killed and hundreds were injured minutes into the FA Cup semi-final between Liverpool and Nottingham Forest at Hillsborough. The tragedy occurred at the Leppings Lane end of the ground when thousands of fans surged on to the terracing. Many perished in the crush in the 30-yard tunnel leading to the terracing but the majority who died were on the terracing from which locked gates and high fences prevented escape. The actions of leading policemen were highly criticized: the police had opened a large metal gate to ease congestion, which led to the surge. The 'Hillsborough Tragedy' was the worst disaster in the history of British sport and resulted in the Taylor Report by Lord Justice Taylor. Among its 76 recommendations was an end to terracing at Football League grounds by 1999. As a result, English football embarked upon a period of reform that resulted in better and safer conditions at sports grounds, changing football in this country for ever.

On 5 May 1992, 15 spectators died and an estimated 1,500 were injured when a temporary stand collapsed during the French Cup semi-final between Bastia and Marseille in Bastia, Corsica.

On 23 April 1993, all but four of the Zambia national squad were killed when the aeroplane taking them to a World Cup qualifying match against Senegal crashed into the ocean shortly after taking off following a refuelling stop in Gabon. The four members of the squad not to perish were signed to European clubs and had not travelled on the aircraft as they were due to link up with the Zambia party in Dakar.

In 2000–01, African football was beset by three tragedies. In April 2001, 43 supporters died and 155 were injured in a crush on overflowing terraces at Ellis Park, Johannesburg, during a game between Orlando Pirates and Kaizer Chiefs. In May, 126 spectators died when rioting broke out during the game between Hearts of Oak and Asante Kotoko in Accra, Ghana. Two months later, 13 fans died in a stampede to avoid tear gas fired by police during a local match in Harare, Zimbabwe.

20

England's first ever international match was against Scotland in Glasgow on 30 November 1872. It was also the first international football match in the world. Bit of a damp squib, though: it ended 0-0.

The first player to score a hat-trick for England was Howard Vaughton (Aston Villa), who in 1882 scored five times in England's 13-0 victory over Ireland. Vaughton scored his hat-trick in the space of only seven minutes; his Villa team-mate Arthur Brown was also on fire that day and scored four. The result stands as England's record victory in an international match.

In 1908, England played their first international matches on foreign soil. On 6 June, England beat Austria 6-1 in Vienna; days later they beat them again, on this occasion 11-1. Having enjoyed two resounding victories, England completed their first Continental tour by beating Hungary 7-0 and Bohemia 4-0.

The last player to score hat-tricks in consecutive matches for England was 'Dixie' Dean, in May 1927 against Belgium (9-1) and Luxembourg (5-2), both matches away from home.

Four players have scored a hat-trick when making their England debut: George Mills (Chelsea), v. Northern Ireland in October 1937; Wilf Mannion (Middlesbrough), v. Northern Ireland in September 1946; Stan Mortensen (Blackpool), v. Portugal in May 1947; and Fred Pickering (Everton), v. USA in May 1964.

England's first defeat at the hands of foreign opposition was on 15 May 1929, when they lost 4-3 to Spain in Madrid, though they could be excused as this was England's third match within seven days as part of a hectic Continental tour.

During the 1920s, 1930s and 1940s, England players made their own way to away matches in the Home International Championship, receiving their match fee, second-class rail fare and what was officially described as 'reasonable expenses'. In 1938, Stan Matthews appeared before an FA Expense Committee for having submitted a claim of one shilling (5p) for a cup of tea and two scones when returning from a game against Wales in Cardiff. As a post-match buffet had been laid on for players at Ninian Park, Matthews was refused the claim on the grounds that it was an 'unnecessary expense'.

England's first defeat on home soil against foreign opposition occurred at Wembley on 25 November 1953 when Hungary won 6-3.

The only man to have played for England and his club on the same day is Danny Clapton. On 26 November 1958, Clapton played for England against Wales at Villa Park in the afternoon and for Arsenal in a prestigious friendly against Juventus in the evening. He and Jack Kelsey (the Wales goalkeeper that day, who also played for Arsenal in the evening) were driven from Birmingham to Highbury by Tommy Docherty, who attended the England v. Wales game on behalf of Scotland caretaker manager Matt Busby, and who also played for Arsenal against Juventus.

In October 1959, for the first time since being appointed manager in 1946, Walter Winterbottom persuaded the FA to allow him to have sole responsibility for team selection for the international against Sweden at Wembley. The crux of his argument was that he wanted to create a young England team that hopefully would win the World Cup. England lost to

Sweden 3-2 – only their second defeat against foreign opposition on home soil. As a result of this defeat, selection of the England team reverted back to the committee, with Winterbottom as an adviser. Four of the young players who appeared in the match against Sweden – Bobby Charlton, Jimmy Greaves, Ron Flowers and John Connelly – and two reserves – Ron Springett and George Eastham – were members of Alf Ramsey's England squad for the 1966 World Cup.

Alf Ramsey was not the FA's first choice to succeed Walter Winterbottom as England manager. The FA at first offered the job to Jimmy Adamson, the captain of Burnley, who turned it down as he wanted to continue his career as a player. Only then was Ramsey offered the post.

On 15 April 1961, England registered their record victory over Scotland, 9-3, at Wembley; England also had a goal disallowed which Jimmy Greaves still maintains was legitimate. The finger of blame was pointed at Scotland goalkeeper Frank Haffey (Celtic), though, in truth, this was an exceptional display by England. During the post-match buffet Haffey suggested the Scottish players should socialize with the England team, saying, 'We lost heavily, but it's only a game of football. We lost to the English at Culloden and that was a battle.' To which Dave Mackay replied, 'Aye, but after Culloden we Scots didn't make small talk with them over sandwiches!' That thrashing of Scotland in 1961 was part of a sensational sequence of results for Winterbottom's team in 1960–61. In six consecutive internationals England scored 40 goals: Northern Ireland 5-2, Luxembourg 9-0, Spain 4-2, Wales 5-1, Scotland 9-3 and Mexico 8-0. During this sequence Bobby Charlton scored two hat-tricks (Luxembourg and Mexico), as did Jimmy Greaves (Luxembourg and Scotland).

England's 9-0 victory over Luxembourg (in Luxembourg on 19 October 1960) was the last occasion on which two England players (Charlton and Greaves) scored hat-tricks in the same international match. England equalled their 9-0 success over Luxembourg on 15 December 1982 in a European Championship qualifying match at Wembley. It was Bobby Robson's fourth game in charge of England.

Jimmy Greaves has scored more hat-tricks for England than any other post-war player. The six he scored came against Luxembourg (October 1960), Scotland (April 1961), Peru (May 1963), Northern Ireland (November 1963), Northern Ireland again (October 1964) and Norway (June 1966).

The first time England played an entire game at Wembley under floodlights was on the evening of 20 November 1963. England beat Northern Ireland 8-3.

Prior to England's game against West Germany at Wembley on 29 April 1972, Sir Alf Ramsey held a team meeting during which he asked certain players if they would volunteer to take a penalty should England be awarded one. Emlyn Hughes, Bobby Moore, Martin Peters and Martin Chivers all declined. Eventually Ramsey asked Rodney Marsh, who informed him he would happily take a penalty. 'That's it then,' said Ramsey. 'If we get a penalty, Rodney will take it.'
    'Only one problem, Alf,' said Marsh. 'You haven't picked me for the team.'

In 1972–73, Alan Hudson (Stoke City) and Colin Todd (Derby County) received a two-year international ban from the FA for preferring to play for their respective clubs rather than join the England squad for an international match. FA secretary Denis Follows said, 'There is no question of an appeal as the players have not been charged with any offence, simply told they will not be required by England for two years.' Ironically, the game Hudson and Todd preferred to play in was between Derby County and Stoke City, a match during which Hudson broke a leg.

I think England will make it to the semi-finals, along with Brazil, Italy, Germany and France.
CHRIS KAMARA

Martin Dobson (Everton) played only five times for England but did so under three different England managers. He made his debut in Alf Ramsey's final game, played for Joe Mercer during his caretaker period, and made his last appearance under Don Revie.

The shortest post-war England career is that of Peter Ward (Brighton), whose only appearance was as a substitute against Australia in 1980, which lasted all of eight minutes.

The shortest England career on record belongs to Frank Hartley (Spurs and Oxford City). Selected to play against France in 1921, Hartley lasted only four minutes before sustaining an injury that forced him to leave the field. He was never chosen for England again as his career with Spurs went off the boil – somewhat appropriately, given that his England career lasted for the same amount of time it takes to boil an egg.

Bobby Charlton holds the record for the most England goals by an individual player – 49 in 106 matches. Next is Gary Lineker with 48 goals in 80 matches. Third is Jimmy Greaves with 44 goals in 57 matches. Michael Owen currently has 40 in 89 matches.

Bloomin' marvellous. The individual record for scoring in successive games for England is held by Steve Bloomer (Derby County). From March 1895 to March 1899, Bloomer scored in ten consecutive England games (19 goals in total).

The highest number of goals scored by an individual for England in the course of a single season is 13, by Jimmy Greaves in 1960-61.

 I gave what I thought was a good interview, but the FA didn't offer me the job as England manager because they thought I'd make too many changes, stir things up and cause them problems . . . and they were bloody right.
BRIAN CLOUGH

The record number of goals scored by an England player in the finals of a World Cup is six, by Gary Lineker, Mexico 1986.

The fastest goal scored by an England player at Wembley came after only 38 seconds of the game against Yugoslavia on 13 December 1989. It was scored by Bryan Robson (Manchester United).

And one can see England's destiny in the World Cup being changed single-handedly and almost by one man – David Beckham.

JOHN MOTSON

The oldest player to have scored for England is Stanley Matthews, who was 42 years and 103 days old when he netted in the 4-1 win over Denmark in Copenhagen on 15 May 1957.

Sir Geoff Hurst is the only player to have scored a hat-trick in a World Cup Final.

When England beat Germany 5-1 in a World Cup qualifying game in Munich on 1 September 2001, all the England goals were scored by Liverpool players: Michael Owen (three), Steven Gerrard and Emile Heskey.

The highest number of goals scored by an individual in a single game for England is five: Howard Vaughton (Aston Villa), v. Ireland in Belfast, 18 February 1882; Steve Bloomer (Derby County), v. Wales in Cardiff, 16 March 1896; Willie Hall (Tottenham), v. Ireland at Old Trafford, 16 November 1938; Malcolm Macdonald (Newcastle), v. Cyprus at Wembley, 16 April 1975.

Hoddle hasn't been the Hoddle we know, and neither has Bryan Robson.

RON GREENWOOD

England have played Australia six times and never scored more than two goals against them. The only occasion when England scored twice against the Aussies was the very first international between the two countries, on 31 May 1981 in Sydney (Australia 1 England 2).

Who is the only man to have managed England twice? Answer: Howard Wilkinson (see below).

Since 1946, when the first appointment was made, England have had 16 managers: Walter Winterbottom (1946–62), Sir Alf Ramsey (1962–1974), Joe Mercer (caretaker manager, 1974), Don Revie (1974–77), Ron Greenwood (1977–82), Bobby Robson (1982–90), Graham Taylor (1990–93), Terry Venables (1994–96), Glenn Hoddle (1996–99), Howard Wilkinson (caretaker, 1999), Kevin Keegan (1999–2000), Howard Wilkinson (caretaker, 2000), Peter Taylor (caretaker, also 2000), Sven-Göran Eriksson (2001–06), Steve McClaren (2006–07), Fabio Capello (2007 to present).

When Bobby and Jack Charlton played against Scotland on 10 April 1965, they became the first pair of brothers to appear together in an England team since Frank and Fred Forman (both Nottingham Forest) in 1899.

When Gary and Phil Neville played against China on 23 May 1996, they were the first brothers to play together for England since the Charltons in the 1970 World Cup match against Czechoslovakia in Guadalajara, Mexico (11 June).

Gordon Banks in goal, Bobby Moore and Jack Charlton at the back – how good were they? Jack made 35 appearances for England and was on the losing side just twice (against Austria and Scotland). Of the 35 games he played, England kept a clean sheet on 23 occasions. Gordon Banks played in 23 consecutive matches for his country between 1964 and 1967 in which England remained unbeaten. He kept 35 clean sheets in a total of 73 appearances for England and was on the losing side on only nine occasions. Bobby Moore won 108 caps for England and scored two goals. When playing in England's 2-0 victory over Greece in Athens (European Championship Qualifier, 1 December 1971), the sole became detached from his right boot during the first-half, and Moore appeared in the second-half wearing odd boots. As he said later, 'It didn't affect my performance, I only use my right leg for standing on.'

Peter Shilton kept 66 clean sheets in his 125 appearances for England. In 1982-83, he kept a record six consecutive clean sheets when on duty with England. Shilton played in a record 37 World Cup matches for England – 20 qualifying games and 17 in the finals.

England's only victory in Brazil came on 10 June 1984 in Rio de Janeiro, when John Barnes scored one of the all-time great England goals and Mark Hateley also netted to give Bobby Robson's side a 2-0 victory. It was Brazil's first home defeat for 26 years.

Since World War Two six players who have an X in their surname have played for England: Lee Dixon (Arsenal), Kerry Dixon (Chelsea), Mike Duxbury (Manchester United), Graeme Le Saux (Chelsea), Albert Quixall (Sheffield Wednesday) and Graham Rix (Arsenal).

David Beckham captained England on 58 occasions; his role as skipper ended following England's elimination from the 2006 World Cup Finals in Germany. Beckham was then ignored by new manager Steve McClaren but recalled in 2007.

Which England manager first appointed David Beckham as captain of the team? Answer: Peter Taylor, then caretaker England manager, who made Beckham captain for the game against Italy in Turin on 15 November 2000. Italy won 1-0.

Fabio Capello's first game as England coach took place on 6 February 2008 against Switzerland at Wembley, and resulted in a 2-1 victory for England. Capello won the domestic league title with every club he managed: AC Milan, Roma, Juventus and Real Madrid. He is a keen collector of fine art and his personal art collection is reportedly valued at £20 million. He is on record as saying his favourite artist is Wassily Kandinsky.

21 The European Cup was first contested in 1956 between the champions of member nations of Europe (though not every nation entered). Originally it was a straight knockout competition with ties played on a home and away basis. In 1991–92 the format featured a league phase for the first time, as well as a later knockout stage, and this has since evolved into what is now commonly termed the UEFA Champions League.

The idea for a European Cup was first aired in 1926, but the competition was not established until 1955–56. In 1955, the former French international and editor of *L'Equipe* Gabriel Hanot invited representatives of the champion clubs of Europe's 15 premier domestic leagues to attend a meeting. UEFA sanctioned the competition on 8 May 1955.

In 1955–56, English champions Chelsea, and Hibernian from Scotland, entered the draw for the first round of the inaugural competition. Chelsea were drawn against Swedish club Djurgården, but later withdrew without playing a game after the Football League and FA refused the club permission to participate. Hibernian reached the semi-finals, losing 3-0 on aggregate to Stade de Reims.

Hibernian were Scotland's representatives in the inaugural European Cup even though Aberdeen were Scottish champions. Hibernian were invited to participate as UEFA regarded the club's playing record in recent years to be superior to that of Aberdeen!

Real Madrid were the first winners of the European Cup, beating Stade de Reims 4-3 in Paris on 13 June 1956.

Real Madrid dominated the tournament in its early years, winning the European Cup in its first five seasons, 1955–56 to 1959–60.

The reigning European Cup holders have always qualified automatically for the next tournament.

The 1958 final between Real Madrid and AC Milan was the first to go to extra-time. Real eventually won 3-2.

The attendance for the 1960 European Cup Final between Real Madrid and Eintracht Frankfurt at Hampden Park was 135,000 – a record for the competition. Madrid's victory that night is considered by many to be the greatest ever performance by the greatest ever club side. The Germans were swept aside 7-3, and to place this performance in some sort of perspective, in the semi-finals Frankfurt had beaten Rangers 6-1 and 6-3 (12-4 on aggregate), and at the time Rangers were considered one of the best teams in British football. The match produced the first double hat-trick of a European final, from Alfredo Di Stefano and Ferenc Puskas. The Hungarian in fact scored four goals.

The first team to inflict defeat on Real Madrid were fellow Spanish club Barcelona (then the Spanish champions), in 1960–61. Following a 2-2 draw in the first leg in Madrid, Barcelona won their home tie 2-1.

Barcelona lost the 1961 final 3-2 to Benfica.

In 1961, Burnley reached the quarter-finals. They beat Hamburg 3-1 in the first leg at Turf Moor but lost the return in Germany 4-1 to go out 5-4 on aggregate. In the last minute of the second leg, a shot from Burnley's Jimmy McIlroy hit the Hamburg post and rolled along the goal-line but was deemed not to have crossed it. With Burnley due to play an FA Cup semi-final three days later, a reporter asked McIlroy, 'Any injuries?'

'No,' replied McIlroy, 'just eleven broken hearts.'

When Hamburg played Burnley in 1961, the German club had not bought a player in the transfer market for seven years. The entire Hamburg team, including German internationals Uwe Seeler and Gert Dorfel, were the product of the club's youth system, put together by manager Gunther Mahlmann.

The 1960–61 semi-final between Benfica and Rapid Vienna was the first tie to be abandoned for reasons other than weather. Benfica won the first leg in Portugal 3-0. The score in the second leg was 1-1 when, ten minutes from time, Rapid were refused what their players believed was a legitimate penalty claim. The Austrians continued to argue with the referee and refused to play; fans spilled on to the pitch and the referee abandoned the game. UEFA awarded the tie to Benfica and banned Rapid Vienna from all European competition for three years.

The first European Cup Final to be decided by a penalty shoot-out was the 1984 final between Liverpool and AS Roma. The tie ended 1-1, Liverpool won 4-2 on penalties.

Liverpool's success in 1984 meant they were the second English club within a week to win a major European trophy by penalty shoot-out. A matter of days earlier Tottenham Hotspur had beaten Anderlecht 4-3 on penalties (after 1-1 and 1-1) to win the UEFA Cup.

Only one final has required a replay, the 1974 encounter between Bayern Munich and Atlético Madrid. The teams drew 1-1 in Brussels and replayed in the same city two days later, Bayern winning 4-0.

The only winner of the European Cup to be stripped of their title is Olympique de Marseille. Having beaten AC Milan 1-0 in 1993 to win what was for the first time referred to as the UEFA European Champions League Cup, Marseilles were ordered to return the trophy after the club was found guilty of match fixing.

Real Madrid have won a record nine European Cups and appeared in 12 finals.

The lowest attendance for a final is 23,009, for the replay between Bayern Munich and Atlético Madrid at the Heysel Stadium, Brussels, in 1974.

The highest average attendance in one single season is 50,545 (1959–60), from an aggregate attendance of 2,780,000.

The record aggregate attendance for a single season is 6,461,112, in 2002–03 – an average of 41,154 per match.

On 13 July 2004, the attendance for the first qualifying round tie between Sliema Wanderers (Malta) and Kaunas (Lithuania) was 445.

Having succeeded Ron Saunders, Tony Barton was only 103 days into the job as manager of Aston Villa when Villa defeated Bayern Munich 1-0 in the European Cup Final of 1982.

In 1986, Barcelona (managed by Terry Venables) paid the penalty for an inept display in the European Cup Final against Steaua Bucharest. Arguably the dullest of all European finals, the game ended goalless after extra-time. In the penalty shoot-out Barcelona proved equally inept, failing to score from any of their spot-kicks.

The 2007 final was Liverpool's fourth consecutive final against Italian opposition: Roma (1984), Juventus (1985) and AC Milan (2005 and 2007).

Francisco Gento (Real Madrid) is the only player to hold six winners medals – a record for the competition.

Paolo Maldini (AC Milan) and Francisco Gento (Real Madrid) have played in a record eight finals. Maldini won in 1989, 1990, 1994, 2003 and 2007, but lost in 1993, 1995 and 2005.

Maldini is the oldest outfield player to have appeared in a final, at 38 years and 331 days, in 2007 against Liverpool.

Maldini's father, Cesare, captained AC Milan when they won the European Cup in 1963 – the only instance of father and son having won the trophy.

The oldest player to have appeared in a final is Dino Zoff (goalkeeper), who was 41 years and 86 days old on the occasion of the 1983 final between Hamburg and Juventus. Hamburg won 1-0.

Clarence Seedorf is the only player to have won the trophy with three different clubs: Ajax (1995), Real Madrid (1998) and AC Milan (2003).

The most goals scored by an individual in a single season is 14 by José Altafini (AC Milan), in 1962–63.

AC Milan have appeared in more Champions League finals than any other club: 2007 was their sixth appearance in the tournament's league format.

21

BRITISH WINNERS OF THE EUROPEAN CUP/CHAMPIONS LEAGUE

Celtic (1967)	Liverpool (1981)
Manchester United (1968)	Aston Villa (1982)
Liverpool (1977)	Liverpool (1984)
Liverpool (1978)	Manchester United (1999)
Nottingham Forest (1979)	Liverpool (2005)
Nottingham Forest (1980)	Manchester United (2008)

England hold the record for the most consecutive trophy wins by teams from a single country: six between 1976–77 and 1981–82.

The countries with the most successes are England, Italy and Spain with 11 wins each.

Real Madrid have won the trophy a record nine times, and appeared in 12 finals; AC Milan have won on seven occasions in total, and Liverpool five times.

When Celtic beat Inter Milan 2-1 in 1967 to become the first British club to win the European Cup, UEFA's official statistics for attempts on goal read Celtic 42, Inter Milan 5.

Manchester United were the second British club to win the trophy, and the first English club, when they beat Benfica 4-1 at Wembley in 1968 after extra-time. Denis Law missed the final due to injury; his place was taken by Brian Kidd, who celebrated his 19th birthday on the day of the final and scored one of the goals. It was arguably the most emotional final of all: it was ten years since the United manager Matt Busby and two of the United team that day, Bobby Charlton and Bill Foulkes, had survived the Munich air disaster.

And who will ever forget Manchester United's epic semi-final against Gornik Zabrze – I beg your pardon, Real Madrid.

BRIAN MOORE

In the 1998–99 final, Manchester United trailed Bayern Munich 0-1 with only one minute of the match remaining. Teddy Sheringham then scored for United, and Ole Gunnar Solskjaer added a second in injury-time to give United a memorable and remarkable last-gasp victory.

In 2001, a replica Manchester United 1968 European Cup Final shirt in red went on sale in the Manchester United megastore. It was quickly withdrawn, as on the night United had played in blue.

Chelsea have appeared in four semi-finals, in 2004, 2005, 2007 and 2008. Leeds United have appeared in three (1970, 1975 and 2001).

Both Dundee clubs have reached the semi-finals, Dundee in 1963 and Dundee United in 1984.

Raúl (Real Madrid) holds the record for the most goals scored by an individual in the competition. At the end of the 2008 Champions League, Raúl had scored 61 goals; Andrij Shevchenko had 59 goals to his name and Ruud van Nistelrooy 57.

Seven players have made more than 100 appearances in the Champions League: Raúl (118), Roberto Carlos (107), Thierry Henry (115), Paolo Maldini (107), Ryan Giggs (104), David Beckham (103) and Oliver Kahn (102).

Bob Paisley (Liverpool) is the only man to have managed one club to three victories (1977, 1978 and 1981).

Marcello Lippi is the only man to have coached a club (Juventus) to four Champions League finals (1996, 1997, 1998 and 2003).

Milan is the only city to have won the Champions League with two different teams – Inter and AC.

Real Madrid hold the record for the most consecutive appearances in the competition – 15, from 1955-56 through to 1969–70.

On only three occasions has the final been contested by clubs from the same country: Real Madrid and Valencia (2000), Milan and Juventus (2003) and Chelsea and Manchester United (2008).

Only four clubs have ever won the European Cup while also winning their domestic championship and cup in the same season: Celtic (1967), Ajax (1972), PSV Eindhoven (1988) and Manchester United (1999).

Ajax went 20 consecutive matches unbeaten in the Champions League: the entire 1994-95 tournament and up to the final of 1995–96 (which they lost to Juventus) – a record for the competition.

The team that took the Champions League trophy having won the fewest matches en route is Manchester United, who won just five games in 1998–99.

Two clubs have won the competition having not won their domestic championship the previous season, Nottingham Forest in 1980, Forest having qualified as holders of the European Cup, and Manchester United in 1999.

Ottmar Hitzfeld and Ernst Happel are the only coaches to have won the trophy with different clubs: Hitzfeld with Borussia Dortmund (1997) and Bayern Munich (2001), and Happel with Feyenoord (1970) and Hamburg (1983).

Nottingham Forest are unique in that they are the only club to have won the European Cup more times than they have won their domestic title. Forest were champions of the Football League for the first and only time in 1978, won the European Cup in 1979, and successfully defended it in 1980.

Five players have scored hat-tricks on their debut in the Champions League: Marco van Basten (AC Milan), Faustino Asprilla (Newcastle United), Aiyegbeni Yakubu (Maccabi Haifa), Wayne Rooney (Manchester United) and Vincenzo Iaquinta (Udinese).

In 2006, Arsenal set a record for the most consecutive clean sheets in the competition – ten matches.

Liverpool (1977) and Porto (2004) are the only clubs to have won the European Cup while in the same season being holders of the UEFA Cup.

Only three clubs have ever won the European Cup with a team entirely comprising players from their own country: Real Madrid (1966), Celtic (1967) and Steaua Bucharest (1986).

In 2002–03, Newcastle United progressed to the next stage of the Champions League having lost their first two matches in the group stage.

The fastest goal scored in the Champions League is 10.2 seconds by Roy Maakay for Bayern Munich against Real Madrid on 7 March 2007.

The biggest win in the Champions League proper is Liverpool 8 Besiktas 0 on 6 November 2007.

The oldest player to have competed in the Champions League is Marco Ballotta, who was 43 years old when keeping goal for Lazio in Group C of the 2007–08 tournament.

Another possible reason for the rejuvenation of Scottish football, and for England's debacle in the qualifying stages of the 2008 European Championship? Though Scotland had only two representatives (Celtic and Rangers) in the 2007–08 Champions League to England's four (Arsenal, Chelsea, Liverpool and Manchester United), Celtic and Rangers had more Scottish players registered to play in the tournament than the combined total of home-grown players registered with the 'big four' from England.

In 2007–08, Champions League places were allocated as follows: England, Italy and Spain – four clubs; France, Germany and Portugal – three clubs; Holland, Greece, Russia, Romania, Scotland, Belgium, Ukraine, Czech Republic and Turkey – two places; all other nations – one entry.

Manchester United's success over Chelsea (7-5 on penalties, 1-1 after extra time) in 2008 was the first occasion two English teams have ever contested the European Cup/Champions League Final.

On 16 January 2008, UEFA announced another change in format to the Champions League from 2009 to 2012. The competition is to include a third qualifying round, while the first knockout round of matches is to be extended over four weeks. The final of the Champions League is to take place on a Saturday afternoon (kick-off 2045 CET).

Reference to the European Cup in the ITV series *Razzamatazz* (1981):

Alistair Pirrie: Even if Newcastle United did play in the European Cup, we wouldn't be able to watch them play away, because Newcastle supporters are banned from travelling abroad.

Suzanne Dando: Why?

Alistair Pirrie: Because of what happened the last time Newcastle qualified for Europe. They travelled by boat, ripped the sails and threw the cannonballs overboard.

European Championship

22 The European Championship is open to all member nations of UEFA and takes place every four years. The competition comprises qualifying groups played over two years and a final tournament played in a host nation or nations.

The competition was originally called the European Nations Cup and was first contested in 1960. The winners were the Soviet Union, who defeated Yugoslavia 2-1. The four home nations declined to participate.

Prior to 1980, only four teams qualified for the final tournament. The host nation was selected by UEFA from the four nations that reached the finals. From 1980, eight teams qualified for the finals. The host nation was now pre-selected by UEFA and enjoyed automatic qualification. The current 16-team format dates back to 1996, when England were the hosts.

Following the break-up of nations such as the USSR, Yugoslavia and Czechoslovakia, Scotland and Ireland proposed increasing the number of teams in the finals to 24. In 2007, UEFA decided that no such expansion would take place until at least after the 2012 finals.

To qualify as hosts of the finals of the European Championship the country in question must have at least one five-star-rated stadium, and the others must be four-star and UEFA-rated. Stadiums must also be situated in at least four different cities. These criteria make it difficult for smaller countries to host the tournament, hence the current vogue for joint hosts.

The European Championship Trophy is named after Henri Delaunay, the first general secretary of UEFA, who first had the idea for the competition. He died in 1955, five years before the competition was launched.

In 2007, UEFA remodelled the trophy, making it larger, which was thought to be more in keeping with the stature the competition now enjoys across Europe. It is made of solid silver and now weighs eight kilograms (a little over 17½lb) and is 60 centimetres in height. A small figure juggling a football was removed from the back and replaced by a plaque listing past winners. The marble plinth was also dispensed with.

Throughout the 1960s and 1970s, the tournament enjoyed nowhere near the importance and kudos it has today. The turning point was 1980 and the increase in the number of teams competing in the finals (to eight) and the 'live' broadcasting on television of all matches across Europe. This attracted sponsorship from global companies. Their products appeared in supermarkets and restaurants bearing the Euro 80 logo and their promotions, offering related prizes, raised the awareness and profile of the championship. Many non-football fans who had never heard of the competition were now aware of its existence, and could follow the drama as it unfolded on television.

No home nation has ever reached the final of the European Championship.

WINNERS OF THE EUROPEAN CHAMPIONSHIP

1960 – USSR	1988 – Holland
1964 – Spain	1992 – Denmark
1972 – West Germany	1996 – Germany
1976 – Czechoslovakia	2000 – France
1980 – West Germany	2004 – Greece
1984 – France	2008 – Spain

Belgium, Italy and France have each hosted the finals on two occasions: Belgium in 1972 and 2000 (the latter as joint hosts with Holland); Italy in 1968 and 1980; and France in 1960 and 1984.

Germany/West Germany have appeared in the most European Championships, on ten occasions; they have appeared in a record six finals; and their three tournament victories is also a record.

The USSR/Russia and Holland have appeared in eight competitions, and England can claim to have reached the finals on seven occasions.

Scotland have reached the final stages of the competition twice, the Republic of Ireland once. Wales and Northern Ireland have never appeared in the finals.

Alan Shearer holds the record for the most goals by an England player in the finals – seven. Wayne Rooney has four goals, Frank Lampard three, and Michael Owen, Paul Scholes and Teddy Sheringham have each scored twice in the final stages. England's other goalscorers in the finals (one goal) are Tony Adams, Trevor Brooking, Bobby Charlton, Paul Gascoigne, Steven Gerrard, Geoff Hurst, Steve McManaman, David Platt, Bryan Robson, Ray Wilkins and Tony Woodcock.

The most goals scored by a Scottish player in the tournament's final stages is one, jointly held by Gary McAllister, Brian McClair, Ally McCoist and Paul McStay. Likewise for the Republic of Ireland – Ray Houghton and Ronnie Whelan.

In the qualifying group stage of Euro 2008, David Healy (Leeds United, later Fulham) scored a record 13 goals.

In the qualifying stages for the 1964 competition, Greece refused to play Albania as the countries were technically at war with each other.

Italy won the championship in 1968. They 'won' through from the semi-finals on the toss of a disc after the tie against Russia ended goalless after extra-time.

In 1976, Czechoslovakia became European champions, defeating West Germany in the first final to feature a penalty shoot-out. At one stage the Czechoslovakians led West Germany 2-0, only for the Germans to pull back to 2-2, which is how it stayed throughout extra-time.

Davor Suker (Croatia) holds the highest individual goalscoring tally in the competition, with 17. Suker also holds the record for having missed the most penalties in the competition – five.

In 1972, Bulgaria fielded an entire team against Belgium whose names ended in 'ov'.

Only 983 spectators turned up for the qualifying group match between the USSR and Finland at the Lenin Stadium on 31 October 1979. The capacity of the stadium was 105,000. The miserly attendance may have had something to do with the weather: the temperature at the stadium was recorded at −10°C.

In 1980, when the format of the competition finals changed, eight teams were divided into two groups with the two group winners contesting the final. Italy beat Belgium 2-1.

In 1984, the format of the finals changed again with the introduction of semi-finals. The group winners and runners-up comprised the four semi-finalists.

The 1988 final between Holland and the Soviet Union was won 2-0 by Holland and produced two of the most memorable goals in the history of the competition: Marco van Basten's exquisite angled volley and Ruud Gullit's bullet header.

A united Germany competed for the first time in the finals of 1992 but were defeated in the final by Denmark.

Denmark won that European Championship in 1992 after failing to qualify for the finals. UEFA had decided that Yugoslavia, riven by civil war, should not take their place in the competition in Sweden, and offered their place to Denmark, who had finished as runners-up to Yugoslavia in their qualifying group. Denmark had only 11 days' notice but, undaunted, went on to become champions.

1992 saw the first semi-final to be decided by a penalty shoot-out. Denmark beat Holland 5-4 on penalties (after a 2-2 draw) in Gothenburg.

England had a miserable time of it in the 1992 finals in Sweden. They drew 0-0 with both Denmark and France and were beaten 2-1 by hosts Sweden to be eliminated from their group. The defeat against Sweden was the last cap earned by Gary Lineker, who was withdrawn during the match by England manager Graham Taylor (and replaced by Alan Smith). Lineker then announced his retirement from International football. He was one goal short of equalling Bobby Charlton's record of 49 goals for England.

In Euro 96, the 'home' side was decided by a draw conducted by UEFA officials. This led to the unique situation of Scotland being drawn at 'home' to England at Wembley.

England topped their group in 1996. After an uninspiring 1-1 draw against Switzerland, they defeated Scotland 2-0 and then enjoyed a sensational 4-1 victory over Holland, in the second-half scoring three goals in 12 minutes including a memorable 'team' goal rounded off by a blistering drive from Alan Shearer. In the quarter-finals, England triumphed 4-2 over Spain on penalties (after a 0-0 draw). England were somewhat fortunate when, in the 34th minute, Spain's Salinas had an effort disallowed for offside. Even ardent England supporters thought this a harsh decision and action replays appeared to show the 'goal' was legitimate.

England reached the semi-finals of the competition for only the second time. The previous occasion was 1968 when England lost 1-0 to Yugoslavia.

In a dramatic repeat of their 1990 World Cup semi-final, England's Euro 96 semi-final against Germany went to penalties (after a 1-1 draw; England goalscorer, Alan Shearer). A total of 12 penalties were taken, and to the nation's angst the outcome was the same as in 1990. Germany triumphed when Gareth Southgate failed to convert penalty number 11 and Andreas Möller scored kick number 12.

There is nothing to be downhearted about, apart from the result.

TERRY VENABLES, finding words of comfort for English supporters following England's Euro 96 defeat by Germany

Germany were crowned Euro 96 champions when they beat the Czech Republic 2-1 in the final. Germany's winning goal was a 'golden goal' scored in extra-time by Oliver Bierhoff.

The 2000 final was contested by Italy and France. France won 2-1. Not one of the French team played his club football in France, whereas all of the Italian team played their club football in Italy.

England again endured a miserable tournament in 2000. In the opening match, England led Portugal 2-0 after 18 minutes (Paul Scholes and Steve McManaman) only to capitulate and lose 3-2. Some pride was restored when England beat Germany 1-0 (Alan Shearer), but then, having led Romania 2-1, England lost their final match 3-2 and were once again eliminated at the group stage of a finals.

The 2000 finals was the first to be staged in two countries – Belgium and Holland. The aggregate attendance was 1,101,650 – an average of 35,537 per match.

Perhaps the most surprising winners of all were Greece, who beat the much-fancied hosts Portugal in 2004 with a goal from Angelos Charisteas. This was Greece's first major international tournament victory. Their coach/manager was Otto Rehhagel, who as a club manager had enjoyed considerable success with Werder Bremen and Kaiserslautern.

In their opening group match against reigning champions France in 2004, England led 1-0 (Frank Lampard) only for David Beckham then to miss a penalty. France scored twice in the final two minutes through Zinédine Zidane (one was a penalty) to win 2-1.

The Charlatans could be forgiven for believing they were the most popular band in the world when they appeared at the 2004 Isle of Wight Festival. When they took to the stage the crowd erupted. Their arrival coincided with pictures of Frank Lampard's goal against France, relayed on the large screens at either side of the stage.

England bounced back to win their final group matches — 3-0 v. Switzerland and 4-2 v. Croatia — and faced hosts Portugal in the quarter-final in the Estádio Da Luz, Lisbon. Having taken the lead after three minutes through Michael Owen, England conceded a goal seven minutes from normal time. Both teams scored in extra-time, then an all too familiar story unfolded: England lost on penalties (6-5) — the second time they had exited the European Championship in such a way.

As England approached their final Euro 2008 qualifying game against Croatia, Steve McClaren's team appeared to have blown the chance of qualification, but when Israel surprisingly defeated Russia, England were given a glimpse of the promised land. A draw against Croatia (who had already ensured their qualification) at Wembley would be enough to take England into the finals. An abject performance saw Croatia take a 2-0 lead, the first goal coming when goalkeeper Scott Carson allowed a 30-yard shot from Nico Kranjcar to evade his grasp. Second-half goals from Frank Lampard (penalty) and Peter Crouch restored parity. England only had to hold out for a draw, but blew it when they allowed Mladen Petric to give his country a 3-2 victory. It cost McClaren his job, and, in all probability, a new umbrella.

For the first time since 1984, in 2008 no home country qualified for the finals. England were widely criticized for their performances in the qualifying stage, but Scotland and Northern Ireland emerged with much credit. Scotland enjoyed a double success over France and only a last-minute goal by Italy in their final match denied them qualification. Northern Ireland too enjoyed notable successes, particularly home victories against Spain, Sweden and Denmark.

History was made when the Republic of Ireland met Wales in Dublin in a 2008 qualifier: it was the first ever football match to be staged at Croke Park, the spiritual home of Gaelic football. The Republic won 1-0. Appropriately, their goal was scored by Stephen Ireland.

In September 2006, Germany created a record score for the competition when they defeated San Marino 13-0. Germany went on to become the highest-scoring team in the qualifying stage with 35 goals.

Is that the German coach or someone out of Depeche Mode?

TOMMY SMITH on Germany coach Joachim Löw

Fons Leweck's last-minute winner for Luxembourg in their qualifying match against Belarus in 2007 ended a run of 55 international matches without a victory for Luxembourg, dating back 12 years.

The Euro 2008 qualifying game between Finland and Belgium was held up for seven minutes when a large owl, known as a *huuhkaja*, perched behind the Finland goal (so, not much in the way of attacking football from Belgium, then). Though the owl was driven away it settled in another area of the stadium and stayed there for the remainder of the game. Finland won 2-0, and the *huuhkaja* has since been adopted as the mascot of the Finnish national team.

The 2012 finals will take place in Poland and Ukraine.

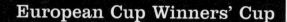

23 This European-wide club knockout competition (over two legs) for the winners of domestic cup competitions began in 1961 and lasted until 1999 when it was absorbed into a revamped and extended Champions League and UEFA Cup.

The decline of the competition was partly due to the expansion of the Champions League. Many clubs that won their domestic cup finished runners-up in their domestic league and opted for the Champions League rather than the European Cup Winners' Cup (ECWC).

Another reason for the competition's decline was the emergence in Europe in the late 1990s of independent states such as Lithuania and Estonia. Many of the bigger clubs thought that entries from such countries served to 'dilute' the overall standard of the ECWC and lessen the public appetite for the competition, and they lobbied UEFA for entry into the UEFA Cup. For example, in 1998–99, the attendance for the first round first leg tie between Vaduz (Liechtenstein) and Helsingborg was a mere 492, and when Hearts visited Lantana Tallinn in Estonia the attendance was 978. Even the semi-finals in 1999 failed to produce good attendances: the crowd for Chelsea's semi-final second leg in Mallorca was 18,848, and the other semi-final between eventual winners Lazio and Lokomotiv Moscow in Rome attracted 24,888.

The ECWC was first contested in 1960–61 by ten clubs. Wolverhampton Wanderers represented England, and Rangers flew the flag for Scotland. Atlético Madrid and Monaco, respective winners of their domestic cups, declined to enter.

The first winners were Fiorentina, who beat Rangers (4-1 on aggregate). Fiorentina qualified as losing Italian Cup finalists; the cup winners, Juventus, were also league champions and therefore qualified for the European Cup. Thus the first winners of the ECWC were not domestic cup holders at all.

The appearance of Rangers in the 1961 final was the first by a Scottish club in the final of a major European competition.

In 1962, the final was played for the first time as a one-off match at a neutral venue, but it went to a replay. Atlético Madrid were the winners against holders Fiorentina after the first match ended 1-1.

In 1962–63, Welsh Cup holders non-league Bangor City were drawn in the first round against Napoli, and won the first leg 2-0. Bangor lost 3-1 in Naples so the tie went to a play-off. Bangor's brave battle came to an end when they lost a closely contested game 2-1.

Tottenham Hotspur beat Atlético Madrid 5-1 in the 1963 final to become the first British club to win a major European competition. Spurs' unlikely hero on the night was winger Terry Dyson who created two goals and scored two, his last effort a scintillating 25-yard drive that followed a run from inside the Spurs half of the field. In the changing room after the game as the players celebrated their success, centre-forward Bobby Smith told Dyson, 'Well done, Terry – fantastic, son. If I were you, I'd 'king well retire now.'

Spurs' victory was a major landmark for British football. It proved how far British football had developed since the mid-1950s and the winning margin of four goals equalled the record margin of victory in any European final, as established by Real Madrid in the European Cup Final of 1960.

In 1963–64, Wales were represented by non-league Borough United who stunned most people by defeating Sliema Wanderers (Malta) in round one, 0-0 and 2-0. Borough were defeated in round two by Slovan Bratislava of Czechoslovakia (0-1 and 0-3).

In 1963–64, two English clubs met for the first time in European competition when Spurs (ECWC holders) were drawn against Manchester United (FA Cup winners). Spurs won the first leg 2-0 at White Hart Lane but lost 4-1 at Old Trafford in a game in which skipper Dave Mackay suffered a broken leg.

In 1965, West Ham United won the trophy defeating 1860 Munich 2-0 at Wembley. West Ham were without regular forwards Peter Brabrook and Johnny Byrne due to injury, but their goals were scored by their respective replacements, Alan Sealey and Brian Dear.

23 West Ham's success was the second step towards Bobby Moore becoming the only captain to ascend the steps to the royal box at Wembley to receive three different major trophies in three successive seasons: FA Cup in 1964, ECWC in 1965 and World Cup in 1966.

In 1967–68, Aberdeen defeated Reykjavik (Iceland) 10-0 in the first round first leg. The following season Scotland's entrants were Dunfermline Athletic, who in their first match defeated Apoel Nicosia (Cyprus) 10-1.

AC Milan won the ECWC in 1968 and the European Cup the following year.

In 1971–72, Chelsea created a record aggregate win in the competition, defeating Jeunesse Hautcharage (Luxembourg) 8-0 and 13-0 to win 21-0 on aggregate.

In 1972, Rangers won the trophy for the first time though it was the club's third appearance in the final (after 1961 and 1967). Rangers beat Moscow Dynamo 3-2 in Barcelona, but their success was marred by some Rangers fans who invaded the pitch at the end and clashed with police. The presentations could not take place as normal, so Rangers became the only winners of a major European competition to be presented with their trophy in their own dressing room. UEFA were far from impressed, and Rangers were banned from defending the title the following season – the first time this had happened, too.

No club has ever won the ECWC in successive seasons. Anderlecht (Belgium) came closest to beating what was termed 'the European Cup Winners' Cup jinx': they won the trophy in 1976, were beaten finalists in 1977, and were winners again in 1978.

The 1980 final between Arsenal and Valencia was the first major European club final to be decided on penalties. Valencia triumphed 5-4 (after a 0-0 draw).

In 1981, Dinamo Tbilisi (Georgia/USSR) beat Carl Zeiss Jena (East Germany) 2-1 to win the cup for the first time. The attendance for this match in Dusseldorf was 7,002, the lowest for any major European final.

In 1983, Aberdeen, managed by Alex Ferguson and featuring the likes of Alex McLeish and Gordon Strachan, beat Real Madrid 2-1 in the final in Gothenburg thanks to an extra-time goal by substitute John Hewitt. It was Aberdeen's first appearance in a major European final and Real's 11th. The following season, Aberdeen defeated European Cup holders Hamburg in the European Super Cup to become the first Scottish club to win two different major European trophies.

In 1985, Everton defeated Rapid Vienna 3-1 in the final in Rotterdam. Everton were the first English club to win the ECWC and the League Championship in the same season, and almost made it a treble. Three days after their success in the ECWC, they lost 1-0 (aet) to Manchester United in the FA Cup Final.

Due to the five-year European ban imposed on English clubs following the Heysel disaster, Everton were not allowed entry into Europe the following season but would not have defended the ECWC anyway: as League champions they would have entered the European Cup.

The Dynamo Kiev team that beat Atlético Madrid 3-0 in the 1986 final supplied 12 players for the USSR squad that went to the Mexico World Cup that summer.

Cardiff City appeared in the competition in a record five successive seasons.

The Ajax team that defeated Lokomotiv Leipzig (East Germany) 1-0 to win the trophy in 1987 included Dennis Bergkamp and Marco van Basten. Ajax was managed by Johan Cruyff who, following the game, predicted a great future for the two young players, only to add, 'But I do not see their future here. The way things are going in football, they will eventually be lured away by big money clubs who will go on to dominate European football . . . even control it.'

In 1989, Cruyff guided Barcelona to success in the trophy when they beat Sampdoria (Italy) 2-0. Cruyff thus became the first manager to win the ECWC with two different clubs – a feat equalled by Alex Ferguson in 1991 when he led Manchester United to a 2-1 victory over Barcelona in Rotterdam (Ferguson had, of course, previously won the trophy with Aberdeen). The final was particularly sweet for Mark Hughes, who scored both United goals, having recently joined the club from Barcelona who at the time of the transfer were on record as saying Hughes was 'now surplus to requirements'. (Although Hughes was credited with both goals, for the first he followed up an effort from Steve Bruce and generously insisted that the ball had crossed the line before he made sure.)

In the 1995 final, Real Zaragoza beat Arsenal in Paris with a bizarre goal scored 20 seconds before the end of extra-time. Real's Nayim hit a speculative lob from the halfway line which deceived Arsenal keeper David Seaman to give his side an extraordinary and, according to many, undeserved 2-1 victory.

In 1998, Chelsea won the trophy for a second time, beating VfB Stuttgart 1-0 in Stockholm with a goal from substitute Gianfranco Zola. After the game, Chelsea manager Gianluca Vialli told reporters, 'This club has a rich history, but now I think the future for this club will be richer still.'

Villa Park staged the last ever ECWC final, the 1999 match between Lazio (Italy) and Real Mallorca (Spain). Sven-Göran Eriksson's expensively assembled Lazio team beat the Spaniards 2-1.

Barcelona won the trophy the most times – four, in 1979, 1982, 1989 and 1997. They were also runners-up in 1969 and 1991.

Three finals in four years saw the holders reach the final again only to lose: Parma in 1994, Arsenal in 1995 and Paris St Germain in 1997.

BRITISH WINNERS OF THE EUROPEAN CUP WINNERS' CUP

Tottenham Hotspur (1963)	Aberdeen (1983)
West Ham United (1965)	Everton (1985)
Manchester City (1970)	Manchester United (1991)
Chelsea (1971, after a replay)	Arsenal (1994)
Rangers (1972)	Chelsea (1998)

Unique ECWC fact: Rangers won the cup in 1972 after being knocked out of the competition in round two. On 20 October 1971, Rangers beat Sporting Lisbon 3-2 at Ibrox, lost the second leg in Portugal 4-3, but won on the away goals rule. Referee Peter van Ravens, however, misinterpreted the rules of the competition. Thinking that the tie had been drawn, he ordered a penalty shoot-out, which Sporting won 2-0. Rangers subsequently protested to UEFA, an inquiry was held, and the Scottish club was reinstated. Mr van Ravens was suspended from officiating at European matches and Rangers went on to beat Moscow Dynamo 3-2 in the final.

24 The FA Cup, or, to give it its official name the Football Association Challenge Cup, is the oldest football club cup competition in the world.

The first ever FA Cup took place in 1871–72 with 12 clubs competing: Barnes, Civil Service, Crystal Palace, Clapham Rovers, Hampstead Heathens, Hitchin, Maidenhead, Marlow, Queen's Park (Glasgow), Royal Engineers, Upton Park and Wanderers. Donington Grammar School (Spalding, Lincs), Harrow and Reigate Priory had also entered the competition but withdrew before playing a game.

The first winners were Wanderers, who beat Royal Engineers 1-0 at the Oval courtesy of a goal scored by M. P. Betts. The attendance was 2,001 – the lowest recorded for any FA Cup Final. *The Times* reported, 'Overall, the Royal Engineers appeared to possess the more skilled football team and offered much evidence they would emerge victorious, however, one has discovered anything may happen in this knockout style tournament.' There can't be many things written about football nigh on 140 years ago that still apply today, but surely that is one.

The first final to go to a replay was the 1875 final between Royal Engineers and Old Etonians. Following a 1-1 draw in the initial match, which did not feature extra-time, the Engineers triumphed 2-0.

The first final to feature extra-time was the 1877 final between Wanderers and Oxford University. The game was goalless at full-time; Wanderers won 2-1 in the extra period. It was Wanderers' fourth FA Cup victory in the six-year history of the fledgling competition. Wanderers won it the following season for a fifth and, pardon the pun, final time. To mark their success in the competition the FA presented the FA Cup to Wanderers to keep for all time, but club officials refused to accept it saying it was only right and proper the cup should be competed for on an annual basis and never be the sole property of a single club.

In 1879–80, Sheffield FC went out of the competition for refusing to play extra-time. Their first round tie against Nottingham Forest ended 2-2 after 90 minutes; thereafter the oldest football club in the world declined to take the field.

Port Vale is the only club to have reached the fifth round of the FA Cup without having to play a game and to have remained unbeaten in the competition yet not win it. In 1886, Vale entered in round three and were drawn against Leek, who subsequently withdrew. Vale were given a bye in round four, and in round five they drew 1-1 at home to Brentwood. Unable to afford the cost of a trip to Essex for the replay, Vale withdrew from the cup.

Blackburn Rovers hold the record for having remained unbeaten in the competition for the longest period of time – three years. They played 24 FA Cup matches without defeat between December 1883 and December 1886.

1887 saw the only instance of an Irish club being knocked out of the FA Cup by a Scottish club when Cliftonville were beaten 11-1 by Partick Thistle.

The most goals scored in a single season of the FA Cup proper by an individual player is 20 by Jimmy Ross of Preston North End in 1887–88.

Crewe Alexandra reached the FA Cup semi-finals in 1888. In round four they drew 2-2 against Swifts (Kensington) but went through when Swifts were disqualified for having a crossbar that was two inches lower than the one in the other goal.

Bolton Wanderers are the only League club to have been beaten in the FA Cup by an Irish club. In 1888–89 (the inaugural season of the Football League), they were beaten 4-0 by Linfield Athletic in a qualifying tie in Belfast.

Preston North End hold the record for the highest score in the FA Cup. They beat Hyde United 26-0 in 1887. Despite the scoreline, it was an even game: Preston scored 13 times in each half. At one point in the proceedings they scored six goals in seven minutes (also a record for the cup).

The only man to have played in and refereed an FA Cup Final is Francis Marindin, who played for the Royal Engineers in the 1872 and 1874 finals and went on to officiate at eight finals between 1880 and 1890.

The highest score achieved by a club in an FA Cup Final is six goals. In 1890, Blackburn beat Sheffield Wednesday 6-1, and in 1903, fellow Lancastrians Bury defeated Derby County 6-0.

When Bury beat Derby County by the record FA Cup Final winning margin of six goals in 1903, their success failed to make the front page of the local newspaper.

In 1905, Crystal Palace, then of the Southern League, beat Second Division Chelsea 7-1. It remains the biggest victory by a non-league club over a League team in the history of the cup.

In 1911–12, Barnsley played a record 12 ties to win the FA Cup. They endured six replays, including both the semi-final and final.

From 1910–11, to the fourth round fourth replay against Barnsley (0-0, 0-0, 0-0, 2-3) in 1912 Bradford City played 12 FA Cup matches without conceding a goal. City won the cup in 1911 for the only time in their history.

The Bradford City team that defeated Newcastle United (1-0 after 0-0) in that 1911 final contained only two English players. The rest of the team comprised eight Scots and an Irishman.

The first monarch to attend an FA Cup Final was George V, who watched Burnley beat Liverpool 1-0 at Crystal Palace in 1914.

The lowest attendance for an FA Cup tie proper is zero. The third round second replay between Norwich City and Bradford City (0-2) in 1915 was played behind closed doors at the government's request. They feared the presence of supporters would interrupt vital war work.

There have been two occasions when three players from the same team scored hat-tricks in the same FA Cup tie. Jack Carr, George Elliott (not also known as Mary Ann Evans) and Walter Tinsley each scored three times in Middlesbrough's 9-3 first round win over Goole in 1915; Les Allen (five goals), Bobby Smith (four) and Cliff Jones also achieved this feat when Spurs beat Crewe Alexandra 13-2 in a fourth round replay in 1962. When the Crewe players left their home town to play Spurs in this tie, their train departed from the station on platform 2 and returned on platform 13.

In 1922, Billy Minter scored seven goals for St Albans City but ended up on the losing side. The score, St Albans 7 Dulwich Hamlet 8.

The construction of Wembley stadium, designated as the home of the FA Cup Final, began in January 1922 and was completed, on schedule and to budget (£750,000), in April 1923. The new stadium was then the largest sporting arena in the world.

Bolton Wanderers and West Ham United met in the very first final to be played at Wembley. Bolton triumphed 2-0, centre-forward David Jack achieving football immortality as the first player to score at the new stadium; Bolton's other goal came from John Smith. Admission by ticket was considered unnecessary as the FA believed there would be 'room for all'. The official attendance was 126,047 – to date the highest in the history of the competition. In the event it was estimated that some 200,000 spectators gained admission and the game was delayed for almost an hour as fans spilled on to the pitch. Order was eventually restored by the police, notably PC George Scorey, whose distinctive white horse was easily recognizable by the thronging crowd, and press.

The oldest player to appear in an FA Cup Final is Walter Hampson, who was 41 years and eight months old when he helped Newcastle United to a 2-0 victory over Aston Villa in 1924.

In 1926–27, Oldham Athletic's third round tie at home to Brentford was halted after 70 minutes due to fog with the home side leading 2-1. Thinking the game had been abandoned, Brentford manager Harry Curtis instructed his players to have a bath. Minutes later the fog cleared sufficiently for the referee to resume play, only for Curtis to explain to the official what had happened and that his players could not now re-take the field as it would be detrimental to their health. The tie was subsequently abandoned and rearranged for midweek. Brentford won 4-2.

2 4 The first teenager to appear in an FA Cup Final was Ernie Curtis (19) for Cardiff City against Arsenal in 1927.

The only occasion on which the FA Cup 'left' England was in 1927, following Cardiff's 1-0 victory over Arsenal. Cardiff's goal was scored by Hughie Ferguson, whose shot squirmed out of the hands of Arsenal keeper Dan Lewis, who attributed his error to the fact that he was wearing a brand new jersey, the shine on which caused the ball to slip off his chest. From 1928 up to the late 1960s it became tradition that no goalkeeper appeared in an FA Cup Final without having had his new jersey washed in the hope of avoiding Lewis's error.

There have been three different trophies in the history of the FA Cup, and there are three in existence today for official use. The original FA Cup was stolen while on display in the window of a Birmingham jeweller's in 1895 and was never recovered. The replacement cup was presented to Lord Kinnaird in 1910 as a token of appreciation of his 21 years' service as FA president. In 1911, a new cup was minted, the one we are familiar with today – only the one presented to the winning captain at Wembley is not the original 1911 trophy. The original is now kept in a bank vault as it is considered too fragile for use. A copy of it is used for presentation to the winning team; a second copy is used for promotional purposes, and for display on television during cup previews and 'live' broadcasts of ties. (A number of clubs that have won the FA Cup also have replica trophies.)

By the time Brighton were knocked out in the fifth round of the FA Cup in 1933 they'd scored a staggering 43 goals. When filling in their application for the 1932-33 competition, Brighton failed to complete the section affording League clubs exemption from the qualifying rounds. As a consequence they began their run in the qualifying rounds, beating Shoreham 12-0, Worthing 7-1, Hastings 9-0 and Barnet 4-0. In the first round proper they accounted for Crystal Palace (2-1), in round two they beat Wrexham 3-2 (after a 0-0 draw), they triumphed 2-1 against Chelsea in round three, then accounted for Bradford Park Avenue by the same scoreline in round four. Brighton were eventually beaten in a replay in round five by West Ham United (1-0 after 2-2).

Portsmouth held the FA Cup for seven years! Having won it in 1939, Pompey retained the trophy for the duration of World War Two until 1946.

Pub football? When Derby County beat Charlton Athletic 4-1 (after extra-time) to win the cup in 1946, their manager, Stuart McMillan, was only part-time. McMillan divided his time between managing County and running the Nag's Head public house in Derby.

The third round draw of January 1947 involved ten London clubs but necessitated only one having to travel outside the capital. Brentford, Charlton Athletic, Chelsea, Fulham, Millwall, QPR, Spurs and West Ham United all received home ties, and Arsenal were drawn at Chelsea; Crystal Palace were handed a trip to Newcastle.

Colchester United's record attendance is 19,072 for a game that lasted only 35 minutes. United's FA Cup first round tie against Reading in November 1948 was the attraction for the bumper crowd, but the match was abandoned due to fog.

Manchester United won the FA Cup in 1948 by playing every tie away from home even when they had originally been drawn at home. United's Old Trafford ground was still unavailable due to bomb damage suffered during the war. United's fourth round tie at home to Liverpool was played at Goodison Park.

Four players by the name of Harrison appeared in cup finals immediately after World War Two – Reg Harrison (Derby County, 1946), a different Reg Harrison (Burnley, 1947), and James and Walter Harrison (both for Leicester City in 1949) – but no Harrison has played in an FA Cup Final since.

Arsenal won the FA Cup in 1950 without ever having to leave London. They defeated Sheffield Wednesday, Swansea City, Burnley and Leeds United at Highbury, Chelsea after a replay in the semi-finals at White Hart Lane, and Liverpool (2-0) at Wembley.

That triumphant Arsenal side of 1950 holds the record for being the team with the oldest average age to have won the FA Cup, at 31 years and seven months.

The 1950–51 competition was the last in which a non-league club failed to reach the third round.

Scunthorpe United are the only Football League club to have been eliminated from the FA Cup before the first round proper. In 1950–51, they were elected to Division Three (North), but prior to this the FA had already completed plans for the preliminary rounds of the FA Cup, which involved Scunthorpe. The newly elected members of the Football League were beaten 1-0 at non-league Hereford United.

The last amateur to appear in an FA Cup Final was Bill Slater, for Blackpool against Newcastle United in 1951. Slater played inside-left but went on to enjoy an illustrious career with Wolves at centre-half, captaining the Molineux club in their FA Cup success of 1960.

Newcastle United were the first club in the 20th century to win successive finals, in 1951 and 1952. Their manager, Stan Seymour, became the first man to win FA Cup Finals both as a player and as a manager. He scored one of Newcastle's goals when they beat Aston Villa in the 1924 final.

The first time the FA Cup left Great Britain was in the summer of 1952 when Newcastle United took the trophy with them on a close-season tour of South Africa.

In 1953, each member of Blackpool's FA Cup-winning team received a match fee of £20 plus a cup final winning bonus from the club in the form of a cigarette lighter. Blackpool's Stan Mortensen became only the third, and to date last, player to score a hat-trick in an FA Cup Final; the other two players to have achieved this feat are Bill Townley (Blackburn Rovers, 1890) and Jimmy Logan (Notts County, 1894). A sign of the times, perhaps, but for all the rarity of Mortensen's feat his name did not feature in a single headline on the match reports carried by the Saturday evening, Sunday and Monday morning newspapers.

THE FOOTBALL ASSOCIATION CHALLENGE CUP COMPETITION

FINAL TIE

BLACKPOOL v BOLTON WANDERERS

SATURDAY, MAY 2nd, 1953   KICK-OFF 3 pm

EMPIRE STADIUM
WEMBLEY
Chairman and Managing Director : SIR ARTHUR J. ELVIN, M.B.E.
OFFICIAL PROGRAMME · ONE SHILLING

The highest number of goals scored in a final by a side that did not win the cup is three, by Bolton Wanderers in 1953.

Revenge is sweet. In 1954–55, non-league Boston United were thrilled to be drawn against Derby County in round two as the Boston side contained six players who had been released by Derby, including outside-right Reg Harrison, who had won a winners medal with the Rams in 1946. Boston caused the cup sensation of the season, beating their supposed superiors 6-1. Geoff Hazeldine, who little over a year earlier had been told by Derby he was surplus to requirements, netted a hat-trick.

Jimmy Delaney (Celtic, Manchester United and Crusaders) is the only player ever to have won English, Scottish and Northern Irish cup winners medals. He nearly made it a quartet, gaining an FAI losers medal with Cork City.

The longest FA Cup tie ever to have taken place was the fourth qualifying round match between Alvechurch and Oxford City in 1971-72 which produced five replays and four periods of extra-time. The six matches produced over 11 hours of football, Alvechurch eventually emerging winners by a goal to nil in the fifth replay.

The third round tie between Bury and Stoke City in 1955 stands as the longest tie in the competition proper. A total of nine hours and 22 minutes of football (over five matches) was played before Stoke triumphed 3-2. Three other ties have gone to five matches: Chelsea v. Burnley (fourth round, 1955–56; Chelsea won 2-0), Hull City v. Darlington (second round, 1960–61; Hull won 3-0), and Arsenal v. Sheffield Wednesday (third round, 1978–79; Arsenal won 2-0). The Bury–Stoke tie holds the record courtesy of the amount of extra-time played.

Arsenal have never beaten Sunderland in the FA Cup. In fact, they have only met three times in the competition. In 1893, Sunderland won 6-0 (Arsenal's heaviest defeat in the FA Cup); in 1961, Sunderland triumphed 2-0 at Roker Park; and in the 1973 semi-final at Hillsborough they won 2-1.

In 1958, Stan Crowther played for Manchester United in the competition even though he was cup-tied having previously appeared in an earlier round for Aston Villa. United were given special dispensation to play Crowther in the wake of the Munich air disaster. He remains the only player to have appeared in an FA Cup Final (v. Bolton Wanderers) having played for another club in an earlier round.

In 1958, Alex Dawson scored a hat-trick for Manchester United in their semi-final victory over Fulham (5-3, replay) – he remains the last player to have scored a hat-trick in the semi-finals of the competition.

The Bolton Wanderers team that beat Manchester United 2-0 in that 1958 final were the last side to win the cup without a single player to have cost a transfer fee. All 11 players came through the ranks, and five of them were internationals.

The last Football League club to play an FA Cup match off mainland Britain are Shrewsbury Town, who drew 0-0 with Newport (Isle of Wight) in the first round of the 1958–59 competition. Shrewsbury won the replay 5-0. Newport (IoW) did reach the first round proper of the FA Cup in both 1995 and 1996, but on both occasions they were defeated by fellow non-league opposition (Enfield and Aylesbury respectively).

The 1959 finalists Luton Town and Nottingham Forest fielded unchanged teams throughout the competition – the only instance of contesting finalists having done this.

I won an FA Cup winners medal with Wolves in 1960, but I was madly jealous of our captain Billy Wright. Not because he went up to receive the cup. In those days everyone called him Mr Wright, and I was jealous of him because every woman I met told me she was looking for him.

EDDIE CLAMP, former Wolves and Stoke wing-half

On 28 January 1961, Denis Law scored all six of Manchester City's goals in an FA Cup fourth round tie at Luton Town. With City leading 6-2 the game was abandoned due to a waterlogged pitch. Law scored again for City in the rearranged tie, but Luton won 3-1.

The longest period of time a League club has gone without winning an FA Cup tie is 11 years. In 1952, Leeds United beat Bradford Park Avenue 2-0 in round four but did not win again until 1963 when they beat Stoke City in round three.

When Preston North End were beaten by a last-minute West Ham goal in the 1964 final, the Deepdale club acquired the unenviable record of being the only club to have been beaten in three FA Cup Finals after having taken the lead in all of them. The other two instances came against Sunderland in 1937 and West Bromwich Albion in 1954.

In winning the FA Cup in 1964, West Ham created the unique record of having scored three times in every round, including the final. The Hammers' record reads: Charlton Athletic (3-0), Leyton Orient (3-0), Swindon Town (3-1), Burnley (3-0), Manchester United (3-1, semi-final), Preston North End (3-2, final).

The first time two Scots came face to face as captains in the FA Cup Final occurred in 1965, when Ron Yeats skippered Liverpool and Bobby Collins led Leeds United.

What might have been! In 1966, Vic Mobley withdrew from Sheffield Wednesday's team to play Everton in the final due to an injury which also caused him to miss his international debut for England. Mobley was destined never again to play in an FA Cup Final and was never recalled to the England squad.

Saturday, 11 March 1967 saw the first FA Cup tie to be shown on closed-circuit TV. A crowd of 64,581 was at Goodison Park to see Everton beat Liverpool 1-0 (Alan Ball) while 40,149 paid admission at Anfield to watch the game on eight large TV screens. The combined attendance of 104,730 remains the largest for a single tie other than the final.

Not remembered for being a perpetrator of rough-house play, Brian Kidd (currently assistant manager at Sheffield United) was the first player to be sent off three times in an FA Cup competition. Kidd first received his marching orders when playing for Manchester United against Spurs in 1968, and then twice in 1980 when playing for Everton: against Wigan Athletic, and later in the semi-final against West Ham United.

The first substitute to be used in an FA Cup Final was Dennis Clarke, who came on for West Bromwich Albion against Everton in 1968. That final was also the first to be broadcast in colour on television, and the first to realize six-figure match receipts (£110,000).

In 1968–69, Billy Best scored a hat-trick in three minutes for Southend United against Brentford (round two). The fastest officially recorded hat-trick in any round of the competition stands at two minutes 20 seconds, by Andy Locke for Nantwich Town against Droylesden, first qualifying round, 9 September 1995.

The 1970 final between Chelsea and Leeds United (2-2) was the first Wembley final to go to a replay. In the match programme, 18 football journalists offered their prediction of the score and only one, Graham Taylor of *Sporting Life*, opted for a draw.

Peter Osgood scored in every round of the FA Cup in 1969–70 including the final replay victory over Leeds United. When Osgood won a second FA Cup winners medal with Southampton in 1976 he failed to score in any round.

Twelve players have scored in every round of the FA Cup in a single season: Archie Hunter (Aston Villa, 1887), Sandy Brown (Spurs, 1901), Harry Hampton (Aston Villa, 1905), Harry Blackmore (Bolton Wanderers, 1929), Ellis Rimmer (Sheffield Wednesday, 1935), Frank O'Donnell (Preston North End, 1937), Stan Mortensen (Blackpool, 1948), Nat Lofthouse (Bolton Wanderers, 1953), Charlie Wayman (Preston North End, 1954), Jeff Astle (West Bromwich Albion, 1968) and Peter Osgood (Chelsea, 1970).

The highest tally of goals by an individual player in a single game in the FA Cup proper is nine by Ted McDougall for Bournemouth against Margate (11-0, 1970–71). McDougall had previously scored six in a first round replay against Oxford City.

The first substitute to score in a final was Eddie Kelly, who, having replaced Peter Storey, scored Arsenal's first goal in their 2-1 victory over Liverpool in 1971.

The first player to appear in five FA Cup Finals for the same club was Arsenal's Pat Rice. Now assistant to Arsène Wenger, Rice played for the Gunners in the finals of 1971, 1972, 1978, 1979 and 1980.

Two players have scored ten goals in a single game in the preliminary rounds of the competition: Chris Marron for South Shields against Radcliffe Borough (1974), and Paul Jackson for Stocksbridge Park Steels (Sheffield), who beat Oldham Town 17-1 in 2002. Jackson scored five in each half.

Prior to Portsmouth and Cardiff City in 2008, the last FA Cup Final not to feature a club from London, Manchester or Liverpool was the 1973 final between Leeds United and Sunderland.

The last team to win the FA Cup whose side did not include a single international were Sunderland (1-0 v. Leeds) in 1973. The only Sunderland player who had ever been to Wembley prior to the final was defender Richie Pitt, who had once attended an England Schoolboys international at the stadium.

Sunderland's winning goal against Leeds was scored by Ian Porterfield, a gifted but compulsively left-footed player. It was the only goal he ever scored with his right foot.

Vic Halom ended the 1972-73 season as an FA Cup winner with Sunderland but as the leading goalscorer with another club. Halom scored ten goals for his previous club, Luton Town, before joining Sunderland. No other Luton player managed double figures that season.

The last team to win the FA Cup with 11 Englishmen were West Ham United in 1975. United's opponents, Fulham, fielded ten English-born players, the exception being Irishman Jimmy Conway.

Three non-league clubs reached round four in 1974-75 – Leatherhead, Stafford Rangers and Wimbledon – equalling the record set in 1957 by New Brighton, Peterborough United and Rhyl.

When Martin Buchan led Manchester United to victory over Liverpool in the 1977 final, he became the first player to captain teams to success in both the English and Scottish FA Cups. Buchan skippered Aberdeen when they won the Scottish FA Cup in 1970.

Roger Osborne scored the only goal of the 1978 final between Ipswich Town and Arsenal and was so overcome by tension and exhaustion he immediately fainted and had to be substituted.

Dixie McNeill (Wrexham) is the only player to have scored in eight successive rounds of the FA Cup: 11 goals in rounds one to six in 1977–78, and the following season (1978–79) he scored four times in rounds three and four.

1977–78 saw a record number of non-league clubs reach the third round proper. The six clubs were Blyth Spartans, Enfield, Scarborough, Tilbury, Wealdstone and Wigan Athletic.

Arsenal played 11 FA Cup matches in the course of winning the trophy in 1979, one short of the record set by Barnsley in 1912.

Seven clubs have won the FA Cup when in the Second Division (the equivalent of the current Championship): Notts County (1894), Wolves (1908), Barnsley (1912), West Bromwich Albion (1931), Sunderland (1973), Southampton (1976) and West Ham United (1980). Tottenham Hotspur won the FA Cup in 1901 when members of the Southern League.

The longest ever semi-final was the match between Arsenal and Liverpool in 1980. The original tie at Hillsborough ended goalless, then the teams drew the replay 1-1 at Villa Park. The venue and the scoreline remained the same in the second replay. Arsenal eventually reached the final when a Brian Talbot goal gave them a 1-0 victory at Coventry in the third replay – the only instance of an FA Cup semi-final taking place at Highfield Road.

Alan Davies (Manchester United) made his debut in the FA Cup in the 1983 final against Brighton – the first instance of this happening.

When non-league Burton Albion met Leicester City in the FA Cup in 1985, the tie was switched to the Baseball Ground, home of Derby County. Something was definitely brewing as both Burton and Leicester boasted the same sponsor, Ind Coope, while the sponsor of the Baseball Ground was Bass, the Burton-based brewery.

Aberdeen hold the British record for the number of FA Cup ties without defeat. The Dons were unbeaten in 20 Scottish FA Cup ties between 1982 and 1985.

The 1985 final between Everton and Manchester United was the first to produce match receipts of £1 million plus (£1,100,000). It was also the first million-pound gate in British football. By way of comparison, match receipts for the 2007 final between Chelsea and Manchester United were in excess of £5 million, not including corporate hospitality, commercial sales, etc.

The Liverpool line-up for the 1986 final against Everton, the first team to win the FA Cup without an Englishman in the starting XI, comprised four Scots, three Irishmen, and one each from Wales, Denmark, Zimbabwe and Australia. The only English player in the squad was substitute Steve McMahon. Liverpool's Kenny Dalglish also became the first player-manager of a cup final team.

History was made in the 1986–87 quarter-finals when every tie was won by the away team – the only instance of this ever happening: Arsenal 1 Watford 3; Sheffield Wednesday 0 Coventry City 3; Wigan Athletic 0 Leeds United 2; Wimbledon 0 Spurs 2.

In 1987, Spurs' Ray Clemence set a new 'long distance' record for FA Cup Final appearances. He'd first played in a final 16 years earlier when keeping goal for Liverpool against Arsenal in 1971.

In 1988, Dave Beasant (Wimbledon) became the first goalkeeper to captain a team to success in an FA Cup Final, a feat subsequently matched by David Seaman (Arsenal, 2003).

In the third round replay between Watford and Newcastle United in

1988–89, Watford took the lead with their first touch of the ball. From the kick-off Newcastle worked the ball back to goalkeeper Dave Beasant who was penalized for holding the ball outside his penalty area. Watford were awarded a direct free-kick from which Neil Redfearn scored.

A crowd of only 1,833 attended the third round tie between Chester City and Bournemouth in 1991. The match was played at Moss Rose, the home of Macclesfield Town, the club with whom Chester were ground-sharing at the time. The attendance is the lowest for any third round tie involving two League clubs.

The FA Cup is indeed unpredictable. In 1991, West Bromwich Albion were drawn at home to non-league Woking in round four. The Albion had not lost in the cup to a non-league club since before World War One; Woking, on the other hand, had never beaten a League club or reached round four before. Woking created a major cup shock, winning 4-2 at the Hawthorns, with striker Tim Buzaglo scoring a hat-trick.

In 1991–92, the FA decreed that ties still level after one replay and extra-time would be decided by a penalty shoot-out, thus breaking with the tradition of multiple replays until a winner was decided through open play.

The only two players named Rush to appear in FA Cup Finals did so in the same one, in 1992, when Liverpool's Ian came up against David of Sunderland.

The Liverpool team that beat Sunderland in the 1992 final are the only team to have won the FA Cup and been presented with losers medals; conversely, Sunderland are the only team to have lost a final and collected winners medals. The mix-up occurred during the royal box presentation but was later rectified when the players swapped medals in the dressing rooms.

Paul Bracewell, a member of the Sunderland team that lost to Liverpool in 1992, was making his fourth appearance in an FA Cup Final at Wembley. He was on the losing side every time.

Peterborough United's Tony Philliskirk scored five times against Kingstonian in a first round replay in 1992, though there is no mention of this in the official records of the competition. With Peterborough leading 3-0 (final score 9-1), the Kingstonian goalkeeper was replaced when he left the field due to an injury sustained when he was hit by a coin thrown from the crowd. The FA ordered the tie to be replayed behind closed doors, Peterborough won 1-0, and Philliskirk's five-goal haul was expunged from the records.

In 1992–93, Hartlepool United produced a minor cup shock when they beat Crystal Palace 1-0 in round three. Pool manager Alan Murray was quoted as saying, 'Hopefully this result will prove a turning point for this club.' Following their success over Palace, Hartlepool did not score again for 13 matches, which spanned a period of just over two months (1,227 minutes of football without a goal).

Sheffield Wednesday fan Bob Montgomery was so disgusted with his team's performance in the 1993 final against Arsenal he sued the club under the Trades Description Act claiming they had obtained money under false pretences. He lost his case.

In reaching the fifth round in 1993–94, Kidderminster Harriers equalled the record for the furthest progress by a non-league club in the competition. Other non-league clubs to have reached round five are Colchester United (1948), Yeovil Town (1949), Blyth Spartans (1978) and Telford United (1985). Yeovil Town accomplished this feat when managed by Alec Stock, the first player-manager in professional football.

Ian Wright played in four FA Cup Finals, one each for Crystal Palace (1990) and Arsenal (1993), both of which went to replays. However, he never completed a game. He appeared twice as a substitute and, having been named in the starting line-ups, was substituted twice.

The first Frenchman to lift the FA Cup was Eric Cantona, captain of Manchester United and scorer of the only goal of the final against Liverpool in 1996.

The fastest goal scored in an FA Cup Final was Roberto Di Matteo's effort for Chelsea after only 43 seconds in 1997. Middlesbrough lost to Chelsea that day and were also relegated from the Premiership – only the fourth club to reach an FA Cup Final and be relegated in the same season. The others are Manchester City (1926), Leicester City (1969) and Brighton (1983).

The highest number of FA Cup goals scored in an individual 'modern' career is 44 by Ian Rush (39 for Liverpool, four for Chester City and one for Newcastle United). The cup's individual goalscoring record, however, remains with Harry 'Hot Shot' Cursham of Notts County – 48 goals (1880–87). Ian Rush also holds the record for the most goals scored in FA Cup Finals: five for Liverpool (two in 1986, two in 1989 and one in 1992).

 One of the things I love about the FA Cup is the democracy of the competition. You get major clubs from the big cities and small clubs from villages where they still point at aeroplanes.

EDDIE CLAMP, former Wolves and Stoke wing-half

In 1999, the FA declared there would be no more FA Cup Final replays. Should the final end in a draw after extra-time, the winners were to be decided by penalty shoot-out.

The result of the fifth round tie between Arsenal and Sheffield United in 1999 was declared void on the grounds of unsporting behaviour on the part of Arsenal. With Arsenal leading 2-1, Sheffield United's Lee Morris sustained an injury. Seeing Morris prostrate on the pitch, United goalkeeper Alan Kelly kicked the ball into touch to allow his team-mate to receive medical attention. Arsenal maintained possession from the throw-in and Marc Overmars scored. The tie was held up for some five minutes as United players and management protested. Arsenal manager Arsène Wenger refused to accept the result and offered to replay the tie. His suggestion was subsequently supported by the FA. Arsenal won the rearranged tie 2-1.

In the 1999 final between Manchester United and Newcastle United, Teddy Sheringham scored within one minute and 36 seconds of having been introduced as a substitute by Manchester United – the fastest goal ever scored by a substitute in a final.

In 1999–2000, the FA once again broke with tradition by scheduling the third round prior to Christmas rather than in the first week of January, as was customary. Attendances plummeted, and such was the criticism that the following season the FA reinstated round three to its traditional New Year slot.

When Wycombe Wanderers reached the semi-finals in 2001, they became only the eighth club from outside the top two divisions to reach this stage of the FA Cup. The other clubs to have achieved this feat are Millwall (1937), Port Vale (1954), York City (1955), Norwich City (1959), Crystal Palace (1976), Plymouth Argyle (1984) and Chesterfield (1997).

When Yeovil Town beat Blackpool 1-0 in 2000–1, it was the 20th time as a non-league club that they had beaten League opposition in the FA Cup – a record for a non-league club triumphing over Football League clubs.

 ## Matches don't come any bigger than FA Cup quarter-finals.

NEIL WARNOCK, former Sheffield United manager

In 2004, Dennis Wise became only the fourth player to have appeared in the FA Cup Final for three different clubs. Wise achieved this feat with Wimbledon (1988), Chelsea (1994, 1997 and 2000) and Millwall (2004). The other players are Harold Halse for Manchester United (1909), Aston Villa (1913) and Chelsea (1915); Ernie Taylor for Newcastle United (1951), Blackpool (1953) and Manchester United (1958); and John Barnes for Watford (1984), Liverpool (1988, 1989, 1996) and Newcastle United (1998).

In the first final to be staged at the 'new' Wembley, in 2007, Chelsea beat Manchester United 1-0. One traditional aspect of the final that disappeared with the reconstruction of Wembley was the 'gladiatorial' walk by teams, managers and match officials from the tunnel. Nowadays, teams simply step out on to the pitch from doors situated near the halfway line.

The youngest player to have appeared in the FA Cup proper is Luke Freeman, who was 15 years and 233 days old when he appeared as an 83rd-minute substitute for Gillingham in their first round defeat at Barnet on 10 November 2007. Later in the season Freeman was transferred to Arsenal.

In 2007–08, only 11 Premiership clubs reached the fourth round of the FA Cup – the lowest number since the Premiership began. A record was also set when Portsmouth became the only Premiership club to reach the semi-finals, the first time since 1908 that only one club from the top division featured at this stage of the competition, also the first time that no club from the top six of the top division had not appeared in the semi-final stage.

From 1950 until 1997, Wembley's capacity was set at 100,000. Today, the 'new' Wembley boasts a capacity of 92,000.

What has been taken to every FA Cup Final since 1878 but never been used? Answer: the losers' ribbons.

This European-wide club competition began life in 1955 as the Inter-Cities Fairs Cup. The competition was known simply as the Fairs Cup between 1960–61 and 1971–72, when it became the UEFA Cup.

The inaugural competition (1955–58) was open to cities that had staged European Trade Fairs since World War Two. As both Birmingham and London had held such trade fairs, both were invited to enter teams. London fielded a team comprising players primarily from the capital's First Division clubs, whereas Birmingham City represented their city.

In 1958, the London XI were the first English team to reach a major European final, losing 8-2 on aggregate to Barcelona. Jimmy Greaves was the first English player to score in a major European final when he opened the scoring for the London XI in the first leg (2-2). He was unavailable for the second leg of the final, which Barcelona won 6-0.

In the following competition (lasting 1958–60), Birmingham City reached the final but lost 4-1 on aggregate, also to Barcelona.

In 1960–61, UEFA decided the cup would be competed for on an annual basis. Birmingham City again reached the final, and lost a second time, 4-2 on aggregate to Roma. Thus, Birmingham City was the first British club to appear in two major European finals.

Leeds United were the first British club to win the Fairs Cup, beating Ferencvaros (Hungary) 1-0 on aggregate in 1968. Leeds had lost the previous year's final to Dinamo Zagreb (Yugoslavia) 2-0 on aggregate.

Leeds United were also the first club to win the cup without actually winning the final. In 1971, the first meeting between Leeds and Juventus (26 May, Turin) was abandoned after 51 minutes with the score at 0-0. The teams then drew 2-2 in Turin and 1-1 at Elland Road, so Leeds won the trophy on the away goals rule. Having drawn the second leg of their semi-final against Liverpool 0-0, Leeds had the further distinction of becoming the winners of a European knockout competition despite not having won any of their final three games.

The first winners of the newly termed UEFA Cup were Tottenham Hotspur, who beat Wolverhampton Wanderers 3-2 on aggregate in 1972 – the first instance of two English clubs contesting a major European final. Having won the Cup Winners' Cup in 1963, Spurs became the first British club to win two different major European club competitions.

Noel Parkinson was a 'European veteran' in the UEFA Cup without ever making his Football League debut for Ipswich Town. In 1979–80, Parkinson played for Ipswich in their matches against Skied Oslo (Norway), went out on loan to Bristol Rovers, returned to Portman Road, was a member of the Ipswich squad for the tie against Grasshoppers (Switzerland), then left the club.

Tottenham Hotspur were the first club to win the UEFA Cup on a penalty shoot-out. They beat Anderlecht (Belgium) 4-3 on spot-kicks in 1984 after the two-legged final ended 2-2 on aggregate.

When Tottenham Hotspur won the UEFA Cup in 1984, that season they finished eighth in Division One – the lowest final League placing of any English club to have won the UEFA Cup.

In 1989, the two-legged final between Napoli (Italy) and Stuttgart (Germany) was attended by a record aggregate crowd of 151,899.

The last winners of a two-legged final were Schalke 04 of Germany, who in 1997 beat Inter Milan 4-1 in a penalty shoot-out after 1-0 and 0-1.

In keeping with the finals of 1964 and 1965, the 1998 final reverted to a single match played at a neutral venue. Inter Milan beat fellow Italian club Lazio 3-0 in Paris.

The highest aggregate goal tally for a single-match final is nine – Liverpool 5 Alavés (Spain) 4 in 2001.

Who scored Liverpool's winning 'golden goal' during extra-time against Alavés? Answer: Geli. It was an own-goal.

BRITISH WINNERS OF THE FAIRS/UEFA CUP

Leeds United (1968)	Liverpool (1973)
Newcastle United (1969)	Liverpool (1976)
Arsenal (1970)	Ipswich Town (1981)
Leeds United (1971)	Tottenham Hotspur (1984)
Tottenham Hotspur (1972)	Liverpool (2001)

The number of entrants (seemingly endless!) is now based on final domestic league placings and the past performances of the country's clubs in European competition. To complicate matters, UEFA also allows entry to the competition for clubs that entered the group stage of the Champions League but finished third, and for the top 11 performing clubs in its summer InterToto Cup competition. To 2009–10, entry was also afforded to the previous winners of the trophy, the winners of the League Cup in England and France, and a Fair Play winner. In 2007–08, the number of clubs entering the UEFA Cup was 157. The first round involved 80 clubs, with another eight clubs later 'parachuting' in, following elimination from the Champions League.

The one-club-per-city rule for the UEFA Cup was dropped in 1975 following a protest from Everton. Everton finished fourth in Division One but were denied entry because Liverpool were runners-up. Everton appealed to UEFA saying the rule was an anachronism and unfair, and UEFA agreed.

Only four clubs have won the UEFA Cup in the same season they won both their domestic league championship and cup. The 'treble' winners are Gothenburg (1982), Galatasaray (2000), Porto (2003) and CSKA Moscow (2005). When Liverpool won the trophy in 2001 they completed a UEFA Cup, FA Cup and League Cup treble.

Liverpool hold the distinction of having won the UEFA Cup and the League Championship in the same season on two occasions – 1973 and 1976.

There have been two occasions when the single-match final has been played on the home ground of one of the finalists. Feyenoord defeated Borussia Dortmund (3-2) at their De Kuip Stadium in Rotterdam in 2002, and Sporting Lisbon lost to CSKA Moscow (3-1) at their José Alvalade Stadium in 2005.

Spain boast the most winners of the UEFA Cup – 11. Spanish clubs have also been runners-up on seven occasions. England and Italy are joint second as far as winners are concerned, both countries with ten winners and, coincidentally, eight runners-up.

No Scottish club has ever won the Fairs/UEFA Cup. Dundee United were the first to reach the final, in 1987; they were beaten 2-1 by Gothenburg (Sweden). Celtic reached the final in 2003 and were beaten 3-2 (aet) by Porto in Seville.

Five clubs jointly hold the record for having won the trophy on three occasions: Liverpool (1973, 1976, 2001), Juventus (1977, 1990, 1993), Barcelona (1958, 1960 and 1966), Inter Milan (1991, 1994 and 1998) and Valencia (1962, 1963 and 2004). Juventus have also been beaten finalists three times, in 1965, 1971 and 1995.

Nine finals have featured clubs from the same country: 1962, Valencia and Barcelona (Valencia 7-3 on aggregate); 1964, Real Zaragoza and Valencia (Zaragoza 2-1 on aggregate); 1972, Tottenham and Wolves (Tottenham 3-2 on aggregate); 1980, Eintracht Frankfurt and Borussia Moenchengladbach (3-3 on aggregate, Frankfurt won on away goals); 1990, Juventus and Fiorentina (Juventus 3-1 on aggregate); 1991, Inter Milan and Roma (Inter 2-1 on aggregate); 1995, Parma and Juventus (Parma 2-1 on aggregate); 1998, Inter Milan and Lazio (Inter 3-0); 2007 Espanyol and Seville (Seville 3-1 on penalties after 2-2).

In 1979–80, West Germany had five entrants (a record for the competition), four clubs that qualified and holders Borussia Moenchengladbach. All five teams reached the quarter-final stage and both semi-finals were contested by West German teams. Eintracht Frankfurt beat Borussia Moenchengladbach in the final on away goals. Not one of the five West German teams was eliminated by a non-West German team.

Five clubs have reached consecutive UEFA Cup Finals: Borussia Mönchengladbach (1979, 1980), Anderlecht (1983, 1984), Real Madrid (1985, 1986), Inter Milan (1997, 1998) and Seville (2006, 2007). Seville won the trophy in 2006 and retained it in 2007.

The only country to boast three consecutive UEFA Cup successes is Italy, and they have done so twice: 1989 to 1991 (winners Napoli, Juventus and Inter Milan) and 1993 to 1995 (winners Juventus, Inter Milan and Parma).

English clubs set a record for the Fairs/UEFA Cup by winning it in six consecutive seasons, from 1967–68 to 1972–73. The winners (in order) were Leeds United, Newcastle United, Arsenal, Leeds United, Tottenham Hotspur, Liverpool. Tottenham nearly made it seven consecutive winning seasons for English clubs: they lost the 1974 final to Feyenoord 4-2 on aggregate.

Newcastle United's success in 1969 over Ujpest Dozsa of Hungary (6-2 on aggregate) came in the club's first ever season in European competition. Whisper it quietly, it remains Newcastle's last major trophy success. For Sunderland and Middlesbrough supporters only, IT REMAINS NEWCASTLE'S LAST MAJOR TROPHY SUCCESS!

Club Brügge boast the record for the most consecutive seasons in the competition – ten, from 1996–97 through to 2005–06.

The record for consecutive seasons in the competition for a British club belongs to Celtic, who appeared in eight UEFA Cups from 1996–97 to 2003–04.

Competing in both the Champions League and UEFA Cup in the same season is common now since the 'parachuting' into the UEFA Cup of teams eliminated from the first group stage of the Champions League. The club that has appeared in the Champions League and UEFA Cup in the same season the most times is Shakhtar Donetsk (Ukraine) who have done so on six occasions (2000–01 to 2005–06).

Celtic and Rangers have appeared in both the Champions League and UEFA Cup in the same season on four and three occasions respectively – the most of any British club (Rangers 1999–2000 to 2001–02, and Celtic 2000–01 to 2003–04).

The lowest domestic league placing of any club to have won the UEFA Cup is 13th (Inter Milan in Serie A, 1993–94).

The record win in a single UEFA Cup tie is Ajax 14 Red Boys (they certainly were) Differdange (Luxembourg) 0, in 1984-85. The first leg ended in a goalless draw.

The record aggregate win in the competition is Feyenoord (Holland) 21 Rumelange (Luxembourg) 0 (9-0 and 12-0).

The Fairs/UEFA Cup has a history of great comebacks in two-legged ties. In 1958, having lost 6-3 in Leipzig, Lausanne Sports (Switzerland) won the home leg 7-3 to win the tie 10-9 on aggregate. In 1987–88, Honved beat Panathinaikos 5-2 in Hungary, but Panathinaikos won the return 5-1 in Greece to take the tie 7-6 on aggregate.

On their way to their first ever European final in 2006, Middlesbrough made something of a habit of coming back from what was seemingly a hopeless position. In the quarter-finals, Basle beat Middlesbrough 2-0 in Switzerland and took the lead in the return at the Riverside, but Middlesbrough stormed back to win 4-1 on the night and 4-3 on aggregate. In the semi-finals they were at it again. Having lost 1-0 away to Steaua Bucharest, Middlesbrough conceded a 2-0 lead to the Romanians at the Riverside only to stage another remarkable comeback and win 4-2 on the night and 4-3 on aggregate.

The 2008 UEFA Cup Final at the City of Manchester Stadium was the first European final to be staged in Manchester.

In January 2008, UEFA announced changes to the UEFA Cup for 2009 to 2012. The restructured format for the group stage will involve 48 teams split into 12 groups of four.

The first brothers to play in a World Cup match were Manuel and Filipe Rosas of Mexico (Argentina v. Mexico, 1930).

In the 1930s and 1940s, brothers Frank and Hugh O'Donnell played together for ten clubs, five of them in senior football: Celtic, Preston North End, Blackpool, Hearts and Liverpool. The only team the O'Donnells did not play for together was Scotland; Frank was the only brother to represent his country (six caps, 1937 to 1938).

The first set of twins to score in the same League match for the same team were Bill and Alf Stephens, who netted Swindon's goals in a 2-0 victory over Exeter City in 1946–47, giving a whole new meaning to the term 'twin strikers'.

The Milburns are a famous football family from Ashington in Northumberland. Jackie Milburn was a legendary centre-forward in the 1940s and 1950s with Newcastle United and England. Jackie's nephews were Bobby and Jack Charlton, World Cup winners with England in 1966. Bobby and Jack's uncles, Jim and Jack Milburn, were a full-back pairing for Leeds prior to World War Two. Jim and Jack's younger brother George also played for

Leeds, while their brother-in-law, Jim Potts, was the Leeds goalkeeper. The Milburn lineage also included Jim and Jack's other brother, Stan, who played for Chesterfield and later became a trainer with the Saltergate club.

The Allen family is another famous football dynasty. Les Allen played for Chelsea in the 1950s and was a member of Spurs' double-winning team of 1961, while his brother, Dennis, played for Charlton Athletic, Reading and Bournemouth. Les's son Clive served several clubs including Spurs and Manchester City and was also an England international; Les's other son, Bradley, played for, among others, QPR. Les's nephew, Paul Allen, played for West Ham and Spurs, and his other nephew, Martin, turned out for QPR and West Ham before entering management.

The Feeneys are the only family who can boast three generations of international caps. James Feeney (Linfield and Swansea) won caps for Northern Ireland in the late 1940s and early 1950s; his son, Warren senior (Glentoran), was capped in 1976; and Warren senior's son, Warren junior (Bournemouth), played for Northern Ireland in 2007.

The first father and son to win caps for England were George Eastham senior (Bolton Wanderers) in 1935 and George Eastham junior (Arsenal) in 1963. While his father won only one cap, George junior played 19 times for England and was a member of the victorious 1966 World Cup squad.

There have been three instances of fathers and sons winning caps for England since World War Two. Brian and Nigel Clough were capped when playing, respectively, for Middlesbrough and Nottingham Forest; Frank Lampard and Frank junior were chosen for England when, respectively, with West Ham United and Chelsea; and Ian Wright (Arsenal) and son Shaun Wright-Phillips (Chelsea).

On the final day of the 1950–51 season against Hartlepool United, Stockport County included in their team father and son David Herd (39) and David Herd junior (17). On 21 April 1990, Ian Bowyer, aged 39, and his son Gary (18) played together for Hereford United against Scunthorpe United.

Johnny Aston senior won a championship medal with Manchester United in 1952. In 1967, his son, John junior, also won a championship medal with United, and the following season a European Cup winners medal too.

In the 1950s, Barrow were keen to promote themselves as a family club. On 31 August 1953, the Barrow team against Port Vale (Third Division North) included three brothers, Jack, Alan and Bert Keen.

In 1953–54, Swansea had four sets of brothers on their books: Ivor and Len Allchurch, Cyril and George Beech, Bryn and Cliff Jones, and Colin and Alan Hole.

George Eastham senior and George Eastham junior played together for Irish club Ards throughout the 1954–55 season.

Wales fielded two sets of brothers in their international match against Northern Ireland on 20 April 1955: John and Mel Charles and Len and Ivor Allchurch. John Charles scored all three goals in Wales's 3-2 victory.

In the late 1950s, the Chelsea full-back pairing was brothers Peter and John Sillett. This is not the only instance of brothers forming a full-back pairing for a club: in the late 1930s, there were Jack and Frank Taylor at Wolves, and, of course, more recently, Phil and Gary Neville at Manchester United, who also played together for England.

St Mirren's Gerry Baker scored ten goals in his team's 15-0 victory over Glasgow University in the first round of the Scottish FA Cup in 1960. The following season, Gerry's brother Joe scored nine for Hibernian in their 15-1 victory over Peeble Rovers, also in the Scottish FA Cup.

Twin brothers David and Peter Jackson could not be parted football-wise: they played together for Wrexham, Bradford City and Tranmere Rovers between 1954 and 1962.

From 1964 to 1968, twins Ian and Roger Morgan played regularly for Queens Park Rangers, occasionally operating on opposite wings.

The Worthingtons were obviously a fit and healthy family. In 1970–71, Frank was with Huddersfield Town while brothers David and Bob played, respectively, for Grimsby Town and Notts County. That season all three brothers were ever-presents for their clubs.

In 1970–71, Leeds United drew 2-2 with Manchester United at Elland Road. One of the Leeds goals was scored by Jack Charlton, one of United's goals by brother Bobby.

In November 1970, Fulham faced Bristol Rovers at Craven Cottage in the first round of the FA Cup. The Fulham manager was Bill Dodgin and the Bristol Rovers manager his son, Bill Dodgin junior. Bristol Rovers, and Bill junior, won 2-1.

Sibling rivalry on the pitch was in evidence on 17 February 1973 in the game between Wolves and Newcastle United at Molineux. Wolves' Kenny Hibbitt had a shot cleared off the goal-line by his brother Terry, who was playing for Newcastle, and Terry had a shot headed off the Wolves goal-line by Kenny. The match ended 1-1. The Wolves goal was scored by Kenny and the Newcastle goal by Terry.

In the early 1970s, Stoke City were managed by Tony Waddington; included in the Stoke squad was his son, Steve. In the 1990s, Lou Macari was manager of Stoke City and the Stoke squad included his sons Mike and Paul. In 2007, Tony Pulis was manager of Stoke and he included in the Stoke squad his son Anthony.

The first father and son to score in a major cup final were Alfie Conn senior, who netted for Hearts in the Scottish FA Cup Final of 1956, and Alfie Conn junior, for Rangers in 1973. Both also received winners medals.

The only instance of brothers being sent off for the same team in the same match came when Tom and Tony English were dismissed while playing for Colchester United against Crewe Alexandra on 26 April 1986.

Southampton included three brothers in their team against Sheffield Wednesday at the Dell on 22 October 1988 – Danny, Ray and Rodney Wallace. Despite this historic milestone it was something of a Grommit day for the Wallace brothers: Wednesday won 2-1.

The Wallaces are not the only instance of three brothers playing together in the same team in the Football League. In the early 1920s, Bill, John and George Carr made 24 appearances together for Middlesbrough in Division One. Also in the early 1920s, David, Donald and Robert Jack played together in the same Plymouth Argyle team.

Brothers who have played in the same FA Cup Final team: Jack and Bill Smith (Portsmouth, 1934), Frank and Hugh O'Donnell (Preston, 1937), Denis and Leslie Compton (Arsenal, 1950), George and Ted Robledo (Newcastle United, 1952), Allan and Ron Harris (Chelsea, 1967), Brian and Jimmy Greenhoff (Manchester United, 1977), Gary and Phil Neville (Manchester United, 1996 – Gary came on as a substitute, replacing David Beckham – and 1999).

On 13 January 1990, Bury entertained Preston in a Division Three match. The Bury goalkeeper was Gary Kelly, the Preston goalkeeper was his brother, Alan Kelly junior. Alan Kelly senior, who also played in goal for Preston North End, flew from the USA to see his sons oppose each other.

In 1991, there were four Linighan brothers with Football League clubs. Andy was a player with Arsenal, David with Ipswich Town, while their younger twin brothers Brian and John were both with Sheffield Wednesday.

On 14 September 1996, a father and son faced each other in the FA Cup for the very first time. In the first qualifying round tie between Bishop Auckland and Pickering, Bobby Scaife (ex-Hartlepool United), aged 41, played for Bishop Auckland and the Pickering team contained his son, Nick. Bishop Auckland won 3-1.

On 24 April 1996, in the international between Iceland and Estonia in Tallinn (Iceland won 3-0), 35-year-old Arnor Gudjohnsen started the game for Iceland and was substituted in the second-half by his son Eidur (aged 17 years and six months).

In 1999, Adam and James Chambers became the first twins to play together in an England team, against Cameroon in the World Youth Championship. In September 2000, they made their West Bromwich Albion debuts together against Derby County in the League Cup.

In 2007–08, the Manchester United manager was Sir Alex Ferguson, the Peterborough United manager his son, Darren.

Blackburn Rovers left-half James Forrest (19) was the first professional to play for England. Forrest was selected to play against Scotland in 1885, despite a protest from the Scottish FA which believed all international players should be strictly amateur.

In 1892, Lincoln became the first club to add the suffix 'City' to their club name.

Top teams devoid of English players is nothing new. When Liverpool played their first ever Football League match against Middlesbrough on 2 September 1893, the side featured ten Scots, and the only Englishman sounded like a Scot – Bill McOwen.

The first footballer to own a car was Bob Crompton (Blackburn Rovers and England), who in 1908 bought one from a local dealer and subsequently drove to daily training and home matches.

The first international played in South America took place on 16 May 1901 – Uruguay 2 Argentina 3. It was the first official international match to take place outside Great Britain.

The first members of the royal family to attend a Scottish League match were the Duke (later King George VI) and Duchess (later Queen Elizabeth the Queen Mother) of York, who in 1923 accepted an invitation from the Earl of Strathmore to attend the game between Forfar Athletic and Albion Rovers. The Duke must have enjoyed the game: weeks later he was at Hampden Park for a Scottish Cup tie between Queen's Park and Bathgate.

West Bromwich Albion was the first club to win the FA Cup and promotion in the same season (1930-31). The Baggies beat Birmingham City 2-1 at Wembley and finished runners-up in Division Two.

Scotland's first defeat against foreign opposition (home nations apart) occurred in May 1931 when they were beaten 5-0 by Austria in Vienna. They lost their first home match against a foreign team on 13 December 1950 – to Austria.

Wigan Borough was the first club to resign from the Football League during a season. After only six matches of the 1931–32 campaign, they resigned due to 'extreme financial difficulties', and their record was expunged.

Millwall became the first Division Three side to reach the FA Cup semi-finals in 1936-37, losing to Sunderland, the eventual winners. Millwall had reached the semi-finals on two previous occasions, in 1900 and 1903, when a Southern League club.

The first and to date only Second Division club to win the Scottish FA Cup is East Fife, who beat Kilmarnock 4-2 in a replay in 1938 after the original tie had been drawn 1-1.

The first player to represent England while not attached to an English League club was Charlie Rutter (Cardiff City), who in March 1952 played for England 'B' against Holland 'B' in Amsterdam.

The first official match to take place under floodlights since an experimental game back in 1878 took place at Highbury on 19 September 1951 when Arsenal beat Hapoel Tel Aviv of Israel 6-1 in a friendly match. The attendance for the game was 44,357.

The first floodlit match between League clubs in a senior competition took place on 28 November 1955 when Carlisle United and Darlington met in an FA Cup second round replay at St James' Park (Newcastle).

The first League match to take place under floodlights was Portsmouth v. Newcastle United at Fratton Park on 22 February 1956.

Though floodlights were installed there in 1957, England's first international to be played at Wembley entirely under lights took place on 20 November 1963. England beat Northern Ireland 8-3.

The first club to field a team in a League match that did not include a single English player were Accrington Stanley, who in 1955–56 fielded 11 Scots in their opening match against Gateshead United (Third Division North).

In their first season following election to the Football League in 1960-61, Peterborough United were champions of Division Four. The Posh scored a record 134 times, centre-forward Terry Bly amassing a post-war record 52 League goals.

Bill Horton's first three appearances for Aldershot came in three different competitions: the FA Cup in 1961–62, and the League Cup and Football League in 1962–63.

The first Sunday matches in English football took place on 6 January 1974 when four FA Cup ties were staged. Cambridge United and Oldham Athletic were first up, kicking off at 11 a.m.

On 31 May 1977, Wales beat England 1-0 to record their first ever victory at Wembley.

Contrary to common opinion, Viv Anderson (Nottingham Forest) was not the first non-white player to represent England at full international level. Stoke City's Hong Yi Soo (commonly referred to as Frankie Soo), of Chinese descent, played eight matches for England in the 1940s.

The first manager to lead a team up the Wembley steps to the royal box to receive a trophy was Liverpool's Bob Paisley following his team's 2-1 victory over Manchester United in the 1983 Milk (League) Cup Final. It was Paisley's 12th and last visit to Wembley in charge of a Liverpool side and the gesture was afforded him as a token of gratitude and respect by his players.

In 1982–83, following their 1-0 defeat of Rangers (after extra-time), Aberdeen, managed by Alex Ferguson, became the first club in the 20th century other than Celtic or Rangers to win the Scottish FA Cup in successive seasons. The following season Aberdeen defeated Celtic 2-1 (again after extra-time) to become only the fourth club to win the Scottish FA Cup three times in a row (after Queen's Park, Vale of Leven and Rangers).

The first high-profile Catholic player to sign for Rangers was Mo Johnston, brought in by manager Graeme Souness in a £1.2 million deal from Nantes on 10 July 1989.

Wood you believe it, a lumbering striker. On 12 September 1990, the Faeroe Islands played their first competitive international match, a qualifying game for the European Championship against Austria. The match was a home game for the Faeroes but UEFA decreed the game should take place in Landskrona in Sweden as all 12 pitches in the Faeroes were made of synthetic material. Only 1,544 spectators were present, but they saw history made: the Faeroe Islands beat Austria 1-0 with a goal from striker Torkil Nielsen, a sales assistant in a timber and lumber shop.

The first manager to receive the award of Manager of the Year, following promotion the previous season, was George Burley, Ipswich Town, 2000–01. A season in which Gérard Houllier guided Liverpool to three major trophies.

Scotland's first foreign national team manager was Berti Vogts (Germany), appointed on 13 February 2002. Later, commenting on when George Bush controversially won the state of Florida to beat Al Gore in the race for the presidency, on the day after Scotland had lost a crucial World Cup qualifying match, a Democrat appearing on a Scottish TV chat programme said, 'We lost because of some stupid votes.' To which fellow guest Scottish comic Frankie Boyle replied, 'So did we.'

First is first and second is nowhere.

BILL SHANKLY

The first country to win successive World Cups was Brazil – 1958 and 1962.

The first time England played an international match indoors was during the 2002 World Cup, in the Sapporo Dome on 7 June. England beat Argentina 1-0, courtesy of a penalty from David Beckham.

The first all-seated England match at Wembley took place on 28 March 1990. England beat Brazil 1-0.

The first team to have played in the Premiership, all four divisions of the Football League and, in the days of regionalization, both the Third Division South and North were Coventry City.

The first club to win successive promotions from the Third Division to First Division were Charlton Athletic, between 1934 and 1936.

The first club of the modern era to win the League Championship (Premiership) by remaining unbeaten throughout the season were Arsenal in 2003–04.

Scotland was the first to launch a League Cup, in 1945–46.

The first time every match of a weekend programme in the Scottish Premier League ended in a draw was 22 January 1994.

The first time goal nets – and penalties – were introduced to British football was in 1891.

The first football pools coupons were printed in 1923.

The first international match at Wembley was in 1924 – England 1 Scotland 1.

Stanley Matthews was the first footballer to be awarded the CBE (1957) and the first to be knighted (in 1965, when still playing for Stoke City). Stan was also the first European Footballer of the Year (1956) and the first (and only) player to play in top-flight English football at the age of 50 (Stoke City v. Fulham, First Division, February 1965). He also claimed to be the first octogenarian to buy a Robbie Williams CD!

Middlesbrough were formed in 1875 and won their first major trophy, the League Cup, in 2004.

The first winners of the Premiership, in 1992–93, were Manchester United.

The first (and only) club other than Arsenal or Manchester United to win the Premiership in the first 12 years of its existence were Blackburn Rovers (1994–95).

The first club to be automatically relegated from the Football League to the Conference were Lincoln City in 1986–87.

The first player to be transferred for a five-figure fee (£10,890) was David Jack, from Bolton Wanderers to Arsenal in 1928.

The first six-figure transfer fee paid by a British club was shelled out by Manchester United to Torino for Denis Law in 1962 (£115,000). Coincidentally, the first six-figure transfer fee received by an English club was when Torino paid £100,000 to Manchester City for Law in 1961.

Should one include VAT, the first million-pound transfer fee was paid by Nottingham Forest to Birmingham City for Trevor Francis in 1979. The total amount paid was £1,180,850.

The first £20 million transfer involving an English club occurred in 1999 when Arsenal sold Nicolas Anelka to Real Madrid for £23.5 million.

The first Football League ground to install undersoil heating was Goodison Park (Everton) in 1958, at a cost of £7,000.

 The first time Manchester United fans saw George Best they were singing 'One George Best, there's only one George Best'. Six years later they were singing, 'One, George Best, have only one, George Best!'

WILF McGUINNESS

28

The Football League was formed on 22 March 1888 and began on 8 September the same year. It is the oldest football league in the world.

The Football League was founded when W. G. Grace captained the England cricket team for the first time, Vincent Van Gogh was still painting, Oscar Wilde was making a name as a writer, Wyatt Earp was still shooting from the hip, and Florence Nightingale was still dispensing nursing care to soldiers.

The first meeting on 22 March 1888 took place at Anderton's Hotel in London's Fleet Street. A second meeting took place at the Royal Hotel, Manchester, on 17 April, when the composition of the League was agreed upon with 12 clubs being accepted: Accrington Stanley, Aston Villa, Blackburn Rovers, Bolton Wanderers, Burnley, Derby County, Everton, Notts County, Preston North End, Stoke, West Bromwich Albion and Wolverhampton Wanderers. No club from the south of England was invited to join as at the time there was no professional football south of Birmingham.

The oldest League club is Notts County, formed in 1862. Stoke were formed in 1863 (later to become defunct and to re-form as Stoke City). Nottingham

Forest were formed in 1865 but did not become members of the Football League until 1892.

The first Football League results on 8 September 1888 were Bolton 3 Derby 6, Everton 2 Accrington 1, Preston 5 Burnley 2, Stoke 0 West Bromwich Albion 2, Wolverhampton Wanderers 1 Aston Villa 1. Blackburn Rovers' first match took place on 15 September (5-5 v. Accrington Stanley), as did Notts County's (1-2 v. Everton).

The first player to score in the Football League was Jack Gordon, for Preston North End against Burnley.

The first southern club to join the Football League was Woolwich Arsenal in 1893.

The Scottish Football League was formed in 1890, with 11 founder members: Abercorn, Celtic, Cowlair, Cambuslang, Dumbarton, Hearts, Rangers, Renton, St Mirren, Third Lanark and Vale of Leven. Renton were expelled after only five matches when it was discovered they had made payments to their players, the Scottish League at the time being strictly amateur.

The Scottish Football League accepted professionalism in 1893, the year a ten-club Second Division was introduced.

Professionalism was accepted in England in 1885. The first players to be paid (officially!) were those of Blackburn Rovers.

The first team to score 100 goals in a Football League season were Sunderland in 1893.

On only one occasion have teams finished in a joint position in the Football League. In 1907–08, Blackburn Rovers and Arsenal (Woolwich) were declared 'joint 14th' after finishing with identical records: won 12, drawn 12, lost 14, goals for 51, conceded 63, points 36.

On 12 March 1892, Aston Villa beat Accrington 12-2 at Wellington Road (Perry Barr, prior to the club moving to Villa Park) – a record goal tally by a club in a single First Division match.

In the late nineteenth/early twentieth century it was popular for supporters to apply nicknames to players, such as 'Nudger' Needham (Sheffield United and England), 'Fatty' Foulke (Sheffield United and Chelsea), 'Whackit' Wilson (Sunderland) and, arguably most stupefying of all, 'Eggcup' Emberton (Notts County).

After Peterborough United's 134 (Division Four, 1960–61), the highest number of goals scored by a team in a single Football League season is 128, by Bradford City (Division Three North, 1928–29) and Aston Villa (First Division, 1930–31). Following promotion, Peterborough scored 107 goals in their first season in Division Three, missing out on promotion by a single point.

On 23 March 1895, Lincoln City arrived late at Hyde Road for their Second Division match against Manchester City which resulted in the match kicking off at 11 minutes past three. Final score: Manchester City 11 Lincoln City 3 – a record aggregate score for a Football League Division Two match. You can imagine a Lincoln player thinking, 'If only we'd arrived eight minutes earlier, we would have got a draw.'

The highest aggregate score in a single match in the First Division since 1900 is Tottenham Hotspur 10 Everton 4 (11 October 1958).

The record number of goals conceded by a team in a single season is 141 by Darwen (34 matches, Division Two, 1898–99).

Striking a blow for Blew. Horace Blew made only one appearance for Manchester United in 1905–06, in the Good Friday game at Chelsea. United drew the match, the point gained helping to seal promotion to Division One. Blew's performance against Chelsea was such that United applied to the Football League for an additional Second Division runners-up medal to be struck for him, and he was subsequently awarded it for playing only one first-team game in the season.

At the outbreak of World War One (1914) there were 13,000 registered football clubs in England involving over half a million players, the vast majority local amateur players.

In 1914–15, for the first and only time, the clubs occupying the first five places in the First Division on the final day were all from the same county (Lancashire): Everton (champions), Oldham Athletic, Blackburn Rovers, Burnley and Manchester City.

When Chesterfield played Accrington Stanley in 1930, all three of Chesterfield's half-backs (Horace Wass, Harold Wightman and Dick Duckworth) scored – the first time this had ever happened in the history of the Football League.

In 1930–31, Blackpool conceded 125 goals in Division One but won 11 and drew ten of their 42 matches to avoid relegation.

In the 1930s, Arsenal manager Herbert Chapman, much to the delight of the Football League, persuaded London Underground to change the name of Gillespie Road station to Highbury. It proved to be some undertaking as all tickets and machines on the system had to be altered, in addition to station signage and maps.

On 2 January 1932, 209 goals were scored in the Football League's four divisions – an all-time record: Division One – 56, Division Two – 53, Division Three (South) – 57, Division Three (North) – 43.

In 1935–36 the Football League attempted to sabotage football pools coupons (the League received no revenue from pools companies). In February, on the pretence of having changed them, the League withheld the fixture list until the Friday prior to the matches on Saturday. The scheme proved a dismal failure and lasted for only three weeks.

In January 1939, during a Second Division fixture between West Ham United and Tottenham Hotspur at Upton Park, a Spurs shot was rolling towards West Ham's open goal when a supporter, wearing an overcoat and cap, ran on to the pitch and cleared the ball by kicking it upfield. The miscreant supporter then disappeared back into the terraces to shouts of 'Sign him up!'

The 1939-40 season was abandoned after three matches due to the outbreak of World War Two, and 'official' League football was suspended until the war ended. The first League tables of 1939–40 showed Blackpool at the top of Division One, where the Seasiders stayed for six long years.

When the Football League resumed in 1946–47, the first champions of Division One were Liverpool, who included in their team Bob Paisley.

In 1946–47, Doncaster Rovers set a new League record by winning 18 of their 21 away matches in Division Three (North).

Average match receipts for Arsenal home matches in 1948–49 were £7,500, and the club made a profit of £59,125 – at the time a record for a Football League club. In 2007, average match receipts for a home game at the Emirates Stadium were an estimated £2.1 million, not inclusive of catering, commercial sales, etc.

In 1952–53, the Port Vale right-half was the Reverend Norman Hallam, thought to be the only minister playing professional football. Bet he gave his forwards a good service.

On 12 September 1953, playing for Sunderland against Arsenal at Roker Park, Len Shackleton rounded the Arsenal keeper, took the ball to the goal-line, turned to face upfield and back-heeled the ball into the net.

In 1956–57, Charlton Athletic were relegated from Division One having conceded 120 goals (the last club to concede 120 goals in top-flight English football). The following season in Division Two, Charlton scored 107.

Brian Clough (Middlesbrough) was the leading goalscorer in the Second Division for three consecutive seasons: 1957–58 (40 goals), 1958–59 (42) and 1959–60 (39).

In 1963–64, Carlisle United were runners-up in Division Four, scoring 113 goals. Champions Gillingham only managed 59.

In 1964–65, Chester finished mid-table in Division Three despite scoring 40 more goals (118) than promoted Millwall (78).

The record number of goals conceded by a post-war team is 123 (Accrington Stanley, 46 matches, Division Three, 1959–60).

The last team to concede 100-plus goals in the Football League was Stockport County (102 goals, Division One, 2001–02).

On 23 September 1958, eight of the 12 matches played in Division Three resulted in away wins – the record number of away victories for a single division of the Football League on a single day.

In July 1959, the Football League finally established copyright on their fixture lists. As a result, pools companies such as Littlewoods, Vernons and Zetters collectively agreed to pay the League a minimum of £240,000 per annum for ten years in return for reproducing fixtures on their coupons.

In 1971–72, Mansfield Town created a Football League record by not scoring at home until their game against Plymouth Argyle on 18 December – a total of 883 minutes at Field Mill without a goal from the start of the season. John Fairbrother broke the barren spell, but Mansfield were beaten 3-2 by Plymouth. As the joke went: 'A Mansfield fan bought a "Golden Goal" ticket at the last home match. When he opened it to see the time of the first goal scored by Mansfield, it said "February".'

In 1975–76, the Football League decided to abolish goal average for determining League positions for clubs finishing on the same number of points, and replaced it with the simpler system of goal difference.

In 1978–79, the Football League adopted the FIFA dictum on the offside rule whereby a player could be adjudged to be played onside if the ball was deflected off an opponent.

In an effort to encourage more attacking football, in 1981–82, the Football League decided to award three points for a win instead of the traditional two.

In 1983–84, the Football League agreed to allow two substitutes to be named and, if necessary, to participate in matches, in accordance with international and European matches.

In 1983–84, Cambridge United endured the longest sequence without a win in the history of the Football League – 31 matches. The dire run began on 8 October and ended on 23 April, when Cambridge managed to beat a Newcastle United team that included Kevin Keegan, Peter Beardsley, Chris Waddle and Terry McDermott 1-0 at the Abbey Stadium.

In 1984–85, Stoke City set a record for the fewest points by a team in Division One: 17 from 42 matches.

Guy Whittingham was the last player to score in excess of 40 goals in a single season of the First Division since the restructuring of the Football League in 1992–93. Whittingham scored 42 goals in 46 matches for Portsmouth, including four hat-tricks (away at Bristol City and Luton Town and at home to Bristol Rovers and Peterborough United). Of Whittingham's 42-goal haul only one came from the penalty spot (against Tranmere Rovers). He signed for Portsmouth from non-league Yeovil Town and the Army. Following his retirement as a player, he became a coach for the PFA, working with prospective coaches.

In 1998–99, in what was then referred to as Division One (now the Championship), Sunderland set a new record points total of 105.

Since 1992 and the formation of the Premiership, the Football League has been the second tier of English senior football.

The Football League headquarters moved from Lytham St Annes to Preston in 1998. The Football League remains a registered company and has 100 shares valued at 5p each. Each member club is issued with one share; thus there are 72 shares issued to member clubs.

Brian Clough once famously said, 'It only takes a second to score a goal,' but it takes nine seconds to score two. On 23 September 2000, Wycombe Wanderers scored twice within nine seconds in their 2-0 defeat of Peterborough United (Division Two). Jamie Bates scored with the last kick of the first-half, and eight seconds into the second-half Jermaine McSporran made it 2-0.

In 2001–02, First Division champions Manchester City scored 108 goals. Nigh on half of City's goals were scored by two players, Shaun Goater (28) and Darren Huckerby (20). Goater also scored four goals in cup matches, and Huckerby six.

On 16 March 2002, the game between Sheffield United and West Bromwich Albion at Bramall Lane was abandoned after 82 minutes by referee Eddie Wolstenholme when United were reduced to six players after three had been red-carded and two had left the field injured after all substitutes had been used. West Brom were leading 3-0 at the time and the result was allowed to stand.

On 17 January 2004, prior to their match at Ipswich Town, Crewe Alexandra manager Dario Gradi informed BBC Radio Stoke that he had ordered his players to 'go out and score more goals'. The Alex players did just that, scoring four at Portman Road. Unfortunately, Ipswich scored six.

In 2007–08, the Bury team contained a Parrish and a Bishop, Mansfield Town had a Brown and a White, and arguably the most workmanlike side was Grimsby Town whose team included a Bore, a Whittle, a Painter, a Wheeler and a Hunt.

Footballer of the Year

The decision to form a Football Writers Association was made on board a boat on 27 September 1947 by a group of journalists returning from England's game against Belgium. One of the founder members was former Sunderland and Arsenal player Charles Buchan, who also founded *Charles Buchan's Football Monthly* magazine.

The entrance fee and subscription for the original members of the Football Writers Association was five guineas (£5.25p) with a subsequent annual subscription of two guineas (£2.10p).

There were 42 original members of the Football Writers Association.

The Footballer of the Year award is presented annually by the Football Writers Association. The first recipient was Stanley Matthews in 1948; the runner-up was his Blackpool team-mate, Stan Mortensen. The pair were presented with their awards during a dinner held at the Hungaria Hotel in London, the night before both appeared for Blackpool in the 1948 FA Cup Final against Manchester United.

Following the death of Sir Stanley Matthews in 2000, one of his Footballer of the Year awards was found in a skip behind a public house in Stoke. Several years earlier Stan had loaned the trophy to the pub which had since changed hands. The new owners, not knowing the significance or value of the trophy, threw it out. Fortunately it was recognized and recovered by a 'skip hunter' and returned to Sir Stan's daughter Jean and her husband Bob.

The award takes the form of a bronze statuette which originally cost £20.

Tom Finney (Preston North End) was the first player to be voted Footballer of the Year twice (1954 and 1957). The other double winners are Stanley Matthews (1948 and 1963), Danny Blanchflower (1958 and 1961), Kenny Dalglish (1979 and 1983), Gary Lineker (1986 and 1992), John Barnes (1988 and 1990) and Christiano Ronaldo (2007 and 2008). In 1969, Dave Mackay (Derby County) and Tony Book (Manchester City) shared the award – the only time this has ever happened.

The first overseas player (excluding Ireland) to be voted Footballer of the Year was Bert Trautmann, Manchester City's German goalkeeper, in 1956. Five overseas players in a row won the award between 1995 and 1999.

In 1964, Charley Hurley of Second Division Sunderland was runner-up to Bobby Moore by a single vote.

In 1980, Terry McDermott did not receive his award as he was unable to attend the annual dinner and presentation. The award was accepted on his behalf by Liverpool manager Bob Paisley.

The last goalkeeper to be voted Footballer of the Year was Neville Southall in 1985.

No player from a north-east club has ever won the award.

Liverpool players have won the award on ten occasions, Tottenham Hotspur players on eight occasions, and Manchester United players eight times.

The last Liverpool player to win the award was John Barnes in 1990.

Only one English player won the award between 1995 and 2004 – Teddy Sheringham, in 2001.

Notable players who were never voted Footballer of the Year: Jimmy Greaves, Denis Law, Alan Ball, Alan Hansen, Geoff Hurst, Peter Shilton, Ray Clemence, Glenn Hoddle, Bryan Robson, Ryan Giggs and David Beckham.

In the first 23 years of the Footballer of the Year, London-based players won the award on four occasions. In seven years up to and including 2008, London-based players have won the award on five occasions.

FOOTBALLERS OF THE YEAR

1948   Stanley Matthews (Blackpool)
1949   Johnny Carey (Manchester United)
1950   Joe Mercer (Arsenal)
1951   Harry Johnston (Blackpool)
1952   Billy Wright (Wolves)
1953   Nat Lofthouse (Bolton Wanderers)
1954   Tom Finney (Preston North End)
1955   Don Revie (Manchester City)
1956   Bert Trautmann (Manchester City)
1957   Tom Finney (Preston North End)
1958   Danny Blanchflower (Tottenham Hotspur)
1959   Syd Owen (Luton Town)
1960   Bill Slater (Wolves)
1961   Danny Blanchflower (Tottenham Hotspur)
1962   Jimmy Adamson (Burnley)
1963   Stanley Matthews (Stoke City)
1964   Bobby Moore (West Ham United)
1965   Bobby Collins (Leeds United)
1966   Bobby Charlton (Manchester United)
1967   Jack Charlton (Leeds United)
1968   George Best (Manchester United)
1969   Tony Book (Manchester City) and
          Dave Mackay (Derby County)
1970   Billy Bremner (Leeds United)
1971   Frank McLintock (Arsenal)

1972	Gordon Banks (Stoke City)
1973	Pat Jennings (Tottenham Hotspur)
1974	Ian Callaghan (Liverpool)
1975	Alan Mullery (Fulham)
1976	Kevin Keegan (Liverpool)
1977	Emlyn Hughes (Liverpool)
1978	Kenny Burns (Nottingham Forest)
1979	Kenny Dalglish (Liverpool)
1980	Terry McDermott (Liverpool)
1981	Frans Thijssen (Ipswich Town)
1982	Steve Perryman (Tottenham Hotspur)
1983	Kenny Dalglish (Liverpool)
1984	Ian Rush (Liverpool)
1985	Neville Southall (Everton)
1986	Gary Lineker (Everton)
1987	Clive Allen (Tottenham Hotspur)
1988	John Barnes (Liverpool)
1989	Steve Nicol (Liverpool)
1990	John Barnes (Liverpool)
1991	Gordon Strachan (Leeds United)
1992	Gary Lineker (Tottenham Hotspur)
1993	Chris Waddle (Sheffield Wednesday)
1994	Alan Shearer (Blackburn Rovers)
1995	Jürgen Klinsmann (Tottenham Hotspur)
1996	Eric Cantona (Manchester United)
1997	Gianfranco Zola (Chelsea)
1998	Dennis Bergkamp (Arsenal)
1999	David Ginola (Tottenham Hotspur)
2000	Roy Keane (Manchester United)
2001	Teddy Sheringham (Manchester United)
2002	Robert Pires (Arsenal)
2003	Thierry Henry (Arsenal)
2004	Thierry Henry (Arsenal)
2005	Frank Lampard (Chelsea)
2006	Thierry Henry (Arsenal)
2007	Cristiano Ronaldo (Manchester United)
2008	Cristiano Ronaldo (Manchester United)

FOOTBALLER OF THE YEAR

1965
Bobby Collins

The Players' Player of the Year Award

An award given to the top player in English senior football as voted for by his fellow players in the Professional Footballers Association.

First awarded to Norman Hunter (Leeds United) in 1974.

The first goalkeeper to be voted Players' Player of the Year was Pat Jennings (Tottenham Hotspur) in 1976.

The first Scot to win the award was Andy Gray (Aston Villa) in 1977. The first Welshman, Ian Rush (Liverpool) in 1984.

The first non-British recipient of the award was Liam Brady (Arsenal and Republic of Ireland) in 1979.

In 1981, for the very first time, three players from the same club took first, second and third places: John Wark, Frans Thijssen and Paul Mariner, all Ipswich Town.

The first player to win the award twice was Mark Hughes (Manchester United) in 1989 and 1991.

The first overseas player to be voted the PFA's Player of the Year was Eric Cantona (Manchester United and France) in 1994.

In 2004, Thierry Henry (Arsenal) became the first player to win the award in two successive seasons. He was also voted Footballer of the Year in 2004.

In 2007, Cristiano Ronaldo (Manchester United) became the first player to win four major awards for an individual player in the same year: Footballer of the Year, PFA Players' Player of the Year, Young Player of the Year and Fans' Player of the Year.

Scottish Football Writers Association Footballer of the Year Award

The first recipient of the SFW Footballer of the Year award was Billy McNeill (Celtic) in 1965.

The first goalkeeper to win the award was Ronnie Simpson (Celtic) in 1967.

In 1968, the award was won for the first and only time by a player from Raith Rovers – Gordon Wallace.

In 1974, the award was presented to Scotland's World Cup squad – the only occasion when a team has won the award.

In 1976, John Greig (Rangers) became the first player to win the award twice (also in 1966).

In 1978, Derek Johnstone (Rangers) became the first player to be voted SFW Footballer of the Year and the Scottish Professional Footballers Association Player of the Year in the same year.

In 1979, Andy Ritchie became the first, and to date only, Morton player to be voted SFA Footballer of the Year.

In 1986, Sandy Jardine became the first player to win the award with two different clubs (Rangers and Hearts).

The first English player to win the award was Mark Hateley (Rangers) in 1994.

In 1995, Brian Laudrup (Rangers and Denmark) became the first overseas player to win the award.

The first non-European to win the award was Celtic's Shunsuke Nakamura (Japan) in 2007.

European Footballer of the Year Award
An award presented annually to the best player in European football as voted for by football journalists.

The accolade was first awarded in 1956 by the magazine *France Football* and was originally named 'Ballon d'Or'.

Until 1994, only players from European national teams were eligible; since 1995, any player, regardless of nationality, has been eligible as long as he plays his club football with a European team.

Originally, votes were cast by readers of *France Football*; now they are cast by football journalists, one from each member country of UEFA. Each journalist chooses his top five players and points are awarded on a sliding scale (five points for player number one, four for player number two, and so on).

The first winner of the award was Stanley Matthews (Blackpool).

Alfredo Di Stefano (Real Madrid, who was born in Argentina but had acquired Spanish citizenship) was the first player to win the award twice, in 1957 and 1959.

The first Scot to win the award was Denis Law (Manchester United) in 1964. Law was the first of three Manchester United players to be voted European Footballer of the Year within a five-year spell, the others being Bobby Charlton (1966) and George Best (the first Irishman to win the accolade) in 1968.

The first player to win the award in successive years was Johan Cruyff (Barcelona), in 1973 and 1974. Cruyff had also won the award when at Ajax in 1971.

Kevin Keegan was the first British player to win the award in successive years, 1978 and 1979. He was playing for Hamburg at the time.

Michel Platini (Juventus) was the first player to win the award in three successive years, 1983 to 1985.

The last British player to be voted European Footballer of the Year was Michael Owen (Liverpool) in 2001 – the first time the award had gone to a British player since 1979 (Kevin Keegan) and the first to a British player with an English club since George Best in 1968.

FIFA World Player of the Year

This annual award is presented to the top player in world football as voted for by national team coaches.

First awarded in 1991 for men, and in 2001 for women.

Since its inception, Brazilian players have dominated the FIFA World Player of the Year with eight winners in the first 17 years of the award.

No British player has ever been voted FIFA World Player of the Year.

Lothar Matthäus (Inter Milan and Germany) was the first winner of the award in 1991. Gary Lineker (Tottenham Hostpur) finished third.

In 1999, David Beckham (Manchester United) was runner-up to Rivaldo (Barcelona and Brazil).

The youngest recipient is Ronaldo (Barcelona and Inter Milan and Brazil), who was 20 when he received the award in 1996. In 2002, he became the first player to win the award on three occasions.

Zinédine Zidane has also won the award on three occasions.

The oldest player to be voted FIFA World Player of the Year is Fabio Cannavaro in 2006, aged 33.

In 2007, Manchester United's Cristiano Ronaldo was voted third-best player in the world. The runner-up was Lionel Messi (Barcelona and Argentina) and the winner was Kaká (AC Milan and Brazil).

No player should accept an award given by a tabloid newspaper, or have done anything that deserves one.

TOMMY DOCHERTY

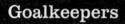

He had to be made of hardy stuff . . . In 1906, Chesterfield goalkeeper Sam Hardy conceded six goals against Liverpool. Liverpool obviously saw something in the keeper as they subsequently signed Hardy, and he went on to win a League Championship medal with the Anfield club and to play for England.

No need to ask 'Who ate all the pies?' The largest goalkeeper to have played in the Football League is Billy 'Fatty' Foulke (Sheffield United and Chelsea), who at one point during his career weighed in at 20 stone.

The tallest goalkeeper to have played in the Football League is Albert Ironmonger (Notts County and Lincoln City, 1905 to 1927), who stood six feet seven inches tall.

He had to wait for his chance in the first team. In 1935–36, Walsall's first-team goalkeeper was Harry Wait and the reserve keeper his son, Harold G. Wait.

Heard the one about the Englishman, Irishman, Scotsman and Welshman? They all played for Wrexham in 1952–53 and they were all goalkeepers: Bob Connor (Englishman), Bill Hayes (Irishman), Archie Ferguson (Scotsman) and Earl Godding (Welshman).

Who is the only goalkeeper to have kept a clean sheet when his team lost 7-0? The answer is John Wright of Chester. On 25 April 1953, Wright was keeping goal for Chester against Wrexham (Division Three North) when, with the game goalless, he sustained an injury that forced him to leave the field. Ralph Morement deputized, but proved to be no goalkeeper.

In 1954, teenager Jim Furnell was out of work. During an interview at his local 'dole' office he informed a clerk he was an unemployed goalkeeper. The office arranged for Furnell to have a trial with Burnley and he impressed sufficiently for the club to offer him a contract in November 1954. Furnell went on to keep goal for several clubs, including Liverpool and Arsenal, and made over 400 Football League appearances.

Blackburn Rovers goalkeeper of the 1950s and 1960s Fred Else enjoyed a reputation as a sharp wit and a sharp dresser; he was often to be seen in Italian suits. Prior to one game at Highbury, a rather large Arsenal supporter asked Else for his autograph. Else duly obliged, but on receipt of the autograph the burly Arsenal fan commented, 'I wouldn't be seen dead in that suit.' To which Else replied, 'You'd have to be dead for six months before it would fit you!'

Peter Grotier's rise in the game was meteoric to say the least. Over a period of only eight days during April 1959, the 18-year-old played for West Ham United 'A' team, youth team and two matches for the reserves, and then made his first-team debut.

Dogged by bad luck? Chic Brodie was a highly respected keeper in the 1960s whose clubs included Wolves, Aldershot, Northampton Town and Brentford. During one game between Brentford and Colchester United at Layer Road, a stray dog ran into Brodie's penalty area and collided with him. Unfortunately, Brodie sustained cartilage damage so bad that he had to retire from full-time football. He became a taxi-driver, but soon returned to football, playing on a part-time basis for Margate. He was in goal when Margate lost 11-0 in the FA Cup to Bournemouth in 1971–72. After retirement from the game he concentrated on taxi-driving. One day, while driving through Westminster, he had to swerve to avoid a stray dog and his taxi was hit by another vehicle – driven by England's 1966 hat-trick hero Geoff Hurst.

Lightning strikes! In 1963, Middlesbrough goalkeeper Arthur Lightning (formerly with Coventry City) was given special permission to take seven days' leave to travel to South Africa to attend his brother's wedding. He never came back. Middlesbrough made various attempts to contact him in South Africa, but no one at the club ever heard from him again.

On 22 August 1964, on the opening day of the season, goalkeeper Derek Foster made his Sunderland debut in the First Division against Leicester City. At 15 years and 185 days, Foster remains the youngest player to have appeared in top-flight English football. Result: Sunderland 3 Leicester City 3.

On 12 August 1967, in the Charity Shield match between Manchester United and Spurs at Old Trafford, Spurs goalkeeper Pat Jennings scored with an 80-yard punt from his own goalmouth which bounced over the head of United keeper Alex Stepney and into the net. The match ended in a 3-3 draw and was watched by a crowd of 63,500.

Gordon Banks enjoyed a trouble-free game when playing for England against Malta at Wembley on 12 May 1971. He did not receive the ball directly from a Malta player at any time during the game and only touched the ball twice in the course of the 90 minutes, when fielding back-passes from team-mates.

On 17 February 1993, in a World Cup qualifying match against San Marino at Wembley, Chris Woods emulated Gordon Banks by not having to execute a save in an England match. Whereas in creating the record Banks touched the ball only two times, Woods touched the ball on six occasions, once to collect a wayward through-ball, the other five times to field back-passes.

On 10 October 1972, Carl Gilbert scored twice for Rotherham United against Bournemouth; then, following an injury to Rotherham goalkeeper Jim McDonagh, Gilbert took over in goal and conceded three. Bournemouth won 7-2 at Millmoor.

In 1972–73, Walsall created a Football League record by calling on the services of seven different goalkeepers throughout the season: Keith Bell, Jimmy Inger, Glen Johnson, John Osborne, Dennis Peacock, Ian Turner and Bob Wesson.

On 19 August 1975, while playing for Manchester United against Birmingham City, United goalkeeper Alex Stepney suffered lockjaw as a result of shouting at his defenders and had to be taken to hospital – prompting Manchester comedian Bernard Manning to quip, 'I should be so lucky that should ever happen to the wife.'

When Ron Greenwood was manager of England (1977-82), he could not decide who was his best goalkeeper, Peter Shilton or Ray Clemence, so for much of his tenure he played them in alternative international matches. Shilton eventually got the nod for the 1982 World Cup Finals in Spain.

Come the end of 1979–80, goalkeeper Dave Felgate had clocked up 61 Football League appearances yet had never played for his club. Felgate was with Bolton Wanderers, who loaned him to Rochdale. He played 35 games for them before returning to Bolton, who then loaned him to Bradford City. Felgate did not make a first-team appearance for City, so he was brought back to Bolton, who then loaned him to Crewe Alexandra, for whom he played 14 matches. When his spell at Crewe ended, Felgate returned to Bolton yet again but, unable to break into the first team, he was loaned for a second time to Rochdale. He played a further 12 games for the Spotland club, and then Bolton sent him off to Lincoln City, which is where he made his 62nd Football League appearance without ever having played a League game for his club, Bolton Wanderers. Lincoln were so impressed with Felgate's performances that at the end of his month-long loan spell they signed him from Bolton on a permanent basis. But it does not end there! Felgate enjoyed four seasons with Lincoln (1980–81 to 1984–85) but then lost his place in goal to Stuart Naylor, so Lincoln loaned him to Cardiff City. When Felgate returned to Lincoln, Naylor was still the number one choice, so he was loaned to Grimsby Town, who signed him. Felgate made a total of 24 appearances in goal for Grimsby and his performances were such that he became the subject of transfer speculation, and in 1987 he was sold – to Bolton Wanderers! Between 1985 and 1987 Felgate made 35 appearances in goal for Bolton, only to be loaned again, this time to Rotherham. Without having made a first-team appearance for Rotherham, Felgate was recalled by Bolton and was an ever-present in the side during 1987–88 and 1988–89. He made 40 appearances the season after that too, and was again an ever-present in 1990–91. He remained at Bolton until 1993–94, when he was transferred to Bury. Later, he also played for Chester City and Wigan Athletic.

Aston Villa goalkeeper Jimmy Rimmer sustained an injury after nine minutes of Villa's 1982 European Cup Final against Bayern Munich. Rimmer's replacement was teenage keeper Nigel Spink who, in only his second senior game, kept a clean sheet, helping Villa to beat Bayern 1-0 and win the European Cup.

Leicester City used three different goalkeepers during their sixth round FA Cup tie against Shrewsbury Town in 1982. Mark Wallington (in his 333rd consecutive match for Leicester) was injured and replaced by Alan Young, only for Young also to sustain an injury; his place in goal was taken by Steve Lynex. Leicester won the tie 5-2. There were so many injuries in the game that the referee played 14 minutes of added time – a record for an FA Cup tie.

In 1985–86, Tottenham's first-choice goalkeeper was Ray Clemence with over 1,000 senior games to his name. Spurs' reserve keeper was Pat Jennings, who had played in 1,087 senior matches. Two goalkeepers at the same club whose combined appearances totalled over 2,000 first-class matches – a record.

In the early seventies, in addition to myself, there was Peter Shilton and Ray Clemence; also Peter Bonetti, Jim Montgomery, Paul Cooper, Colin Boulton, Gordon West and Joe Corrigan; and Alex Stepney, David Lawson, Jimmy Rimmer, Phil Parkes, John Osborne and Peter Springett – all top-class English goalkeepers. After which Alf Ramsey was pretty much struggling to find a keeper good enough to play at international level.
GORDON BANKS

John 'Budgie' Burridge is English football's most travelled goalkeeper. No other player has been attached to more clubs than Burridge, who began his 29-year career as a goalkeeper with Workington Town in 1968. He then played for (in order) Blackpool, Aston Villa, Southend United (loan), Crystal Palace, QPR, Wolverhampton Wanderers, Derby County (loan), Sheffield United, Southampton, Newcastle United, Hibernian, Newcastle United (second spell), Scarborough, Lincoln City, Enfield, Aberdeen, Newcastle United (third spell), Dumbarton, Dunfermline, Falkirk, Manchester City, Notts County, Witton Albion, Darlington, Grimsby Town, Northampton Town, Queen of the South, Purfleet, Blyth Spartans, Scarborough (second spell) and, finally, Blyth Spartans again. Burridge played 771 first-class matches in England and Scotland and 121 in non-league. He is now the goalkeeping coach of Al-Ain in the United Arab Emirates. When he was appointed, a spokesperson for Al-Ain said, 'We are delighted John has decided to join our club, he is an experienced goalkeeper' – arguably one of football's most understated comments.

In 1985–86, Pat Jennings came out of retirement and rejoined Spurs as a 'cover' goalkeeper for League matches. He also signed on a non-contract basis for Everton as cover for Neville Southall, but for FA Cup matches only. Thus Jennings achieved a unique position in English football: he was eligible to play for two different clubs. As it turned out, he wasn't called upon to play for either.

On 16 October 1993, in a Division Three match between Colchester United and Hereford United at Layer Road, Colchester goalkeeper John Keeley was sent off as a result of a 'professional foul'. Colchester replaced outfield player Steve Brown with substitute goalkeeper Nathan Munson, only for Munson to be dismissed for committing a 'professional foul'. Colchester lost the game 5-0 and are the only League club to have had two recognized goalkeepers sent off in the same match.

Between January and April 1994, Mark Leonard (Chesterfield) did not concede a goal in eight consecutive away matches in Division Three – a record for a goalkeeper in away matches in English football.

Can you name the goalkeeper who played at Wembley on the occasion of 12 cup finals? On 23 April 1995, singer Jess Conrad kept goal for the Show Biz XI in a charity match at Wembley prior to the Auto Windscreens Shield Final between Birmingham City and Carlisle United. Conrad was 59 years old and it was the 12th time he had appeared at Wembley prior to a domestic final. Among his hits as a singer was, fittingly for a goalkeeper, 'My Pullover' and, just to prove that Albert Camus does not have sole claim on philosophizing goalkeepers, 'Why Am I Living?'

In 1995–96, Gillingham's Jim Stannard achieved 29 clean sheets in 46 League matches. As he joked, 'Which is more than some of the bedrooms in the hotels we've had the dubious pleasure of staying at when playing away.'

Arguably the most sensational, audacious and acrobatic save ever executed by a goalkeeper – albeit the whistle had already blown for a free-kick – occurred during the England–Colombia international at Wembley in September 1995. Faced with an England shot at goal, instead of simply catching the ball, Colombian goalkeeper René Higuita flung his torso forward, kicked up his feet behind him and cleared the ball with the heels of both boots. The press dubbed Higuita's amazing save 'the scorpion kick'.

Neville Southall was 41 years old when he kept goal for Bradford City in the Premiership against Leeds United (1-2) on 12 March 2000.

In 1995–96, John Burridge signed for Gateshead United whose other goalkeepers were Steve Sherwood (ex-Watford) and Sean Musgrave. Burridge was 44 years old and Sherwood 42 – a combined age of 86. Sean Musgrave, at 21, was young enough to be the son of either of his senior keepers.

On 22 December 1996, Peter Shilton made his 1,000th League appearance, for Leyton Orient against Brighton at Brisbane Road. Shilton, who won 125 caps for England, had begun his career with Leicester City in 1966 on a wage of £8 a week.

On 27 September 2002, Dave Beasant signed for Bradford City, at the age of 42. One month later, to the day (27 October), Beasant joined Wigan Athletic.

In 2003, Gordon Banks met Jairzinho for the first time since England and Brazil's classic encounter in the 1970 World Cup Finals. The pair had been invited by Sky Sports to re-enact the moment when Jairzinho scored the only goal of the match. It took five takes as Banks continually saved the Brazilian's efforts. As Banks commented, 'If only that had happened in 1970.'

In 2006–07, Wayne Hennessey (on loan from Wolverhampton Wanderers) kept nine clean sheets in his first nine matches for Stockport County. Nine games without conceding a goal is also a Football League record.

In 2007–08, Kevin Poole was keeping goal for Burton Albion in the Conference at the age of 44. Poole began his career at Aston Villa in 1981, prior to Villa winning the European Cup.

Mark Schwarzer has been wearing the same pair of shinguards in games since he was six years old.

On 19 April 2008, Chris Mann made his League debut in goal for Port Vale against Swindon Town – Vale lost 6-0.

31 Nottingham Forest and West Bromwich Albion share the record for the biggest-margin wins in top-flight English football (First Division). On 4 April 1892, West Bromwich Albion beat Darwen 12-0. On 21 April 1909, Nottingham Forest beat Leicester Fosse 12-0.

Morton created a goalscoring record in 1912–13 that exists to this day. They used 21 players during the course of the season in the Scottish Division One and every player scored, including the goalkeeper, who successfully converted a penalty.

Right-back Jimmy Evans was Southend United's leading goalscorer in 1921–22 (Third Division South) with ten goals. This tally was equalled by Stan Lynn, Birmingham City's right-back, who was City's leading goalscorer in 1964–65.

The most goals scored by a goalkeeper in a single season is five, by Arthur Birch for Chesterfield (Division Three North) in 1923–24. All Birch's goals came from the penalty spot.

Maker rather than a taker? Fred Hopkin made 133 appearances as a forward for Liverpool between 1921 and 1928 and failed to score a single goal.

One for the book. W. H. Smith was the first player to score direct from a corner-kick. He did so when playing for Huddersfield Town against Arsenal in August 1924. The rule making such a feat possible had only been introduced the previous June.

During 1928–29, Rotherham United suffered the ignominy of conceding double figures in two League matches (Third Division North). On 25 August they were hammered 11-1 at Bradford City, and on 10 March they lost 10-1 at South Shields.

In the same season (1928–29), Bradford City scored a (then) League record 128 goals. In addition to beating Rotherham United 11-1, Bradford also scored eight goals on three occasions, including once away from home. City scored 82 goals at home – an average of little under four per game.

Chesterfield hold the record for having scored in the most successive Football League matches. Starting on Christmas Day 1929 and ending on 27 December 1930, they netted in 46 consecutive matches in Division Three (North).

In September 1929, Joe Bradford (Birmingham City) scored three hat-tricks in eight days, against Newcastle United, for the Football League v. Irish League, and against Blackburn Rovers.

In 1937–38, Raith Rovers scored a British record 142 goals in their 34 League matches – an average of 4.1 per match. Raith were champions of Division Two, and in 17 away matches scored a staggering 74 goals – an average of 4.3 per match.

The fastest goal scored by an England player came during England's match against Portugal in Lisbon on 25 May 1947, when Tommy Lawton netted after only 17 seconds. England went on to win 10-0.

Tommy Lawton and Jackie Sewell both scored hat-tricks in a 12-minute spell of the second-half of the game between Notts County and Exeter City (Third Division South) on 16 October 1948. Notts County won 9-0.

The record number of goals disallowed for offside in a single first-class game in Britain is six, during the match between Swindon Town and Southend United (Third Division South) in 1949. Swindon won 2-1.

In 1951–52, Derek Dooley scored 46 goals in only 30 League matches for Sheffield Wednesday, who finished champions of Division Two.

The record for the longest-distance headed goal is held by Peter Aldis. Playing for Aston Villa against Sunderland at Villa Park on 1 September 1952, Aldis beat Sunderland goalkeeper Harry Threadgold with a header from 35 yards. Villa won the match 3-0.

Away teams were very much in the ascendancy in the second round of the Scottish FA Cup in 1953–54. Partick Thistle won 9-1 at Tarff Rovers, Buckie Thistle won 7-2 at Peeble Rovers, Dundee scored four without reply at Albion Rovers, Aberdeen travelled to Duns and won 8-0, and Raith Rovers enjoyed a 10-1 victory at Coldstream.

The record number of goals scored by a winger in a single League match is seven, achieved by Stoke City outside-right Tim Coleman in his club's 8-0 victory over Lincoln City (Division Two, 23 February 1957).

Not a hope. During 1957–58, Hope and O'Neill both scored for Sunderland in Division One, yet they were the same player. On 4 September, Alan Hope scored twice in Sunderland's 3-2 victory over Leicester City at Roker Park. The player then received official notification from Somerset House that his request to change his name by deed poll had been granted. Hope changed his surname to that of his stepfather, O'Neill, and on 7 September he scored for Sunderland in a 1-1 draw with Aston Villa. During the course of the season the goals he had scored under the name Hope were altered in official records to O'Neill to avoid confusion.

Jimmy Harris scored a hat-trick for Everton in their match against Tottenham Hotspur at White Hart Lane in 1958–59, only for Everton to lose 10-4.

Wolves are the only team to have scored in excess of 100 goals in four consecutive seasons in top-flight English football. They scored 103 in 1957–58, 110 in 1958–59, 106 in 1959–60 and 103 in 1960–61.

On 15 August 1959, Motherwell centre-forward Ian St John scored a hat-trick in two minutes and 27 seconds against Hibernian.

The only player to have scored hat-tricks on successive days is Cliff Holton. On Good Friday 1960, the Watford centre-forward scored three against Chester; the following day he hit another hat-trick against Gateshead United.

The highest number of hat-tricks scored by an individual in a single post-war season in top-flight English football is six – Jimmy Greaves (Chelsea), First Division, 1960–61.

There have been only two occasions since World War Two when three players from the same team have scored hat-tricks in the same League game: Ron Barnes, Roy Ambler and Wyn Davies in Wrexham's 10-1 victory over Hartlepool on 3 March 1962; and Paul Stewart, Tony Adcock and David White in Manchester City's 10-1 defeat of Huddersfield Town on 7 November 1987.

Boxing Day 1963 saw 66 goals scored in ten First Division matches – a post-war record for English top-flight football. The results were as follows: Blackpool 1 Chelsea 5; Burnley 6 Manchester United 1; Fulham 10 Ipswich Town 1; Leicester City 2 Everton 0; Liverpool 6 Stoke City 1; Nottingham Forest 3 Sheffield United 3; Sheffield Wednesday 3 Bolton Wanderers 0; West Bromwich Albion 4 Spurs 4; West Ham United 2 Blackburn Rovers 8; Wolves 3 Aston Villa 3.

The fastest hat-trick scored in post-war top-flight English football was notched by Graham Leggat, who scored three in three minutes for Fulham against Ipswich Town on Boxing Day 1963. Final score: Fulham 10 Ipswich Town 1. In the return fixture at Portman Road two days later, Ipswich won 4-1.

The fastest goal scored in a Football League match was netted by Jim Fryatt of Bradford Park Avenue on 25 April 1964. Fryatt scored after just four seconds of Bradford's match against Tranmere Rovers, as confirmed by the stopwatch carried by referee Mr R. Simon.

Mistakes in defence cost West Brom dear in 1965. Brian Dear scored five goals in 20 minutes for West Ham United against West Bromwich Albion (6-1) on 16 April 1965.

Centre-forward Ronnie Allen (West Bromwich Albion) scored goals in 21 successive seasons (1944–45 to 1964–65) – the longest sequence by any player.

On 20 November 1969, Pelé scored his 1,000th first-class goal from the penalty spot during Santos's 2-1 victory over Vasco Da Gama at the Maracana Stadium.

After serving a four-week suspension in 1969, George Best returned to play for Manchester United in their fifth round FA Cup tie against Northampton Town at the County Ground. Best scored six in United's 8-2 victory, prompting Denis Law to say, 'Heaven knows how many he would have scored if he had been match fit.'

In 1972–73, Bolton Wanderers beat Rotherham United courtesy of an extraordinary goal by Gary Jones. Rotherham goalkeeper Jim McDonagh thought the ball had gone out of play, placed it on the six-yard box and stepped back to take a goal-kick. Jones didn't panic. Realizing that the referee had not signalled that the ball had gone out of play, he simply walked up and, much to McDonagh's chagrin, kicked the ball into the net.

Liverpool hold the British record for the most scoring players in a senior competitive match. Nine different players netted in Liverpool's 11-0 win over Stromsgodset (Norway) in the first round first leg of the European Cup Winners' Cup on 17 September 1974: Alec Lindsay, Phil Boersma (two), Phil Thompson (two), Steve Heighway, Peter Cormack, Emlyn Hughes, Ian Callaghan, Tommy Smith and Ray Kennedy. The only players not to score were goalkeeper Ray Clemence and midfielder Brian Hall.

On 8 December 1984, during Stirling's 20-0 Scottish Cup win over Selkirk, eight different Stirling players got their names on the scoresheet; Thompson (seven), Irvine (five), Walker (two), Watt (two), Maxwell, Ormond, Dawson and McTeague. The following Saturday, the same Selkirk team won their next match in the Borders League 4-1.

> ## It seemed only a matter of time before a goal would come, then, with the very last kick of the game, Bobby McDonald scored with a header.
> ALAN PARRY

On 21 April 1986, centre-back Alvin Martin scored a hat-trick in West Ham United's 8-1 victory over Newcastle United – against three different goalkeepers. Original Newcastle keeper Martin Thomas sustained an injury and was replaced by Chris Hedworth, who in turn was replaced by Peter Beardsley. Three other players have achieved this feat: Jock Dodds for Lincoln City v. West Ham United (18 December 1948) against Ernie Gregory, Tommy Moroney and George Dick; David Herd for Manchester United v. Sunderland (26 November 1966) against Jim Montgomery, Charlie Hurley and John Parke; and Brian Clark for Bournemouth v. Rotherham United (10 October 1972) against Jim McDonagh, Con Gilbert and Michael Leng.

On 5 September 1987, Chesterfield travelled to Gillingham boasting a record of not having conceded a goal in their four League matches since the start of the season. Result: Gillingham 10 Chesterfield 0.

The highest aggregate score in the Scottish Premier League is 11 goals: Celtic 8 Hamilton Academical 3 (3 January 1987) and Motherwell 5 Aberdeen 6 (20 October 1999). The record modern aggregate for Scottish senior football is 12 goals: Brechin City 5 Cowdenbeath 7 (Division Two, 18 January 2003).

The last player to score in excess of 100 goals across two consecutive seasons was Steve Bull (Wolverhampton Wanderers). In all competitions, Bull amassed 52 goals in 1987-88 and 50 in 1988-89.

Hodge scored for Forest after only 22 seconds, and I have to say it was completely against the run of play.

PETER LORENZO, BBC Radio

When Liverpool beat Crystal Palace 9-0 on 12 September 1989, their goalscorers were Steve Nicol (two), Steve McMahon, Ian Rush, Peter Beardsley, John Barnes, John Aldridge, Gary Gillespie and Glen Hysen – the first time in the history of the Football League that eight players scored for one team in a single game.

A Leyland DAF Cup match between Southend United and Torquay United on 26 February 1991 stood goalless after 55 minutes. Southend then scored seven goals in 29 minutes without reply to win 7-0.

On 6 February 1993, Tottenham Hotspur trailed Southampton 0-1 at White Hart Lane, then scored four goals in four minutes and 40 seconds (and won the game 4-2).

The fastest international goal was scored against England. In the World Cup qualifying match between San Marino and England in Bologna on 17 November 1993, San Marino's Davide Gualtieri scored after only 8.3 seconds. England, however, went on to win 6-1. Not that it did Graham Taylor's side any good: they failed to qualify for the 1994 finals in the USA.

The fastest hat-trick scored in the Premiership stands at four minutes and 33 seconds (26, 29, 31), by Robbie Fowler for Liverpool against Arsenal on 28 August 1994. They were the only goals of the game.

When Oxford United beat Shrewsbury Town 6-0 (Division Two) on 23 April 1996, all six Oxford goals came from headers, the heads belonging to Paul Moody (two), Stuart Massey, David Rush, Joey Beauchamp and Matt Murphy.

A fabulous taker of chances is Zola, as one would expect from a player with two feet.

DAVID PLEAT, FiveLive

The fewest number of goals scored in a weekend of Premiership fixtures is ten, in the ten matches played on 24/25 November 2001. The most goals scored in the Premiership on a single day is 47, in nine matches on 8 May 1993.

To be honest, Coventry never looked like scoring.

ALEX FERGUSON, following a 3-2 defeat for Manchester United at Coventry

In 2001–02, Arsenal scored in every match they played (38 matches) – a record for the Premiership.

The goals made such a difference to the way this game went.

JOHN MOTSON

The fastest goal scored in the finals of a World Cup was netted by Hakan Sukur, after only 10.8 seconds of the game between Turkey and South Korea in 2002, beating the record of 16 seconds set by Vaclav Masek, for Czechoslovakia against Mexico (Chile, 1962).

PLAYER'S CIGARETTES

SHOOTING ON THE RUN

The honour of the fastest goal scored by an England player in the finals of a World Cup goes to Bryan Robson, who netted after just 27 seconds of the group match against France (Spain, 1982) – a game England won 3-1.

On 7 May 2003, Robert Pires and Jermaine Pennant both scored hat-tricks in Arsenal's 6-1 Premiership win against Southampton at Highbury.

The fastest hat-trick in the history of the Football League was scored by James Hayter, officially timed at two minutes 20 seconds. Hayter, a second-half substitute for Bournemouth in their Divsion Two match with Wrexham on 24 February 2004, scored in the 86th, 87th and 88th minutes of the game. Bournemouth won 6-0.

In 2003–04, Ruud van Nistlelrooy scored 15 goals in ten successive matches for Manchester United – a Premiership record for the longest sequence of scoring in consecutive matches. Prior to van Nistelrooy, the last player to score in ten consecutive matches in top-flight English football was John Aldridge (Liverpool, 1986–87). Prior to Aldridge, two other players had achieved this feat: Billy McAdams (Manchester City, 1957–58) and Ron Davies (Southampton, 1966–67).

 Van Nistelrooy, imperious, sublime, sensational, the prime predator of the penalty box. Two goals now for him in three games, and you can't beat that.

STUART HALL, FiveLive

The fewest goals conceded in a Premiership season is 15 (Chelsea, 38 matches, 2004–05).

Jimmy Greaves scored goals with all the fuss and commotion of someone closing the door of a Rolls-Royce.

GEOFFREY GREEN, football writer

Inter-League matches were first introduced in 1891. The first Inter-League game was between the Football League and the Alliance (Southern) League.

The first Football League v. Scottish League game (2-2) took place in 1892 at Bolton. Over the years, fixtures between the Football League and sides representing the leagues of Scotland, Northern Ireland ('Irish League'), Ireland ('League of Ireland') and Italy became part of the annual fixture list.

The heyday of Inter-League matches was the 1930s, 1940s and 1950s when such fixtures drew healthy attendances. The record attendance is 90,987 for the Scottish League v. the Football League (0-3).

In the 1950s, England manager Walter Winterbottom was also in charge of the Football League representative side for Inter-League matches.

In the 1950s, Walter Winterbottom often used Inter-League matches as a means of compromising the England selection committee. Frustrated at having to field players who had been selected for England not on merit but, as Winterbottom once put it, 'because the FA selection committee wished to reward a player for being a decent sportsman', Winterbottom persuaded the

FA to 'reward' such players with an appearance for the Football League representative side rather than the national team. That is not to say, of course, that all players representing the Football League did so as a 'reward'.

Nat Lofthouse (Bolton Wanderers) scored six for the Football League against the League of Ireland at Molineux on 24 September 1952 – an individual scoring record for Inter-League matches.

The wonderfully named Barney Battles scored five for the Scottish League against the Irish League at Firhill (Glasgow) on 31 October 1928.
Final result: 8-2.

On 18 October 1950 at Bloomfield Road, Blackpool, Albert Stubbins (Liverpool) scored five for the Football League against the Irish League. Result: 6-3.

Brian Clough, who had been averaging a goal per game for Middlesbrough, scored all five goals for the Football League in the 5-0 defeat of the Irish League in Belfast on 23 September 1959.

In 1960, German goalkeeper Bert Trautmann (Manchester City) played for the Football League against the Scottish League – the only overseas player to have represented the Football League. Welsh internationals Jack Kelsey (Arsenal) and Cliff Jones (Spurs) along with Northern Ireland international Peter McParland (Aston Villa) were also chosen to represent the Football League.

The Italian League beat the Scottish League 3-2 at Hampden Park on 1 November 1961. Included in the Italian team were Scotsman Denis Law (Torino), Englishman Gerry Hitchens (Inter Milan) and Welshman John Charles (Juventus).

In 1952, the Welsh League played the Scottish League at Ninian Park. This was the only match involving a Welsh League XI, though the title was a misnomer as the players were Welsh but played for clubs in the English Football League. The Welsh League won 3-0 with two goals from Ivor Allchurch (Swansea) and one from Reg Parker (Newport County).

In 1952–53, the Football League and Scottish League both played the Danish League – the only instances of Inter-League matches involving the Danes. The Football League beat the Danish League 4-0 in Copenhagen.

Dave Mackay (Spurs) once played for the Football League against the Scottish League, having previously played in his days with Hearts for the Scottish League against the Football League.

International rules were much stricter in the 1950s and 1960s. For example, a player attached to a Scottish club could play for the Scottish League but not for Scotland if he had been born in England or another country. This resulted in Joe Baker (Hibernian) playing for the Scottish League but for England at international level, and his brother Gerry (St Mirren) also playing for the Scottish League but at international level for Canada, the country in which he was born.

In 1966, the Football League beat the Irish League 12-0 at Home Park (Plymouth) – the record score in the history of Inter-League matches. The Football League goalscorers were Johnny Byrne (West Ham, four), George Eastham (Stoke City, two), John Connelly (Manchester United, two), Geoff Hurst (West Ham, two), Terry Paine (Southampton, two).

In 1967, the Football League played the Belgian League for the first and only time. The match in Brussels ended 2-2.

RECORD OF FOOTBALL LEAGUE REPRESENTATIVE MATCHES

FOOTBALL LEAGUE V. SCOTTISH LEAGUE:
Played 69, England won 38, Scotland won 18, 13 drawn.
FOOTBALL LEAGUE V. IRISH LEAGUE:
Played 61, England won 54, Northern Ireland won 3, 4 drawn.
FOOTBALL LEAGUE V. LEAGUE OF IRELAND:
Played 21, England won 18, Republic of Ireland won 1, 2 drawn.
FOOTBALL LEAGUE V. ITALIAN LEAGUE:
Played 4, England won 1, Italy won 3.

Due to fixture list pressure and declining interest, Inter-League games were dispensed with in 1976.

The last Inter-League match saw the Football League play the Scottish League in Glasgow in 1976. The Football League line-up was: Shilton (Stoke City), Cherry (Leeds), Mills (Ipswich Town), Doyle (Manchester City), McFarland, Todd (both Derby County), Wilkins (Chelsea), Channon (Southampton), J. Greenhoff (Stoke City), Currie (Sheffield United) and Tueart (Manchester City). The Scottish League side featured: Stewart (Kilmarnock), Rolland (Dundee United), Wark (Motherwell), Forsyth, Jackson (both Rangers), Miller (Aberdeen), Duncan, Bremner (both Hibernian), Craig (Partick Thistle), McDonald and McKean (both Rangers). The Football League won 1-0 (Trevor Cherry), and the attendance was 8,874.

Landmarks

33

1857	Sheffield FC formed – world's oldest football club
1863	Football Association formed
1863	Initial rules of football laid down
1871	FA Cup begins
1872	First international: Scotland v. England
1873	Scottish FA formed
1874	Shin pads first worn, by Sam Widdowson (Nottingham Forest)
1875	Crossbar replaces tape between goalposts
1876	Welsh FA formed
1878	Referee's whistle introduced
1880	Irish FA formed
1883	Two-handed throw-in made part of rules
1885	Professionalism legalized
1886	FA International Board formed
1888	Football League founded
1889	Preston first to win double
1890	Scottish League formed
1890	Irish League formed
1891	Goal nets introduced
1891	Penalties introduced

1892	Football League forms Second Division
1893	FA Amateur Cup comes into being
1894	Southern League formed
1895	FA Cup stolen – never found
1896	Second FA Cup trophy minted
1897	Players form union – PFA
1897	Aston Villa win double
1898	Football League introduce promotion/relegation
1901	Maximum wage introduced (£4)
1901	Tottenham (Southern League) win FA Cup
1902	Current dimensions of penalty area laid down
1902	Welsh League formed
1904	FIFA formed
1905	First £1,000 transfer
1911	New FA Cup trophy (third) introduced
1914	First reigning monarch at FA Cup Final (George V)
1914–18	Official football suspended due to war
1919	Football League increased to 44 clubs
1920	Third Division South formed
1921	Third Division North formed
1922	Second Division formed in Scotland
1923	Wembley Stadium opens
1923	First FA Cup Final at Wembley
1924	First England match at Wembley
1925	New offside law introduced
1926	Huddersfield champions for third successive season
1927	First match broadcast on radio
1928	First £10,000 transfer
1930	First World Cup
1933	Players numbered for first time (in FA Cup Final)
1935	Arsenal win third successive championship
1936	Joe Payne scored ten for Luton Town
1937	British record attendance of 149,547 at Hampden
1938	Laws of football rewritten
1938	First coverage of FA Cup Final by television
1938	Pitch markings adjusted – arc on penalty box
1939	All players to wear numbered shirts

33

1939–45	Official football suspended due to war
1946	Scottish League Cup begins
1946	First England manager appointed
1950	Football League increased from 88 to 92 clubs
1950	England enter World Cup for first time
1950	Scotland's first home defeat by foreign opposition
1951	White ball introduced
1953	England's first home defeat to foreign opposition
1956	First League and cup matches under floodlights
1957	Last full Christmas Day fixture list
1958	Munich air disaster
1958	Football League overhauled – four divisions
1959	Football League establish copyright on fixtures
1960	League Cup launched
1961	Spurs complete first double of century
1961	Maximum wage abolished
1962	First £100,000 transfer paid by British club (Man Utd)
1963	FA centenary; Football League 75th anniversary
1963	ITV in deal to show match highlights on regional TV
1963	Pools panel formed
1964	BBC (2) introduce *Match of the Day*
1965	Stanley Matthews first player to be knighted
1965	Substitutes introduced for League and cup matches
1966	England win World Cup
1967	Celtic win European Cup (first British team)
1970	UEFA/FIFA introduce penalty shoot-outs
1973	Three-up/three-down promotion and relegation
1974	First League and cup games on Sunday
1975	Scottish Premier League formed
1975	Goal difference to replace goal average
1978	Restriction on foreign players in England lifted
1979	First £1 million transfer
1981	Three points for a win introduced
1983	Clubs vote to keep own match receipts
1983	First League matches 'live' on TV
1984	FA Cup rounds to include Friday and Sunday as part of TV deal
1985	Bradford Fire disaster

1985	Heysel disaster
1985	English clubs banned from Europe (five years)
1986	Football League sponsored – by *Today* newspaper
1987	Play-offs introduced
1987	Re-election abolished
1987	Two substitutes per team
1987	First Division reduced to 21 clubs
1988	First Division reduced to 20 clubs
1989	Hillsborough disaster
1990	Both FA Cup semi-finals on Sunday to accommodate TV
1990	Wembley venue for play-off finals
1990	Player 'level' no longer offside
1990	English clubs readmitted to Europe
1991	Penalty shoot-outs in FA Cup after one replay
1992	Premiership launched (22 clubs)
1993	Premiership – squad numbers/names on shirts
1994	FA Cup sponsored for first time
1995	Bosman ruling
1995	Premiership reduced to 20 clubs
1999	FA buy Wembley for £103 million
1999	Oxford v. Sunderland first pay-per-view TV match
2004	Arsenal complete entire League season unbeaten
2007	Premier League agree record £1.7 billion deal with Sky/Setanta
2008	Premier League proposal for some matches to be played overseas

34

The League Cup was the 'brainchild' of Football League secretary Alan
Hardaker, who borrowed the idea from Scotland. Whereas the Scottish League
Cup took place prior to the domestic season, the English League Cup was to
be a creature of the night, ties (including the final) being played midweek
under floodlights.

The League Cup trophy is unique in that it has three handles.

Players participating in the final were presented with winners and losers
tankards as opposed to medals.

The League Cup was first contested in 1960–61. Five First Division clubs –
Arsenal, Sheffield Wednesday, Tottenham Hotspur, West Bromwich Albion
and Wolves – declined to enter on the grounds the season was already over-
burdened with fixtures.

The first winners of the League Cup were Aston Villa (1961) who defeated
Rotherham United 3-2 (after extra-time) in a two-legged final – 0-2 and 3-0.
Due to concerns about fixture congestion, this final was not played until the
following season (August and September 1961).

The first player to score in a League Cup Final was Rotherham's Barry Webster in the aforementioned match (first leg) against Aston Villa at Millmoor.

The attendance for that first League Cup Final at Millmoor was 12,226. The attendance at Villa Park for the second leg was 27,102.

The only Fourth Division club to reach the final – and that of any major English domestic cup competition – is Rochdale, who lost 3-1 on aggregate to Norwich City in 1961–62.

In that match, Derek Lythgoe scored what at the time was the fastest goal in a League Cup Final, timed at two minutes 58 seconds, for Norwich City.

As the 1962 League Cup Final was played within the season as scheduled, and the previous season's final between Aston Villa and Rotherham United had been held over, two different League Cup Finals were staged in the same season – the only time this has happened in any major domestic cup competition.

The first League Cup tie to be staged on a Saturday afternoon was Sunderland v. Aston Villa at Roker Park (semi-final, first leg, 12 January 1963). That day, Sunderland were scheduled to play a Second Division match at Swansea and Aston Villa a First Division match at Blackpool. Both matches were postponed, so Sunderland and Villa hastily rearranged their semi-final. A crowd of 33,237 attended Roker Park to see Villa win 3-1 on a frost-bound pitch. The second leg at Villa Park was goalless; thus Aston Villa became the first club to reach two League Cup Finals.

Birmingham City's victory in the 1963 final against Aston Villa (3-1 and 0-0) remains the club's only major domestic trophy success. (Birmingham City's only other trophy successes are the Leyland DAF Cup and the Auto Windscreens Shield.)

In 1962–63, Leyton Orient defeated Chester 9-2 in round three but scored only 37 League goals that season and finished bottom of Division One.

In the 1965 final, Chelsea defeated Leicester City 3-2 on aggregate. Chelsea did the job in the first leg, winning 3-2 at Stamford Bridge. In the weeks preceding the final, Chelsea left-back Eddie McCreadie had been badgering manager Tommy Docherty to try him as a centre-forward. Docherty surprised everyone by selecting him at centre-forward for the final against Leicester, and McCreadie scored Chelsea's winning goal, a thunderbolt shot from 25 yards.

Following the second leg of that 1965 final, at Leicester's Filbert Street, Chelsea players were not presented with their tankards immediately after the game as League officials had misplaced the box in which they were contained. They were eventually located and, somewhat ignominiously, Chelsea club secretary John Battersby handed them out from a cardboard box in the dressing room.

In 1964–65, Leicester City won 8-1 at Coventry City (fifth round) on the same night that Aston Villa defeated Bradford City 7-1.

The last League Cup Final to be staged over two legs and scheduled in midweek was West Bromwich Albion v. West Ham United (1965–66). West Brom triumphed 5-3 on aggregate (1-2 and 4-1).

The first League Cup Final to be staged at Wembley was in 1967. Third Division Queens Park Rangers came from 2-0 down to defeat West Bromwich Albion 3-2. The attendance at Wembley of 98,000 was, at the time, a record for the competition. QPR became the first Football League club from outside the top two divisions of English football to win a major domestic trophy, albeit Tottenham Hotspur won the FA Cup in 1901 when members of the Southern League.

In 1966–67, UEFA decreed that the winners of the League Cup would qualify for Europe (Fairs Cup). However, Queens Park Rangers were denied entry as UEFA stipulated that only League Cup winners from the First Division were admissible.

The only player to have scored in every possible round of the League Cup is Tony Brown (West Bromwich Albion), whose nine goals helped Albion win the cup in 1965–66. Albion were exempt from round one, but Brown then scored in every tie Albion were scheduled to play.

The first club to win the League Cup twice were Tottenham Hotspur, in 1971 and 1973.

Fifteen of the players who played in the League Cup Final between Arsenal and Leeds United in 1968 also played in the 1972 FA Cup Final between these clubs, Leeds repeating their success and scoreline from the League Cup Final (1-0).

In 1968–69, Swindon Town upset the odds and became only the second Third Division club to win the League Cup when they defeated Arsenal 3-1 at Wembley (aet). As with QPR before them, Swindon were denied entry to the Fairs Cup due to their lowly status.

The first League Cup Final to attract a six-figure attendance (100,000) was the 1971 final between Tottenham Hotspur and Aston Villa (2-0).

In the 1960s, George Graham played in four League Cup Finals for three different clubs: Aston Villa (v. Birmingham City, 1963 – lost), Chelsea (v. Leicester City, 1965 – won) and Arsenal (v. Leeds United, 1968 – lost; v. Swindon Town, 1969 – lost).

In 1971–72, Stoke City and West Ham United were involved in the longest semi-final in the history of the competition. It began on 8 December and was not resolved until 26 January. This epic started with Stoke City losing 2-1 at the Victoria Ground. They then won the second leg at Upton Park 1-0, the aggregate score locked at 2-2 after extra-time. A winner did not emerge until the third replay, at Old Trafford, which Stoke won 3-2.

The oldest League Cup winner is George Eastham (35 years and 161 days), who scored Stoke City's winning goal in their 2-1 victory over Chelsea in 1972.

Eight of the Chelsea team that lost to Stoke in the 1972 League Cup Final had also appeared for Chelsea in the 1970 FA Cup Final and 1971 European Cup Winners' Cup Final: Peter Bonetti, Ron Harris, John Hollins, John Dempsey, David Webb, Charlie Cooke, Peter Osgood and Peter Houseman.

In 1975–76, Southport were drawn at home to Newcastle United in round two. Southport, however, conceded home advantage in the hope of receiving a financial windfall from a tie at St James' Park. Southport lost the match 6-0 but the attendance of 23,352 was almost the aggregate total of the club's first 18 League matches of the season.

The first League Cup tie to be decided on a penalty shoot-out was Lincoln City v. Doncaster Rovers (first round replay, 24 August 1976). The first leg between these two sides at Doncaster was drawn 1-1, and the second leg at Lincoln also ended 1-1. The replay was held at a neutral venue (City Ground, Nottingham), it ended 2-2 after extra-time, and Doncaster won 4-2 on penalties. The following evening (25 August), the first round replay between Colchester United and Millwall ended 4-4 and it too went to a penalty shoot-out. Millwall won 4-2 – the only instance in English football when the aggregate score of the penalty shoot-out was less than that from open play.

The 1977 final between Aston Villa and Everton was the first to go to a replay – not once, but twice. Having drawn 0-0 at Wembley, Villa and Everton then drew 1-1 (aet) at Hillsborough. The second replay took place at Old Trafford and it too went to extra-time. After five and a half hours of football Villa eventually triumphed 3-2, their winning goal scored by Brian Little 90 seconds from the end of extra-time.

In 1976–77, Bobby Moore was sent off while playing for Fulham at Bolton Wanderers (third round replay) for protesting about the amount of injury-time allowed by referee Kevin McNally, during which Bolton equalized to make the score on the night 2-2. When the whistle blew for the end of normal time, the Fulham players took to the dressing room and refused to re-take the pitch for extra-time. It was only on being told that should they continue with their protest they would forfeit the tie that the players eventually relented. Extra-time could not separate the teams. The tie went to a second replay (at St Andrews) which Bolton won 2-1.

Nottingham Forest were the first club to win the trophy in successive seasons – 1978 and 1979; they repeated this feat in 1989 and 1990. Liverpool surpassed this achievement by winning the trophy in four successive seasons, 1981 to 1984.

Somewhat surprisingly, 20 years after the competition was inaugurated Liverpool won the League Cup for the first time, though it took Bob Paisley's team two matches to dispense of West Ham United. The 1981 final finished 1-1 (aet), and Liverpool won the replay 2-1 at Villa Park.

Liverpool did not lose a League Cup tie between February 1980 and October 1985.

Six players appeared for Liverpool in all of their four consecutive League Cup Finals from 1981 to 1984: Phil Neal, Alan Kennedy, Alan Hansen, Kenny Dalglish, Sammy Lee and Ian Rush.

In 1983–84, a Third Division club reached the semi-finals of both major domestic cup competitions for the first time in the history of English football. Walsall reached the semi-finals of the League Cup, but after securing a 2-2 draw at Anfield they lost 2-0 at Fellows Park. Later in the season, Plymouth Argyle were beaten 1-0 by Watford in the semi-finals of the FA Cup.

Norwich City defeated Sunderland 1-0 in the 1985 final only for both clubs to be relegated from Division One. Norwich is the only club to have won a major domestic trophy and suffered relegation in the same season. What's more, Norwich won the cup without scoring a goal: their winner was an own-goal by Sunderland's Gordon Chisholm. The Sunderland captain was Barry Venison, who at 20 years and seven months became the youngest captain of a team competing in a major British cup final.

Gordon Chisholm is the only player to have appeared in the finals of the English and Scottish League Cups in the same year. In 1985, having appeared for Sunderland against Norwich City in March, Chisholm was subsequently transferred to Hibernian and in October of that year played in the 1986 Scottish League Cup Final against Aberdeen. He ended on the losing side again: Aberdeen defeated Hibernian 3-0.

In 1986, Oxford United won their first major domestic trophy, beating Queens Park Rangers 3-0 at Wembley. In Oxford's League Cup-winning team that day were John Aldridge and Ray Houghton. Oddly, Aldridge failed to score, the Oxford goals coming from Houghton, Trevor Hebberd and Jeremy Charles.

The highest number of goals scored by an individual player in a single season of the competition is 12, by Clive Allen of Tottenham Hotspur (1986–87).

The fewest goals conceded by the eventual winners of the competition is three, a record shared by three clubs: Leeds United (1967–68), Tottenham Hotspur (1970–71) and Aston Villa (1995–96).

On 25 October 1983, West Ham United defeated Bury 10-0 at Upton Park (second round second leg) – a record victory in the League Cup. This was equalled on 23 September 1986 when Liverpool beat Fulham by the same score (second round first leg, Anfield). In the second leg at Craven Cottage, Liverpool won 3-2 to establish the record aggregate victory (13-2) for the competition.

In 1986–87, the League Cup acquired a new sponsor, Littlewoods, who lent their name to the competition and introduced a new trophy – though the trophy itself was far from new. The 98-year-old cup hailed from Cumbria, was originally called the Viscountess Furness Football Cup, and was contested by teams from local shipbuilding companies. Listed among the previous winners inscribed on the plinth was 'The Platers Helpers, 1923'. Appropriate, then, that one newspaper described the 1987 final between Arsenal and Liverpool (2-1) as 'riveting'.

Luton Town went nigh on three years without losing a League Cup tie. They did not enter the competition in 1986-87, won the cup in 1988 (3-2 v. Arsenal) and were defeated finalists in 1989 (1-3, Nottingham Forest).

In 1989–90, Sheffield Wednesday were held to a 0-0 draw by Aldershot at Hillsborough. In the second leg at the Recreation Ground, Wednesday thrashed Aldershot 8-0 – a record away victory for the League Cup.

The record for the most goals scored by an individual in a single League Cup tie is six, by Frankie Bunn for Oldham Athletic against Scarborough (third round, 1989–90).

Arsenal's Steve Morrow is the only player to have been injured at Wembley after a game. In 1993, Arsenal beat Sheffield Wednesday 2-1 to win the Coca Cola (League) Cup. At the end of the game, as the Arsenal players celebrated victory on the pitch, Morrow, scorer of the winning goal, was hoisted on to the shoulders of skipper Tony Adams but fell off and broke an arm.

Goalkeeper Chris Woods and full-back Viv Anderson played for Sheffield Wednesday in the 1993 final against Arsenal, 15 years after they had appeared for Nottingham Forest in the 1978 final against Liverpool.

In 1995–96, a Manchester United team containing David Beckham, Ryan Giggs, Denis Irwin, Lee Sharpe, Gary Pallister, Phil Neville, Brian McClair and Steve Bruce lost 3-0 at home to York City (second round first leg). One would imagine that was a 'hair-dryer' night in the United dressing room. United saved some face by winning the return 3-1 at Bootham Crescent, even if they did lose the tie 4-3 on aggregate.

In 1997–98, Ian Rush equalled Sir Geoff Hurst's record of 49 League Cup goals when the Welsh international scored in Newcastle United's 2-0 victory over Hull City. Rush also holds the record for having won the most League Cup winners medals (tankards still doesn't sound right, does it?) – five. He also shares the record, with Liverpool team-mate Kenny Dalglish, of having appeared in the most League Cup Finals – six.

The lowest attendance for a League Cup tie is 612, for Halifax Town v. Tranmere Rovers (first round second leg) on 6 September 2000. Having lost the first leg 3-0 at Tranmere, Halifax fans were seemingly resigned to the fact that their club was going out of the competition. They weren't wrong: Tranmere also won the second leg, 2-1.

The lowest recorded attendance for a tie played at a top-division ground is 1,987, for Wimbledon v. Bolton Wanderers (second round second leg) on 6 October 1992 – a surprisingly low turnout by the Dons fans given that their team had won the first leg 3-1. Bolton saved some face winning 1-0 at Plough Lane, but it was not good enough to win the tie.

The League Cup has assumed various names courtesy of sponsors. It was simply the League Cup from 1960 to 1981, but then the Milk Cup (1982–86), Littlewoods Cup (1987–90), Rumbelows Cup (1991–92), Coca-Cola Cup (1993–98), Worthington Cup (1999–2003), and the Carling Cup (2004 to present). What is it with the League Cup and drinks sponsors? Little wonder the trophy has three handles.

On 24 February 2002, the League Cup Final between Blackburn Rovers and Tottenham Hotspur at the Millennium Stadium created English football history by being the first major domestic cup final to take place under cover. The stadium's retractable roof was closed due to 'inclement weather' – or rain. And football is supposedly an outdoor game to be played in all weathers.

In 2001–02, Notts County goalkeeper Steve Mildenhall scored from his own half of the field with a free-kick against Mansfield Town at Field Mill (first round, 21 August). The score at the time was 3-3, and Mildenhall's long-range punt proved to be the winning goal. The embarrassed Mansfield keeper was Kevin Pilkington.

Manchester United manager Sir Alex Ferguson caused a sensation prior to United's 2005 semi-final second leg against Chelsea at Old Trafford by dropping Wayne Rooney to the substitutes bench. Rooney, who had played in the first leg, replaced Quinton Fortune in the second-half but could not prevent United losing 2-1 (after 0-0 at Stamford Bridge).

Having taken the lead after only 59 seconds of the 2005 final at the Millennium Stadium (fastest goal in a League Cup Final), Liverpool succumbed to Chelsea 3-2 in extra-time. Chelsea had Steven Gerrard to thank for the extra-time: the Liverpool skipper put through his own net after 79 minutes to gift Chelsea their equalizer.

35 It's easy to be a good manager. All you have to do is sign good players. You don't have to tell good players what to do, they know. The most difficult thing about being a good manager is signing the good players.

BOB STOKOE

Since their formation in 1900, West Ham United have only had one non-English manager, Lou Macari (Scottish), who remained at the club for just one season (1989–90). West Ham can also lay claim to having had the fewest managers: only eleven up to and including Alan Curbishley.

The longest-serving manager in English football is Fred Everiss, who led West Bromwich Albion for 46 years (1902 to 1948). Halfway through his lengthy appointment, Everiss began to manage players who had not been born when he was first appointed.

The youngest manager of a Football League club is Ivor Broadis, who was 23 years old when appointed player-manager of Carlisle United in August 1946.

Lure of the lire? In 1951–52, four top Italian clubs boasted English managers: Jes Carver (Juventus), Ted Crawford (Bologna), Denis Neville (Atalanta) and 'Frankie' Soo (Padova).

Bill Nicholson, himself a former Spurs player, was appointed manager of Tottenham Hotspur in 1958–59. In his first game in charge, Spurs beat Everton 10-4 – a case of 'over and in'.

Sir Alex Ferguson is the most successful British manager of all time. He is the only one to have won the treble of Premiership, FA Cup and European Champions Cup. His managerial career began at East Stirling (1974), and from there it reads St Mirren (1974–75), Aberdeen (1978–86 – also Scotland, 1981), Manchester United (1986 to present).

SIR ALEX FERGUSON'S TROPHY HAUL AS A MANAGER (TO 2008)

Aberdeen
Scottish Championship 1980, 1984, 1985
Scottish FA Cup 1982, 1983, 1984, 1986
Scottish League Cup 1986
European Cup Winners' Cup 1983
European Super Cup 1984

Manchester United
Premiership champions 1993, 1994, 1996, 1997, 1999, 2000, 2001, 2003, 2007, 2008
FA Cup 1990, 1994, 1996, 1999, 2004
League Cup 1992, 2006
Charity/Community Shield 1990, 1993, 1994, 1996, 1997, 2003, 2007
European Champions Cup 1999, 2008
European Cup Winners' Cup 1991
European Super Cup 1992

FA Premiership Manager of the Year 1994, 1996, 1997, 1999, 2000, 2003, 2007, 2008
League Managers Association Manager of the Year 1999
League Managers Association Manager of the Decade – 1990s

Sir Alex Ferguson's 1,000th game as manager of Manchester United was against Lyon in the Champions League on 23 November 2004.

Jock Stein is the most successful manager in Scottish football. Having cut his managerial teeth at Dunfermline and Hibernian, he was appointed manager of Celtic in 1965. Between 1966 and 1977, under Stein, Celtic won the European Cup (1967), the Scottish League Championship ten times, the Scottish Cup on eight occasions and the Scottish League Cup six times.

Hear the one about the Englishman, Irishman, Scotsman and Welshman? They were successive managers at Queens Park Rangers: Archie Mitchell (English, 1931–33), Mick O'Brien (Irish, 1933–35), Billy Birrell (Scottish, 1935–39) and Ted Vizard (Welsh, 1939–44).

Joe Smith [Blackpool] was a very good manager with great man-management skills. All the Blackpool players had implicit belief in everything Joe said. If he'd told us to 'Go to hell' we would have actually looked forward to the journey.
STANLEY MATTHEWS

Alf Ramsey's first match as manager of England on 27 February 1962 ended in a 5-2 defeat by France in Paris. To compound Ramsey's misery his luggage was lost in transit, and for the duration of the trip the new England boss had to wear the clothes he had on when the England party left Heathrow.

In 1968–69, Tommy Docherty managed three clubs in six weeks. On 6 November the Doc resigned as manager of Rotherham United to become manager of Queens Park Rangers. He left Rangers after four weeks following a disagreement with chairman Jim Gregory, and on 18 December was appointed manager of Aston Villa.

Bob Paisley was associated with Liverpool as a player, coach, manager and director for over 50 years. In nine years as manager of Liverpool, between 1974 and 1983, he won six League Championships, three European Cups, one UEFA Cup, three League Cups, five Charity Shields, and the European Super Cup. No other British manager has won the European Cup three times. He was also voted Manager of the Year in 1976, 1977, 1979, 1980, 1982 and 1983.

Bob Stokoe is unique in Football League management in that he managed five clubs twice: Bury (1961–65 and 1977–78), Blackpool (1970–72 and 1978–79), Carlisle United (1968–70 and 1980–85), Rochdale (1967–68 and 1979–80) and Sunderland (1972–76 and 1987 as caretaker manager following the dismissal of Lawrie McMenemy). He was also manager of Charlton Athletic (1965–67).

Dario Gradi was appointed manager of Crewe Alexandra in 1983 and was, up to 2007, British senior football's longest-serving manager. In July 2007, he became technical director at Crewe, Steve Holland assuming the role of first-team coach. Neil Baker has been assistant manager at Crewe Alexandra since 1992. Dario Gradi never played League football; he played non-league football, for Sutton United, Tooting and Mitcham, and Wimbledon.

Arsène Wenger is Arsenal's longest-serving manager in terms of matches and the club's most successful manager in terms of trophies won. He is the only non-British manager to have won the double of Premiership and FA Cup, and he achieved this with Arsenal on two occasions (1998 and 2001). In 2003–04, he guided Arsenal to an unbeaten season in the Premiership.

AS Monaco
Ligue 1 Champions 1988, 1990
Coupe de France 1989, 1990, 19901

Grampus Eight (Japan)
J-League Super Cup 1996
Emperor's Cup 1996

Arsenal
Premiership champions 1998, 2002, 2004
FA Cup 1998, 2002, 2003, 2005
Community Shield 1998, 1999, 2002, 2004

Manager of the Year 1998, 2002, 2004

35 Norman Dodgin once signed a player for two different clubs only for the player not to play a single game under him. In the summer of 1957, Dodgin was manager of Yeovil Town and signed Andy Torrance from junior football. Before the 1957–58 season started, however, Dodgin was appointed manager of Barrow. During 1957–58, Dodgin made several attempts to sign Torrance from Yeovil and eventually landed his man a few weeks before the end of the season. Days after signing Torrance, Dodgin left Barrow when offered the manager's job at Oldham Athletic.

 I always tell the players things will happen in matches, and I'm not wrong. Things happened in that match today.
RON ATKINSON

In November 1970, Billy Lucas was appointed manager of Newport County for a fifth time – for the third time as the club's full-time manager, and he'd also managed the club twice on a caretaker basis.

When Arsenal won the League and cup double in 1971, the Gunners' manager was Bertie Mee who had been on the books of Derby County in the late 1930s but whose playing career was cut short due to injury which resulted in him never establishing himself in the Derby first team. Mee became a qualified physiotherapist, a position he had held at Highbury for six years prior to being appointed manager.

On 2 December 1972, Bob Stokoe was appointed manager of Sunderland when the club was third from bottom in Division Two. Stokoe signed only three new players (Ron Guthrie and David Young from Newcastle United, and Vic Halom from Luton Town) but Sunderland revived to finish sixth in Division Two and win the FA Cup, beating Leeds United 1-0 at Wembley.

 José Mourinho says no one in this country likes him, which is not true. Not everyone in this country has met him yet.

TOMMY SMITH

In 1972–73, the Welsh FA fined Cardiff City manager Jimmy Scoular £50 for having handed the referee of his team's match against Bristol City an optician's advert from the local newspaper as he left the pitch.

Jimmy Sirrell managed two Football League clubs at the same time. In 1975, he was manager of Notts County when he accepted the role of manager of Sheffield United. The two clubs agreed Sirrell would continue to manage both until County found a replacement, which they did in Ron Fenton, four weeks later. The only other instance of this occurring is the case of David Steele, who left Bradford City to become manager of Huddersfield Town in September 1943, his departure coinciding with that of City manager Fred Westgarth. In addition to his new role at Huddersfield, Steele also fulfilled the managerial duties at Bradford City for three weeks until the club appointed Bob Sharp. Steele returned to Bradford City as their full-time manager from 1948 to 1952.

Alan Ball senior (father of the England World Cup winner) also managed two clubs simultaneously in the mid-1960s. Ball was manager of Cheshire League clubs Oswestry Town and Nantwich Town. When the clubs played each other, he assumed charge of the team that was playing at home.

If we can play like that every week, we'll achieve some level of consistency.

SIR ALEX FERGUSON

It isn't often the supporters of Sheffield United and Sheffield Wednesday unite behind a common cause, but they did when Derek Dooley (who'd had a leg amputated following an injury sustained when playing for Wednesday against Preston North End in 1953) was sacked as manager of Wednesday in 1977. Both sets of supporters were outraged by the timing of Dooley's dismissal – on Christmas Eve. Dooley was subsequently offered a job in United's commercial department and was their chief executive.

As a full-back with Leeds United in the 1960s, Willie Bell gained a reputation for successfully converting penalties. In 1978, he resigned as manager of Lincoln City to join the Campus Crusade for Christ in the USA where his remit was to convert sportspeople to Christianity.

People talk about England playing every match at Wembley in 1966, but that wasn't greatly to our advantage. Winning the World Cup involves much more than simply being able to play matches at Wembley. Winning the World Cup is very, very hard to do, as future England managers will discover.

SIR ALF RAMSEY, in 1974

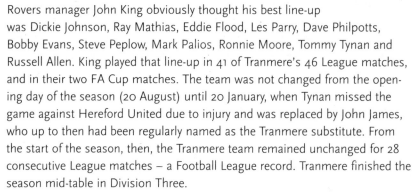

ALF RAMSEY

They say a manager should know what his best team is. In 1977–78, Tranmere Rovers manager John King obviously thought his best line-up was Dickie Johnson, Ray Mathias, Eddie Flood, Les Parry, Dave Philpotts, Bobby Evans, Steve Peplow, Mark Palios, Ronnie Moore, Tommy Tynan and Russell Allen. King played that line-up in 41 of Tranmere's 46 League matches, and in their two FA Cup matches. The team was not changed from the opening day of the season (20 August) until 20 January, when Tynan missed the game against Hereford United due to injury and was replaced by John James, who up to then had been regularly named as the Tranmere substitute. From the start of the season, then, the Tranmere team remained unchanged for 28 consecutive League matches – a Football League record. Tranmere finished the season mid-table in Division Three.

What I said to them at half-time would be unprintable on radio.

GERRY FRANCIS

On 18 August 1980, Steve Murray was appointed manager of Forfar Athletic. Three days later, he tendered his resignation. Two days after that the players were informed of Murray's decision, and his departure was revealed to the press on the 24th. As one Forfar official explained, 'The press were not informed immediately of Steve Murray's resignation as we felt a manager leaving after only three days would reflect badly on the club.'

Malcolm Allison holds the British record for having managed and coached the most clubs during the course of a career. 'Big Mal' began his career coaching at non-league Sutton United; he then went on to manage Wembley, Bath City, Plymouth Argyle (twice), Manchester City (once as coach, twice as manager), Crystal Palace (twice), Galatasaray, Memphis Rogues (though he never took charge of a game), Sporting Lisbon, Middlesbrough, Willington (Northern League), Turkey, Kuwait, Vitoria Setúbal, Farense and Fisher Athletic. Eventually he became director of football at Bristol Rovers.

On 5 November 1990, in an extra-preliminary round tie of the Leyland DAF Cup (how important does that sound?) between Halifax Town and Rotherham United, the referee ordered Rotherham manager Billy McEwan from the dugout for dissent. Rather than take a seat in the stand, McEwan went and stood with the visiting Rotherham fans on the terraces.

In 1993, Malcolm Crosby was sacked as Sunderland manager the day after the pools panel adjudged his side would have lost their postponed match at Tranmere Rovers.

 When clubs have money they send for Ron Atkinson. When they are skint they send for Dave Bassett or me.

DON MACKAY

In July 2007, Leroy Rosenior received a telephone call informing him of his appointment as manager of Torquay United for a second time. Two hours later he received news that the club had been taken over and the new owners no longer required his services.

Given that Rosenior's appointment as manager at Torquay United was never made official, the shortest term of any League manager is three days: Bill Lambton (Scunthorpe United) in April 1959, albeit in 2007–08 Leicester City made a gallant effort to beat this record. From April 2007 to May 2008, Leicester had ten managers: Rob Kelly, Nigel Worthingon (caretaker), Martin Allen, Jon Rudkin, Steve Beaglehole and Mike Stowell (caretakers), Gary Megson, Frank Burrows and Gerry Taggart (caretakers), and Ian Holloway. As Liverpool legend Tommy Smith quipped, 'To qualify for the Manager of the Month Award, Leicester first have to keep a manager for a month.'

Managers who were appointed and gone within a fortnight: Steve Murray (Forfar Athletic), three days in August 1988; Tim Ward (Exeter City), seven days in March 1953; Kevin Cullis (Swansea City), seven days in February 1996; Dave Cowling (Doncaster Rovers), ten days in October 1997; Peter Cormack (Cowdenbeath), ten days in December 2000; Johnny Cochrane (Reading), 13 days in April 1939; Micky Adams (Swansea City), 13 days in October 1997.

Steve Coppell was appointed manager of Manchester City in November 1996 and resigned 32 days later.

Sammy Chung left Doncaster Rovers on the morning of the opening day of the 1996–97 season.

Neil McDonald lost his job as manager of Carlisle United after the first match of 2007–08.

Glenn Roeder was dismissed as manager of West Ham United after only 15 days of 2003–04.

In 1993, Peter Reid was dismissed as manager of Manchester City after only 12 days of the 1993–94 season. Three years later, City sacked manager Alan Ball after only 12 days of 1996–97.

The last Englishman to win the League Championship was Howard Wilkinson with Leeds United in 1991–92, the last season of the Football League in its old format. No English manager has ever won the Premiership.

It looks as if I'm trying to stab Dave Bassett in the back, but I'm not holding a gun to anybody's head.

MICKY ADAMS

Tom Whittaker enjoyed a good start as manager of Arsenal in 1947–48: the Gunners remained unbeaten for their first 17 League matches – a record for a new manager at a club.

Four managers have won the League Championship with different clubs: Tom Watson with Sunderland (1892, 1893, 1895) and Liverpool (1901); Herbert Chapman with Huddersfield Town (1924, 1925, and Arsenal (1931, 1933); Brian Clough with Derby County (1972) and Nottingham Forest (1978); and Kenny Dalglish with Liverpool (1986, 1988, 1990) and Blackburn Rovers (1995).

Bill Walker won the FA Cup as manager of Sheffield Wednesday in 1935 and again as manager of Nottingham Forest in 1959. Herbert Chapman had previously achieved this feat with Huddersfield Town (1922) and Arsenal (1930).

I knew I wasn't going to last long as manager of Preston. On my first day my name was written on the manager's door in chalk . . . and hanging from the door was a sponge.

JOHN McGRATH

The first player-manager in top-flight English football was Les Allen with Queens Park Rangers (First Division) in 1968–69.

Trevor Francis is the only man to have been a player-manager with two clubs in top-flight English football: Queens Park Rangers (1988–89) and Sheffield Wednesday (1991–94).

The first overseas manager to win a major trophy in English football was Ruud Gullit, who won the FA Cup with Chelsea in 1997.

Who would want to become a football manager? Well, people like me who are too old to play, too poor to be a director, and too much in love with the game to be an agent.

STEVE COPPELL

In October 1998, Tottenham Hotspur paid Leeds United £3 million in compensation for manager George Graham.

It was alleged that David O'Leary received £3.7 million compensation from Leeds United when he left the club in June 2002.

When David O'Leary received his pay-off from Leeds United the cheque didn't bounce, the club did.

TOMMY DOCHERTY

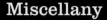

36 Ten 'Celebs' who had Trials With or Were Connected as Players to Clubs

Paul Boardman (Torquay United)
Boris Becker (Bayern Munich)
David Essex (Leyton Orient)
Mike Gatting (Arsenal)
Julio Iglesias (Real Madrid)
Eddie Large (Manchester City)
Des O'Connor (Northampton Town)
Gordon Ramsay (Rangers)
Dr Robert (Blow Monkeys) (Norwich City)
Rod Stewart (Brentford)

Their Jobs Before Becoming Footballers

Vinnie Jones (hod carrier)
Steve Archibald (car mechanic)
Cyrille Regis (builder)
Gordon Banks (hod carrier)

Chris Waddle (sausage maker)
Alan Pardew (window fitter)
Ian Wright (builder)
Kerry Dixon (tool maker)
Steve Bull (warehouseman)
Gérard Houllier (teacher)

Aptly Named Players

Alan Knill (Rotherham United)
Peter Skipper (Wigan)
Nicky Marker (Plymouth)
Kevin Ball (Sunderland)
Gary Speed (Bolton)
Greg Fee (Mansfield)
Nicky Cross (WBA)
David Corner (Sunderland)
Keith Curle (Manchester City)
Lee Sharpe (Manchester United)

A Quick Football Team

Ian Rush (Liverpool)
David Speedie (Chelsea)
Gary Speed (Bolton)
Ray Train (Bolton)
Derek Pace (Sheffield United)
Franz Carr (Nottingham Forest)
Jason Rockett (Scarborough)

Stuart Ryder (Walsall)
Chris Lightfoot (Chester)
Arthur Lightning (Coventry)
Danny Bolt (Fulham)
Phil Driver (Chelsea)

A Team for Monty Don

Tim Flowers (Blackburn)
Mike Rose (Charlton)
Paul Lemon (Sunderland)
Dennis Viollet (Manchester United)
Andy Thorn (Wimbledon)
Rodney Fern (Leicester City)
Jimmy Seed (Charlton)
Ian Plant (Hull City)
Rodney Marsh (QPR)
Graham Branch (Tranmere)
Michael Oakes (Cardiff)

Ten Great Fanzine Titles

The Absolute Game (Scotland – from Skids track of same title)
And Smith Must Score! (Brighton and Hove Albion)
Brian Moore's Head (Gillingham – from Half Man Half Biscuit track of same title, the next line of which is 'Looks uncannily like the London Planetarium')
Dial 'M' for Merthyr (Merthyr Tydfil)
Elm Park Disease (Reading)
There's Only One 'F' in Fulham (Fulham, natch)
They Hang Monkeys Don't They? (Hartlepool United)
Memoirs of Seth Bottomley (Port Vale)
Sing When We're Fishing (Grimsby Town)
When Sunday Comes (Liverpool – ironic reaction to frequency of Sunday games for Liverpool)

In 1910–11, local butcher Duncan McPhail offered a live lamb to each Morton player who scored a goal (perhaps thinking that would bring supporters flocking back to Cappielow). Centre-forward Tommy Gracie was seemingly a little sheepish about it all: he didn't have the heart to have his slaughtered and butchered, so he kept it in a field near his home.

In 1972–73, Hillsborough was the neutral venue for Arsenal's FA Cup semi-final. They paid Sheffield Wednesday £30,000 for tickets prior to the match in order to beat VAT, which came into effect on 1 April.

In 1979–80, Nottingham Forest made a profit of £1,258,000 whereas Manchester City announced a loss of £1,663,000 – the first instance of First Division clubs producing a seven-figure profit and a seven-figure loss.

It takes the biscuit. During 1981–82, Reading were so strapped for cash that as an economy measure the club announced that referees and linesmen officiating at games at Elm Park would no longer receive biscuits with their half-time cup of tea. Reading's nickname? The Biscuitmen.

Not so senior service. On 2 September 1985, Trevor Senior scored a hat-trick in Reading's 3-1 win against Cardiff City at Ninian Park – part of a record-breaking run of 13 consecutive victories Reading enjoyed from the start of the season. Senior, as was the tradition, expected to be presented with the match ball in recognition of his feat, but Cardiff said he could only have it if he agreed to pay the club the £40 it cost them to buy it.

On 11 October 1989, Michael Knighton failed in his bid to acquire Manchester United in a £20 million takeover deal. Previously, when it seemed the deal would go through, Knighton (a former Coventry City apprentice) had appeared on the Old Trafford pitch prior to a League game in a United strip juggling a football.

In 1991, when First Division clubs were discussing forming a breakaway league, a study compiled by Dr Simon Pitt entitled *The Bankrupting of English Football* claimed that Football League clubs had a collective debt of £130 million. Pitt blamed the perilous financial state of the game in England on 'the spiralling cost of players' wages, signing-on fees and transfer fees, allied to a significant drop in spectator interest and, as such, revenue in the past decade'.

In 1998–99, FA chief executive Graham Kelly resigned following allegations that the FA of Wales had been promised a loan of £2 million by the English FA in return for voting for FA chairman Keith Wiseman to become vice-president of FIFA. Mr Wiseman refused to resign amid allegations that the loan had been sanctioned without consultation with other senior FA officials.

On 9 April 1999, Trade and Industry Secretary Stephen Byers and the Mergers and Monopolies Commission blocked BSkyB's £623 million bid to buy out Manchester United. The United board had accepted the offer from Mr Murdoch's company, so the blocking of the deal was reported as 'a victory for the little man which will ensure one of the most famous football clubs in the world remains in British ownership'. No one was reported to have added, 'Watch this space.'

In 2000, ITV outbid the BBC with an £183 million deal to broadcast high-lights of Premiership matches on a Saturday night. It meant an end to *Match of the Day*, though only temporarily, as things turned out.

In 2002–03 the Football League failed in their claim for £131.9 million against Carlton and Granada, parent companies of the ill-fated ITV Digital which had a deal to broadcast 'live' Football League matches on a pay-per-view basis. ITV Digital collapsed following insufficient audience figures, though why viewers did not rush to sign up to watch Grimsby Town v. Bradford City was seemingly a mystery to some ITV Digital executives. The loss of revenue brought increased financial hardship to several League clubs that had already budgeted for the money promised by the ITV Digital deal.

In January 2007, the Premier League negotiated a three-year deal worth £600 million for overseas TV rights to games, and another deal with Sky and Setanta worth £1.76 billion to screen matches in Great Britain and Ireland. The Premier League also has a deal with internet and mobile phone companies that is worth £400 million.

Premiership clubs share £900 million a season from broadcasting rights in a deal that runs to 2010.

Admission prices to Premiership matches are the highest of any top league in Europe.

The best-supported league in the world is the Bundesliga; average attendance in 2006–07 was 40,102. Adult supporters can gain admission to Bundesliga matches for 15 euros (around £10), and there are thousands of tickets like these available every weekend.

In 2007–08, adults could buy tickets for VfB Stuttgart (2007 Bundesliga champions) home matches for 23 euros (around £15).

In 2003–04, Russian oil billionaire Roman Abramovich acquired control of Chelsea for a reported £150 million – a drop in the ocean compared to what he would subsequently spend on transfer fees and wages.

When Stoke City directors Peter Coates and Keith Humphreys sold the club to an Icelandic consortium in 1999-2000, the pair negotiated a deal that ensured they would remain directors of the club for life – the only directors to enjoy such security in the history of English football.

The record damages awarded to a player for injuries incurred during the course of a game is £909,143, awarded by a High Court judge at Newcastle Crown Court to Gordon Watson of Bradford City who sustained a double break to his right leg as the result of a challenge by Huddersfield Town's Kevin Gray on 1 February 1997.

In May 1993, Ladbrokes paid out £654,375 to Jim Wright from Devon who, pre-season, placed a £1,000 each-way fixed-odds bet on the eventual winners of each of the three divisions of the Football League: Newcastle United (8-1), Stoke City (6-1) and Cardiff City (9-1).

Many players have lent their names to advertising products, particularly those of kit manufacturers. Pre-war, 'Dixie' Dean (Everton) promoted Craven A cigarettes. In the late 1940s, Denis Compton (Arsenal and England) was the face – or rather head – of Brylcreem. Other players who have lent their name/image to advertising non-football-related products include Alan Ball (Bisto); George Best (eggs, male hair products, catalogue male fashions); Brian Clough, Jack Charlton, Glenn Hoddle, Paul Gascoigne (Shredded Wheat); Kenny Dalglish (BT, *Yellow Pages*); Tommy Docherty, Steve Coppell, Gordon Hill (Gillette razors); Les Ferdinand (Horlicks); Andy Gray (Snickers bars); Jimmy Greaves (Bovril); Ryan Giggs (Konica films, Quorn burgers); David Ginola (L'Oréal hair products, Renault); Pat Jennings (Solvite); Kevin Keegan (Brut cologne); Gary Lineker (Walkers crisps, Shredded Wheat); Jason McAteer (Wash 'n' Go shampoo); Ally McCoist (Vauxhall); Michael Owen (Walkers crisps); Stuart Pearce (Raleigh bicycles); Stuart Pearce, Gareth Southgate, Chris Waddle (Pizza Hut); Peter Schmeichel (Danish bacon); Alan Shearer (McDonald's, Lucozade); Graham Taylor (Vauxhall); Ray Wilkins (Tango); and Ian Wright (One 2 One, Thomas Cook).

David Beckham has promoted numerous products (he once had a £1 million deal with Pepsi) but now concentrates on his own ranges.

PLAYERS WHO DIDN'T PROMOTE THESE PRODUCTS BUT SHOULD HAVE!

Gordon Banks – Barclays
Dave Bassett – Liquorice Allsorts
Colin Bell – whisky
Mark Bright – Stain Devils
Ian Bowyer – sausages
Jimmy Case – luggage
Perry Digweed – garden forks
Kerry Dixon – electrical goods
Paul Gascoigne – gas meters
Ryan Giggs – rock concerts
Glenn Hoddle – whisky
Paul Parker – pens
Paul Robinson – squash drinks
David Seaman – cross-Channel ferries
Nicky Summerbee – honey
John Terry – plain chocolates
Howard Wilkinson – razors

In December 1994, Tottenham Hotspur were fined a record £1,500,000 for financial irregularities committed in the 1980s which involved making illegal loans to players. Spurs were also barred from the 1994–95 FA Cup and given a six-point penalty in the Premiership.

Sponsorship brings much-needed revenue to the game, particularly major competitions. How easily we forget? Past sponsors of the Football League: Canon (1983–86), *Today* newspaper (1986–87), Barclays (1987–93), Endsleigh Insurance (1993–96), Nationwide (1996–2004), Coca Cola (2004 – ongoing); Premiership – Carling, Barclaycard and Barclays.

In the past, individual clubs were at liberty to set their own admission charges, but in 1939 a minimum adult admission price was laid down by the Football League and FA of one shilling (5p). In 1946 it was increased to 1s 3d (6p); in 1951 it was set at 1s 6d (7.5p); 1952 saw another rise to 1s 9d (8.5p); in 1955 it went up to 2 shillings (10p); in 1960 to 2s 6d (12.5p); in 1965 to 4s (20p); in 1968 to 5s

(25p); in 1970 to 6s (30p); and in 1972 to 40p. In 1974–75, the fixed minimum admission price was abolished and clubs were once again free to set their own.

HOW FIRST DIVISION CLUBS WERE FARING FINANCIALLY IN 1960–61 WHEN THE PFA BEGAN ITS CAMPAIGN TO ABOLISH THE MAXIMUM WAGE

Club	Profit	Loss	Supporters' donation
Arsenal	£32,000	–	–
Aston Villa	–	£15,800	–
Birmingham	£300	–	–
Blackburn	£31,600	–	£4,500
Blackpool	£4,900	–	–
Bolton	£4,200	–	–
Burnley	£13,600	–	–
Cardiff	£8,100	–	–
Chelsea	£200	–	–
Everton	–	£49,500	–
Fulham	£1,118	–	–
Ipswich	£1,150	–	£12,700
Leicester	£3,300	–	–
Man City	£781	–	–
Man Utd	£29,700	–	–
Nottm Forest	–	£13,600	–
Sheff United	–	£11,200	–
Sheff Wed	£24,100	–	£1,000
Spurs	£23,000	–	–
West Brom	£33,800	–	–
West Ham	£150	–	–
Wolves	£77,500	–	–

NB: Everton recorded by far the biggest loss yet were the third best-supported team at the time.

In 1961, only six clubs in Division Two made a profit: Brighton (£3,100), Derby (£75), Huddersfield (£58,300), Luton Town (£40,200), Preston (£7,300) and Rotherham United (£4,700). The biggest loss was incurred by Bury (£25,700).

In Division Three, only four clubs made a profit: Bournemouth (£3,000), Peterborough United (£200), Shrewsbury Town (£15,500) and Torquay United (£700). The biggest loss was incurred by Hull City (£14,300).

In Division Four, seven clubs reported a profit: Carlisle United (£1,500), Colchester United (£579), Gillingham (£150), Stockport County (£800), Workington (£4,500), Wrexham (£8,500) and York City (£2,200). The biggest loss was incurred by Millwall (£15,800).

Compare that to now. In the summer of 2007, Deloitte published the annual review of football finances (2005–06 figures). Arsenal recorded a loss of £6.2 million (the club attributed this to the move to the Emirates Stadium), but Chelsea recorded a loss of £80 million. Premiership wages passed the £850 million mark for the first time (£854 million). Chelsea spent £114 million on wages, Manchester United £85 million, Arsenal £83 million and Liverpool £69 million. The 20 Premiership clubs collectively earned £1.4 billion. It was estimated this would rise to £1.8 billion in 2007–08. Manchester United revenue was £167.7 million, Chelsea £152.8 million, Arsenal £133 million and Liverpool £120 million. Only nine Premiership clubs reported a pre-tax profit.

In September 2007, the Glazer family refuted claims that Manchester United's debts totalled £700 million, though it was alleged at the time that the Glazer takeover saddled the club with debts in the region of £600 million.

In 1983, David Dein paid £295,000 for his shares in Arsenal. In September 2007, it was reported that he sold them for nigh on £60 million.

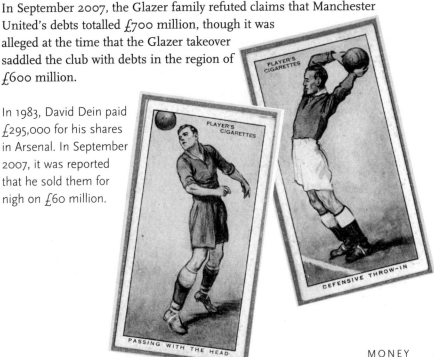

38 The referee's authority is governed by the laws of the game which, strictly speaking, apply when he/she enters the field of play. One of the laws dictates that 'The referee's decision is final' – a phrase often used by players, managers and pundits.

The International FA Board decreed that referees are not liable for injuries incurred by players, officials or spectators during the course of a game. Generally, though, referees will postpone or abandon a game if they think conditions are such that they will make play hazardous, or put players at increased risk of injury.

In the early days of football, games were refereed by two umpires, one in each half of the field, carrying a stick to indicate in which direction a free-kick had been awarded. If a player was not deemed to be behaving like a gentleman the umpire would refer the matter to his team-mates, who would decide whether or not the player should stay on the field – hence the origin of the term 'ungentlemanly conduct'.

The first referee of an FA Cup Final was Alfred Stair in 1872. The first referee of an FA Cup Final at Wembley was Mr. D. H. Aston, in 1923.

The first time a referee used a whistle was in 1878 during a friendly match between Nottingham Forest and Sheffield Norfolk. Prior to this all referees had only used hand signals – a method since adopted by many a supporter when wanting to communicate an opinion to a referee.

In 1879, the FA sanctioned the use of whistles by referees. They were made for the FA by Joseph Hudson of the Acme Whistle Company in London.

The last referee to officiate at more than one FA Cup Final was Mr A. Kingscott, in 1900 and 1901. The FA then decreed that match officials were only to be allowed to referee an FA Cup Final once.

The FA Cup Final referee was given the option of a match fee or a souvenir medal. No referee ever accepted the match fee until the rule was changed in 1978 to provide him with both.

The only occasion when two vicars officiated at the same Football League match was the Second Division game between West Bromwich Albion and Blackpool in December 1910. The referee was the Right Reverend J. Marsh; one of his linesmen was the Right Reverend W. Strange.

On 14 March 1936, one of the linesmen did not turn up for the game between Bradford City and Doncaster Rovers (Third Division North). George Flowers, who had travelled with the Doncaster party, a qualified referee, stepped into the breach and ran the line. Flowers is father to Ron Flowers (Wolves and England) and grandfather of former goalkeeper Tim Flowers (Southampton, Blackburn and England).

The name game. Arthur Bookim was a League referee from 1951 to 1957. Also in the 1950s, the Scottish League had a referee whose name was Charlie Faultless.

One of the most highly respected referees of the 1950s and 1960s was Arthur Ellis who later sat as a member of the pools panel and co-hosted the BBC series *It's a Knockout.*

Double Dutch. Arthur Holland (Barnsley) was the first referee to officiate at two major English domestic Cup finals, the League Cup first leg in 1964 and the 1964 FA Cup. And a good job he did too.

On 26 September 1970, during the First Division match between Chelsea and Ipswich Town at Stamford Bridge, a shot from Chelsea's Alan Hudson hit the stanchion on the outside of the Ipswich goal and the ball rebounded back into the penalty area. Referee Roy Capey thought the ball had hit the stanchion in the back of the net and awarded a goal.

In 1972–73, TV commentator Jimmy Hill (a qualified referee) took over the line during Arsenal's game against Liverpool following an injury to Mike Hunt. The announcer on the Highbury public address system that day was female, so one hopes she didn't mention the injured linesman by name.

Pat Partridge (Middlesbrough) received 42p for refereeing the 1974 FA Cup Final between Liverpool and Newcastle United. Partridge stayed at the Great Western Hotel. Though he had only been booked in for two nights by the FA, Partridge stayed an extra night at the hotel in order to attend the FWA Footballer of the Year Award annual dinner and charged this to the FA. The FA refused to foot the bill for the additional night of accommodation but deducted the sum from the fee Partridge was to receive for officiating in the FA Cup Final. His fee for the Final was £15.95, the extra night's accommodation cost £15.53, thus Partridge was sent a payment of 42p.

In 1978, Elizabeth Forsdick became the first woman to officiate at an FA Cup tie (preliminary round) as an assistant referee.

When Bobby Robson was manager of Ipswich Town (1969–82) he bid £10,000 for non-league Hertford Town's goalkeeper. Hertford turned down the bid as they believed it was far too low. The goalkeeper in question was Mark Halsey, later to become a top Premiership/League referee.

Kim George was the first woman to referee an FA Cup match, a preliminary round tie in 1989.

The fourth official was introduced in 1991. In 1966, referee and administrator Ken Aston had his idea for a named replacement official accepted by the game's governing bodies, but it was not compulsory.

In 1991–92, FIFA legislated that all referees of international matches must be able to speak English to 'conversational level'.

Up to 1954 most referees wore blazers. After that, during a period when football was subject to much change, particularly regarding innovations in kit, referees adopted jerseys for matches. Traditionally, the uniform of match officials was always black. No British club wore all-black shirts so there would never be a colour clash.

With the formation of the Premiership in 1992-93, referees adopted green jerseys as opposed to the traditional black shirt and shorts to help distinguish the Premiership from the Football League.

For the 1994 World Cup, match officials were given the option of wearing burgundy, yellow or white jerseys. This is still a FIFA-approved option.

How long does it take from refereeing your first parks game to taking charge of a League match? On 12 August 1995, former Chesterfield player Steve Baines took charge of Rochdale versus Cardiff City (3-3) exactly six years after taking up the whistle – a record for the elevation of a referee.

Wendy Toms was the first woman to referee a senior League match in England. On 31 August 1996, she took charge of the Conference League match between Woking and Telford United.

Linda Bailey, Karen Ford and Anne Smith created football history when they became the first women to fulfil all three officials' positions in an FA-affiliated competitive match, Broomfield United v. Kent University, on 26 October 1996 (Kent County League).

In 1998, the term 'linesman' was replaced by 'referee's assistant' to better reflect the role of these officials, and to be non-gender specific.

In 1999–2000, Premiership referees were linked to their assistants by means of two-way radios to enable what the Premiership described as 'swifter and better communication'.

> Some people will be pro the referee, and certain people will be for him, but you're always going to have that in football.

TERRY VENABLES

The common view is that the highest honour that can be bestowed upon match officials is to be chosen to officiate at an FA Cup Final. The schedule for match officials is steeped in tradition. They attend an 'Eve of Final' dinner held at the Russell Hotel in London, where they are the guests of honour of the Referees Association, then stay for the night at White's Hotel. FA protocol is such that they are not allowed to overnight anywhere else, though David Elleray broke with tradition by returning on the Friday night to his rooms at Harrow School for 'a good night's sleep'. On the morning of the final it is tradition for the match officials to take a walk in Hyde Park. (One supposes this posed a problem when the FA Cup Final was temporarily staged at the Millennium Stadium.) They are then taken by car to Wembley, where again tradition dictates that during a pre-match reception they autograph the official copy of the match programme.

Only one referee has withdrawn from FA Cup Final duties on the grounds of 'possible partiality'. In 2006, Mike Dean offered to sit out the final involving Liverpool when the press pointed out that he lived on the Wirral. Dean was replaced by Alan Wiley.

At 19, Michael Oliver became the youngest match official ever in the history of the Football League.

In 2004, Clive and Michael Oliver became the first father and son to officiate in the Football League in the same season. Clive was a referee, Michael an assistant referee.

In 2002, the Premier League announced plans for full-time professional referees.

Referee Mark Halsey red-carded Jimmy Floyd Hasselbaink for lashing out at Teddy Sheringham during the Football League Cup semi-final between Spurs and Chelsea in 2002. Unfortunately, Hasselbaink was not the culprit; it was Mario Melchiot. Hasselbaink was subsequently exonerated through video evidence.

During the 2006 World Cup Finals, FIFA assigned five match officials to each game. The role of the fifth official was to stand by to replace the fourth official and assume his/her duties should a designated match official be injured and have to be replaced by the fourth official – and that was official!

In 2007, there were 210 women on the official FIFA-recognized list of referees.

That said, I know referees don't come here with a particularly flavoured shirt on.
STEVE COPPELL

Indirect free kick   Advantage   Substitution   Offside   Throw-in

Direct free kick

Caution   Sending Off   Offside on the near side of the field   Offside in the centre of the field   Offside on the far side of the field

In 2008, in addition to travel expenses, the FA Cup Final referee received a match fee of £525, referee's assistants £300, and the fourth official £225. All officials also took home a commemorative medal.

One of the most highly regarded and respected referees among players was Keith Hackett, who at 36 became one of the youngest men to take charge of an FA Cup Final (Manchester City v. Tottenham, 1981). Mr Hackett was so highly thought of he continued refereeing after the prescribed retirement age of 45, which allowed him to take up duties for in the inaugural season of the Premiership (1992–93). Again, he proved so popular with managers and players that a further extension was afforded. Mr Hackett continued to referee in the Premiership until 1994 when of his own volition he retired, at the age of 50. He is now general manager of Professional Game Match Officials Limited.

The only referee to bear the names of a famous pop duet/group is Phillip Don, as in Phil and Don Everly. This is no coincidence. Mr Don senior was a big Everly Brothers fan, and following the birth of his son he persuaded Mrs Don that their son should be named Phil.

I played full-back in rugby union, wicket-keeper in cricket and goalkeeper in football, the positions in which you stand out. On reflection, refereeing is a bit like that. We're very much loners.

PHILLIP DON

In a Second Division match between Manchester United and Oldham Athletic in 1923–24, Oldham's Sam Wynne scored four goals, two for each team. He scored from a penalty and a direct free-kick for Oldham and also netted two own-goals for United. Oldham won 3-2.

In 1934–35, Middlesbrough defender Bob Stuart scored five own-goals. He also put through his own net twice when playing for Middlesbrough reserves.

On Boxing Day 1952, three Sheffield Wednesday players scored own-goals in Wednesday's match at home to West Bromwich Albion. The unfortunate trio were Norman Curtis, Vince Kenny and Eddie Gannon. West Brom went on to win 5-4.

Christmas presents. On Christmas Day 1954, George Underwood, Kenny Boyle and Danny Murphy of Rochdale all scored own-goals in their team's 7-2 defeat at Carlisle United (Third Division North).

There is definitely something about the festive period and the scoring of own-goals. On 18 December 1954, Leicester defenders Stan Milburn and Jack Froggatt touched the ball simultaneously to put through their own net against Chelsea. It provided a unique moment in English football: both players were credited with 'half an own-goal' each.

On 17 December 1955, Arsenal led Blackpool 4-0 at Highbury when a whistle was blown in the crowd. Thinking this was the full-time whistle, Arsenal left-back Dennis Evans, who had possession of the ball, turned and kicked it into his own net. The referee had no alternative but to award the goal.

Defenders should have told them to remain upfield! On 14 May 1955, England and Scotland schoolboys drew 2-2 at Goodison Park. Both Scotland goals were own-goals by England's centre-forward Joe Baker, and one of the England goals was scored by Scotland centre-forward Alex Dawson.

Between 1956–57 and 1961–62, Danny Malloy played for Cardiff City and Doncaster Rovers. He never scored for either of his clubs but in that time was credited with 14 own-goals.

Aston Villa's Chris Nichol scored all four goals in his side's 2-2 draw with Leicester City on 20 March 1976. Curiously, despite his haul, Nichol was not presented with the match ball.

The fastest recorded own-goal was scored by Pat Kruse, who headed into his own net after only eight seconds when playing for Torquay United against Cambridge United on 3 January 1977 (Division Four).

The 1987 FA Cup Final between Coventry City and Tottenham Hotspur was decided by an own-goal scored in extra-time by Gary Mabbutt. With the score at 2-2, Mabbutt deflected a cross from Coventry's Lloyd McGrath past Ray Clemence.

One-nil against the Arsenal. On 17 February 1990, Arsenal's Steve Bould scored an own-goal after just 16 seconds of the game against Sheffield Wednesday. It was the fastest own-goal of the season.

Frank Sinclair (Leicester) scored an own-goal with what was the last kick of the match between Arsenal and Leicester City at Highbury on 7 August 1999. Arsenal won 2-1. In their next Premiership match, against Chelsea (14 August), Leicester were leading 2-1 when Sinclair put through his own net to equalize for Chelsea, with only seven seconds of the match remaining.

Jamie Carragher scored two own-goals against Manchester United at Anfield in the Premiership on 11 September 1999. United beat Liverpool 3-2.

The record number of own-goals scored in a match is 149! In a league match in Madagascar on 31 October 2002, the players of Olympique De L'Emryne were so incensed by a decision made by the referee that they decided to capitulate by repeatedly putting the ball through their own net. The folly of this was, of course, that even if the referee had made a monumental error, the score at the time was 0-0.

On 1 February 2003, Sunderland scored three own-goals in little over half an hour of their Premiership match at home to Charlton Athletic. Stephen Wright put through his own net after 24 minutes, Mark Proctor after 29 minutes, and Proctor did so again in the 31st minute. Statistics showed Charlton leading 3-0 without having had a single shot on target. Charlton won 3-1.

The luck of the Irish. In 2007, Northern Ireland's hopes of qualifying for the finals of the 2008 European Championship were effectively ended with two last-minute own-goals in consecutive matches. On 8 September, Chris Baird scored in the 90th minute to give Latvia a 1-0 win. Four days later in Reykjavik, with the score at 1-1, Keith Gillespie put through his own goal in the 89th minute to gift Iceland victory.

40

The penalty kick was proposed by William McCrum to the Irish FA in 1890 for a foul or deliberate handball committed within what was then termed the goal-keeper's area. The Irish FA accepted the idea, and it was approved by the International Football Board in 1891.

The first official penalty in a first-class match was taken and converted by Alex McCall for Renton against Leith Athletic (Scottish League, 22 August 1891).

John Heath was the first player to score from a penalty in a first-class match in England, for Wolverhampton Wanderers against Accrington (Division One, 14 September 1891).

The current dimensions of the penalty area were not laid down until 1902. The edge of the penalty area to be 18 yards from the goal-line, and the boundary on each side marked by a line of 18 yards running at right angles from the goal-line and 18 yards to the side of each goal-post. The penalty spot to be 12 yards from the goal-line. The penalty arc (also referred to as the 'D') on the edge of the penalty area, marks the minimum distance any player, excluding the penalty taker and goalkeeper, must be from the ball when the penalty kick is taken. The rules stipulated only that the player taking the penalty kick must play the ball forward (not necessarily shoot), and that the penalty taker must not touch the ball again until it had made contact with a player from either side. The defending goalkeeper was obliged to remain on the goal-line until the ball was kicked.

Walter Scott proved a good talisman for Grimsby Town when it came to facing penalties. In 1909, against Burnley, he became the first goalkeeper to save three penalties in a single competitive game.

The first penalty to be missed in an FA Cup Final was taken by Charlie Wallace for Aston Villa against Sunderland (Crystal Palace, 1913). Wallace's miss from the spot proved not to be decisive: Villa won 1-0.

In 1921–22, Southend United right-back Jimmy Evans finished the season as the club's leading goalscorer in Division Three South with ten goals – at the time the only instance of a full-back having achieved this feat at a club. All ten of Evans's goals came from the penalty spot.

The first player to score a penalty in a World Cup match was Manuel Rocquetas Rosas for Mexico against Argentina (19 July 1930). In the same match, Argentina's Fernando Paternoster became the first player to miss a World Cup penalty, but Argentina went on to win the tie 6-3. Five penalties were awarded during this game – a record for the World Cup Finals.

The first penalty to be awarded in an FA Cup Final at Wembley (1938) proved decisive: George Mutch scored from the spot in the last seconds of extra-time to give Preston North End a 1-0 victory over Huddersfield Town. Indeed, Mutch's penalty proved to be the last kick of the match; there wasn't even enough time left for Huddersfield to kick off again. It was also the first time an FA Cup Final at Wembley had gone to extra-time.

The record for the number of times a player has been requested by a referee to retake a penalty kick is six. In 1945, in a match between Kilmarnock and Partick Thistle, the referee ruled on six occasions that either Partick Thistle players had encroached into the penalty area or the goalkeeper had moved before Kilmarnock left-half 'Jock' White made contact with the ball. The seventh attempt the referee was satisfied with, but not White – he missed.

On 7 January 1947, after an hour of play, Sheffield Wednesday led Chesterfield 2-1 at Saltergate. Wednesday then contrived to concede three penalties and lost the game 4-2.

On 26 August 1953, Sheffield Wednesday goalkeeper Dave McIntosh sustained an injury against Preston North End and had to leave the pitch. Wednesday defender Norman Curtis took over in goal and went on to save two penalties.

Swings and roundabouts? On 13 October 1956, Sheffield United were awarded two penalties in their Second Division match against Notts County at Bramall Lane; United defender Jim Iley successfully converted them both. In the return match at the County Ground, Sheffield United were again awarded two penalties. Naturally Iley elected to take them, but he missed both.

Ronnie Allen was West Bromwich Albion's regular penalty taker in the 1950s. He preferred something to aim at and had an arrangement with photographers from local newspapers or press agencies that one would position himself near a stanchion at the back of the goal and Allen would aim at his camera. When Allen took a penalty against Newcastle United in 1954, the ball burst on its way to goal and the *Birmingham Evening Post* had the sports scoop picture of the year.

In 1960, playing for Sunderland Youth in an International Youth Tournament in Holland, Jim Montgomery faced six penalties in the course of the competition and saved every one.

Walsall's Tony Richards, who played for the club from 1954 to 1963, once scored a penalty and saved a penalty in the same match. Having scored from the spot against Bournemouth, Richards then took over in goal following an injury to the Saddlers' keeper and went on to save a penalty kick.

The penalty shoot-out to decide drawn ties in cup competitions was approved by FIFA and UEFA in the summer of 1970.

Manchester United were the first English club to win a first-class match by way of a penalty shoot-out. On 1 August 1970, they beat Hull City 4-3 on penalties at Boothferry Park in the semi-final of the Watney Cup. The first player to take one of these deciding penalties (and successfully convert it) was George Best. Uncharacteristically, the player to suffer the ignominy of being the first British player to miss from the spot in a penalty shoot-out was Denis Law.

In 1971–72, Francis Lee scored 13 penalties for Manchester City – a Football League record. As Brian Clough once infamously said, 'The only thing not taking a dive at Manchester City is the shares.'

Three Notts County players missed the same penalty during County's game against Portsmouth on 22 September 1973. The initial penalty was missed but was ordered to be retaken because the goalkeeper had moved. The second attempt, by a different player, was also missed and also ordered to be retaken because the referee adjudged that a Portsmouth player had encroached into the penalty area. The third attempt, by a third County player, was placed wide of goal. The three miscreants were Kevin Randall, Don Masson and Brian Stubbs.

On 1 September 1973, Hearts enjoyed a 3-2 away win at Morton. The Hearts hero was Donald Ford, who scored a hat-trick. Each goal came from the penalty spot.

A hat-trick of penalties in a single game is not uncommon. Among those to achieve this feat are Joe Willetts for Hartlepool United against Darlington (Division Three North), Good Friday 1951; Alan Slough for Peterborough United at Chester (Division Three), 29 April 1978 (Slough's efforts were all in vain as Chester won 4-3); Kevin Dillon for Portsmouth against Millwall (second round of Full Members Cup), 4 November 1986; Andy Blair for Sheffield Wednesday against Luton Town (fourth round of the Milk/League Cup), 20 November 1986; and Jan Molby for Liverpool against Coventry City (Littlewoods/League Cup fourth round replay), 26 November 1986. This was the only hat-trick Molby scored for Liverpool.

The first major domestic trophy to be settled by a penalty shoot-out was the 1974 Charity Shield match between Leeds United and Liverpool at Wembley. Liverpool beat Leeds 6-5 (after 1-1). It was also the first time the Charity Shield had been played at Wembley, and the first time it was broadcast live on television.

The first player to miss from the penalty spot in a League Cup Final at Wembley was Ray Graydon for Aston Villa against Norwich City (1975). Villa, however, triumphed, beating Norwich 1-0. Sunderland's Clive Walker also failed from the penalty spot against Norwich in a League Cup Final at Wembley (1985). Walker's effort came back into play off the foot of a post, and this miss proved costly: Norwich won 1-0 courtesy of an own-goal by Sunderland's Gordon Chisholm. The third player to have missed a penalty in a League Cup Final was Nigel Winterburn who, with Arsenal leading Luton Town 2-1, had his spot-kick saved by Andy Dibble. Dibble's save (or, if you like, Winterburn's miss) proved crucial: Luton stormed back to win 3-2.

On 6 June 2001, Henrik Larsson scored a penalty hat-trick in international football, for Sweden against Moldova (World Cup qualifier). Larsson in fact scored four goals in Sweden's 6-0 victory.

In 1979–80, Ipswich Town goalkeeper Paul Cooper saved eight of ten penalties he faced, including two in the game against Derby County on 29 March.

Wrexham's Dixie McNeill is the only player to have been sent off while in the process of taking a penalty. On 19 January 1980, when playing against Charlton Athletic at the Racecourse Ground, and with the score at 2-2, McNeill elected to take a penalty Wrexham had been awarded. He made two attempts at addressing the ball only to be put off by gamesmanship on the part of Charlton players. Frustrated by this, McNeill kicked the ball into the crowd and received his marching orders from the referee. With McNeill in the dressing room, Mick Vinter stepped up to take the penalty and successfully converted to give Wrexham victory.

On 27 December 1980, goalkeeper Tony Coton made his debut for Birmingham City against Sunderland at St Andrews. Just 58 seconds into the game, he saved a penalty taken by Sunderland's Stan Cummins.

There's nothing new in the world. In 1982–83, Ajax were awarded a penalty against Helmond Sport. Johan Cruyff stepped up to take it, but instead of shooting at goal he played the ball forward for Jesper Olsen, who in turn played it back to Cruyff, who then scored. The incident was shown worldwide on television, including the ITV programme *Saint and Greavsie*, which correctly declared that there was nothing in the rules of football to prevent Cruyff doing this. The incident was not a football first, however. In the 1940s, the great Peter Doherty did exactly the same when playing for Derby County against Port Vale at Vale's former home the Recreation Ground.

John Aldridge (Liverpool) was the first player to miss from the penalty spot in a Wembley FA Cup Final (1988) when Wimbledon's Dave Beasant saved his effort. Wimbledon went on to beat Liverpool 1-0, their goal coming from Lawrie Sanchez.

Not a Happy Monday. The most penalties awarded in a single League match is five (Crystal Palace v. Brighton, 4-1, Easter Monday 1989). Palace scored one (Mark Bright) but missed three, whereas Brighton converted the penalty they were awarded (Alan Curbishley). Referee Kelvin Morton awarded three of the penalties inside five minutes.

On 12 September 1989, Liverpool's John Aldridge agreed to join Spanish club Real Sociedad with a view to flying to Spain and signing the following day. Aldridge was named as substitute for Liverpool's evening match on 12 September against Crystal Palace. With Liverpool leading 5-0, manager Kenny Dalglish called Aldridge from the bench when his team was awarded a penalty as a farewell gesture to the Irish striker. Peter Beardsley left the field and Aldridge stepped up and converted the spot-kick for his final goal for Liverpool. Liverpool went on to beat Crystal Palace 9-0.

In 1991, Torquay United became the first club to win promotion via a penalty shoot-out. They beat Blackpool 5-4 at Wembley (after a 2-2 draw) to win the Division Four play-off final.

In 1991–92, penalty shoot-outs were introduced to decide FA Cup ties that were still level after a period of extra-time in the replay. The first team to win an FA Cup tie on a penalty shoot-out was Rotherham United (first round replay, 26 November 1991), who defeated Scunthorpe United 7-6 (after 1-1 and 3-3).

Matthew Le Tissier successfully converted 48 of the 49 penalties taken during his career with Southampton. The only goalkeeper to thwart Le Tissier from the spot was Mark Crossley (Nottingham Forest) during a match at the Dell on 24 March 1993.

Martin Palermo missed a hat-trick of penalties when playing for Argentina against Colombia in the Copa America in 1999.

At the 2000 Olympic Games, Cameroon became the first nation to win a gold medal on a penalty shoot-out. After their final had ended 2-2 (aet), Cameroon beat Spain 5-3.

On 28 November 2001, the drawn FA Cup first round replay between Forest Green Rovers and Macclesfield Town involved 24 penalties. Macclesfield eventually won the shoot-out 11-10.

The longest a player has had to wait from a penalty being awarded to actually taking it is 24 days! In 2003, the game between Defensores de Cambaceres and Atlanta in Argentina was abandoned when spectators rioted following the award of a penalty. The Argentinian FA ordered the game to continue behind closed doors, which it did, over three weeks later. The game resumed with the taking of the penalty by Atlanta's Lucas Ferreiro, who successfully converted to score the only goal of the game.

England do not have a particularly successful record in penalty shoot-outs which has invariably caused the nation much grief and angst: 1990 World Cup semi-final, England lost 4-3 on penalties to West Germany; 1996 European Championship quarter-final, England beat Spain 4-2; 1996 European Championship semi-final, England lost 6-5 to Germany; 1998 World Cup, second round, England lost 4-3 to Argentina; 2004 European Championship quarter-final, England lost 6-5 to Portugal.

 I knew how to take a penalty kick . . . with my head.

LES DAWSON

41

The Premiership came into existence in 1992–93. On 20 February 1992, the FA gave its blessing to the formation of the new league which meant an end to the 104-year-old Football League in its old format.

The Premiership was first mooted in 1990-91 in the FA's 'Blueprint for the Future of Football', a dossier overseen by FA chief executive Graham Kelly, though the FA proposed that such a league should consist of only 18 teams. The 22 that initially contested the Premiership were reduced to 20 at the end of the 1994–95 season.

Notts County and Luton Town were among the signatories to the agreement to form the Premiership.

The first chairman of the Premier League, the governing body of the Premiership, was John Quinton, former chairman of Barclays Bank plc. The chief executive was Rick Parry, a qualified chartered accountant.

The Premiership was linked to the Football League by way of a three-up/three-down promotion and relegation to what was now called the First Division of the Football League (formerly the Second Division).

Lost in the mists of time . . . One of the main advantages cited for the formation of the Premiership was it would reduce the number of matches played by our top players. This, we were told, would be of great benefit to the England national team as players would be 'fresher and more readily available for international duty'. The Champions League put the kibosh on that notion, and the plethora of overseas players has meant that the England manager has never had fewer options available to him in terms of players of international class regularly appearing in top-flight English football.

It was also agreed that the half-time interval in Premiership matches would be extended from ten to 15 minutes. Also, three substitutes (one a goalkeeper) could be named, of which two could be introduced in the course of a game.

The first 22 members of the inaugural Premiership in 1992 were Arsenal, Aston Villa, Blackburn Rovers, Chelsea, Coventry City, Crystal Palace, Everton, Ipswich Town, Leeds United, Liverpool, Manchester City, Manchester United, Middlesbrough, Norwich City, Nottingham Forest, Oldham Athletic, Queens Park Rangers, Sheffield United, Sheffield Wednesday, Southampton, Tottenham Hotspur and Wimbledon.

The first Premiership goal was scored by Brian Deane for Sheffield United against Manchester United on 15 August 1992.

Manchester United hold the records for the biggest home and away victories in the Premiership. On 4 March 1995, United defeated Ipswich Town 9-0 at Old Trafford; on 6 February 1999, they beat Nottingham Forest 8-1 at the City Ground.

The highest aggregate score in the Premiership is Portsmouth 7 Reading 4 (29 September 2007).

The record for the most goals scored by an individual player in a single season of the Premiership is shared by Andy Cole (Newcastle United) and Alan Shearer (Blackburn Rovers). In 1993–94, Cole scored 34 goals (42 games), Shearer likewise in 1994–95 (42 games). Cole and Shearer also share the record for the most number of goals scored by an individual player in a single Premiership match. Cole scored five for Manchester United against Ipswich Town (1994–95), and Shearer matched that for Newcastle United against Sheffield Wednesday (1999–2000).

The most goals conceded by a Premiership side in a single season is 100 (Swindon Town, 1993–94, 42 matches). Swindon went 16 matches from the start of the season before registering their first victory (24 November, 1-0 v. Queens Park Rangers at the County Ground) and won only five Premiership matches. Curiously, this included victory at QPR (3-1) – the club's only double success in the Premiership.

In 1992–93, Norwich City finished third in the Premiership having conceded more goals (65) than they scored (61).

On 26 December 1999, Chelsea created English football history when they became the first club not to include a single English player in their starting line-up, for the Premiership game against Southampton at the Dell. The history-making Chelsea team was Ed De Goey (Holland), Albert Ferrer (Spain), Celestine Babayaro (Nigeria), Didier Deschamps (France), Franck Leboeuf (France), Emerson Thome (Brazil), Dan Petrescu (Romania), Roberto Di Matteo (Italy), Tore Andre Flo (Norway), Gus Poyet (Uruguay) and Gabriele Ambrosetti (Italy).

Only a matter of time before there is a Premiership match which does not feature a single English player? On 26 August 2007, the game between Arsenal and Manchester City at the Emirates Stadium featured only two British players – Micah Richards and Michael Johnson (both English, both for Manchester City).

In 2001–02 Arsenal scored in every one of their Premiership games (38).

In 2002–03, Sunderland created a record for the fewest goals scored in the course of a Premiership season – 21 in 38 matches – prompting one Sunderland fan to quip, 'Osama bin Laden has been hiding out in the Sunderland forward line.' That record was beaten by Derby in 2007–08, when they scored just 20 goals.

The Premiership is ranked the number two league in Europe by UEFA, behind La Liga and ahead of Serie A.

As the Premiership grew in stature and revenue, so did the transfer fees paid by clubs. In June 1993, the record fee paid was £3.75 million, by Manchester United to Nottingham Forest for Roy Keane. In July 1995, Liverpool paid Forest £8.5 million for Stan Collymore. A year later (July 1996), the record fee had jumped to £15 million, paid by Newcastle United to Blackburn Rovers for Alan Shearer. In 2001, Manchester United paid £19 million to PSV Eindhoven for Ruud van Nistelrooy, and then shelled out £28.1 million to Lazio for Juan Sebastian Verón. In June 2006, Chelsea paid £30 million to AC Milan for Andriy Shevchenko.

There has only been one season when not one of the previously promoted clubs was relegated – 2001–02, when Blackburn Rovers, Bolton Wanderers and Fulham all preserved their Premiership status.

Relegated clubs receive a parachute payment for two years to offset loss of broadcasting revenues. In 2007–08, each relegated club received £11.2 million. Parachute payments are a contentious issue with existing Championship clubs who feel it gives relegated clubs a distinct financial advantage – and they're not wrong.

In 2007–08 the average Premiership club received £47 million from broadcasting rights. The average Championship club received £1 million.

There is a sliding scale for payment in accordance with where a club finishes in the Premiership. The club finishing top in 2007–08 received £50 million. The club finishing bottom received £26.8 million. It would take a Championship club such as Plymouth Argyle or Burnley some 27 years to earn in broadcasting revenue what the club finishing bottom of the Premiership earns in a single season.

Forty different clubs have played in the Premiership since the inaugural season of 1992–93 (to 2008).

Seven clubs have enjoyed continued membership of the Premiership since 1992–93: Arsenal, Aston Villa, Chelsea, Everton, Liverpool, Manchester United and Tottenham Hotspur.

In 2000–01, Ipswich Town finished fifth. They were relegated the following season.

TOP-CAPACITY STADIUMS

76,212 – Old Trafford, Manchester United
60,432 – Emirates Stadium, Arsenal
52,387 – St James' Park, Newcastle United
49,000 – Stadium of Light, Sunderland (planning permission has been granted to increase this to 55,000)
47,726 – City of Manchester Stadium, Manchester City
45,362 – Anfield, Liverpool (plans in place to create new stadium)
42,593 – Villa Park, Aston Villa
42,055 – Stamford Bridge, Chelsea

NOBBY STILES

GORDON BANKS

The stadium in the Premiership with the lowest capacity is Fratton Park, Portsmouth at 20,328.

Alan Shearer has scored the most goals by an individual player in the Premiership – 260.

In 2005–06 Thierry Henry (27 goals) finished as the Premiership's leading goalscorer for a third consecutive season, equalling the record set by Alan Shearer (1994–97).

In 2006–07 Didier Drogba (Chelsea) became the first player since Dwight Yorke in 1998–99 to win the Premiership Golden Boot Award without being his club's penalty taker.

Manchester United was the first club to score 1,000 goals in the Premiership, during their 4-1 win against Middlesbrough in 2005–06. At the start of 2007–08, the only other club to have scored 1,000 goals was Arsenal.

Up to 2007–08 only two players had scored in every season since the Premiership began: Gary Speed (Bolton) and Ryan Giggs (Manchester United).

The most consecutive wins by a team in the Premiership is 14, by Arsenal, February to August 2002.

From 7 May 2003 to 24 October 2004, Arsenal went a record 49 games unbeaten in the Premiership.

The most goals conceded by an individual goalkeeper in the course of a Premiership season is 85, by Paul Robinson (Leeds United) in 2003–04.

The fewest goals conceded by a team in the course of a season is 15 (Chelsea, 2004–05).

In 2006–07 from 1 January up to and including the final day of the season, Manchester City did not score a single goal at home (eight games).

The record for the most defeats in a single Premiership season is 29, by Sunderland in 2005–06 and Derby County in 2007–08. Derby County also achieved the fewest points in a 38-game season (11) and the fewest wins (one).

Sunderland nearly went through that 2005–06 season without winning a home match. In February, they trailed 0-1 at home to Fulham but the game was abandoned due to snow. The match was rearranged as Sunderland's final home match of the season, and they beat Fulham 1-0 to record their only home victory.

The player with the most Premiership appearances to his name is Gary Speed who, prior to joining Sheffield United in 2008, had played 537 matches.

The oldest player to have appeared in the Premiership is goalkeeper John Burridge at 43 years and 162 days old, for Manchester City against Queens Park Rangers on 14 May 1995.

The oldest player to make his Premiership debut is Fernando Hierro, who was 36 years and 151 days old when he played for Bolton Wanderers against Fulham on 21 August 2004.

The youngest Premiership player is Matthew Briggs, 16 years and 65 days old when he played for Fulham against Middlesbrough on 13 May 2007.

Frank Lampard holds the record for having played the most consecutive Premiership matches – 164.

The youngest player to score in the Premiership is James Vaughan, who was 16 years and 271 days old when he scored for Everton against Crystal Palace on 10 April 2005.

The oldest player to score in the Premiership is Teddy Sheringham, 40 years and 268 days old when he scored for West Ham United against Portsmouth on Boxing Day 2006.

The quickest Premiership goal was scored by Ledley King after nine seconds of Tottenham Hotspur's game against Bradford City on 9 December 2000.

On 17 March 2007, goalkeeper Paul Robinson scored with a punt from his own penalty area against Arsenal. Only two other goalkeepers have scored in the Premiership: Peter Schmeichel for Aston Villa against Everton, and Brad Friedel for Blackburn Rovers against Charlton Athletic.

In 2004–05, Chelsea goalkeeper Petr Cech kept a record 24 clean sheets.

Aston Villa have conceded the most penalties of any Premiership club. Before the start of the 2008–09 season they had conceded 47 penalties at home and 95 in away matches since 1992–93 – a total of 142.

On 7 February 2008, Premier League chief executive Richard Scudamore announced that the management was exploring proposals to play Premiership matches overseas, in so doing extending the season to 39 fixtures. Scudamore was quoted as saying that this was 'making history', whereas the consensus of opinion among press and supporters was that it was all about making money. Remember, one of the reasons cited for the formation of the Premiership was that such a league would reduce the number of matches played by top clubs, and this in turn would benefit the England team. On 9 February 2008, the Premier League refuted claims that the travel involved in playing matches overseas would tire players and officials and have an adverse effect on performances.

On 10 February 2008, following Manchester United's 2-1 loss at home to Manchester City, United's assistant manager Carlos Queiroz told the press, 'We believe the team was affected by international call-ups. Players were not at their best today, they were still suffering from fatigue.'

From the very beginnings of organized football in the Victorian age, clubs have issued matchday programmes, though in the 19th century these took the form of cards printed black on white. The essence and function of these programmes are still the same today as they were over a century ago: to act as the official mouthpiece of the host club and to contain details of the teams and officials.

Some of the early 'card' programmes listed teams vertically, in much the same way as today's matchday magazines list squads. By the end of the nineteenth century most clubs had taken to setting out teams in a 1-2-3-5 formation, more like how the team would line up and play on the field.

The majority of programmes also served as a means of generating additional revenue for clubs by way of advertisements from local companies as well as well-known branded products. The Notts County programme of 5 December 1908 for the game against Chelsea featured on the front of the card an advert for Bovril, proclaiming it to be 'a splendid preventative of colds and chills, and recommended for those watching the game'.

The early 1900s saw the emergence of what today's supporter would regard as a recognizable programme, comprising two sheets of folded printed A4 paper. The team line-ups usually appeared in the centre pages; some clubs, however, featured the line-ups on the front cover.

As clubs realized that programmes were also a way of expressing club identity, in the years leading up to World War One the front covers of programmes became more personalized and usually featured the colours of the club shirt. For example, Aston Villa entitled their programme *The Villa News and Record* and the cover was printed in claret and blue with a drawing depicting sections of the main stands and packed terraces at Villa Park.

Generally, the 1920s and 1930s saw little development except for, in a number of cases, an increase in size to eight pages, though the programmes of top clubs such as Arsenal and Manchester United contained considerably more and occasionally featured a photograph of a player. Every club programme now had an individual and easily recognizable identity. One could hide the name of the club and still know which club programme it was purely by its design.

For a number of seasons Liverpool and Everton shared a programme, detailing information about the home matches of both clubs.

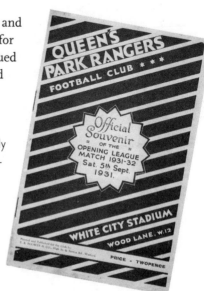

Paper was scarce during World War Two, and programmes adapted accordingly. Those for wartime regional matches, if one was issued at all, consisted of just one sheet of folded poor-quality A5 paper.

The post-war years saw a gradual return to the standard eight-page programme, usually priced at 2d (just under 1p), though a number of First Division clubs charged more (Aston Villa's was 3d). As paper (and advertisers) became more plentiful in the 1950s, many programmes increased in size to 12 pages, printed on matt paper.

For much of the 1950s the design, format and content of many club programmes varied little from season to season. Programmes for the FA Cup Final and England international matches at Wembley, however, were subjected to a new design and format in 1953 which remained more or less unaltered until 1966. The cover was divided into three sections, the upper bearing details of the fixture and names of the competing teams, the centre an aerial view of the stadium, the base a block of green colour which bore in white the words 'Empire Stadium, Wembley', together with the cover price.

Pen pictures of the opposition were supplied by the secretary of the opposing club. Not only did such information enlighten home supporters, occasionally, and unwittingly, it was a source of news to the players themselves. In 1954, when Tommy Docherty was playing for Preston North End, his pen picture in an opposition programme mentioned the fact that Preston had recently turned down an offer of £20,000 from Aston Villa for his services. As Docherty later said in his 2006 autobiography, 'This turned out to be true, but it was the first I'd heard of it!'

Some clubs, such as Aston Villa, issued programmes that covered both a first-team home match and the next reserve team match.

Many printers of programmes in the 1950s and early 1960s used stock 'line images' in their design of front covers. This led to a number of programmes bearing the same layout and image. For example, for a number of seasons the programmes of Wolverhampton Wanderers and Chesterfield displayed an airborne player in silhouette kicking a ball towards a goal in which was a silhouetted goalkeeper at full stretch.

In 1957–58, the Gateshead United (Division Three North) programme contained a large advert on its front cover for 'Hoggett's Pickled Onions, VinHogg, Piccalilli and Pompey Sauce'.

In the late 1950s, the average programme cost 4d (less than 2p).

Local public houses and sports shops regularly took adverts in programmes. Many ex-players had taken to running such establishments and their adverts always reminded supporters of their connection with the local football club – for example, The Travellers Inn, Boldon, Mine Host, Arthur Wright (ex-Sunderland).

Following the Munich air disaster in February 1958, the Manchester United programme for the next home match at Old Trafford against Sheffield Wednesday contained the names of no United players in the team line-ups, just blank spaces.

In pre-motorway Britain many supporters who travelled to watch their team play away from home did so by train. From the 1940s to mid-1960s, just about every club programme carried an advert from the local office of British Railways giving details of a 'Football Excursion' to whichever town or city the club would next visit. For a trip to Bolton Wanderers on 17 October 1959, the return fare for West Bromwich Albion supporters from Birmingham New Street was 13/3d (66p), and the journey to Bolton took three hours and 40 minutes.

For a number of decades the match programme was the only source of information for supporters of what was happening in games elsewhere. Programmes contained a list of fixtures; each was denoted by a letter of the alphabet, and these letters related to the letters and scores displayed on the half-time scoreboard, usually situated high in one corner of the ground. A high half-time score often induced gasps from the home crowd. Sometimes supporters indulged in fun and humour on the terraces if the letter and score spelled a word. B, 0-0 would prompt boos; M, 0-0 would usually result in supporters making the sound of a cow.

In the late 1950s and early 1960s, more and more programmes began to feature photographs. In most cases this was restricted to one shot, though programmes of leading First Division clubs such as Chelsea and Arsenal continued to carry some five or six photographs featuring the opposing team and action images of a recent match – a practice Arsenal had begun in the 1930s.

In the 1950s and 1960s, it was quite common for printers not allied to a club to issue a 'pirate' programme for a big game such as an important FA Cup tie. Such programmes were frowned upon by the clubs because they often contained inferior content and were purchased on the day by unsuspecting supporters. Many such programmes have now become collectors' items.

Many clubs featured well-known local landmarks on their programme covers – Blackpool carried the Blackpool Tower, Exeter City and Lincoln City their respective cathedrals, Grimsby Town the harbour entry lighthouse – but by far the most popular image was that of the football ground itself, usually an aerial view in the form of a photograph or drawing.

In the early 1960s, many clubs, particularly those in the lower divisions, attempted to offset falling attendances by generating more programme advertising. In some instances this led to 60 per cent and more of the programme being given over to adverts. When clubs failed to sell the space set aside it was common to see a quarter- or half-page of the programme blank except for the words 'To Let'.

The adverts themselves tended to be parochial and parsimonious, small local businesses that, like the local football club itself, provided the town with its social glue and identity. Otherwise they promoted breweries, cigarette companies and local industry, all of whom knew their market – the working man. A Chesterfield programme from 1958 is typical. It features a recruiting advert for the National Coal Board – 'Many jobs available in mining, mechanical and electrical for men and boys. Apply now!' – alongside which is an advert for 'Joyce Mullis, ALCM, AIMD (Hons), the gold medallist soprano offering teaching in singing and the piano'.

Unthinkable as it may be now, the only programmes that did not carry any advertising whatsoever were those of Arsenal, Tottenham Hotspur, Chelsea and West Ham United. For many years these clubs adopted the policy that their matchday programme was the official organ of the club. As one Arsenal director put it, we 'do not desire our match programme to be besmirched by the vulgarity of commercialism'.

The Rochdale programme of 1958–59 encouraged supporters to visit the local tea bar with an advert that read as follows:

Walk to the tea bar
Straight as a die,
Count out your coppers
And ask for a pie.

In the days before saturation coverage of football by television, radio and other media, the team line-ups in the matchday programme were the only way of knowing what the teams would be on the day. For a Saturday match, club secretaries submitted the line-ups to programme printers on a Thursday afternoon; barring late changes due to injury, the line-ups in the programme were as they would be for the match. This policy inadvertently prevented managers from telling a player he was to be included in the team for reasons other than injury to another player. In 1947, Stanley Matthews found himself out of favour with Stoke City manager Bob McGrory. On the Friday morning the Stoke manager informed Matthews he was being recalled for the game against Brentford as it was 'a nonsense to have a current England international out of the Stoke team'. On the day of the game Matthews looked at the match programme and saw that his name wasn't included in the Stoke line-up, which alerted him to the fact that he had only been recalled due to late injuries to two other players. This proved to be the case. It soured relations between the pair even more and precipitated Matthews' move to Blackpool.

In 1963, it became something of a vogue to issue mini-programmes some six inches by five inches in size. Ipswich Town, Sunderland, Plymouth Argyle, Hartlepool United, Swindon Town and Walsall were among the clubs that readily embraced the format.

When Sunderland opted for a mini-programme in 1963–64, it was the first change in size, layout and format to the club programme for nine years, but still the cover remained the same. Likewise, the design, layout and format of the Wolverhampton Wanderers programme did not change from 1957 to 1965.

In the early to mid-sixties, the average programme cost 6d (2.5p).

In an attempt to inject more information and quality reading into matchday programmes, the Football League launched its own magazine, *The Football League Review*, which was inserted free of charge in the programmes of most clubs. The first issue appeared on the opening day of 1965–66, though the *Review* contained few photographs and was printed on poor-quality paper in just two colours, orange and black on white.

The 1966 World Cup was a watershed moment for programmes. The official World Cup brochure, applicable to every game up to the final, and the programme for the World Cup Final itself, raised expectations among spectators. To meet this need, the Football League overhauled and relaunched the *Review*. The magazine was now produced in full colour and contained two photographs of League teams, individual players, and a weekly 'guide' to a club as well as a letters page and articles by well-known figures in football. The content of the programmes themselves soon imitated this style.

On 16 November 1965, a Brazil XI played Arsenal at Highbury as part of their preparations for the 1966 World Cup. Arsenal issued a 16-page programme – as usual, advert-free – on page three of which was a photograph of the Duke of Edinburgh, who was the guest of honour at the game. But the first print run had to be aborted and the programmes pulped as the Duke of Edinburgh was referred to as 'His Royal Highness the Duck of Edinburgh'.

The price of the official 1966 World Cup brochure was 2/6d (12.5p) – the same as the price of the programme for the final itself.

The 1966 World Cup Final programme contained a blank page opposite a page featuring a photograph of Her Majesty the Queen, as it was considered disrespectful and in breach of royal etiquette for the image of Her Majesty to appear alongside any general information or, God forbid, advertisements.

The match programme for the 1966 World Cup Final between England and West Germany contained 66 pages and was divided into four parts each containing two sections. The final score was 4-2.

Adverts for cigarettes and alcohol were still predominant in programmes in the 1960s and formed the bulk of the advertising for the 1966 World Cup Final programme, which contained three full-page adverts for cigarettes (Players No. 6, Embassy and Cadets) and eight adverts for Carlsberg, Bass Charrington, Gordon's Gin, Guinness, Johnnie Walker, Martini, Lamb's Navy Rum and Watney Mann. Curiously, the 1966 programme also contained a quarter-page advert for Coleman, the bespoke tailors of Savile Row (By Appointment to Royalty), which, one should imagine, would have had a limited market among football supporters.

Many programmes issued by top clubs in the 1950s and 1960s contained tokens that could be collected over a period of time; for an important all-ticket cup tie, supporters with the required amount of tokens were given preference in the allocation of tickets over non-season ticket holders. Two of the clubs that successfully ran such a scheme were Manchester United and Leeds United.

At the end of the 1960s, the average programme cost one shilling (5p).

The 1970s saw programmes containing more in the way of content and photographs. Some clubs, such as Derby County and Shrewsbury Town, even produced programmes in newspaper format.

In 1975–76, the average cost of a programme for a League match was 10p.

With more and more matches being featured on television, large companies such as banks, motor manufacturers and producers of technical products at last woke up to the fact that football was a cultural phenomenon of the twentieth century. Throughout the 1970s these global companies became increasingly associated with football. In addition to sponsorship, they placed adverts in match programmes at a price local businesses could not compete with. Indeed, the early 1970s saw an end to small businesses advertising in match programmes.

In 1978–79, the average programme cost 20p.

In keeping with a game that was becoming more commercially ambitious, club programmes too became ambitious in the 1980s. Content burgeoned, leading to the emergence of the glossy matchday magazines we know today.

In 1980, the average programme cost 30p. By 1987 this had risen to 50p. In 1990, the average cost of a match programme was £1.

The only known player to have appeared in a team line-up in a matchday programme but who in the event played for the opposition is Bert Sproston. On Thursday, 3 November 1938, Sproston was chosen to play for Tottenham Hotspur against Manchester City at Maine Road on the forthcoming Saturday. Later that day, he was transferred to Manchester City, and he made his debut on the Saturday (5 November) against Spurs. The team line-ups in the programme showed Sproston as playing right-back for Spurs when in fact he played right-back for City.

Many supporters find contemporary glossy matchday magazines too bulky to slip into the pocket. In 2006, Hibernian kicked the trend for cumbersome programmes into touch by reverting to a simple 12-page format for their Scottish Premier League matches at Easter Road.

One feature of the matchday programme has always been an article by the manager of the club. During his two spells as manager of Lincoln City (1978–85 and 1987–90), Colin Murphy gained a certain notoriety for the surreal nature of his 'Manager's Notes'. Here are a couple of examples: 'Promotion from Division Four is all about being first, second, third or fourth'; 'I was left speechless after the game at Brentford and, to me, that says it all.' Bobby Robson could, on occasion, raise eyebrows too: 'If we start counting our chickens before they hatch, they won't lay any eggs in the basket.'

In 2007, programmes for key games at the new Wembley cost £10.

Team line-ups in programmes became redundant with the introduction of squads. In 2007–08, the matchday magazines of some Premiership sides listed the names of up to 40 players for each team – totally useless. This in itself has been a source of humour to some supporters, who bring along a menu from their local Chinese takeaway to a game and relate player squad numbers to the numbers on the menu, thus affording players a 'new' identity.

43 Automatic promotion and relegation between the two divisions of the Football League were first introduced in 1898–99.

Automatic promotion for clubs that finished in the top two places of Division Two replaced the previous system of a series of 'Test' matches – a forerunner of the play-off.

The first clubs to gain promotion to Division One by way of playing Test matches were Sheffield United and Darwen in 1892-93. The beaten teams were Notts County and Accrington, both relegated to Division Two.

Test matches were scrapped in 1898 when Stoke and Burnley realized that should they draw their match they would both retain First Division status. Consequently they played out an uneventful goalless draw.

Glossop North End and Manchester City were the first two clubs to win automatic promotion from Division Two to Division One.

In 1914–15, Woolwich Arsenal finished sixth in Division Two but won promotion to Division One four years later without having played another game. At the end of 1914–15 football was suspended due to the war. In 1919–20, when official football resumed, the Football League was extended and as a result Arsenal were promoted to Division One. They have remained in top-flight football ever since.

The system of three-up/three-down was introduced in 1973–74 and applied only to the first three divisions of the Football League; four clubs were still promoted from Division Four and relegated from Division Three. This was the first change to relegation and promotion in the top two divisions of the Football League since 1892.

Play-offs were introduced by the Football League in 1986-87, primarily in the hope of sustaining the interest of players and supporters of clubs whose League position towards the end of the season left nothing to play for other than pride. It was hoped the possibility of appearing in the play-offs would result in increased attendances at end-of-season matches and that the play-offs themselves would also attract large crowds.

The first play-offs in 1986–87 involved the team finishing fourth from bottom in Division One (Charlton Athletic) playing the team that finished fifth in Division Two (Ipswich Town), and the teams that finished third and fourth in Division Two, Leeds United and Oldham Athletic, playing each other. A similar system operated for the play-offs involving Divisions Two and Three.

No club won promotion from Division Two to Division One in the first season through the play-offs. Charlton retained their First Division status by beating Leeds United 2-1 (after a replay) in the 'Divisions One and Two' final.

Aldershot became the first club to win promotion via the play-offs when they beat Wolverhampton Wanderers (2-0 and 1-0) in the 'Divisions Three and Four' final.

Swindon Town, who had finished third in Division Three, secured promotion to Division Two when they beat Gillingham 2-0 (in a replay after 0-1 and 2-1) in the 'Divisions Two and Three' final.

In 1989, the promotion play-offs system was changed to include only the four clubs that had just missed automatic promotion.

In 1990, the play-off finals were switched to Wembley. The first club to secure promotion at Wembley were Cambridge United (from Division Four), who beat Notts County.

In 1990 at Wembley, Swindon Town beat Sunderland 1-0 in the Division Two final only for Swindon subsequently to be found guilty of financial irregularities. As part of their punishment they were denied promotion, and Sunderland took their place in Division One. They remain the only club to have lost a play-off final and still won promotion.

Rules in Scotland stipulate that promotion is not mandatory: 'In the event of either or both clubs in the Third/Second Division refusing to go into the First/Second Division, either or both of the two lowest clubs in the Second/First Division shall remain in that Division.'

The highest score in a play-off final is Charlton Athletic 4 Sunderland 4 (1998 Division One final); Charlton won promotion to the Premiership 7-6 on penalties. Three of Charlton's goals from open play were scored by Clive Mendonca, who was born in Sunderland. The game was watched by a record play-off attendance of 77,739. Sunderland hold the dubious honour of having achieved the highest points total by a team that didn't win promotion (90).

 Promotion play-offs? I love them. A team finishes 15 points ahead of another in the League then loses to that team on a penalty shoot-out in a play-off final. It's a just and fair system that rewards the clubs who have produced the most consistent form over the course of a season – not!!!

PETER REID

In the 1950s, Sheffield Wednesday were promoted four times to and relegated four times from Division One.

Redfern Froggatt quite literally had his ups and downs as a player. He suffered three relegations with Sheffield Wednesday (1951, 1955 and 1958) but also enjoyed four promotions (1950, 1952, 1956 and 1959).

Northampton Town were the first club to win promotion through from Division Four (1960) to Division One (1965). Unfortunately they then equalled this feat in reverse, enduring successive relegations, until by 1969 they were back in Division Four.

Within ten years (1964 to 1974), Carlisle United won promotion from Division Four to Division One. They began this period at the bottom of Division Four and within a decade found themselves top of Division One, albeit only for one weekend.

Swansea City won three promotions in four seasons (1977–78 to 1980–81) to rise from Division Four to Division One, under the management of John Toshack.

When Wimbledon won promotion to Division One in 1985–86 it completed a remarkable sequence for the club which began with 'promotion' from the Southern League to the Football League only nine years earlier.

Wimbledon's promotion to the First Division in 1985-86 earned their players an unusual bonus: they no longer had to take their kit home and wash it themselves.

In 1962–63, Stoke City were champions of Division Two and Chelsea runners-up. The Stoke team had the oldest average age (32 years and 98 days) of any team to win a Football League divisional championship, and at the time the Chelsea team had the youngest average age (20 years and 291 days) of any team to win promotion in the Football League. As Tommy Docherty (Chelsea manager at the time) later said in his autobiography, 'I know this should tell us something about football but, over the years, I have never been able to work out what it could be.'

In the 1960s and 1970s, Willie Carlin won five promotions with five different clubs: Liverpool (Second Division), Carlisle United (Third), Derby County (Second), Leicester City (Second) and Notts County (Third).

In 1966–67, Middlesbrough won promotion from Division Three having lost only five fewer matches (14) than Swansea (19), who were relegated.

In February 1968, the Football League expelled Port Vale for making unauthorized payments to players, the punishment to come into effect at the end of the season. The knowledge that they were doomed irrespective of how they played did not affect the Port Vale players; on the contrary, Vale finished the season in Division Four in 18th place, three places higher than they had been when the expulsion was announced. They were immediately re-elected back into the Football League.

In the same season (1967–68), Peterborough United had 19 points deducted for offering irregular bonuses to their players. Posh were relegated to Division Four.

In 1972–73, Cambridge United won only one of their first six League matches, but from then on lost only four from 40 to win promotion from Division Four.

Southend United were champions of Division Four in 1980-81, in the process breaking 14 club records: most home points (42); most victories in the League (30); 18 successive home wins (19 in all); 15 successive home victories from the start of the season; only six goals conceded at home (also a Football League record for Division Four); undefeated at home; only 31 goals conceded in the season; 11 away wins; 25 clean sheets; ten successive home matches without conceding a goal; a total of 17 clean sheets at home; goalkeeper Mervyn Crawston went 985 minutes without conceding a goal at home; ten 'doubles' over the opposition; and fewest defeats in a season (nine). The Southend manager was Dave Smith, who left the club by 'mutual agreement' two years later.

In 1985–86, Swindon Town won promotion as champions of Division Four. They finished 18 points ahead of runners-up Chester City, 23 points ahead of Port Vale, who also won automatic promotion, and 30 points ahead of Orient, who just failed to make the automatic promotion places.

Going to the wire. On 19 April 1986, with three matches remaining, Hamilton clinched promotion from Scottish Division One to the Premier Division, while Alloa Athletic were relegated to Division Two. All the other 12 clubs in Division One were embroiled in a battle either for promotion or against relegation. Eventually Falkirk clinched the remaining promotion place, finishing one point ahead of Kilmarnock and Forfar and two ahead of East Fife and Dumbarton.

Between 1996 and 2006, Sunderland won promotion to the Premiership four times.

Between 1997 and 1999, Watford won successive promotions from Division Two via Division One to the Premiership – a feat equalled by Manchester City (1998–2000).

In 2003–4, the First Division play-off final between Crystal Palace and West Ham United drew a crowd of 72,523 to the Millennium Stadium – 1,173 more than attended the FA Cup Final between Manchester United and Millwall at the same venue. Palace won 1-0 to earn promotion to the Premiership.

Roy Keane was appointed manager of Sunderland in September 2006 when the club was bottom of the Championship and had just suffered an exit from the League Cup at Bury. Sunderland finished the season as champions, winning promotion to the Premiership – the only instance of a manager taking over the reins at a club at the bottom of a division and leading them to the championship in the same season.

'Are your players aware of the rules?' (FIFA OBSERVER prior to Derby County v. Zeljeznicar, European Cup tie)
'Are you?' (reply from BRIAN CLOUGH)

Of course Tommy Docherty has his weaknesses. For a start, he can't knit.
BILL SHANKLY

They tore down all the fences at Football League grounds but, credit to Mark Bright, he still always manages to sit on them.
FRED TRUEMAN

At eight o'clock I settle into my armchair to watch an England game on TV. An hour and a half later, I look at my watch and it says a quarter past eight.
JIMMY GREAVES, commenting on England under Sven-Göran Eriksson.

Football in the national press is like a swimming pool: all the screaming and shouting is at the shallow end.
BOB PAISLEY

Tommy, since you left Chelsea some people at this club have said some harsh things about you, but I want to assure you, I have never, never ever, told anyone you now live in the north of England.
Chelsea director VISCOUNT CHELSEA to Tommy Docherty on his return to Stamford Bridge as manager of Manchester United

The FA does bugger all, and they don't start till noon.
BRIAN CLOUGH

Dimitar Berbatov's agent said he wants to leave Spurs to join a club that will 'match his ambition'. He should go to Newcastle. They're overly ambitious and only perform four times a season.
KEN BOLAM, TV/music producer

It was as if one had discovered Shakespeare, Picasso and the Beatles for the first time, and all on the same night. A stunningly formative experience from which there was no going back.
JIMMY GREAVES, recalling Real Madrid's 7-3 victory over Eintracht Frankfurt in the 1960 European Cup Final

It's perfect, Stan. You're not so low dogs will piss on you, and you're not so high that pigeons will shit on you.
Former Wolves and Stoke City wing-half EDDIE CLAMP replying to Stan Matthews when asked what he thought of the statue of Stan at the unveiling in Hanley city centre (Stan roared with laughter at this)

Wayne Bridges has defended McClaren's defensive tactics against Croatia? It's a pity he didn't do that at Wembley.
TOMMY SMITH

Football is all about teamwork these days, which gives a player the opportunity to blame someone else.
LEN SHACKLETON

I look at John Fashanu, and think, 'Is there no beginning to this player's skill?'
BOB STOKOE

One of George Best's problems was he was a light sleeper. When it got light he went home and went to sleep.
TOMMY DOCHERTY

David Icke says he's here to save the world. Well, he saved bugger all when he was in goal for Coventry City.
JASPER CARROTT

These days you're not allowed to use the word 'piccaninny'. I don't know why not. Everyone's familiar with the FA's policy for selecting an England manager.
ANDY HAMILTON, comedy writer

The second he's brave enough, big enough, gets a bloody shave and doesn't walk like a spiv, then I'll sue him if he repeats it.
BRIAN CLOUGH, responding to Alan Sugar's bung allegation

44

Geoff Thomas can trap a ball further than I could kick it.
GEORGE BEST

If only Stan Bowles could pass a betting office like he passes a ball.
ERNIE TAGG, Bowles' former manager at Crewe Alexandra

I'm a Sunderland supporter, through thin and thinner.
AUTHOR

Long ball, short ball, it doesn't matter as long as it's the right ball.
NEIL BAKER, when manager of Leek Town, now assistant manager at Crewe Alexandra

These tournaments come round every four years and we can't expect to win them every year.
MICHAEL OWEN

The World Cup is every four years, so it's going to be a perennial problem.
GARY LINEKER

Football management is like nuclear war. There is only one winner, the rest are survivors or casualties.
TOMMY DOCHERTY

We lost to both cup winners last year, and you can't do more than that.
NEIL WARNOCK

Andy Ritchie has now scored 11 goals – exactly double the number he scored last season.
ALAN PARRY

Thank you for evoking memories, particularly of days gone by.
MIKE INGHAM, BBC Radio

Gheorghe Hagi has a left foot like Brian Lara's bat.
DON HOWE

The ball only has to get near the penalty area for Alan Green to sound like a man whose pants are on fire.
JIMMY GREAVES

It is going to be difficult for me. I've never had to learn a language, and now I do.
DAVID BECKHAM

In the end, Alan Ball's voice got so high he could only be heard on the pitch during floodlit games by bats.
TOMMY DOCHERTY

Bristol Rovers lead four-nil at half-time, all those goals coming in the first-half.
TONY ADAMSON. BBC Radio

It's the curtain raiser to the end of the season.
PETER WITHE

Newcastle can still make sure their hands are in their own destiny.
MARK SAGGERS, BBC FiveLive

Champions League action takes over centre stage from football tonight.
GARRY RICHARDSON, BBC Radio 4

It's about the two 'M's – movement and positioning.
RON ATKINSON

Just remind me again, who did Gary Mabbutt play for?
SKY SPORTS NEWS presenter to co-anchor

United seem to be in total, if not complete, control.
JON CHAMPION, commentator

That's the sort of save David James is capable of.
TREVOR BROOKING

Jimmy Greaves was a great goalscorer. Perhaps not a natural goalscorer like Michael Owen.
SKY SPORTS NEWS PRESENTER

Liverpool, wearing an unaccustomed strip of all white, with black shorts and red stockings.
DAVE WOOD, BBC Radio

We've reached a crossroads: one road leads to success, the other to a cul-de-sac and failure. (EDDIE BAILY, Spurs coach)
That's not a crossroads, Eddie, it's a T-junction. (reply from JIMMY GREAVES)

Had we not got that second goal the score might have been different.
DAVID PLEAT

Steve Brooker has been outstanding for Port Vale today. (GEORGE ANDREWS, Signal Radio)
Yes, he has, he's been the best player on the pitch. (SUMMARIZER)
So, who is your man of the match? (ANDREWS)
Neil Brisco. (SUMMARIZER)

I've always been a childhood fan of Liverpool.
HARRY KEWELL

Come on you Bury fans, you've got your night in the sun.
ADRIAN CHILES

Football is much harder if you don't have the ball.
SVEN-GÖRAN ERIKSSON

So very different from the scenes in 1872 at the cup final none of us can remember.
JOHN MOTSON

Northern Rock eventually turned to Arsenal for help. They'd heard Arsène Wenger had a surplus of foreign reserves.
AUTHOR

That's a typical Ipswich move, O'Callaghan crossing for Mariner to drive over the bar.
JOHN MOTSON

Toshack also had a spell managing Sporting Lesbian.
Leek Post and Times

I definitely want Brooklyn to be christened, but I don't know into what religion yet.
DAVID BECKHAM

Chesterfield 1 Chester 1, so that local 'derby' ending in a draw.
DES LYNAM

The problem we have here at Wimbledon is, we seem to have suffered a loss of complacency.
JOE KINNEAR

I'll give you an Arsène Wenger answer. I didn't see it.
KELHAM O'HANLON, Preston caretaker manager

Well, as the saying goes, football is an old, funny game.
GIANLUCA VIALLI

The goalkeeper parried the ball or, as we used to say in my day, he couldn't hold it.
GORDON BANKS

Brazil, so good it's as if they are running around the pitch playing with themselves.
JOHN MOTSON

Barnsley have started the way they mean to begin.
CHRIS KAMARA

Paolo Wanchope scoring after 67 minutes. That's exactly the start Manchester City would have wanted.
DAVE BASSETT

Chris Armstrong is going nowhere, he's staying at Crystal Palace.
ALAN SMITH, Palace manager

Our first goal was pure textile stuff.
JOHN LAMBIE, Partick Thistle

Thierry Henry, exploding like the French train he is.
DAVID PLEAT

You seemed to be in control in the first-half, you certainly looked comfortable. You created chances in that first period, bossed the first 45 minutes. Would you say, given your domination of the first-half and the fact you weren't troubled, you were disappointed to go in goalless after a first 45 minutes in which you had the upper hand?
GARTH CROOKS

I have a number of alternatives and each one gives me something different.
GLENN HODDLE

If Glenn Hoddle had been any other nationality, he would have had 70 or 80 caps for England.
JOHN BARNES

He got a yellow card for the dive and a red card for the sending-off.
STEVE McCLAREN

The final? If United and Arsenal get through the quarter-finals and can avoid themselves in the semi-finals . . .
MARK LAWRENSON

And the town of Macclesfield is rocking tonight, like only Macclesfield can.
BBC RADIO STOKE

I think in the end it will be down to Manchester United and Arsenal.
(BRYAN HAMILTON, former Northern Ireland manager)
So, you clearly haven't ruled out Liverpool then?
(VICTORIA DERBYSHIRE, BBC FiveLive)

[David] James is comfortably one of the most articulate in the England squad – an amateur painter, a campaigner for healthy eating among children – but he really seems to have hit upon something here. Catch-22 was the old trick the US Army Air Force played on its pilots [after] Joseph Heller's novel. The double bind was that if you objected to flying absurdly dangerous life-threatening missions, then you must be sane and therefore of a stable enough mind to fly those very missions you objected to. The only way to prove you were mad was to fly the missions. It is certainly a more eloquent variation on the lame old football cliché that goalkeepers are different. The way things are going, any English goalkeeper of international pedigree and of a sane and stable mind would object to playing for his national team on the grounds of likely damage to his own reputation.
SAM WALLACE, 'Football Correspondent' of the *Independent* (2007).
And they wonder why sales are poor

When you're down, you Palace fans, the fickle finger of fate rarely smiles on you.
JONATHAN PEARCE

It's real end-to-end stuff, but unfortunately it's all up at Forest's end.
CHRIS KAMARA

He's such an honest player it's untrue.
BRIAN LITTLE, former Aston Villa manager

They say the universe is expanding, but the Derby front two still can't find space in that penalty area.
RODNEY MARSH

Those days at White Hart Lane – the taste of dirt, grit, sawdust and sweat in my mouth . . . and that was only the burgers.
JIMMY GREAVES

If it wasn't for bad luck, we'd have no luck at all.
NEIL WARNOCK

I like a drink as much as the next man – unless, of course, the man next to me happens to be George Best.
WILF McGUINNESS

Players complain about playing too many games, but one year I played 15 months of football.
FRANZ BECKENBAUER

I took a knock on the head. Doctors have given me a brain scan but they didn't find anything.
GORDON HILL, Manchester United

From the almost sublime to the ridiculous? . . . Unacceptable.
PETER KENYON, chief executive, comments on Chelsea's season on parting with Avram Grant – a season in which Chelsea finished runners-up in both the Premiership and European Champions League.

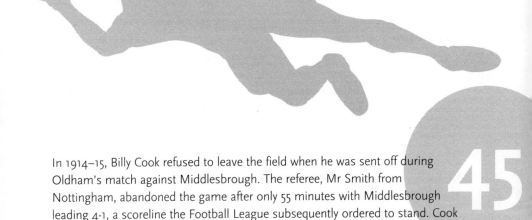

In 1914–15, Billy Cook refused to leave the field when he was sent off during Oldham's match against Middlesbrough. The referee, Mr Smith from Nottingham, abandoned the game after only 55 minutes with Middlesbrough leading 4-1, a scoreline the Football League subsequently ordered to stand. Cook was suspended from all football for a year and Oldham were fined £350. They finished the season as runners-up to champions Everton by a single point.

The only instance of a referee being sent off occurred during the annual British Challenge match between a Glasgow XI and a Sheffield XI on 22 September 1930. Referee Mr J. Thompson (Burnbank) was wearing a white shirt and black shorts – the same strip as the Sheffield team. After 15 minutes of play the Sheffield captain, Jimmy Seed, protested, saying his players were mistaking the referee for one of their own. Mr Thompson was ordered from the field by Scottish FA officials, and asked to don a jacket. Upon his return, the game recommenced with him in charge.

In the entire 1946–47 season, only 12 players were sent off in the Football League. The following season the number of dismissals was 13, and in 1949–50 it was 14.

Stan Anderson (Sunderland) was the first player to be dismissed while on duty for England. He received his marching orders when playing for England Under-23s against Bulgaria in Sofia on 19 May 1957.

Only three other players have been sent off while playing for England Under-23s: Alan Ball (Blackpool), v. Austria in 1965; Kevin Keegan (Liverpool), v. East Germany in 1972; and Steve Perryman (Spurs), v. Portugal in 1974. These dismissals all occurred when England were playing away.

The first player to be dismissed while playing for England Under-21s was Sammy Lee (Liverpool v. Hungary in 1981). Again, this occurred on foreign soil.

As a result of his dismissal for a foul on Alan Ball during the Northern Ireland–England game at Windsor Park in 1967, Billy Ferguson (Linfield) became the first Irish footballer to be sent off in an international match and the first player ever to be dismissed in the Home International Championship.

Trevor Hockey was the first Wales player to be sent off in an international match. He was dismissed during Wales's match against Poland on 26 September 1973.

The first England player to be dismissed in an international match was Alan Mullery (Spurs), who was sent off during the 1-0 defeat against Yugoslavia on 5 June 1968.

The first Scotland player to be sent off in an international match was Bertie Auld, against Holland on 27 May 1959, in the third minute of injury-time. It was his first international.

The first player to be sent off while playing for the full England team in England was Paul Scholes (Manchester United), against Sweden at Wembley in a European Championship qualifying match on 5 June 1999.

In 1962–63, Mansfield Town had ten players booked during their second round FA Cup tie against Crystal Palace at Selhurst Park, but not one was sent off. The tie ended 2-2, and Mansfield won the replay 7-2.

In 1972, Stockport County centre-forward Ian Lawther had his suspension as a result of being sent off against Hull City reversed following evidence given by John Bingham, a Methodist minister who attended the match.

Chelsea were fined by the FA in 1972–73 for having played Ron Harris in a friendly against the British Police at Hartley Wintney in Hampshire when the Chelsea skipper was serving a suspension as a result of a sending-off. Commenting on the situation in the *Daily Mirror*, Harris said, 'I was only playing against a team of policemen. I don't think we [Chelsea] did anything to break the law.'

The first double sending-off involving English clubs at Wembley occurred in the Charity Shield match between Leeds United and Liverpool in August 1974. Billy Bremner (Leeds) and Kevin Keegan (Liverpool) were both dismissed following a fracas. It was the first time the Charity Shield match was televised live.

The record number of dismissals in an international match is 19. On 25 June 1975, in the game between Chile and Uruguay, Chile had ten players sent off and Uruguay nine. The match had been abandoned and some of these dismissals occurred as the remaining players left the field.

Red cards for a sending-off and yellow cards for a booking (caution) were introduced in the Football League on 2 October 1976. Prior to this referees simply gave a verbal instruction and hand indication for a sending-off.

George Best was the first player to receive a red card, when playing for Fulham against Southampton. He was dismissed for foul and abusive language to a match official on the very day red cards were introduced.

On 9 January 1979, during Charlton Athletic's third round FA Cup tie against Maidstone United, referee Brian Martin dismissed Charlton's Derek Hales and Mike Flanagan for fighting each other.

The first player to be sent off in an FA Cup Final was Kevin Moran, who was dismissed during Manchester United's 1-0 victory over Everton in 1985. Moran received his red card following a 'professional foul' on Everton's Peter Reid. The referee was Peter Willis, a policeman.

During 1987–88, Dave Caldwell was red-carded five times, twice when playing for Chesterfield and three times when playing for Torquay United.

Not worth his salt? Nigel Pepper was sent off three times while playing for York City in 1990-91, on each occasion against the same opposition – Darlington. Pepper was dismissed in both League games and when the teams met in the FA Cup.

The fastest ever sending-off came after only ten seconds of Bologna's Serie A match against Parma on 9 December 1990 when Giuseppe Lorenzo was red-carded for retaliation.

In March 1996, John Neilson of Scottish junior side Easthouses Lily appeared before the Scottish FA after being sent off against Civil Service Strollers. After being shown the red card, Neilson had entered the dressing room of the match officials and cut referee Kenny Low's socks in half with a pair of scissors. The Scottish FA was not amused. Neilson received a ban lasting from April 1996 to the end of the 1997-98 season.

Off his trolley. In 1996, during a cup tie between Ecuador clubs Espoli and Barcelona, Espoli's Ataulfo Valencia was so incensed when a trolley being used to carry off an injured player knocked him over that he got up and punched the driver, for which he was immediately red-carded.

Pushed for time. On 7 February 2008, Cameroon defender Andre Bikey was red-carded in added time during his team's Africa Cup of Nations semi-final against Ghana for pushing over a medic who was attending to team-mate Rigobert Song. With Cameroon trailing, Bikey seemingly took exception to the amount of time the medic was taking to attend to Song and place him on a stretcher.

On the opening day of the 2000–01 season, Sheffield Wednesday goalkeeper Kevin Pressman was red-carded after only 12.7 seconds of his team's game against Wolves at Molineux – the quickest ever sending-off in an English League match.

On 5 January 1997, during the third round FA Cup tie between Everton and Swindon Town at Goodison Park, Swindon's Ian Culverhouse was red-carded after only 52 seconds for deliberate handball – the fastest sending-off in the history of the FA Cup.

> So, Culverhouse sent off and back in the dressing room all within the first minute of the game. I suspect he'll be taking no further part in this match.

BBC RADIO SWINDON

As the Crowe flies. Jason Crowe (Arsenal) holds the dubious record(s) of the fastest sending-off of a player making his debut, and the fastest dismissal in the history of the League Cup. On 14 October 1997, Crowe appeared as a substitute for the Gunners in their third round League Cup tie against Birmingham City and was red-carded after only 38 seconds.

Vinnie Jones was booked after only three seconds of Chelsea's fifth round FA Cup tie at home to Sheffield United on 15 February 1992 – the fastest booking in English senior football. Later in the same match, he was cautioned again and red-carded.

In the Scottish FA Cup quarter-final match between Celtic and Rangers at Parkhead on 17 March 1991, Rangers had three players red-carded, all of them English – Terry Hurlock, Mark Walters and Mark Hateley.

The first player to be red-carded in a League match while sitting on the substitutes bench was Ben Rowe of Exeter City. On 27 October 1990, Rowe was dismissed during a game against Fulham for constant dissent.

The only club to have had two players red-carded while playing at Wembley are Stockport County. Mike Wallace and Chris Beaumont were dismissed during County's Division Two play-off final against Burnley in May 1994.

Playing for Manchester United against Crystal Palace at Selhurst Park on 25 January 1995, Eric Cantona was red-carded for a foul on an opponent. As he left the field he was subjected to verbal abuse from a Palace supporter; incensed, the Frenchman leapt into the crowd and aimed a kick at the abusive fan. Later, when Cantona announced his retirement from the game and informed the media he wished to pursue a career as an actor, it prompted one wag to say that Cantona was to appear in a new BBC sitcom, *One Foot in the Crowd*. (For this offence, and that of bringing the game into disrepute, Cantona received the longest suspension in modern British football – eight months – and was fined £20,000. Apart from the punishment meted out by his club and the football authorities, Cantona also received a two-week jail sentence which was reduced on appeal to 120 hours' community service.)

Eric Cantona was sentenced to do 120 hours' community service, which has been reduced to 80 hours on appeal – from the community.
JIMMY GREAVES

On 6 September 1992, Hereford United had four players red-carded in a game at Northampton Town yet still managed to draw 1-1.

In 1994–95, in a Scottish League match, Stranraer led Airdrie 1-0. Stranraer then had four players red-carded – a record number of dismissals for a Scottish League game. They finished the game with seven players and lost the match 5-1. Two years later, Hearts had the dubious honour of equalling Stranraer's record when they had four players dismissed against Rangers (14 September 1996).

On 16 December 1996, a record for the Scottish Cup was set when two teams had three players red-carded on the same day but in separate cup matches – Albion Rovers away to Forfar Athletic, and Huntly away to Clyde.

On 26 September 1998, Sheffield Wednesday's Paolo Di Canio was sent off and immediately suspended for pushing referee Paul Alcock to the ground during Wednesday's game against Arsenal at Hillsborough. Those who witnessed the referee tumble, however, might have been grateful it was not a windy day, as Mr Alcock might have had trouble staying on his feet.

The record number of dismissals in England and Scotland on the same day occurred on 16 October 1999 when 14 players were red-carded in England and 11 in Scotland.

Total football and the Beautiful Game? In the international between Brazil and Holland in Goiania on 6 June 1999, Holland had three players red-carded and Brazil two.

13 December 2003 saw a record number of red cards issued on a single day in English football: 19 players were dismissed, two in the Premiership and 17 in the Football League.

The highest number of players red-carded by a female official refereeing a men's game is five. During the international Island Games Cup match in Guernsey between Guernsey and Rhodes, Wendy Toms dismissed five players from the Rhodes team.

Apart from the obvious exception of one-club players, Carlton Palmer is the only player to have been red-carded with every Premiership club he played for – Sheffield Wednesday, Leeds United, Southampton, Nottingham Forest and Coventry City.

Rigobert Song was singing from the same hymn sheet at the 1998 World Cup. When the Cameroon defender was red-carded against Chile he became the first player to be dismissed in two World Cup Finals, having also been sent off during USA 94.

On 23 November 2002, five players were red-carded in the last minute of the game between Exeter City and Cambridge United. Exeter won 3-2.

Roy Keane must have turned over a new leaf when, as manager of Sunderland, he encouraged his players to demonstrate discipline on the field and not contend decisions made by referees. During his playing career, Keane was red-carded 13 times including once at Wembley, for Manchester United against Chelsea in the 2000 Charity Shield, and received 95 yellow cards.

On 20 January 2007, Keith Gillespie (Sheffield United) was sent off for elbowing a Reading player at Bramall Lane after being on the pitch for zero seconds of play. Gillespie appeared as a second-half substitute, committed the offence, and was red-carded before play resumed.

British football's red-card rogues are Willie Johnston and Roy McDonagh, both of whom were dismissed 21 times in their playing careers. Johnston's dismal dismissal record reads Rangers (seven), West Bromwich Albion (six), Vancouver Whitecaps (four), Hearts (three), Scotland (one); McDonagh's encompassed 13 dismissals in the Football League (Birmingham City, Walsall, Chelsea, Colchester United, Southend United, Exeter City, Cambridge United) and eight in non-league football.

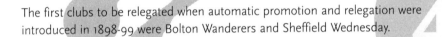

The first clubs to be relegated when automatic promotion and relegation were introduced in 1898-99 were Bolton Wanderers and Sheffield Wednesday.

The closest and most extraordinary First Division relegation battle occurred in 1927–28, when come the last day of the season two points separated 13 clubs from the top half to the bottom of the table. Seven clubs finished on 39 points; Tottenham were relegated with 38 points along with bottom club Middlesbrough (37). Only seven points separated Middlesbrough from Derby County, who finished in fourth place.

In 1928–29, Cardiff City were the only team in Division One to concede fewer than 60 goals (59 – three fewer than champions Sheffield Wednesday). They also conceded the fewest goals away from home (43), but finished the season bottom of the table and were relegated.

Pride comes before a fall. In 1957–58, the cover of the Sunderland matchday programme carried the proud boast 'The only League club not to have played in any Division other than Division One'. Sunderland were relegated that season for the first time, ending an unbroken 68-year run in Division One since their election to the Football League in 1890.

Kiss of death. In the summer of 1963, Mr Geoff Osborne of Crewe placed a double bet of four shillings (20p) on Crewe Alexandra and Wrexham to win promotion from Division Three. Both clubs were relegated. In the summer of 1964, Mr Osborne placed an identical bet, this time on Port Vale and Luton Town to win promotion from Division Three. Both were relegated. Undaunted, in the summer of 1965, Mr Osborne placed a five shilling double bet on Port Vale and Wrexham to win promotion from Division Four. Port Vale finished sixth from bottom (19th) and Wrexham bottom, and had to apply for re-election to the Football League.

Blackpool began the 1966–67 season in sensational style, beating Newcastle United 6-0 at Bloomfield Road. It proved to be their only home win, and at the end of the season they were relegated to Division Two.

The Clarke family enjoyed many a success in English football, but also endured more relegations than any other footballing family. Allan Clarke was a member of the Fulham team relegated in 1967–68; Frank went down with Carlisle United (1974–75), Derek with Oxford United (1975–76), Kelvin with Walsall (1978–79) and Wayne with Wolves (1981–82).

In a dramatic finale to the 1982–83 season, with Swansea and Brighton already relegated from Division One, the remaining place rested on the outcome of the game between Manchester City and Luton Town, who met at Maine Road on the final day of the season. Luton won 1-0, their goal scored by substitute Raddy Antic in the 86th minute. When the final whistle sounded, Luton manager David Pleat could not contain his joy and relief, running and jumping on the pitch to embrace his players. The most striking aspect of this performance was his beige shoes.

Lincoln City were the first club to lose Football League status automatically when they were relegated to the Conference in 1986–87. This meant Lincoln became the only club to have experienced four spells outside the Football League. They were voted out of the League in 1908, gained re-election the following season, only to be voted out again in 1911. They were readmitted in 1912 but were voted out for a third time in 1920, only then to become founder members of Division Three North in 1921.

Between 1962 and 1966, Carlisle United appeared in five different divisions in as many seasons. Promoted from Division Four, Carlisle were relegated from Division Three in their first season but won promotion back to Division Three at the first attempt, which was followed by promotion to Division Two. Wimbledon's feat of playing in seven different divisions in seven seasons encompassed only two relegations, from Division Three to Four (1980 and 1982).

Relegation was introduced in Scotland in 1921–22.

How the mighty did fall. Preston North End were the first champions of the Football League in 1888-89 and the first club to achieve the League and cup double. In 1986, Preston finished in the bottom four of Division Four and had to apply for re-election to the Football League. There was to be some success at last for Preston: the club was readmitted.

Wolverhampton Wanderers, the most successful club of the 1950s, suffered between 1984 and 1986 the ignominy of successive relegations from Division One to Division Four.

In 1960–61, Newcastle United scored 86 goals in the First Division, eight more than runners-up Sheffield Wednesday, yet Newcastle were relegated.

Very disappointed to have gone down, but there was nothing between us and Bradford City, except three points.
EGIL OLSEN, Wimbledon manager

In 1962–63, Carlisle United (Division Three) won only five games fewer than fourth-placed Coventry City yet finished second from bottom and were relegated to Division Four.

In 1966–67, Ayr United were relegated from Scottish Division One having won only one of their 34 League matches, a 1-0 home victory over St Johnstone.

In 1972–73, Norwich City scored the fewest goals in the First Division (36) and conceded the most (63) yet still avoided relegation by two points.

In 1974–75, Aldershot (Division Three) had three points deducted for playing an unregistered player, which was reduced to one point on appeal. Come the end of the season, Aldershot and Bournemouth finished level on 38 points but Bournemouth were relegated on goal difference.

 When I said even my missus could save Derby from relegation I was, of course, exaggerating.
PETER TAYLOR

Middlesbrough is the only club in English football to have appeared in two major cup finals and suffered relegation in the same season. In 1996–97, Middlesbrough were beaten by Chelsea in the FA Cup Final (2-0) and Leicester City in the League Cup Final (1-0 after 1-1) and were relegated by a margin of two points. Earlier in the season they had been docked two points for calling off their game against Blackburn Rovers, citing illness to players.

Carlisle United needed victory over Plymouth Argyle at Brunton Park on the last day of 1998-99 to avoid relegation to the Conference. With the score 1-1 and the game deep into time added on, Carlisle won a corner. Their goalkeeper, Jimmy Glass, came up into the Argyle penalty area and scored with only ten seconds of the match remaining to ensure Carlisle's survival at the expense of Scarborough. On hearing of the Carlisle goalkeeper's winning goal, a Scarborough director told his local radio station, 'When the news came through of Glass's goal, I was shattered.'

Airdrie go, Airdrie go, Airdrie go! In 2001–02 Airdrie were runners-up in Scottish Division One but folded due to financial problems. Their demise meant that Falkirk would not be relegated to Division Two, nor Stenhousemuir to Division Three. With a vacancy in Division Three, Gretna were elected to the Scottish League. Days after Gretna's election, Clydebank folded due to financial problems. Their place was taken by a newly formed Airdrie.

Stockport County were relegated from Division One on 16 March 2002 with seven matches still to play. This ignominious record was equalled by MK Dons, who with seven games to play in the 2003–04 season were relegated from Division One (6 April).

The earliest relegation in First Division football was that of Queens Park Rangers, whose fate was sealed on 29 March 1969 with five games remaining. Queens Park Rangers won only four of their 42 League matches that season. In 2005–06, Sunderland's relegation from the Premiership was confirmed when the club also had five matches to play.

I was guest speaker at Sunderland's end-of-season dinner. That was in October.

TOMMY DOCHERTY

47 The first football agent can be said to have been Bagenal Harvey, who in 1946 represented Denis Compton, who played football for Arsenal and cricket for Middlesex and appeared for England at both sports. Harvey negotiated a deal with County Perfumery for Compton to promote Brylcreem, for which the Arsenal player received £1,000 for three days' photographic work and the rights to use his image in advertisements. Harvey looked after Compton's commercial interests outside football but was never involved in contract negotiations with Arsenal or Middlesex. In 1958, Harvey began to represent Fulham inside-forward Johnny Haynes. Haynes succeeded Compton as the 'Brylcreem Boy', but again, Harvey had no dealings with Fulham regarding Haynes's contract and wages.

In 1959, a similar arrangement was struck between agent Stan Thomlin and Jimmy Greaves, then of Chelsea. Thomlin represented Greaves in what were then termed 'peripheral interests' – that is, work Greaves took outside football. The first contract Thomlin negotiated was for Greaves to advertise Bovril. The advert regularly appeared on the back page of Wembley match programmes from 1959 to 1961.

Throughout the 1960s and 1970s, players personally negotiated wages and contracts with the club manager. Should a team reach, for example, the FA Cup Final, the bonus for doing so was negotiated on behalf of the team by either a committee of players or a designated individual, usually the team captain. At Liverpool in the 1960s, skipper Ron Yeats did it, and thereafter Tommy Smith, who replaced Yeats as team captain.

In the 1970s, John Holmes and Jeff Pointon, who ran a management company called Pointon and York, began to represent the interests of Peter Shilton (Leicester City). Initially, Holmes and Pointon negotiated a sportswear endorsement deal with Admiral Sportswear, but soon they were acting on behalf of the England goalkeeper in relation to contract and wage negotiations. Holmes negotiated Shilton's transfer from Leicester to Stoke City in 1974 for a then record fee for a goalkeeper of £300,000.

Seemingly, Nottingham Forest manager Brian Clough was not enamoured of agents. When John Holmes attended a meeting in Clough's office to discuss Shilton's move, Clough was hiding behind the door as Holmes entered and tripped him up with a badminton racket.

The first agent to gain public recognition can be said to have been Eric 'Monster' Hall, who in 1987 began to represent the interests and negotiate contracts on behalf of a number of Tottenham Hotspur players, the first of whom was Steve Perryman. Hall had no background in football; his business was in the music and entertainment industry. He was introduced to the Spurs players by Terry Venables.

In the early 1990s, as football gained popularity and became more commercially viable due to increasing TV coverage, mainly through the advent of Sky Sports and the Premiership, nigh on every player in the top divisions deemed it necessary to have an agent to handle wages, contracts and the burgeoning commercial opportunities coming their way. Overseas players were by now common in British football, and agents were also required to negotiate on their behalf.

Following the Bosman ruling, in 1995 the European Court of Justice ruled that an out-of-contract player over the age of 24 was to be automatically entitled to a free transfer. This allowed players over that age to negotiate larger signing-on fees when moving to a new club; often this fee was similar in size to the transfer fee itself. With such sums now in millions of pounds, it was essential that footballers had professional representatives in what had become a complex, high-stakes arena.

In 1992, Rachel Anderson became the first FIFA-registered female football agent; she represented Julian Dicks (West Ham United) and, later, David Seaman (Arsenal). In 1998, Anderson was banned from attending the annual Professional Footballers Association dinner because she was a woman, which resulted in Sports Minister Tony Banks declining an invitation to attend in protest.

In 1997, there were 286 FIFA-approved licensed agents. In 2007, the figure was put at 1,980.

Each agent is required to post a £100,000 bond with FIFA before he or she is allowed to act as an agent.

FIFA states that agents must not have a significant financial interest (greater than 10 per cent) in deals involving players, or be an official of a club.

Football agents have had a chequered history. In recent years the profession has often been termed a 'murky world'. In 2006, *Panorama* revealed that illegal payments, known in football parlance as 'bungs', were regularly being paid to facilitate the transfer of players from one club to another. These allegations led to the Premier League commissioning an investigation under the chairmanship of Lord Stevens (a former Metropolitan Police Commissioner). In 2007, Lord Stevens identified 39 transfers as requiring 'further investigation'.

There have been instances of agents representing both a club and a player in the same deal. Known as 'dual representation', it contravenes Article 14(d) of the FIFA Players' Agents Regulations, and in 2006 led to a case involving Newcastle United plc (appellant) and Her Majesty's Customs and Revenue. After concluding new contracts with players, clubs are required to submit two forms to the FA stating the parties involved in the negotiations. It was alleged that Newcastle United plc often approached a player's agent and asked him to persuade his player to sign a contract favourable to the club; the club would then pay the agent on the basis of how close to the club's terms he managed to get. The player was often 'unaware' of the dual representation. In such instances the agent is in breach of his fiduciary duty to the player to obtain for him the best possible contractual terms. In July 2007, it was alleged that Newcastle United (along with Portsmouth and Rangers) were under investigation by the police regarding possible 'irregularities regarding the transfer and signing of players'.

The Professional Footballers Association (Players Union) will act as agent/representative for any footballer in the negotiation of wages, contracts, etc. for no commission, though, should they so wish, players may make a voluntary contribution to the PFA Players Fund. In 2005, former Port Vale and Birmingham City defender Phil Sproson was appointed as the PFA's first 'Player Representative'.

Some former players who have become agents: Keith Bertschin (Ipswich Town, Birmingham City, Norwich City and Stoke City), Paul Beilby (Hartlepool United), Tony Dorigo (Leeds United and England), John Duncan (Dundee and Spurs), Mel Eves (Wolves), John Hawley (Leeds United and Sunderland), Cyrille Regis (Coventry City and West Bromwich Albion), Barry Silkman (Manchester City and Crystal Palace), Mel Sterland (Sheffield Wednesday).

Responding to a question about agents inciting players to move clubs after the departure of Gabriel Heinze, on 25 August 2007 Manchester United manager Sir Alex Ferguson was quoted as saying, 'What has happened in the last few months is only the culmination of the drip, drip, drip effect of dealing with agents who only have one thing in mind – to make money for themselves.'

48 In 1920–21, Stockport County endured a disastrous season. Not only were they relegated from Division Two, they also had their ground suspended by the Football League as it did not meet requirements. On the final day of the season, Stockport played Leicester City at Old Trafford. The official attendance was 13 – the smallest ever recorded for a Football League match. The game ended in a drab goalless draw.

The smallest man to have played League football is Harold Ibrans, who turned out for New Brighton in the 1920s. Ibrans measured four feet and ten inches.

In March 1927, Scotland fielded a five-man forward line against England at Wembley that was the smallest ever to represent the country. The tallest among them was Alex Jackson at five feet seven inches. He scored a hat-trick and Scotland won 5-1.

The Preston North End team that won the FA Cup in 1938 had a five-man forward line with a combined height of only 27 feet and eight inches – an average height of five foot six. Opponents Huddersfield Town were considered to have aerial superiority, and were the bookies' favourites. Preston, however, triumphed 1-0.

At five foot four, Bobby Kerr is the smallest captain of an FA Cup-winning team. He skippered Sunderland's triumphant side in 1973.

On 6 May 1969, only 7,843 spectators were at Hampden Park to see Scotland play Northern Ireland – the smallest ever attendance for an international match at Hampden.

Small Simba play in the Zanzibar League and were originally the football team of the Zanzibar Army. They have been champions on five occasions and, despite their name, have the largest-capacity stadium of any Zanzibar club at 10,000.

The smallest town or city in Britain to boast a club in senior football is Brechin, whose population in 2006 was 7,989.

The smallest attendance at an FA Cup semi-final since World War Two is 17,987 for the replay between Crystal Palace and Manchester United at Villa Park on 12 April 1995.

The smallest attendance for a third round FA Cup tie between League clubs is 1,833 for the tie between Chester City and Bournemouth on 5 January 1991.

The smallest attendance at an international match involving home nations is 2,315 for Wales v. Northern Ireland at the Racecourse Ground, Wrexham, on 27 May 1982.

The smallest attendance at a post-war England match is 2,378 for the match against San Marino in Bologna on 17 November 1993.

The smallest attendance at a match in the World Cup Finals is 300 for Romania v. Peru at Pocitas Stadium, Montevideo, Uruguay, on 14 July 1930.

The smallest attendance at an international match involving any of the home nations is 221 for Poland v. Northern Ireland on 13 February 2002. The game was played in Limassol, Cyprus, as the Poland team were based there in preparation for the forthcoming World Cup.

The fewest goals scored by a team in a 46-match season is 27, by Stockport County in Division Three, 1969–70.

In the 1990s, Brian Small played for Aston Villa, Birmingham City and Bolton Wanderers. He was five feet eight inches tall.

In 1992–93, Arsenal scored the fewest goals of any team in the Premiership (40 in 42 matches) yet won both domestic cup competitions.

The fewest goals scored in top-flight English football in a 42-match season is 24, by Stoke City in Division One, 1984–85.

In 2007–08, the club with the smallest-capacity stadium in the Football League was Accrington Stanley whose Fraser Eagle Stadium accommodated just 5,057. This eclipsed Barnet, whose Underhill ground capacity was for a number of years set at 4,800, though in 2007 it rose to 5,300.

East Stirling's Firs Park has the smallest capacity of any ground in British senior football – just 1,880. It also boasts the fewest seats – 200.

49

The oldest song associated with a League club is 'On the Ball City', a popular music hall ditty of the 1890s adopted by Norwich City supporters in the 1900s, and still heard at Carrow Road today. Another song adopted by football supporters dating back a century or so is 'Pompey Chimes' – 'Play up Pompey, play up Pompey' – still synonymous with Portsmouth and their fans today.

'Traditional' songs adopted by football clubs and their supporters include 'Blaydon Races' (Newcastle United), 'I'm Forever Blowing Bubbles' (West Ham United) and 'You'll Never Walk Alone' (Liverpool).

How did Liverpool supporters come to adopt 'You'll Never Walk Alone' as their club anthem? In 1963, Gerry Marsden of Gerry and the Pacemakers, a big Liverpool fan, was friends with the Liverpool players and manager Bill Shankly. Before setting off for a pre-season tour in July 1963, Marsden presented Shankly with a tape on which was the group's version of the Rodgers and Hammerstein song 'You'll Never Walk Alone', which was going to be their next single. Shankly played the song on the club coach as they toured the Continent and was so taken with the sentiment and message of the song, which he felt embodied the spirit he had created at the club, that he told the Liverpool players, 'From now on, "You'll Never Walk Alone" will be our song.' Reporters from local newspapers, keen to file a story of any sort back to their editors between matches, penned pieces to the effect that Liverpool had adopted the number as the official club song, and the rest is history.

In the 1960s, Coventry City fans took to singing 'The Eton Boating Song'. Manager, Jimmy Hill even penned alternative lyrics for the fans to sing, though sadly, they never really caught on.

The only footballer ever to have appeared on the same bill as the Beatles is Colin Grainger (Sheffield United, Sunderland, Port Vale and England). Grainger was a winger with Port Vale in 1963 but also enjoyed a career outside football as a singer. While still a regular member of the Port Vale squad, he appeared as the support act to the Beatles in a concert given by the 'Fab Four' at the Southern Sporting Club in Manchester on 13 June 1963. From which point their paths diversified: the Beatles went on to find world fame while Grainger went to Doncaster Rovers.

49 The first football song to reach number 1 in the charts was 'Back Home', recorded by the 1970 England World Cup squad. The 'B' side was a song entitled 'Cinnamon Stick'.

In February 1972, Chelsea players reached number 5 in the charts with 'Blue is the Colour'. Later Chelsea teams were less successful with recordings: the 1994 FA Cup Final squad's 'No One Can Stop Us Now' (Manchester United did, 4-0) charted at a high of 23, and the 1997 team (featuring Suggs!) reached number 22 with 'Blue Day', as did the 2000 squad with 'Blue Tomorrow'.

Sunderland's song for the 1973 FA Cup Final, penned by Bobby Knoxall, contained the generic line 'We've got Jimmy Monty, he stops all the goals.' Now, not wishing to be pedantic, but, given a goal is a goal, how come . . .

In 1979, Kevin Keegan reached number 31 with 'Head Over Heels in Love' – described by NME as 'as good a song as you're going to get . . . from Kevin Keegan'.

In 1982, the England squad for the World Cup in Spain reached number 2 in the charts with a song entitled 'This Time We'll Get It Right'. Needless to say, they didn't.

In 1987, Glenn Hoddle and Chris Waddle (Spurs) reached number 12 with 'Diamond Lights', the mere mention of which conjures up images of rolled-up jacket sleeves on *Top of the Pops*. Coventry City exacted ample revenge by beating Spurs in the FA Cup Final.

Songs were recorded by Tottenham's FA Cup Final squads of 1981, 1982, 1987 and 1991 and were, respectively, 'Ossie's Dream' (number 5 in 1981); the imaginatively titled 'Tottenham, Tottenham' (number 19 in 1982); 'Hot Shot Tottenham' (a misnomer, surely, which reached number 18 in 1987); and 'When the Year Ends in 1' (which, rather than make it to number 1, could do no better than 44 in 1991). According to the *Guinness Book of Hit Singles and Albums*, all four of these songs 'feature the vocal and instrumental talents of Chas and Dave' – again, surely a misnomer.

The Cockerel Chorus (sadly minus the vocal and instrumental talents of Chas and Dave) reached a high of number 14 in 1973 with 'Nice One Cyril', in reference to Spurs full-back Cyril Knowles, though the title of the song was derivative. 'Nice One Cyril' had previously established itself in the nation's consciousness as the strapline for a TV advert for Mother's Pride bread featuring the character of a baker called Cyril.

Manchester United and Liverpool have enjoyed the most success in the charts with songs recorded by squad players. United's were the imaginatively titled 'Man United' (number 50 in 1976), 'We All Follow Man United' (number 10, 1985), 'Glory, Glory Man United' (number 13, also 1985), 'Come On You Reds' (number 1, 1994), 'We're Gonna Do It Again' (unfortunately they did; number 6, 1995) and 'Lift It High' (number 11, 1999). Liverpool's were 'We Can Do It' (number 15, 1977 – they did), 'We're Never Gonna . . .' (but they did; number 40, 1983), 'Sitting on Top of the World' (but not the charts – number 50, 1986), 'Anfield Rap' (number 3, 1988) and 'Pass and Move' (number 4, 1996).

Vinnie Jones recorded his version of the old Sam the Sham and the Pharaohs hit of the sixties 'Woolly Bully', which was as about as woolly a version of the song as you could wish for.

Football-oriented songs were given a semblance of street cred in 1990 when New Order reached number 1 with 'World in Motion', released to coincide with Italia 90. When re-issued in 2002, it reached number 2.

Far from being a football song but inexorably linked to the sport for many people, 'Nessun Dorma', recorded by Luciano Pavarotti, reached number 2 in the charts in 1990. The song was chosen by the BBC as the theme for their Italia 90 World Cup coverage. In 1998, Pavarotti reached number 35 in the charts with his version of 'You'll Never Walk Alone' – again, not strictly a football song but inextricably linked to the English game, and Liverpool in particular.

Hell bent on replicating the success enjoyed by Pavarotti, in the 1990s, Paul Gascoigne joined forces with Lindisfarne (yes, they were still going!) to record a version of the band's seventies hit 'Fog on the Tyne'. It reached number 2 in the UK. The record also did well in Japan, where it fitted the parking meters.

I don't give a damn about records. Kylie Minogue makes records.

JASON McATEER, seemingly unconcerned that Sunderland was in the midst of the worst losing streak in the club's history

Sing when you're fishing, you only sing when you're fishing . . .

Lincoln City fans' song aimed at travelling Grimsby supporters

An eclectic mix? '5-8-6' was recorded by Englandneworder, which comprised Keith Allen (actor, and father of Lily), John Barnes and New Order!

In 1995–96, Brentford divided their ticket allocation for their FA Cup tie at Charlton Athletic between 'singing' and 'non-singing' supporters. The singers were allocated the rear seats of the South Stand at the Valley, the non-singers the front rows.

Never one to knowingly hide his light under a bushel, in 2000, Andy Cole recorded an r'n'b cum rap song entitled 'Outstanding'. It wasn't.

A Love Supreme, who took their name from the Sunderland fanzine who in turn took it from the title of an album by jazz legend John Coltrane, once released a song entitled 'Niall Quinn's Disco Pants'. They didn't trouser much in the way of royalties.

The last 'football' songs to register as chart hits (for this small mercy one must be very thankful) were 'Daydream Believer' (aka 'Cheer Up Peter Reid'), recorded by Simply Red – and White (you couldn't make it up, could you?), which reached the top 40 in 1996; 'Three Lions' (the official England song for Euro 96) by David Baddiel, Frank Skinner and the Lightning Seeds, which reached number 1 in 1996 and which, sadly, was re-issued in 1998 to coincide with the World Cup with the snappy new title of 'Three Lions 98' (it reached number 1 again); and the cult 'football' hit of that 1998 summer, 'Vindaloo' by Fat Les (Keith Allen again).

In 2006, England's official song for the World Cup was recorded by Embrace and was called 'Song for England'. To cut a long story short (Spandau Ballet), Embrace are damned lucky still to be around today with a modicum of street cred.

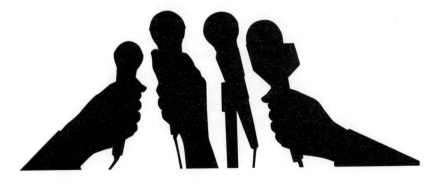

50

Curious settings for grounds . . . Villa Park (Aston Villa) was built on the site of an amusement park, Britannia Stadium (Stoke City) on a former colliery, Burnden Park (former home of Bolton Wanderers) on a chemical works, Fratton Park (Portsmouth) on a market garden, St James' Park (Exeter City) on a pig farm, White Hart Lane (Tottenham), on a plant nursery, Pittodrie (Aberdeen) on a manure heap, and Underhill (Barnet) on a duck pond.

Fourteen Football League clubs suffered serious bomb damage to their grounds during World War Two which resulted in them having to be closed for varying periods of time: Arsenal (Highbury), Birmingham City (St Andrews), Charlton Athletic (the Valley), Fulham (Craven Cottage), Leicester City (Filbert Street), Leyton Orient (Brisbane Road), Manchester United (Old Trafford), Millwall (the Den), Notts County (Meadow Lane), New Brighton (Tower Ground), Plymouth Argyle (Home Park), Sheffield United (Bramall Lane), Sunderland (Roker Park) and West Ham United (Upton Park).

The first all-seater stadium in first-class British football was Aberdeen's Pittodrie, which was converted to total seating in 1978. The first all-seater stadium in England was Ipswich Town's Portman Road.

Arsenal's former home of Highbury was the setting for the 1939 film *The Arsenal Stadium Mystery*, which also featured Arsenal's 1938 championship-winning side. Slade of the Yard paced the marble halls in search of the killer of an opposition player murdered during a friendly match – quite literally gunning among the Gunners. They don't make 'em like that any more.

With many clubs in the process of converting their grounds to all-seater stadiums in line with the recommendations of the Taylor Report, Arsenal began 1992–93, the inaugural season of the Premiership, with the North Bank closed for reconstruction. To blank the building work, Arsenal erected a huge mural across the face of the North Bank on which were painted seated specta-tors. Between 1998 and 2000, Arsenal switched their Champions League home matches to Wembley Stadium, but in six matches only won twice.

Highbury was witness to many great achievements over the years. In 2000, it was the venue for what remains the fastest goal scored in English football. Owen Price of Ernest Bevan College had the sauce to score after only 4.07 seconds of his team's Heinz Ketchup Cup Final against Barking Abbey.

Arsenal's first grandstand at their Plumstead Ground (1886) was a line of army wagons. In those days, Arsenal players were multi-tasking long before the term had been invented. One of Arsenal skipper David Danskin's duties was to collect admission money on the gate before joining his team-mates 'on the wagon' prior to the game.

Architects Rinder and Lietch's original plans for Villa Park were for the ground to have a capacity of 104,000. The plans also provided for a bowling ground, which was built and existed until 1980.

Legend has it that gypsies who were displaced when Birmingham City began work on what was to become St Andrews put a curse on the ground. A similar legend was connected with Derby County's former home the Baseball Ground, though anyone who ever played there in winter might have been forgiven for thinking the curse was the work of St Swithin, the Baseball pitch being a forerunner to many a scene since witnessed at the Glastonbury Festival.

The oak panelling in the boardroom at Blackpool's Bloomfield Road came from Lord Nelson's flagship HMS *Foudroyant*. The ship was wrecked in a Force 10 gale just off Blackpool pier when making its way from Portsmouth to the River Clyde.

The East and West Stands at Bloomfield Road were famous for having large adverts painted along the length of the roof, so that they were visible from the top of the tower. One of the most durable was for Dutton's Beer, which proclaimed in large letters on the West Stand 'Oh, be joyful'.

Cardiff City's Ninian Park was another ground where large adverts were emblazoned on the roof of a stand. The Bob Bank Stand got its name because originally that was the admission price for supporters – a bob being a shilling (5p).

Brentford's main stand at Griffin Park also displayed an advert on its roof. In 1995, it read 'Next Time . . . Fly KLM' and was at the time the largest advert in Great Britain.

The original pitch at Bolton's Burnden Park was laid on barrels and cotton bales; it eventually became a quagmire and had to be dug out and relaid in 1896.

Crewe Alexandra acquired their first floodlights from Coventry City in 1958 and mounted them on telegraph poles around Gresty Road. The poles survived until 1995 when the club acquired new floodlights.

When Chelsea's Stamford Bridge pitch was relaid in the new millennium, one of the contract workers, a Sunderland supporter, buried a Sunderland shirt deep below the centre spot.

Chesterfield was the last Football League club to acquire fully pyloned floodlights that met Football League requirements. They were installed at Saltergate in 1963–64.

It's a wonder they didn't run up a cricket score. On 29 December 1923, Darlington's game at home to Chesterfield (Third Division North) was postponed two hours before kick-off because their Feethams pitch was frozen. The watery winter sun, however, had penetrated the adjoining cricket pitch of Darlington CC. Having travelled all the way from Derbyshire, Chesterfield agreed to Darlington's suggestion of playing the match on the cricket pitch. The goals were erected, the pitch marked out, and with the blessing of the referee the game went ahead.

Estonia players and officials were not happy with the standard of the floodlights at the Kadriorg Stadium in Tallinn, the venue for their World Cup qualifying match against Scotland in 1996-97. The Estonia team failed to turn up for the rescheduled afternoon match, Scotland kicked off facing a deserted half of the pitch, and once the game was under way the referee promptly abandoned it. FIFA awarded the game to Scotland, then reneged on that decision and ordered the game to be played in neutral Monaco. Following this fiasco, the tie in Monaco was an uneventful goalless draw.

Everton's Goodison Park was opened in 1892, but the first three events to be staged there did not include a football match. First up was an athletics meeting, followed by a musical concert and then a firework display. The first match then took place, a friendly against Bolton Wanderers.

The original cottage at Fulham's Craven Cottage was built in 1780 by Baron Craven in hunting woods once owned by Anne Boleyn. In the 19th century it was the home of writer Edward Bulwer-Lytton. The cottage was destroyed by fire in 1888 but rebuilt in 1894 when Fulham took up residency.

Four times FA Cup finalists Royal Engineers used to play at a ground close to Gillingham's Priestfield Stadium.

Hartlepool United's Victoria Park was bombed by a Zeppelin during World War One. When football resumed after the war, Hartlepool took up temporary residence at a local ground, the wonderfully named Foggy Furze Park.

Hull City's former home at Boothferry Park was easily located by visiting supporters as it had six towering floodlight pylons as opposed to the normal four. It also boasted its own railway station, constructed in the early sixties.

During World War One, Leeds United's Elland Road pitch was used by the army for shooting practice. (Yes, yes, it still is.)

Leyton Orient's Brisbane Road ground had been in use as a football and sports stadium for 30 years before the club set up home there in 1937.

The flagpole that stood for many years at Anfield was taken from Brunel's ship *Great Eastern*.

Lincoln City's Sincil Bank was once a regular venue for cricket, athletics and cycling.

Eleven different London grounds have staged England internationals: Crystal Palace, Craven Cottage, the Den, Highbury, the Oval, Queens Club, Richmond Athletic Sports Ground, Selhurst Park, Stamford Bridge, Wembley and White Hart Lane.

In 1959, Luton Town's FA Cup replay against Blackpool took place on a Wednesday afternoon because the Seasiders exercised their right, as stated in FA rules, not to play under floodlights. The match attracted a record crowd of 30,069 to Kenilworth Road, and Luton won.

Manchester City's City of Manchester Stadium was originally used for the 2002 Commonwealth Games.

When Manchester United moved into their new home Old Trafford in 1910, the total cost of their new ground was £60,000.

Sir Bobby Charlton coined the term 'Theatre of Dreams' for Old Trafford during the course of an interview in 1976.

The first half-time scoreboard was put up at Middlesbrough's Ayresome Park ground in 1902.

When Millwall moved out of the Den they invited families to picnic on the pitch and buy sections of turf and items from the ground in an auction.

The Poplar Side at Newcastle United's St James' Park was so called because of the row of poplar trees across the road visible above the top of the terracing.

When Northampton Town's new Sixfields Stadium was built, it included venting tubes around the perimeter of the stadium for the release of methane.

Norwich City's Carrow Road took its name from Carrow Abbey, which once stood close to where the ground was constructed.

Nottingham Forest are one of only two English clubs (the other is Crystal Palace) to have derived their club name from the ground at which they were formed – the Forest Recreation Ground in Nottingham.

Oldham Athletic is the only club to have suffered a home defeat in the League while playing at their opponents' ground. Oldham were due to play Blackburn Rovers at home on Boxing Day 1981 but their Boundary Park pitch was declared unfit. The fixture was switched to Ewood Park and resulted in a 3-0 win for Blackburn, but the Football League registered it as a home defeat for Oldham – their first of the season. On 9 April, Oldham returned to Ewood Park for their away match against Blackburn and secured a goalless draw.

Partick Thistle's Firhill Stadium once staged a European Cup tie. Hibernian played Djurgården (Sweden) in the second round of the 1955–56 competition and won the first leg 3-1 at Easter Road. But severe winter weather in Sweden prevented Djurgården from playing the second leg on their home ground so UEFA switched the tie to Firhill, where on 28 November Hibernian won 1-0 to clinch the tie 4-1 on aggregate – the only instance of a club playing home and away ties in the European Cup against foreign opposition in their home country.

During World War Two, the main stand at Plymouth Argyle's Home Park was totally destroyed by bombs and the pitch was riddled with craters, one 20 feet deep.

In the late 1940s, when Port Vale revealed plans for a new ground at Vale Park it was hailed as 'The Wembley of the North'. Vale moved into their new ground in 1950, but there had only been sufficient funds to build the tunnel and paddock of the proposed main stand.

The first footballer to be 'imprinted' on the seating of a ground was Tom Finney, whose image appears in the seating contained within the 'Italianate' Tom Finney Stand at Deepdale, home of Preston North End.

In the 1970s, Rochdale were so strapped for cash that the club installed seats from an old cinema in their main stand at Spotland.

When Tommy Docherty was first appointed manager of Rotherham United in 1967, chairman Eric Purshouse took the Doc on a tour of the Millmoor ground and its facilities, informing him that now he was the manager, Docherty could make any changes he wished. At the rear of the main grandstand Docherty's gaze fell on a ramshackle old shed. 'Well, that eyesore will go for a start,' said Docherty. 'That's your office,' Purshouse informed him.

The first ever football match under floodlights took place at Bramall Lane, Sheffield, on 14 October 1878 between two Sheffield representative teams.

Sheffield United's Bramall Lane and Northampton Town's former home at the County Ground were both three-sided stadiums as they also contained a county cricket pitch. As a result of this, in the past it was often the case that both clubs had to play away matches at the start of the season to accommodate county cricket fixtures.

Sheffield Wednesday's Hillsborough boasted the first cantilever stand (built in 1961) in British football.

The 'Chocolate Boxes' of Southampton's East Stand at the club's previous home the Dell formed the only uncovered upper-tier stand in British football. In the early days of the Dell, an adjoining building was so close to the touchline that the wall had to be padded so that players did not injure themselves on the brickwork.

Southend United's Roots Hall boasted the only double-barrel roofed stand (the West Stand) in English football.

The ashes of Sir Stanley Matthews are buried in the pitch at Stoke City's Britannia Stadium.

Stranraer's Stair Park is on the same latitude as Newcastle-upon-Tyne yet nearer Ireland than Glasgow.

Graffiti is a blight on urban landscapes, but occasionally it has to be admired. In 1975–76, an advertising hoarding on the street side of Sunderland's main grandstand bore an advert for Charlie perfume with the catchphrase 'Who Says Women Are Fickle?' Underneath, someone had scrawled in red and white spray paint, 'Verdi!'

Sunderland named their new home the Stadium of Light not after Benfica's famous ground but for the fact that the ground was built on an old colliery site at Monkwearmouth which was thought to have been the first to use the miners' lamp as designed by Sir Humphry Davy.

Having lost the first leg 3-1, West Ham United enjoyed a 5-1 victory over Castilla (Spain) in the second leg of the 1980–81 European Cup Winners' Cup at Upton Park but did so without the vocal encouragement of their supporters. The official attendance at Upton Park was zero, West Ham having been ordered to play the game behind closed doors as punishment for their fans' disruptive behaviour during a previous tie in the Bernabéu Stadium in Madrid.

The only club to have had to move because their stadium was engulfed by lava from a volcano is IB Vestmannaeyjar of Iceland in 1973. It was two years before Vestmannaeyjar reclaimed their stadium and returned home.

In the 1980s and 1990s, Viktoria Zizkov (who played Chelsea in the 1994–95 European Cup Winners' Cup) staged home league matches on a Sunday morning with a 10.15 a.m. kick-off. In 1994, Zizkov's 10,000-capacity stadium in Prague was covered in snow and a home game was in danger of being postponed. Supporters turned up at the ground at five a.m. and spent over four hours clearing snow from the pitch and terraces to allow the game to go ahead. Minutes into the match, one of Zizkov's supporters/snow-clearers fired a flare which embedded itself in the roof of a sausage stand selling *klobása*, a favourite of home fans and a local delicacy. The stand was set ablaze, the pitch was engulfed in smoke, and the game was abandoned due to fears for public safety.

West Bromwich Albion's ground the Hawthorns is actually in Staffordshire as opposed to the city of Birmingham which is encompassed, in the main, by Warwickshire.

In 1991, when Wrexham revealed plans for a £44 million development at their Racecourse Ground, Frank Keating was prompted to write in the *Guardian*, 'Surely the sky has never contained a bigger pie?'

The new Wembley is an iconic football stadium. It contains 90,000 seats and is the largest stadium in the world with every seat under cover. The arch is 133 metres above the level of the concourse. The London Eye would fit between the top of the arch and the pitch. The circumference of the stadium is one kilometre. If you laid the seating out end to end, it would stretch for 54 kilometres. The roof weighs 7,000 tonnes. The volume of the stadium is 4,000,000 cubic metres – the equivalent of 7 billion pints of beer. Each of the large screens inside the stadium is the equivalent of 600 domestic flatscreen TVs patched together. There are 2,000 toilets – more than in any other building in the world. And there is more space between every seat than there was in the old royal box. So, still the venue of legends but no longer the venue of no leg room.

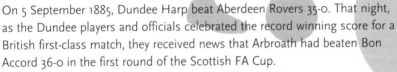

On 5 September 1885, Dundee Harp beat Aberdeen Rovers 35-0. That night, as the Dundee players and officials celebrated the record winning score for a British first-class match, they received news that Arbroath had beaten Bon Accord 36-0 in the first round of the Scottish FA Cup.

In 1888, FA Cup winners West Bromwich Albion met Scottish Cup winners Renton in a game billed as 'The Match to Decide the Football Championship of the World'.

On 15 March 1890, England fielded two different international teams on the same day. One defeated Wales 3-1 at Wrexham, the other beat Ireland 9-1 in Belfast. And to think, England fielded but one team against Croatia in the final match of their Euro 2008 qualifying group and still couldn't achieve the draw they needed.

In 1890–91, the inaugural season of the Scottish Football League, 90 matches produced 409 goals and not one game ended in a goalless draw.

England's most prolific pre-war goalscorer, Steve Bloomer (Derby County), retired as a player in 1914 and accepted a coaching post in Germany. Five days into his new job Great Britain and Germany declared war. Bloomer was interned by the German authorities and spent the duration of World War One in a camp in Ruthleben. Undaunted, he coached other internees and formed a team that played regular matches against local German sides.

During 1914–15, due to World War One, the Scottish FA banned midweek matches. Following a winter in which many games were postponed as a result of bad weather, several clubs found themselves pushed to complete their League fixtures. On 15 April, this led to both Celtic and Motherwell playing two matches on the same Saturday. In the afternoon, Celtic beat Raith Rovers 6-0 at Parkhead while Motherwell lost 3-0 at home to Ayr United. Immediately after their victory over Raith, Celtic travelled to Motherwell and that evening beat the home side 3-1. It remains the only instance of two clubs playing two League matches on the same day.

In 1929, Andrew Smailes was invited for a month's trial by Rotherham United manager Bill Heald. During that month, Heald was replaced as manager by Stan Davies. The new manager thought Smailes was a regular player and not just 'on trial', and Smailes played for Rotherham for over four years. In 1934, the Rotherham trainer retired and Smailes was asked to 'fill in' until a new one could be found by the manager. Two weeks later, Stan Davies left the club and was replaced as manager by Reg Freeman who believed Smailes to be the regular trainer and never questioned it. Smailes continued as the Rotherham trainer for 18 years until Freeman left the club. The Rotherham board asked Smailes to stand in as manager. 'You know you're only on trial,' one director informed him. 'Yes,' said Smailes, 'have been for twenty-three years!' Smailes was offered the post of manager on a permanent basis and remained in the role until 1958.

All my trials, Lord, soon be over . . . In 1931, Bradford Park Avenue (Second Division) gave trials to two players from local team Manningham Saints whose names were Albert Lord and Tommy Trial.

Andy Wilson and Alex Cheyne were the first players to be transferred from English clubs to a Continental club. In 1932, Cheyne left Chelsea and Wilson left Queens Park Rangers to join French club Nîmes. At the time the English FA was not a member of FIFA so, despite their disapproval, the FA could do little about the moves.

The match between Newcastle United and Portsmouth on 5 December 1931 ended goalless, but was unique in that during the course of the 90 minutes not one corner-kick was awarded. The final score was 0-0.

On 30 January 1937, not one away win was recorded in the entire fixture programme of FA Cup ties and Football League games.

In 1937–38, both Arsenal and Wolverhampton Wanderers entered the Colchester Challenge Cup, though why they did so appears to be lost in the mists of time. As one might expect, both reached the final, which Wolves won 1-0 before a Layer Road crowd of 17,500.

Hibernian's Johnny Paterson had a real 'club or country' dilemma in the 1940s. The Hibs centre-forward was serving with the Black Watch when his photograph appeared on army recruiting posters.

In June 1946, 14 clubs applied to join the Football League in place of New Brighton who had resigned during the war. Among the applicants were Colchester United, Gillingham, Shrewsbury Town and Workington Town (Divisions Three North and South would be expanded by two clubs each in 1950). Among the other clubs that applied were Lindsey United and Petters United. Lindsey became Scunthorpe United and Petters amalgamated with Yeovil to form Yeovil Town.

In winning the FA Cup in 1947–48, Manchester United played First Division opposition in every round – the first instance of this ever happening. What's more, because Old Trafford was bomb-damaged and therefore unavailable, United had to play every tie away from home.

On 21 September 1949, Peter Desmond was a member of the Republic of Ireland team that enjoyed a historic 2-0 victory over England at Goodison Park. Three days later, Desmond played for Middlesbrough reserves against Horden Colliery Welfare. Weeks after that, Desmond played for the Republic in a World Cup qualifying match against Finland in Helsinki. His next game was again for Middlesbrough reserves, against Hetton-le-Hole in the North Eastern League.

World heavyweight champion Joe Louis signed for Liverpool but never played a first-team match. Britain's greatest ever tennis champion, Fred Perry, signed for Arsenal.

In 1946–47, Jesse Pye made his Football League debut for Wolverhampton Wanderers, as did George Robledo for Barnsley, Maurice Owen for Swindon Town, Dennis Thompson for Hull City and Mel Daniel for Luton Town – and they all scored hat-tricks.

In 1949–50, Arsenal had a staff of 59 professional players – the highest number registered with any club in the history of the Football League.

In the 1950s, Darlington had a winger called Baden Powell who later became a scout for the club.

On 22 November 1952, the Leyton district of London staged three first round FA Cup ties – the only time a district in London has ever done so: Leyton Orient 1 Bristol Rovers 1, Leyton 0 Hereford United 0, and Leytonstone 0 Watford 2.

The fourth round FA Cup tie between Wolves and Bournemouth at Molineux in 1957 was held up when Bournemouth outside-left Reg Cutler collided with a goalpost which resulted in the post and crossbar collapsing. Cutler recovered to score the winning goal.

On 22 March 1958, Walsall's Tony Richards missed a penalty in the game against Swindon Town at the County Ground. In the second-half, Walsall goalkeeper John Savage was injured, Richards took over in goal, and he saved a penalty. Walsall won 3-2.

Stan Anderson is the only player ever to have captained all three of the major north-east clubs – Sunderland, Newcastle United and Middlesbrough – all in the 1960s.

In 1968, West Bromwich Albion became the first British club to visit Communist China. The tour was so ground-breaking it was the subject of a TV documentary. During a visit to the Great Wall of China, Albion skipper John Wile was awestruck. The interviewer then turned to John Trewick for his impressions. 'It's a wall, innit?' said Trewick to camera. 'And when you've seen one wall, you've seen them all.'

Eric Cantona and Vinnie Jones, eat your heart out. In the 1960s, the entire Alloa Athletic team and Hibernian's centre-forward appeared in a BBC drama, *Dr Finlay's Casebook* (based on the novels by A. J. Cronin). The Alloa team played the parts of the fictional Tannochbrae FC in a match which featured Brian Marjoribanks who, in addition to playing centre-forward for Hibernian, was also an actor.

In 1965, Sunderland winger George Mulhall, whose shot was once timed at 72mph, broke an ankle and was sidelined for two months. He'd fallen asleep at home in an armchair with his feet up on the fireplace, they'd fallen on to the hearth, and one of his ankles had sustained a fracture.

In the summer of 1964, during England's tour of South America, Alan Mullery wrenched his back while brushing his teeth.

In 1993, goalkeeper Dave Beasant was sidelined for eight weeks with an injury sustained when he dropped a jar of salad cream on his foot.

In 1996, Grimsby Town's Ivano Bonetti's jaw was broken by his manager, Brian Laws, who took exception to Bonetti throwing food at him during a post-match discussion in the dressing room.

In 2000, Barnsley's Darren Barnard sustained ligament damage when he slipped on a pool of wee deposited on his kitchen floor by his newly acquired puppy.

On 5 December 2004, Servette's Paulo Diogo jumped into the crowd to celebrate scoring a goal against Schaffhausen in the Swiss League, caught his wedding ring on the fencing and tore off the top half of his finger.

In March 2008, Derek Lyle fell through a glass table at home and sustained injuries that ruled him out of Dundee's Scottish FA Cup semi-final against Queen of the South.

When he was a player with Leeds United, Rio Ferdinand strained a tendon in his knee while putting his feet up on a coffee table at home.

On 11 May 2008, Rochdale's Lee Thorpe missed his club's League Two Play-Off semi-final against Darlington when he broke his arm in three places while arm-wrestling with a team mate prior to the match.

Colchester United were the first club to stage a sponsored game, against Crewe Alexandra in 1973. The game was sponsored by the local newspaper, the *Evening Gazette*.

The First Division match between Leicester City and Newcastle United in 1972–73 was postponed because of a bug that had given in 24 Leicester players and administrative staff acute diarrhoea. As one Foxes fan told *Football Weekly News*, 'The way City have been playing of late, there is more than a touch of irony about this.'

In 1967–68, the Aberdeen strip featured numbers on the front of the players' shirts as opposed to the back. A wag remarked that this was because Aberdeen did so much defending it gave the impression they were on the attack.

In 1969, the Queen named one of her racehorses Charlton after Jack and Bobby Charlton.

The oldest club competition for European clubs is the Mitropa Cup. It began in 1927 with clubs from Austria, Czechoslovakia, Hungary and Italy competing; the first winners were Sparta Prague. Later, clubs from Romania, Switzerland and what was Yugoslavia also entered. From 1980 to its demise in 1992, the trophy was contested by the champions of the second division of each country. In 1982, the Mitropa Cup was won by AC Milan; other winners include Torino, Pisa, Bari, Vasas Budapest and Banik Ostrava.

On 9 October 1976, the attendance at Wrexham's Racecourse Ground for the game against Lincoln City was 7,753. On 18 March 1977, the attendance at Sincil Bank for the return fixture between the clubs was 7,753.

On 21 December 1979, Bruce Grobbelaar made his debut in English football for Crewe Alexandra against Wigan Athletic. It was also the day his native country Zimbabwe (formerly Southern Rhodesia) was first officially recognized by the British government.

Eamon O'Keefe (Everton, Wigan and Port Vale) is the oldest player to have represented an Under-21 international team. In 1983, O'Keefe scored four goals for the Republic of Ireland against China during an Under-21 tournament held in Toulon, France. He was only months short of his 30th birthday, but eligible to play as each team was allowed to field one over-age player.

Jack and Bobby Charlton retired as players on the same day, the final day of the 1972–73 season. On 4 May 1973, Bobby was appointed manager of Preston, and three days later, Jack was appointed manager of Middlesbrough.

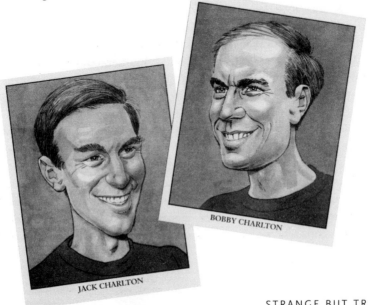

BOBBY CHARLTON

JACK CHARLTON

In 1980–81, Scottish Second Division side Arbroath won only three matches at home, but ten away from home.

Prior to the 1974 Charity Shield match between Leeds United and Liverpool at Wembley, the crowd were 'entertained' by a game involving two teams of Jack Russell dogs.

In 1980, Dumbarton manager Sean Fallon attempted to sign Johan Cruyff. The great Dutchman declined.

In 1982–83, Kevin Bremner scored against Reading three times, once each for Wrexham, Plymouth Argyle and Millwall.

In December 1982, Leicester City beat Burnley 4-2 in a game that featured four goalkeepers (two deputies due to injuries), three penalties (two of which were missed), two sendings-off and eight cautions. And the floodlights failed for a time.

Carlisle United played cricket, Orient a banjo; Sheffield United played hockey, Brighton preferred badminton; Walsall opted for Shakespeare and Wolves played Macbeth; Bournemouth went to town, Derby County had a curry, Nottingham Forest paid cash and bought rice; Dundee United bought a Ferrari, Blackburn bought flowers, Oxford got moody, and the Luton defence appeared before a judge . . . Norman Cricket played for Carlisle United, Tunji Banjo for Orient; Trevor Hockey turned out for Sheffield United, Roger Badminton for Brighton; Craig Shakespeare played for Walsall and Andy Macbeth for Wolves; Bournemouth signed David Town from local junior football, Bill Curry played for Derby County, Stuart Cash (at Nottingham Forest) bought Brian Rice from Hibernian; Dundee United bought Juan Ferrari from Defensor Sporting Club in Uruguay, Blackburn bought Tim Flowers from Southampton, Oxford signed Paul Moody from Southampton, and Alan Judge played in goal for Luton Town. (Author's note: and the winter nights just flew by . . .)

The oldest football club in France is Le Havre, founded in 1872. The club won its first trophy, the Coupe de France, in 1959 but is still waiting for its second.

On 9 February 1985, the Division Two match between Sheffield United and Oldham Athletic was postponed when workmen found an unexploded World War Two bomb while digging up the road outside Bramall Lane.

The third round of the 1988–89 Welsh FA Cup produced the longest result in the history of British football: Kidderminster Harriers 3 Llanfairpwllgwyngyllgocerychwyndroiswllilantysiliogogogoch 0.

On the orders of the local police, Torquay United's 1999 Worthington (League) Cup tie against Portsmouth was postponed because it clashed with the solar eclipse. Torquay's finest felt they could not cope with both the League Cup tie and the number of visitors wanting to view the eclipse from the town's seafront.

One of the top clubs in Botswana in the 1990s was Lobatse Cash Stores Gunners. The club's official name is Lobatse Extension Gunners, but from 1992 to 1995 they were sponsored by Lobatse Cash Stores.

Arguably the most exotically named team to take the field in 2008? Caps United of the Zimbabwe National League (who share their ground with fellow National League club Blackpool). The Caps squad included: goalkeepers Witness Monkulee and Energy Mubaagadoro; Lloyd Chittibengu, Method Majani, Laughter Chilembay, Marvellous Semanaka, Takeshore Gwangee, Gift Lunga, Wanda Unkoko, Limited Chikarfay and Danger Fourpence.

There is a club in the northern division of the Finnish Second Division called FC Santa Claus. Try as they might, the club has failed to win promotion to the First Division – but their supporters continue to believe in them.

On 9 October 1993, Reading won 6-4 at Exeter City. The result is unique in English football as five players each scored two goals: Jimmy Quinn, Scott Taylor and Stuart Lovell for Reading, Ronnie Jepson and Mike Ross for Exeter City.

On 14 October 1995, Mick Gooding was playing for Reading against Huddersfield Town at Elm Park. During the game a tannoy announcement conveyed a police message that a car must be removed as it was causing an obstruction. When the registration was read out, Gooding realized it was his.

In the summer of 1995, Dutch side Roda JC Kerkrade won the Maspalomas tournament in Gran Canaria but their captain didn't pick up the cup – because he couldn't. The Maspalomas trophy, modelled on a local lighthouse, was so large and heavy it took four Roda players to lift it.

In 1996–97, the secretary of the Screwfix Direct League (formerly Western League) was Maurice Washer.

In September 1996, Atletic Bucharest (Romania) were losing 16-0 when all their players suddenly left the pitch. Some gypsies had vowed that the Atletic players would leave the stadium naked if they lost the match 18-0. The club were subsequently fined the equivalent of £10,000 by the Romanian FA.

In December 1995, Brentford's Marcus Bent bought a mirror for his mum as a Christmas present. Unfortunately, as he carried it through the front door, Bent slipped and dropped the mirror, which shattered. He fell on the broken glass and sustained injuries that required 24 stitches. Dismissive of the proverb that to break a mirror results in seven years of bad luck, Bent recovered from his injuries in time to travel with the Brentford team to Carlisle on 10 February. On the train, Bent was buying teas for himself and the club physio when boiling hot water was knocked over and scalded his foot. The following Saturday (17 February), Bent played in Brentford's 2-2 draw with Bristol City and sustained an injury that resulted in his being substituted, and which subsequently required three stitches. Though injured, four days later Bent travelled with Brentford for the game at Swindon Town – a game that kicked off 15 minutes late because of a floodlight failure. Bent did not play another first-team game for Brentford for the remainder of the season.

Ipswich Town are the only club to have provided two England managers – Alf Ramsey and Bobby Robson. (Glenn Hoddle and Terry Venables both managed Tottenham Hotspur and England, but Hoddle did not assume the England role direct from Spurs.)

Prior to joining Southampton, Alan Shearer had been on the books of Newcastle United. He was released after failing to impress the club with his performance in a youth match. He played in goal.

52

In their early days as a club in the late 1860s, the only piece of kit that was the same for every player at Scottish club Queen's Park was an armband.

Following the formation of the Football League in 1888, clubs adopted a regular strip for a clearer distinction between teams, and to establish club identity. In the 1890s, shirts were made of wool with laced collars. Shorts took the form of breeches which came down to the knee.

In 1889–90, Lord Rosebery, a well-known English racehorse owner, attended the Scotland–England international at Parkhead and persuaded the Scottish FA to have the Scotland team wear shirts in his racing colours of primrose and pink.

In 1893, Tottenham Hotspur's Harold Payne lost his boots while travelling home from a game. Payne was provided with a new pair out of club funds. Southern League officials ruled, however, that Payne, by accepting the 'gift', was in breach of his amateur status. Tottenham were suspended indefinitely from all competitions, and in protest the club countered this ruling by turning professional.

In 1895, a number of Nottingham Forest players joined Woolwich Arsenal and brought with them the red shirts they used when playing for Forest. Woolwich Arsenal officials liked the idea of red shirts and adopted them as the Arsenal colours.

In the 1930s, Arsenal manager Herbert Chapman changed the club strip from deep red shirts to a lighter red with white sleeves.

In the 1890s, the style of heavy cotton shirts with buttoned starched collar and sleeves was adopted by many clubs, and by England.

In the Edwardian era, long shorts made of thick cotton replaced breeches. In 1907, accounts show the cost of the Woolwich Arsenal strip to have been as follows: flannelette shirts 2s 5d (12.5p), shorts 3s 3d (16p), russet calf boots 8s 6d (42.5p).

Laced shirts remained popular, and were worn by many clubs into the late 1920s.

Numbered shirts were worn for the first time in a Football League match by Arsenal, against Sheffield Wednesday, and by Chelsea in their home match against Swansea. Both matches took place on 25 August 1928.

Numbered shirts were worn in an FA Cup Final for the first time in 1932-33. Everton (the winners) wore shirts numbered 1 to 11 while opponents West Bromwich Albion wore numbers 12 to 22, the latter being that of the Albion goalkeeper. Shirts were numbered simply to help spectators identify players.

In 1939–40, a season that lasted for only three matches due to the outbreak of World War Two, the Football League decreed that numbers should feature on the backs of shirts at all times.

In the early 1930s, cotton shirts with collars, buttoned fronts and buttoned sleeves became the vogue. Along with long cotton shorts and wool socks, this style of strip was to remain largely unchanged until the mid-1950s.

When England and Hungary took to the field at Wembley for the 1953 international match that was to prove a watershed for English football, many journalists commented on the different styles of strip. The England kit had remained largely unchanged since the 1930s. Hungary wore light cotton shirts, much shorter shorts and lightweight boots cut off below the ankle. As Geoffrey Green commented, 'It was the old world walking out alongside the new world, and we knew the old world had had its day.'

In 1956, Manchester City appeared at Wembley in the FA Cup Final against Birmingham City wearing V-necked shirts with short sleeves, 'skimpy' cotton shorts, socks made of a wool/cotton combination and a new low-cut type of boot. Birmingham wore more traditional kit with collar and buttons. Following City's appearance (and victory) in this final, English clubs adopted their new style of strip.

This style of strip remained in vogue until 1964, when players began to wear round-collar cotton shirts with long sleeves, shorts made of nylon or other light synthetic material, and light cotton socks. Silk materials for shirts also became popular.

In the 1960s, it was common even for First Division teams to get a whole season out of one set of kit – sometimes longer.

 At Spurs I wore the same shirt for nigh on three seasons – in the end the round collar was all but hanging off – and Mike England was wearing shorts whose crotch had been stitched and mended countless times. I wore the same pair of moulded boots for four years. Clubs were very stingy where expense on strips was concerned. When we played in Europe, trainer Cyril Poynton would say, 'Whatever you do, at the end of the game, don't you lot go and swap shirts with the opposition.' We didn't, not least because we would have been too embarrassed.

JIMMY GREAVES

In the mid-1960s there was a fashion for a formulaic strip of a single colour that resulted in many clubs dispensing with the club badge on their shirts. For example, Carlisle United wore blue shirts, shorts and socks, which made their strip indistinguishable from that of Oldham Athletic, who for a time wore the same.

Also in the mid-1960s, some goalkeepers wore green jersey, shorts and socks. The first goalkeeper to be kitted out in such a way was Peter Bonetti of Chelsea. It was a style many other clubs adopted.

In the 1970s, when clubs were waking up to the commercial possibilities of 'branding', many who had dispensed with the club badge reintroduced it, though often the badge was redesigned; a town or city's official coat of arms, which often featured on a football club badge, was considered passé. In the 1990s, when clubs began fully to exploit branding and the sale of replica shirts, commercial managers were keen to establish club identity and to link modern commercialism to club tradition. This resulted in many of the 'old style' coat-of-arms badges being reintroduced to shirts.

In the 1980s, strips became lighter and shorts shorter. The style and design of strips changed annually as club commercial departments looked to cash in on the vogue of selling replica shirts to fans, who wore them as leisurewear.

Commercial departments of clubs say replica shirts are fashionable. You ever seen David Beckham, or any footballer, wearing a football shirt other than when he was on a pitch? Look at the sort of guy who wears a replica football shirt when he takes his wife or partner out. You telling me that guy is cutting-edge fashion?

JIMMY GREAVES

Players first wore names on the backs of shirts in the League Cup and FA Cup Finals of 1992–93. The Premier League took up the idea in 1993–94 as a means of helping viewers watching matches on Sky TV who might not be familiar with the players. Supporters realized that when buying a replica shirt they could align themselves with their favourite player by having his name printed on the back. What had been a 'trickle' market suddenly took off. Between 1993–94 and 1995–96 sales of replica shirts rose by 640 per cent. By pure accident the Premier League had opened up a new commercial market that was to be worth millions of pounds to clubs.

Such was the volume of sales of shirts bearing the names of top players, it was widely thought that Real Madrid signed David Beckham in 2003 principally for his commercial potential rather than his ability as a footballer.

The downside to having players' names on the backs of shirts was the end of traditional numbering. If tops bore players' names and were numbered 1 to 11, what would happen if a manager made a late change to the team? To overcome this problem the Premier League introduced squad numbers, later to be adopted by the Football League. The last team to take to the field for a Premiership match wearing traditional numbers were Charlton Athletic, for their first two matches of 1998–99.

As a result of commercial sponsorship deals with clubs, in the 1990s kit manufacturers became so powerful in football that the company's own logo became an integral part of kit design.

It has now become the vogue for teams to wear gold stars on their shirts to indicate past achievements. This idea came from Italy, where clubs that had won Serie A ten times or more were allowed to signify this by wearing a gold star on their shirts. The first Italian club to do so were Juventus in 1958.

In 1971, Brazil adopted three gold stars on their shirts to signify the winning of three World Cups.

Athletic Bilbao play in red and white striped shirts because the club was formed in 1898 by local businessman Arthur Pentland, a British mining engineer and Sunderland supporter.

In 1949, Bolton Wanderers arrived for a First Division match at Middlesbrough only to discover that the players' shinguards had been left behind at Burnden Park. The Bolton trainer, Bill Ridding, went to a bookshop and bought 22 paperbacks which the players used as temporary replacements. As one might expect, it made for a good story in the local press.

In 1953, Arsenal wore a strip of black and white striped shirts and black shorts when playing at home to Blackpool in the FA Cup.

Amazingly, Celtic did not have numbers on their strip until 1960. They first wore them for a friendly match against Sparta Rotterdam in May of that year, and even then, the numbers appeared not on the backs of the players' shirts but on their shorts.

Liverpool first adopted their famous all-red strip in 1965 for a European Cup tie against Anderlecht at Anfield.

In 1967–68, Sporting Lisbon arrived in Belgium for their first round Fairs Cup tie against Club Brugge KV only to discover that the skip containing their kit had been sent in error to Stockholm. Sporting borrowed a strip from their hosts, and players had to buy boots and shinpads from a local sports store.

After much wrangling and consultation with lawyers, in January 1976, non-league Kettering Town won the right to carry a sponsor's logo on the front of their shirts – Kettering Tyres – and became the first English club to do so. It was the idea of Kettering chairman Derek Dougan who, despite fierce opposition from the FA and various football governing bodies, achieved his aim and opened the door to blanket commercialism in English football.

The first League club to feature the name of a sponsor on the front of their shirts was Derby County in 1977–78. The sponsor was Saab.

Initially, television did not want to broadcast matches in which clubs wore sponsored shirts as they believed it to be 'free advertising'. In 1980, Brighton refused to wear shirts that did not carry their sponsor's name for a televised game against Aston Villa. ITV sidestepped the issue by broadcasting highlights from another League match.

In 1980, Nottingham Forest were fined £7,000 for wearing a sponsor's logo on their shirts for a televised match. Clubs lobbied the Football League and FA who in turn lobbied TV companies. In July 1983, television agreed to the broadcast of matches featuring teams wearing sponsored shirts.

In 1995, the shirt of Carlisle United's David Currie was sponsored by The Viceroy, a local Bangladeshi restaurant.

In 2002–03, Burnley bucked the trend by playing the entire season in shirts that bore no sponsor's logo. The official club line was that 'sponsor logos vulgarize the club's traditional claret and blue shirt'. Failed to do a deal with a sponsor then?

At the start of 1995–96, the commercial shop at Crystal Palace had an advert for a 'home hanging kit'. The previous season Palace had been relegated from the Premiership.

In 2002, Italy wore a new style of shirt introduced by kit manufacturer Kappa. Its stretchable Lycra called Kombat 2000 was tight-fitting to improve aerodynamics (though this could also have been to prevent shirt-pulling) and had underarm panelling. The style was widely adopted.

PLAYER'S CIGARETTES

DEFENSIVE THROW-IN

PLAYER'S CIGARETTES

HEADING

Substitutes

53 Substitutes were widely used on the Continent from the 1930s.

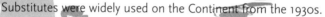

The first substitutes used by England took to the field during the game with Mexico in Mexico City on 24 April 1959. Warren Bradley of Manchester United replaced Doug Holden (Bolton Wanderers), and Ron Flowers (Wolverhampton Wanderers) replaced Wilf McGuinness (Manchester United). England lost 2-1.

Substitutes were first allowed in Football League matches in 1965–66. Initially, clubs were allowed to name just one substitute who was only permitted to replace a player suffering from injury. Within weeks, however, managers were introducing the substitute for tactical and other reasons. One often saw a substituted player feigning a limp when being replaced.

The first player to come on as a substitute in a Football League match was Keith Peacock of Charlton Athletic against Bolton Wanderers at Burnden Park on the opening day of the 1965–66 season. Peacock replaced injured Charlton goalkeeper Mike Rose. John Hewie took over in goal and Peacock assumed Hewie's outfield position.

Opportunity Knox – twice! The first substitute to come on and score in a League match was Bobby Knox, who netted for Barrow against Wrexham on the opening day of 1965–66. Not content with making this little piece of English football history, four months later, on 27 December, Knox also became the first substitute to come on and save a penalty in a League match, after replacing injured keeper Ken Mulholland in Barrow's 1-0 victory at Doncaster Rovers.

Archie Gemmill was the first substitute in Scottish football. On 13 August 1966, playing for St Mirren against Clyde, Gemmill replaced Jim Clunie who had sustained an injury after 24 minutes of the game.

The number of substitutes allowed in a match is governed by the particular rules of the competition, or as agreed upon by both managers if it is a friendly. For any match played under FIFA rules or under the jurisdiction of international federations such as UEFA or CONCACAF, teams may name up to seven substitutes of which three can be called upon to play.

From 1986, clubs were allowed to use two substitutes for FA Cup and League Cup matches. The rule was extended to Football League matches in 1987–88.

When the Premiership was formed in 1992–93, initially it allowed for three substitutes to be named, of which two could be called upon to play. The rule was also adopted by the Football League in 1993–94. In 1995–96 the substitutes rule was again amended: three substitutes could be named for Premiership and Football League matches and all three could be called upon to play. The current substitutes rule for the Premiership and Football League is that five per team may be named, of which three can be called upon to play. One of the designated substitutes may be a recognized goalkeeper, though this is not mandatory.

In 1995–96, the public address system at Moss Rose during a Vauxhall Conference game informed supporters of a Macclesfield Town substitution by announcing, 'Macclesfield substitution: Power is off, so Coates on.'

Substitute boards were introduced in Football League games in 1975. Initially, the boards denoting the number of the player to be substituted were held up by the trainer or coach of the team in question. It is now part of the role of the fourth official to hold up the substitute board and to ensure the smooth exchange of players on and off the field.

Rules state that any player who has been substituted may not take any further part in the game.

The only player ever to be substituted because he was too cold is Ayrton Ignacio, a Brazilian who played for Clydebank in 1966–67. During the second-half of Clydebank's game against Forfar Athletic at Station Park, Ignacio complained to the bench that he could not continue as he was freezing, and was promptly substituted. Clydebank won 3-0.

In the late 1960s, Ian Ross was often named as the Liverpool substitute. Fed up with never being given a full game he took manager Bill Shankly to task on the matter. 'Jesus Christ, Ian, son,' said Shankly, 'when you started out in this game you would have more than settled for being the twelfth-best player in the world!'

The first player to appear as a substitute in the finals of a World Cup was Anatoly Puzach, for the USSR against Mexico in the opening match of the 1970 World Cup.

On 8 September 1973, Arsenal's Eddie Kelly was so upset at being substituted against Leicester City that as he left the field he removed his shirt and threw it at the bench. Kelly retained his place for Arsenal's next match against Sheffield United, and when they took to the pitch the Arsenal players did so bare-chested.

In the 1970s, Leicester City centre-forward Alan Birchenall, who had missed a chance in a previous game that resulted in City fans criticizing him for 'being asleep', took to the field in the next home match wearing a dressing gown over his strip.

In 1975–76, David Fairclough was dubbed 'Super Sub' for the sheer number of goals he scored and created when coming on as a substitute for Liverpool. Fairclough was a sub for six of Liverpool's last seven League matches of that season, scored eight goals, and was credited with setting up two others. He also scored vital goals as a substitute in cup matches.

What might have been. In one of the final interviews he gave before his death in 1999, Sir Alf Ramsey told the *Evening Sentinel* (Stoke-on-Trent) that had substitutes been allowed during the 1966 World Cup, Jimmy Greaves, who had recovered from injury, would have been one. And had that been the case, with the final going into extra-time, in all probability Ramsey would have replaced Geoff Hurst with Greaves.

GEOFF HURST

One ploy of Liverpool under the management of Bob Paisley was to wait until they won a corner or a free-kick around their opponents' penalty box before making a substitution. Paisley believed that the opposition, when defending, were vulnerable when a new player was introduced as they did not have the time to sort out who was going to mark him.

On 8 October 1983, Darlington met Chester at Feethams. Darlington kicked off the game and the ball was played back to midfielder Colin Ross who, in moving towards it, injured his knee. Ross left the pitch after only four seconds of play and was substituted by Peter Cartwright, who subsequently created goals for David Barton and Tim Gilbert, Darlington winning 2-1. In an interview with the Northern Echo, Cartwright quipped, 'It was good to come off the bench and get a run-out, though I could have done with getting on a little earlier.'

On 15 September 1990, Andy Rammell, a recent signing from Manchester United, made his debut as a substitute for Barnsley against Blackburn Rovers in a Division Two match. Rammell was introduced in the 81st minute but did not touch the ball for a full six minutes. Eventually he did make contact with the ball, with his head, to score Barnsley's winning goal. Result: Blackburn 1 Barnsley 2. Rammell's winning goal failed to secure him a place in the team for Barnsley's next match at Notts County, for which he was a substitute again, and for the following two Barnsley matches. On 29 September, he came on as a substitute and scored Barnsley's only goal at Charlton Athletic with his second touch of the ball. Thereafter Rammell became a regular in the side, ending the season as the club's leading goalscorer.

The first time all four substitutes scored in a game occurred in the Division Three match between Barnet and Torquay United at Underhill on 28 December 1992. Nicky Evans and Mark Carter came on and scored for Barnet, and Duane Derby and Paul Trollope did likewise for Torquay. Barnet won 5-4.

On 12 April 1993, Phil Starbuck was called on to play as a substitute for Huddersfield Town against Wigan Athletic (Division Two) and scored three seconds after taking to the field.

On 12 October 1994, John Jensen appeared as a substitute for Denmark in a European Championship qualifying match against Belgium and scored after being on the pitch for only five seconds – the fastest goal by a substitute in an international match.

On 6 October 2001, Teddy Sheringham was introduced as a substitute by England in a crucial World Cup qualifying match against Greece at Old Trafford and scored after being on the pitch for only ten seconds. Having trailed Greece 0-1 and then 1-2, England went on to draw 2-2 and qualify for the World Cup Finals in Japan/South Korea. England's other goal was, of course, scored by David Beckham.

Teddy Sheringham also holds the record for the fastest goal scored by a substitute in an FA Cup Final. Playing for Manchester United against Newcastle United at Wembley on 22 May 1999, Sheringham scored after one minute and 36 seconds of coming on in place of Roy Keane. Result: Manchester United 2 Newcastle United 0.

The fastest recorded goal scored by a substitute for any England team stands at 3.6 seconds. It was netted by Jermain Defoe (West Ham) for England Under-21s against Holland Under-21s in 2001–02.

On 6 February 1999, Manchester United substitute Ole Gunnar Solskjaer scored four times in the final 13 minutes of United's 8-1 victory against Nottingham Forest at the City Ground.

Stan Collymore scored for five different Premiership clubs after having been introduced as a substitute: Nottingham Forest, Liverpool, Aston Villa, Leicester City and Bradford City.

In 2003, the International FA Board accepted FIFA proposals to cut the number of substitutes allowed during friendly internationals to six players. This despite protestations from England coach Sven-Göran Eriksson who advocated 'total freedom to experiment in non-competitive international matches'. On 12 February 2003, Eriksson changed the entire England team at half-time during the 3-1 defeat by Australia at Upton Park.

54

I go to every Stoke City game home and away. I watch every midweek reserve-team home game and quite a number of reserve away matches as well. On a Saturday morning I watch the youth team play at home. But the way Stoke have been playing lately has affected my support. I used to be a fanatic.

PHIL MELLOR, Stoke City supporter, tells *The Sentinel* that he is now not so keen

Sunderland supporters were so incensed by the performance of the referee in their 1-0 defeat against Sheffield Wednesday in 1903 that they stoned the match official's carriage as it left the ground. The Football League punished the club by ordering Roker Park to be closed for a period of seven days and Sunderland to find an alternative venue for games – which did not really affect the club or its supporters as they did not have a home match during that particular week.

From the 1930s to the 1970s, many smaller clubs depended on annual donations from their supporters clubs in order to survive. Often such sums of money were in excess of those invested by club directors, yet supporters were continually frustrated in their attempts to gain representation in the boardroom. Here are some examples of the substantial donations to clubs made by supporters associations in 1961: Barrow – £18,800, Bournemouth – £12,000, Carlisle United – £13,300, Grimsby Town – £11,100, Shrewsbury Town – £24,100, Workington Town – £16,600, Wrexham – £20,555.

Shrewsbury Town moved to Gay Meadow in 1910, but the ground was an open site. In the 1930s, Gay Meadow became an enclosed ground and new stands were built, the money for which was donated by their supporters club.

In 1932, it was with money from Swindon Town supporters (£4,500) that the club were able to erect a roof on the Town End of the County Ground.

In 1958, Tranmere Rovers Supporters Club provided the club with £15,000 towards the installation of floodlights at Prenton Park.

Between 1945 and 1999, Lincoln City Supporters Club donated £1.8 million to their football club.

In 1962, Portsmouth Supporters Club donated the money for the erection of new floodlights on corner pylons at Fratton Park.

In 1965, Ipswich Town Supporters Club donated £42,000 to their football club for general running costs and improvements to Portman Road.

In 1968–69, Rochdale Supporters Club were presented with an award for being the best-behaved supporters in the Football League. A week later, the FA ordered Rochdale to post warning notices around their ground after some fans threw missiles on to the pitch during the award ceremony.

Just the message Southampton supporters wanted to hear from chairman Rupert Lowe as their club faced up to the inevitability of relegation from the Premiership. In the matchday programme for the game against

Manchester United in 2004–05, Mr Lowe wrote, 'It is always easy to forget the progress we have made at this club over the past decade when, as now, results go badly. Our academy has continued to flourish, our community and educational activities have made progress, our shop is doing well, our matchday and non-matchday catering is the envy of other clubs, and our radio station has made great progress . . .' Well, that's all right then.

In his playing days with Blackburn Rovers, Ally McLeod (later to manage Scotland) had two Blackburn supporters living either side of him and his family. One of them continually told Ally he was the best winger Blackburn had ever had. One day Ally happened to mention this when talking to his other Blackburn-supporting neighbour. 'Well, that's right, he's always saying that about you,' said neighbour number two, 'but he also believes his radio works because there are little people inside it.'

One of the joys of attending football is the wit of supporters. In the 1950s, Newcastle United supporters dubbed their hero, centre-forward Jackie Milburn, 'Wor Jackie'. Following Milburn's retirement, Newcastle signed another forward, George Hannah, whom, with characteristic humour, Newcastle fans dubbed 'Wor Palindrome'.

In 1969, fanatical 19-year-old Huddersfield supporter Dan Tagg watched his team play at Leeds Road from his bed. Dan had been bedridden for eight years. On hearing of his plight, the club arranged for a removals van to collect him and his bed and transport them to Leeds Road for the home match against Blackpool. Propped up by pillows, Dan watched the game from the perimeter track. Huddersfield won 2-0.

During a game between Stoke City and Tottenham Hotspur at the Victoria Ground in the mid-1960s, Stoke goalkeeper Lawrie Leslie stepped forward, stretched out his arms and wafted each to either side to indicate that his full-backs should push out wide on the wings. 'He's bloody swimming now!' shouted one Stoke fan. 'He's not swimming,' shouted another. 'Poor blind sod's trying to feel for his posts.'

In the mid-1990s, John Rundle and his sister Florence's support of Northern League club South Shields went beyond the call of duty. The siblings remortgaged their house and raided their life savings to finance redevelopment of the South Shields ground and provide money for players' wages and team strengthening, and by 1995 they had given the club £280,000.

In 1995, Huddersfield Town supporter and lorry driver Chris Armitage dialled the Huddersfield club-call phone line only to fall asleep while listening to the tape. He awoke four hours later to find it still chattering away at a cost of 39p a minute. Mr Armitage received a bill from British Telecom for £93.60 and appealed against the charge but was unsuccessful. Still, he could always go on *Mastermind* – specialist subject, 'Injuries to Huddersfield Town players, 15 to 16 December 1995'.

In 1994–95, every home match at Newcastle United's St James' Park was sold out with the exception of two seats that remained empty from the first home match of the season until Newcastle entertained Manchester City on 2 January 1995. On that day they were occupied by a Newcastle supporter and his young son. The season ticket holder who occupied the seat next to the father asked why he and his son had missed so many matches. 'You won't believe it,' said the father. 'My wife bought my son and me season tickets back in July and kept them for Christmas presents.'

The oldest mascot to lead out a team is Harold Farnell, who was 90 years old when he did the honours for Bradford City in their match against Bolton Wanderers on 21 September 1996.

The early 1990s saw the establishment of supporters trusts, the aim of which was to give ordinary fans a say in the running of their football club, and in some cases to obtain outright or majority ownership of their club.

The first supporters trust was established at Northampton Town in 1992.

The largest supporters trust in existence today is the Manchester United Supporters Trust (pre-Glazer known as Shareholders United), with some 30,000 members. The Reading and Tottenham Supporters Trusts have, respectively, some 3,000 and 5,000 members. Glasgow Rangers Supporters Trust has in the region of 6,000 members.

Supporters Direct is an organization with full government and cross-party support whose aim is to promote the formation of supporters trusts and democratic support in football clubs.

Up to 2007, supporters trusts had prevented 20 football clubs from going into administration, the majority in the aftermath of the collapse of ITV Digital.

There are five Football League Clubs that are now run and controlled by supporters trusts: Bournemouth, Brentford, Chesterfield, Exeter City and Stockport County. There are ten senior non-league clubs run by and in the ownership of supporters trusts: Ebbsfleet United, York City, AFC Wimbledon, Telford, Newport (IoW), Enfield Town, FC United of Manchester, Scarborough Athletic, Runcorn and Cambridge City. There is just one Scottish club in the ownership of a supporters trust – Clydebank.

In 2007, over 40 supporters clubs or fans organizations had representation on the boards of their respective clubs.

54 Radio Head. London-based Scot and former police officer John Taylor is a fanatical supporter of football and obsessed with collecting radio match commentaries. The first recording he did was Scotland's 3-2 victory over England at Wembley in 1967. Since then he has recorded and catalogued over 7,000 radio match commentaries, many of which he utilizes in his voluntary work with blind people.

CELEBRITY SUPPORTERS (GENUINE SUPPORTERS, THAT IS)

Keith Allen – Fulham
Sir Richard Attenborough –
  Chelsea
David Baddiel – Chelsea
Danny Baker – Millwall
Sean Bean – Sheffield United
Ian Bell (Gomez – lead singer)
  – Everton
Melvyn Bragg – Arsenal
Chuckle Brothers – Rotherham
  United
Geezer Butler (Black Sabbath)
  – Aston Villa
Jasper Carrott – Birmingham
  City
Steve Cram – Sunderland
Noel Gallagher – Manchester
  City
Helen Chamberlain – Torquay
  United
Adrian Chiles – West
  Bromwich Albion
Elvis Costello – Liverpool
Ray Davies – Arsenal
Colin Firth – Arsenal
Michael Grade – Charlton
  Athletic

Nick Hancock – Stoke City
Paul Heaton – Sheffield United
Charlie Higson – Arsenal
Elton John – Watford
Nigel Kennedy – Aston Villa
Eddie Large – Manchester City
Mike Lewis (Lost Prophets) –
  Everton
Warren Mitchell – Spurs
Mike Osman – Southampton
Kele Okereke (Bloc Party) –
  Chelsea
Maximo Park – Newcastle
  United
Nigel Pearson – Spurs
Leslie Phillips – Spurs
David Mellor – Chelsea
Robert Plant – Wolves
Tim Rice – Sunderland
Chris Shiflet (Foo Fighters) –
  Arsenal
Frank Skinner – West
  Bromwich Albion
Delia Smith – Norwich City
Dave Stewart – Sunderland
Pete Waterman – Walsall
Robbie Williams – Port Vale

Cambridge United fanatic Peter Woor cycles around the country to watch his favourite team. In October 2007, Mr Woor (57) cycled 168 miles to watch Cambridge United play at Altrincham, only to arrive late and find all the gates and doors locked. Cambridge won 3-0 but Mr Woor missed the goals; he only gained entry to the ground when the exit gates were opened some 20 minutes before the end. By January 2008, Mr Woor had visited 58 different grounds on his bicycle and estimated he had cycled 8,000 miles in the process.

In February 2008, a group of Liverpool supporters announced that they were attempting to raise the necessary finance for a takeover of their club.

The first match to be broadcast on radio was the First Division game between Arsenal and Sheffield United on 22 January 1927. It was broadcast on the BBC Home Service, and in addition to the match commentator, an assistant called out numbers relating to areas of the pitch as depicted on a chart given away free with the *Radio Times*. Surprisingly for a company that prides itself on being impartial, the commentator was George Allison, an Arsenal director, who later went on to manage the club. Allison's co-commentator was Derek McCulloch, who went on to become 'Uncle Mac', the presenter of BBC Radio's popular request programme of the 1950s and 1960s *Children's Favourites* (later renamed *Junior Choice*).

The first League match to be shown on television in the form of brief highlights was the Division One game between Arsenal and Everton on 29 August 1936 which was broadcast on the BBC (the only TV channel at that time). As very few people owned a television set in 1936, the audience would have been minimal.

The first live match to be shown on television was a 'staged' friendly between Arsenal and Arsenal reserves at Highbury, broadcast by the BBC on 16 September 1937. Again few people would have seen this.

The first FA Cup Final to be broadcast in its entirety on radio was Preston North End v. Sunderland (1-3) in 1937.

To coincide with the first full-length radio commentary of an FA Cup Final, the BBC broadcast 'limited highlights', so that the 1937 final was also the first to be screened on television.

In 1938, the FA Cup Final between Huddersfield Town and Preston North End was the first to be broadcast live and in its entirety on the BBC.

With only seconds remaining of extra-time in that 1938 FA Cup Final, as Preston staged one final attack radio commentator Commander Tom Woodaroofe informed listeners, 'If Preston score now I'll eat my hat.' Preston were awarded a penalty, and George Mutch scored. More's the pity, Woodaroofe never did eat his hat, though he did pose at a table holding a knife and fork with a hat on a plate for publicity photographs.

55 The first live transmission of a senior British game other than an FA Cup Final took place on 8 February 1947 when the BBC screened the FA Cup fifth round tie between Charlton Athletic and Blackburn Rovers.

The first Scottish FA Cup Final to be broadcast live on television in Scotland was Celtic v. Clyde on 23 April 1955 (1-1), but not the replay (0-1).

The first Scottish League game to be broadcast live on television in Scotland was Clyde v. Aberdeen on 3 September 1955.

The first Football League match to be broadcast live on television was the Division One match between Bolton Wanderers and Blackpool on 9 September 1960. The game took place on a Friday night as a joint 'experiment' by the Football League and the BBC. The League feared that television coverage of matches, even in the form of highlights, would affect attendances so the 'experiment' was dropped.

As television was broadcasting only the FA Cup Final and England matches, for much of the 1950s and early 1960s supporters were starved of football on television. So much so that when ITV broadcast live charity fund-raising matches featuring a Show Biz XI against amateur and works teams, these matches drew large audiences.

Sportsview was first broadcast in 1954, initially on a Tuesday night. One regular aim of the programme was to focus on a topical issue, an aspect of technique, or a rule relating to football. *Sportsview* also went 'behind the scenes' at famous clubs such as Arsenal and Wolverhampton Wanderers. With no League matches on television even in highlights form, these 'strands' proved very popular with supporters.

From 1957 to 1967, the BBC broadcast *Junior Sportsview*. The original programme was anchored by Cliff Michelmore and presented by Danny Blanchflower (Tottenham) and Billy Wright (Wolves).

Sportsview switched to Wednesday nights, and in 1973 was relaunched as *Sportsnight*, broadcasting highlights of midweek encounters in the FA, League and European Cups. One of the flagship aspects of the programme was the annual BBC Sports Personality of the Year award.

The main presenters of *Sportsview/Sportsnight* were Peter Dimmock (1954–64), Frank Bough (1964–68), David Coleman (1968–72), Tony Gubba (1972–75), Harry Carpenter (1975–85), Steve Rider (1985–91), and Des Lynam (1991–97).

Grandstand was for many years the BBC's flagship sports programme, though the majority of viewers tuned in for news of football. *Grandstand* was first broadcast on 11 October 1958, presented by Peter Dimmock.

Until the early 1960s, the Football League prevented *Grandstand* from broadcasting updates of scores and even half-time scores as they felt that relating such information would affect attendances at matches. Pardon the pun, but as a result of this, in its early days *Grandstand* broadcast only final results followed by match reports. Incoming results were brought to the screen by a digital device known as a Teleprinter, each character of the result displayed one at a time in much the same way as a typewriter.

The classified results were broadcast at five p.m. In the history of *Grandstand* only two men ever read the classified results: Len Martin from the outset until his death in 1995, and then Tim Gudgin. Both read the results with the same gravitas. Viewers became so familiar with this style it was possible to know if a game was a home win, an away win or a draw just by the tone of voice applied to the name of the first club and its score.

The *Grandstand* theme was composed by Keith Mansfield.

'Football Focus' was aired at the head of the *Grandstand* programme and was a preview of the day's top matches. In 1974, *Football Focus* was launched as a programme in its own right.

In the 1970s, the BBC was not allowed to reveal the identity of the match/matches it was to feature on *Match of the Day* as the Football League – you guessed it – believed this would affect crowd numbers at the game. Viewers, however, always knew which match would be featured as *Football Focus* would broadcast a preview of a 'top game' live from the ground itself.

In 2005, Prime Minister Tony Blair appeared on *Football Focus* along with presenter Manish Bhasin, John Motson and Mark Lawrenson. Among the topics discussed were the current footballers Mr Blair liked to watch, who included Steed Malbranque (Fulham), Arjan de Zeeuw (Wigan Athletic) and Teddy Sheringham (West Ham United).

The final edition of *Grandstand* was broadcast on 27 January 2007.

Competing with *Grandstand* to bring the public reports and results of Saturday matches was ITV's *World of Sport*, which ran from 2 January 1965 to 28 September 1985. The first presenter was Eamon Andrews, followed by Dickie Davies. Another regular presenter was Fred Dineage.

World of Sport also opened with a football preview, 'On the Ball', presented by Brian Moore. Moore was succeeded in the role in 1981 by Ian St John, who, curiously, had previously entered a BBC competition for football commentators and had come runner-up to a would-be broadcaster by the name of Idwal Robling. St John was later joined by Jimmy Greaves, and so successful were the pair that in 1985 they found themselves presenting *Saint and Greavsie*. Their mix of seriousness and irreverent humour, and a penchant for featuring the quirky and curious, proved immensely popular with viewers. In direct competition with *Football Focus*, in terms of ratings, ITV won hands down.

After covering the 1992 European Championship in Sweden, though *Saint and Greavsie* was still attracting excellent ratings, the programme was axed. The Premiership was about to come into being, and as one ITV executive told Greaves, 'There is no place for a humorous and irreverent programme in what is now the very serious business of football.'

Sports Report is one of the longest-running programmes on BBC Radio. It was first broadcast in 1948 and originally aired between five and six p.m., providing listeners with a full classified results service, match reports, post-match interviews, analysis and a view on a topical football issue by a leading football writer.

The programme was initially broadcast on the Light Programme. From 1964 it went out on the Third Programme and began at the earlier time of 4.42 p.m. In 1970, it was switched to Radio 2, and in September 1990 to Radio 5, now referred to as BBC Radio FiveLive.

Sports Report's main presenters (many of them overlapped) were Eamon Andrews (1950–62), Des Lynam (1969–78), Peter Jones (1968–1990), Mike Ingham (1979–84), Ian Payne (1994–2000). Mark Pougatch is currently in the chair (since 2000). Since 1974, the classified results on *Sports Report* have been read by James Alexander Gordon.

The programme's iconic theme tune, 'Out of the Blue', was written by Hubert Bath and has been introducing *Sports Report* since the first one in 1948. In the 1970s, BBC executives sought to drop it as they felt it was anachronistic. One of the fiercest opponents of this move was Des Lynam. Listeners protested too, and the theme remained.

In recent years the BBC has come under criticism for broadcasting too many live matches on radio to the detriment of *Sports Report*. Often the classified results and match reports are shoehorned into a 15-minute slot between five and 5.15 prior to yet another live commentary.

One aspect of *Sports Report* popular with listeners, but long since dropped, was the personal view on some aspect of football as offered by a well-known football writer such as Brian Glanville, Bryon Butler or Ken Jones, and usually broadcast around 5.30 p.m. As Jimmy Greaves wrote in his book *The Heart of the Game*, 'These vignettes, almost always in prose, were highly entertaining, thought-provoking and a joy to listen to.' Alas, no more.

The first *Match of the Day* was broadcast on 20 August 1964. It featured highlights of a single game, Liverpool v. Arsenal (3-2) from Anfield.

This first *Match of the Day* had been commissioned by the controller of BBC2, David Attenborough, and thus was aired on that channel (at 6.30 p.m.). It wasn't seen by much of the nation as in 1964 BBC2 was only available in London and the Home Counties. On 3 December 1964, BBC2 reached as far north as Birmingham! Within another year, most areas of the UK were able to watch *MOTD*.

MOTD did not switch to BBC1 until 1983.

The first presenter of *MOTD* was Kenneth Wolstenholme, though for a number of years the programme was not studio-based. Wolstenholme's co-presenter/commentator was Wally Barnes (ex-Arsenal and Wales).

To combat increasing coverage by ITV regional companies, which also broadcast highlights of games, in 1968 the BBC successfully negotiated with the Football League to broadcast highlights of two matches on *MOTD*. As part of this agreement the BBC were obliged to show highlights of a minimum of three Second Division matches per season on *MOTD*. This was later expanded to cover two Third Division matches and FA Cup ties.

In 1970, *MOTD* was attracting an audience of 12 million.

In 1970, the programme became studio-based and was presented by David Coleman. Jimmy Hill presented from 1973. Des Lynam joined *MOTD* in 1979 and took over from Hill as the programme's main presenter in 1988. In 1999, Gary Lineker became the main *MOTD* anchorman.

John Motson is *MOTD*'s current longest-serving match commentator (and arguably its most popular). He joined the programme in 1971. Other notable *MOTD* commentators include Barry Davies, Gerald Sinstadt, Alan Weeks, Alan Parry, Tony Gubba and Stuart Hall. On 21 April 2007, Jacqui Oatley became the first female *MOTD* match commentator, for the Premiership match between Fulham and Blackburn Rovers (1-1).

The atmosphere within the Emirates Stadium has really improved since Arsenal moved here.
JOHN MOTSON on *MOTD*, 2007

'Goal of the Month' was introduced to *MOTD* in 1970.

The first colour broadcast of MOTD took place on 15 November 1969 and featured Liverpool against West Ham United (Division One).

The iconic *MOTD* theme tune was written by Barry Stoller, but it was not the original music for the programme. That was written by Major Leslie Statham (sometimes known as Arnold Stock), a band leader with the Welsh Guards. His 'Drum Majorette' was the *MOTD* theme from 1964 to 1970.

Due to contractual negotiations between ITV, the BBC and the Football League which involved the TV companies broadcasting football highlights programmes in alternate seasons, in 1980–81 and 1982–83 *MOTD* was broadcast on a Sunday.

Individual regional ITV companies had negotiated with the Football League to broadcast highlights from a single match in 1962. In 1963–64, most ITV regional companies showed the highlights of a single match on a Sunday – for example, *Shoot* on Tyne-Tees Television.

ITV's flagship highlights programme was *The Big Match*, originally launched by London Weekend Television. It ran from 1968 to 1992.

55 The first live game of the modern era to be broadcast on television (ITV) was Tottenham Hotspur v. Nottingham Forest (2-1) on 2 October 1983.

On 20 December 1985, the BBC and ITV negotiated a deal with the Football League and the FA to broadcast live football matches. The deal, worth £1.3 million, involved four League matches, both Milk (League) Cup semi-finals, four FA Cup ties plus the semi-finals and final.

Ceefax was first developed by the BBC in 1974 but di no begin to broad t in-vision footba news until 1983. Prior to the emergenc o 24 hou tele ion, Ceefa was the prime medium fo support s want g to keep up to date wi the unfoldin events of matche .

The UK's longest-running television football programme is STV's *ScotSport*, which began in 1957 and is still going strong.

Arthur Montford was one of the most respected of all TV football commentators and enjoys legendary status in Scotland. From 1957 to 1989 he commentated on 2,005 matches for *ScotSport*, including 38 'Auld Firm' derbies and 26 Edinburgh derbies. He became a director of Morton in 2001 and is now the club's vice-president.

In a new deal brokered in part by the PFA on 8 August 1988, the Football League accepted ITV's proposal to broadcast a mixture of live matches and highlights of League games for £44 million over four years. The deal involved the PFA receiving £550,000 per annum, First Division clubs sharing £7.3 million per year, Second Division clubs £1.3 million, and £1.3 million being shared annually between Third and Fourth Division clubs. As a result of this deal, MOTD was restricted to showing FA Cup matches.

A record 26.29 billion people worldwide were estimated to have watched the 2006 World Cup in Germany. A record 715.1 million people were estimated to have watched the final between Italy and France.

Unlike Premiership clubs, Real Madrid and Barcelona negotiate their own broadcasting rights. In 2007, they completed individual deals that will result in each club receiving £100 million in 2008–09 in return for broadcasting rights, nigh on twice the amount top Premiership clubs receive.

Far and away the most significant influence on English football has been Sky Sports. Sky was launched in 1990 and originally did not broadcast its own football programmes, having linked up with Eurosport. BSB and Sky TV merged later in 1990 and from this came the Sky Sports channel.

It is widely believed that Sky Sports was influential in persuading the newly formed Premiership to break away from the Football League in 1992.

In 1992, BSkyB and the BBC negotiated a deal worth £304 million (over five years) to broadcast live games and highlights of Premiership matches. Sky would broadcast live matches on Sunday afternoons and Monday evenings, while the BBC would show edited highlights of games on the revived Match of the Day programme on a Saturday night. Sky negotiated to transmit 60 live matches per season, for which viewers would have to pay a subscription.

The influence of Sky has been such that it has been instrumental in many organizational changes in football, particularly regarding revenue for clubs (and therefore wages for players), fixtures and kick-off times. These alterations totally changed the culture of football in England.

There is no doubt that Sky has played a major role in the increased commercialization of football in England, which has resulted in leading clubs with previously unthinkable riches. Sky's saturation coverage of the game has also won many 'new' supporters of football, though a common view is that such supporters are merely 'consumers', watching games purely from their armchairs as opposed to actually attending games.

For all the matches now broadcast and the huge sums of money involved, in August 2007, Sky's audience share in the UK was 2.8 per cent. It does, however, enjoy huge audience figures in pubs and clubs and in those countries in which it is received for its broadcast of live Premiership matches. Such coverage has made players such as David Beckham and Wayne Rooney readily recognizable to football fans throughout the world, and they enjoy a level of fame that would have been impossible prior to the emergence of Sky.

Sky Sports presenter Paul Boardman (son of comedian Stan) spent three years with Torquay United and scored on his first-team debut against Bournemouth.

In the 1970s and 1980s, Jimmy Greaves was involved with the 'Gold Diggers', a group comprising television personalities and former footballers who got together at football clubs to raise money for charities and worthy causes. At one Gold Diggers function at Luton Town, Jimmy fell into conversation with Eric Morecambe. The pair chatted about how both had had to work hard to improve and hone their skills in their respective careers in football and television.

'And what would you have been if you had not had a talent for football and scoring goals?' asked Eric at one point.

'When I left school, I had a job lined up as a compositor with *The Times*,' replied Jimmy. 'And what would you and Ernie have been if you had not been funny?'

'Mike and Bernie Winters.'

Although a season-ticket holder at Sunderland, writer/veterinarian James Alfred Wight decided upon the name of Birmingham City's Scottish-born goalkeeper Jim Herriott as his nom de plume. Wight, alias James Herriott, wrote the books which were adapted for the BBC series *All Creatures Great and Small*.

Jimmy Perry and David Croft were such fans of Sir Stanley Matthews that they named one of the characters in their successful TV comedy series *Hi-De-Hi*! after the legendary Stoke City, Blackpool and England winger. Stanley Matthews was one of the yellowcoat entertainers. Coincidentally, he was played by an actor whose name was also that of a famous former footballer, David Webb (Chelsea). He was always credited alongside his twin brother, who also played a yellowcoat in the series, as 'The Webb Twins'.

Play 'Spot the lazy TV/radio reporter on FA Cup day'. When a team from a higher division meets one from a lower division, or a non-league club, in the FA Cup, the reporter who can't be bothered to research a revealing fact about the tie will, for ease, simply work out how many League places separate the two clubs – an easily accessible statistic that supposedly puts the tie into perspective, but meaningless as the majority of viewers/ listeners know a gulf separates the two clubs. A good game to play, and one at its most rewarding on the occasion of the third round.

Or play 'Spot the emotive statement' when listening to TV or radio match commentators or reporters. For example, it is now seemingly inadequate for a TV or radio sports reporter to say a player has been 'left out of the England team', or even 'dropped'. To gain maximum emotional effect the player is said to have been 'snubbed by the England coach'.

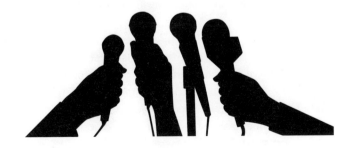

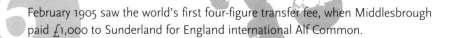

56 February 1905 saw the world's first four-figure transfer fee, when Middlesbrough paid £1,000 to Sunderland for England international Alf Common.

The transfer deadline was introduced by the Football League in 1911 to prevent clubs challenging for honours or battling against relegation by 'buying' themselves out of trouble.

In October 1920, Leeds City of the Second Division were expelled from the Football League for financial irregularities. The club decided to auction all their players at the Hotel Metropole. They fetched a total of £10,000, the transfer fees ranging from £250 to £1,250. Following the demise of Leeds City, Leeds United was formed and the new club, operating from City's Elland Road, was duly elected the following season to the newly formed Division Three of the Football League.

Falkirk once laid claim to the record British transfer fee paid – £5,000 to West Ham United for Syd Puddefoot in 1922.

Frozen asset. In 1927, Manchester United signed defender Hughie McLenahan from Stockport County in exchange for three freezers of ice cream that were later sold at Stockport's club fundraiser fayre.

In June 1947, Billy Steel was transferred from Morton to Derby County for a British record fee of £15,500. Some weeks later, a County supporter wrote to the 'Letters Page' of the *Derby Evening Telegraph*, 'When I heard how much Derby had paid for Steel, I thought English football had gone mad. Now, having seen him play, I reckon we've got a bargain.'

In 1947–48, Tom Hartley was at five different clubs in five months. In September 1947, he was transferred from Chesterfield to non-league Stockton; in December, he was transferred from Stockton to North Shields; on 1 January he was transferred from North Shields to Leicester City; and on 28 January he was transferred from Leicester City to Watford.

Freddie Steele's transfer from Mansfield Town to Port Vale in December 1951 was the first instance of a player-manager being transferred from one League club to another.

Generally speaking, a free transfer turns out to be worth every penny the club paid for him.

LEN SHACKLETON

In December 1961, Spurs broke the British transfer fee record when they paid AC Milan £99,999 for Jimmy Greaves. For all that Greaves was British football's most expensive player, Spurs refused to supply him with a club house on his return to England. Jimmy and his family lived for two months in the Dagenham council house home of his wife's parents until they found a home of their own.

Within a 12-month spell in 1963, Third Lanark transferred ten players to English League clubs: Willie Clarkson (Oxford United), Gavin Fletcher (Bradford City), David Grant (Reading), Matt Gray (Manchester City), Alex Harley (Manchester City), Dave Hilley (Newcastle United), Peter Kerr (Reading), John McLaughlin (Shrewsbury Town), Jim Robb (Charlton Athletic) and Robbie Stenhouse (Crewe Alexandra).

When Alan Ball was transferred from Blackpool to Everton in August 1966 for a record fee between British clubs of £110,000, he received a telephone call from Liverpool manager Bill Shankly, who told him, 'Congratulations, Alan, son, you're going to be playing your football next to the greatest club in the world.'

In 1967, the Football League introduced temporary transfers (loans), originally limited to two players per club per season.

Within a 12-month period, June 1968 to June 1969, Allan Clarke featured in two record British transfer fees. In June 1968, he was transferred from Fulham to Leicester City for £150,000, and in June 1969 from Leicester City to Leeds United for £165,000.

In 1972–73, Frank McMahon was transferred from Lincoln City to Darlington for a new set of goalposts.

On 29 January 1975, Paul Smith was transferred from Huddersfield Town to Cambridge United for a fee of £1.

I'm aware of the situation here, the club doesn't have ten million to spend. In fact it doesn't have 10p.

TONY ADAMS, Wycombe Wanderers manager

Contrary to common belief, Trevor Francis was not the first million-pound transfer in British football. Francis's fee when he joined Nottingham Forest from Birmingham City was £999,999.99p. The Birmingham board demanded £1 million for Francis, but the Forest management team of Brian Clough and Peter Taylor did not want their new signing to carry the burden of being Britain's first million-pound player. Taylor offered to pay the balance of one pence in cash, a gesture the Birmingham board declined.

1980–81 witnessed one of the most bizarre, some were given to say dubious transfers in the history of English football. On 13 August, Clive Allen, who had not played a game for Arsenal following his transfer from Queens Park Rangers, was transferred to Crystal Palace along with reserve-team goalkeeper Paul Barron in exchange for Palace full-back Kenny Sansom. Allen was valued at £1.2 million, Sansom at £1 million, and Palace paid £400,000 for Barron.

Just as Clive Allen never played a game for Arsenal, Peter Beardsley signed for Manchester United but never played a first-team game for the club.

In 1981–82, non-league Crockenhill sold striker Tony Cascarino to Gillingham for a set of tracksuits. Cascarino went on to play for Millwall, Aston Villa, Celtic, Chelsea, Marseille and Nancy, and won 88 caps with the Republic of Ireland.

In 1982, Dumbarton received £125,000 from Everton for the services of Graeme Sharp. It is still the record fee received by the club.

In 1985–86, Viv Williams, who played as a part-time professional for Bangor City and whose day job was in frozen-chicken packing, was the subject of a £25,000 transfer to La Liga club Atlético Madrid. Unfortunately for Williams, the deal fell through. A case of Atlético Madrid crying 'fowl'?

The player who paid his own transfer fee. In 1986–87, Ian Bennyworth was transferred to Scarborough from Nuneaton for a fee of £1,500. Strapped for cash, Scarborough were unable to come up with the money for the fee, so Bennyworth paid it himself.

'Stoke in for O'Sullivan – A Loan Again, Naturally'

Evening Sentinel headline on occasion of Stoke City trying to get Wayne O'Sullivan on loan from Swindon Town

Some distance for a loan deal. In 1994, Oldham Athletic goalkeeper Ian Gray went out on loan – to Brunei, who play in the Malaysian League.

On transfer deadline day in 1994, a fax was received at Football League headquarters in Lytham St Annes. The fax, on Bristol City headed notepaper, read 'Confirm transfer of Eric Cantona from Manchester United to Bristol City for a fee of £750,000'. Suitably suspicious, Football League officials rang Bristol City who confirmed it was a hoax. City launched an internal inquiry but the identity of the prankster was never discovered.

If you are a player recently released from a club, you may take heart from this. Phil Babb (Liverpool), John Beresford (Newcastle United), Lee Dixon (Arsenal), John Fashanu (Wimbledon, Aston Villa, etc.), Ray Houghton (Aston Villa, etc.), Brian McClair (Manchester United), Dean Saunders (Aston Villa, Liverpool, etc.), David Seaman (Arsenal), John Sheridan (Leeds United, Sheffield

Wednesday, etc.) and Dennis Wise (Chelsea) were some of the top players of the 1990s. With the exception of Seaman, all were the subject of free transfers from their first club. The clubs that gave a free transfer to a gem were Millwall (Babb), Manchester City (Beresford), Burnley (Dixon), Cambridge United (Fashanu), West Ham United (Houghton), Aston Villa (McClair), Swansea (Saunders), Manchester City (Sheridan) and Southampton (Wise) – while Leeds United sold David Seaman to Peterborough United in 1982 for a fee of just £4,000.

I'm going to have to listen to offers for all my players, and the club cat, Benny, who is pissed off because there are no mice to catch because they have all died from starvation.

JOHN MCGRATH, Halifax Town manager

The 'transfer' that has had the greatest effect on football involved a player few if any British fans had ever heard of – Jean-Marc Bosman. In 1995, Belgian footballer Bosman went to the European Court of Justice in Luxembourg claiming that the existing transfer system was a restraint of trade. He took the Belgian FA, UEFA and FC Liège to court when Liège blocked his transfer to French club Dunkirk after his contract with the Belgian club had ended. Bosman won his case. The court ruled that players were free agents once their contract with a club had expired and they could sell themselves to any club that wanted their services. Historically, transfer fees were paid for players even if they were out of contract with their club. The Bosman ruling put an end to this.

Current UEFA rules stipulate that a 'compensation' fee must be paid for a player under 23 years of age.

The 'transfer window' is a period when a club can transfer a player to another club. It was introduced after talks between FIFA, UEFA and the European Commission. FIFA made the transfer window mandatory in 2002–03.

There are two windows per season, from the close season to midnight on 31 August, and from midnight on 31 December for one month until 11 p.m. on 31 January. The final day of the transfer window is known as 'deadline day'. To complicate matters further, Football League and Conference clubs can negotiate the loan of players from 8 September to 23 November, and from 8 February to 23 March.

Two notable 'deadline day' transfers. In 2006, when Ashley Cole moved from Arsenal to Chelsea for £5 million plus William Gallas, the deal was reputedly agreed within five minutes of the August deadline. Exactly two years earlier Wayne Rooney was transferred from Everton to Manchester United on deadline day.

On 31 January 2008, Portsmouth striker Benjani (Zimbabwe) was the subject of a deadline day move to Manchester City. The paperwork was quickly completed, only for Benjani to fail a medical. City still wanted the deal to go through but the situation was further complicated when concerns were expressed about whether or not all the necessary paperwork had actually been completed on time. The deadline passed, but Premiership officials eventually confirmed that all the paperwork was as it should be and the £7.6 million deal was completed (though they also stated that some of the 'original details' of the transfer were subsequently changed).

 West Ham United are paying millions of pounds for players who back in the sixties wouldn't have got a game in the reserve team.

JOHN LYALL, former Hammers manager

It is unusual. Former Chelsea apprentice Tom Jones played for several clubs in the 1980s and 1990s: 207 games for Swindon Town, and others for clubs including Reading, Aberdeen, Woking and Weymouth. He may as a result lay claim to the longest transfers in terms of distance. He went from Weymouth to Aberdeen (595 miles), from Aberdeen to Swindon (565 miles) and from Swindon to Busan in North Korea (player-coach) – a distance of 5,400 miles. In 2007–08, Jones was coach to the Armenian national team.

The transfer of Carlos Tevez from West Ham United to Manchester United in 2007 was a long-drawn-out and complicated affair. There was much debate over who actually owned the player's registration, West Ham or his agent. In the end, the deal went through, though the consensus of opinion was that the matter was still far from clear.

In 1999, *The Times* reported that Liverpool manager Gérard Houllier was to sign French Under-21 striker Didier Baptiste. The only problem was that Baptiste didn't exist. He was a character played by actor Tom Redmond in the Sky TV programme *The Dream Team*.

In 2002, Darlington announced that they had signed Faustino Asprilla, who was a free agent at the time, following his release from Atlético Nacional (Colombia). Darlington successfully applied for a work permit and Asprilla was paraded in front of Quakers fans before a home game. Unfortunately, the day before he was due to make his debut, without informing the club he flew out of the country and has never been seen in Darlington since.

56

THE WORLD'S TOP TRANSFERS
(AS AT 2007–08 AUGUST DEADLINE)

Zinédine Zidane from Juventus to Real Madrid in 2000 – £46 million
Luís Figo from Barcelona to Real Madrid in 2000 – £37 million
Hernán Crespo from Parma to Lazio in 2000 – £35.5 million
Gianluigi Buffon from Parma to Juventus in 2001 – £32.6 million
Christian Vieri from Lazio to Inter Milan in 1999 – £32 million
Andriy Shevchenko from AC Milan to Chelsea in 2006 – £30 million
Rio Ferdinand from Leeds to Manchester United in 2002 – £29.1 million
Gaizka Mendieta from Valencia to Lazio in 2001 – £29 million
Ronaldo from Inter Milan to Real Madrid in 2002 – £28.5 million
Juan Sebastian Verón from Lazio to Manchester United in 2001 –
  £28.1 million

MILESTONE TRANSFERS INVOLVING BRITISH CLUBS

Alf Common from Sunderland to Middlesbrough in 1905 – £1,000
Syd Puddefoot from West Ham United to Falkirk in 1922 – £5,000

Bob Kelly from Burnley to Sunderland in 1925 – £6,500
David Jack from Bolton to Arsenal in 1928 – £10,890
Bryn Jones from Wolves to Arsenal in 1938 – £14,500
Billy Steel from Morton to Derby County in 1947 – £15,000
Tommy Lawton from Chelsea to Notts County in 1947 – £20,000
Eddie Quigley from Sheffield Wednesday to Preston in 1949 –
    £26,500
Trevor Ford from Aston Villa to Sunderland in 1950 – £30,000
Eddie Firmani from Charlton to Sampdoria in 1955 – £35,000
John Charles from Leeds to Juventus in 1957 – £65,000
Denis Law from Manchester City to Torino in 1961 – £100,000
Denis Law from Torino to Manchester United in 1962 – £115,000
Alan Ball from Blackpool to Everton in 1966 – £110,000
Allan Clarke from Fulham to Leicester City in 1968 – £150,000
Martin Peters from West Ham to Tottenham in 1970 – £200,000
Alan Ball from Everton to Arsenal in 1971 – £220,000
David Nish from Leicester to Derby County in 1972 – £250,000
Bob Latchford from Birmingham to Everton in 1974 – £350,000
Kevin Keegan from Liverpool to Hamburg in 1977 – £500,000
David Mills from Middlesbrough to West Brom in 1979 – £550,000
Trevor Francis from Birmingham to Nottingham Forest in 1979 –
    £1 million
Steve Daley from Wolves to Manchester City in 1979 – £1,450,000
Bryan Robson from West Brom to Manchester United in 1981 –
    £1,500,000
Ray Wilkins from Manchester United to AC Milan in 1984 –
    £1,550,000
Mark Hughes from Manchester United to Barcelona in 1986 –
    £2,300,000
Ian Rush from Liverpool to Juventus in 1987 – £3,200,000
Chris Waddle from Tottenham to Marseille in 1989 – £4,250,000
David Platt from Aston Villa to Bari in 1991 – £5 million
Paul Gascoigne from Tottenham to Lazio in 1992 – £5,500,000
Andy Cole from Newcastle to Manchester United in 1995 –
    £7 million
Stan Collymore from Nottingham Forest to Liverpool in 1995 –
    £8,500,000

Alan Shearer from Blackburn to Newcastle in 1996 – £15 million
Nicolas Anelka from Arsenal to Real Madrid in 1999 –
  £23.5 million
Juan Sebastian Verón from Lazio to Manchester United in 2001 –
  £28.1 million
Rio Ferdinand from Leeds to Manchester United in 2002 –
  £29.1 million

Wayne Rooney became British football's most expensive teenager when he joined Manchester United from Everton in 2004 for an initial fee of £27 million paid over two years, plus further payments depending on appearances and the success of United, which could realize a final fee in the region of £31 million by 2010.

David Beckham was transferred from Manchester United to Real Madrid in 2003 for an initial fee of £12 million. Beckham became the third Englishman to be transferred to Real, after Laurie Cunningham and Steve McManaman. Following Beckham's transfer, Jonathan Woodgate became the fourth Englishman to be transferred to Real Madrid.

In my days as a player, football was a simple game played largely by semi-illiterates. Now, with colossal broadcasting deals, huge transfer fees, astronomic wages and what have you, it's a multi-billion-pound industry . . . played largely by semi-illiterates.
BOB STOKOE

Big-money transfers dominate the news, but many of the record transfer fees paid by individual clubs are still very modest, and of some years' standing (in Clyde's case, as you'll see, 42 years' standing).

ENGLAND

Barnet, £130,000 for Greg Heald from Peterborough United in 1997
Hereford United, £80,000 for Dean Smith from Walsall in 1994

Leyton Orient, £175,000 for Paul Beesley from Wigan in 1989
Macclesfield Town, £40,000 for Danny Swailes from Bury in 2005
Rochdale, £150,000 for Paul Connor from Stoke City in 2001
Rotherham United, £150,000 for Martin Butler from Reading in 2003
Shrewsbury Town, £100,000 for Mark Blake from Southampton
   in 1990
Tranmere Rovers, £450,000 for Shaun Teale from Aston Villa in 1995
Walsall, £175,000 for Alan Buckley from Birmingham City in 1979
Wrexham, £210,000 for Joey Jones from Liverpool in 1978
Wycombe Wanderers, £200,000 for Sean Devine from Barnet
   in 1999

SCOTLAND

Aberdeen, £1 million for Paul Bernard from Oldham Athletic in
   1995 (the club states £1 million was the initial fee paid; this
   rose slightly in relation to games played)
Albion Rovers, £7,000 for Gerry McTeague from Stirling Albion
   in 1989
Alloa Athletic, £26,000 for Ross Hamilton from Stenhousemuir
   in 2000
Arbroath, £20,000 for Dougie Robb from Montrose in 1981
Brechin City, £16,000 for Sandy Ross from Berwick Rangers in 1991
Clyde, £14,000 to Sunderland for Harry Hood in 1966
Dumbarton, £50,000 for Charlie Gibson from Stirling Albion
   in 1989
East Fife, £70,000 for John Sludden from Kilmarnock in 1991
East Stirling, £6,000 for Colin McKinnon from Falkirk in 1991
Elgin City, £10,000 for Russell McBride from Fraserburgh in 2001
Forfar Athletic, £50,000 for Ian McPhee from Airdrieonians in 1991
Hamilton, £60,000 for John McQuade from Dumbarton in 1993
   (also Paul Martin)
Montrose, £17,500 for Jim Smith from Airdrieonians in 1992
Queen of the South, £30,000 for Jim Butter from Alloa in 1995
Stenhousemuir, £20,000 for Ian Little from Livingston in 1995
Stirling Albion, £25,000 for Craig Taggart from Falkirk in 1994
Stranraer, £15,000 for Colin Harkness from Kilmarnock in 1989

57 In 1907–08, Bradford Park Avenue were elected to the Southern League. Their nearest away match was against Northampton Town, over 130 miles away.

Raith Rovers are the only club to have been shipwrecked on their way to a game. On 23 July 1920, Raith were travelling to the Canary islands to play a series of friendly matches when their ship, *Highland Loch*, ran into a violent storm off Curruedo in northern Spain. The ship was grounded on a sandbank and began to sink, and the Rovers party were taken by lifeboat to the port of Vigo. A tug managed to re-float the *Highland Loch* and her passengers returned to her some days later. Apparently unaffected by their ordeal, Raith Rovers sank all opposition on the Canaries, winning every one of their five matches.

Viv Gibbins holds the distinction of being the first player to be flown to a Football League match as an individual. In 1932–33, Gibbins, an amateur on the books of Bristol Rovers, was a schoolteacher in Essex. On 7 September, Rovers had an injury crisis, selected Gibbins as centre-forward for their midweek game against Southend United, and arranged for him to be flown from Romford to Bristol. Gibbins concluded his day of teaching, boarded the plane and arrived 30 minutes before the scheduled kick-off. Rovers won 3-1.

On Good Friday 1936, Swansea won 2-1 at Plymouth Argyle; the following day, Swansea lost 2-0 at Newcastle United. Swansea travelled from Plymouth to Newcastle by train, a distance of 413 miles – a record for a club travelling between League games played on consecutive days. Swansea's journey from their home town to Plymouth, from Plymouth to Newcastle, then back to Swansea totalled 881 miles. That and two League matches, all in the space of three days.

Brighton had little in the way of Christmas 'presents' in 1940. On Christmas morning 1940, they travelled to Norwich City with only five players, having arranged to pick up other players on Christmas leave from the armed services along the way. But with the nation at war, these players opted to spend Christmas with their families, and Brighton arrived at Carrow Road with just the original five players. They made up a full side by recruiting some Norwich reserves and two soldiers from the crowd – but were beaten 18-0.

On Christmas Day 1941, Bristol City players set off in cars for a game at Southampton. A car containing two City players and the team kit arrived at the Dell in time for the game, but the other two vehicles failed to arrive. Southampton offered to help provide City with a full team, which eventually comprised the two Bristol City players who had managed to get there, plus the Southampton trainer, a number of their reserves, and three spectators who responded to an announcement over the public address system appealing for players. The game went ahead with Bristol City fielding this cobbled-together team. The missing City players eventually turned up at the Dell over an hour late. It transpired that one of the cars had sustained a puncture and the other had stopped to offer assistance, after which both had taken a wrong turning and got lost. Southampton won the game 5-2. One of the Bristol City goals was scored by the Southampton trainer, who apparently never let his players forget that he had scored against them.

In 1947, Aston Villa were returning by train from a pre-season friendly against Hearts. As their train approached Preston station, Harry Parkes volunteered to run to the station refreshment bar to buy a tray of teas for the team. As the train slowed down, Parkes jumped down on to the platform and ran into the refreshment bar, only to turn and see the train pick up speed again and continue its journey to Birmingham.

George Middleton had the longest journey for home games of any player in the history of the Football League. Middleton spent 1946–47 playing in goal for Plymouth Argyle while in the week he lived and trained in Sunderland.

For the first round of the FA Cup of 1951–52, the FA attempted to regionalize the draw to minimize travel expenses for clubs. But the draw could not accommodate in every instance. Non-league Folkestone found themselves drawn away to fellow non-leaguers Stockton – a round trip of some 644 miles. To compound their misery, Folkestone lost 2-1.

In 1957, Chelsea became the first club to travel to a Football League match by air, for their game against Newcastle United.

When Brian Clough and Peter Taylor took over at Hartlepools United in 1965, the club was so destitute it could not afford a coach to take players to away matches. Taylor borrowed a coach from a pal for Hartlepools' match at Southport; Taylor himself drove it to Southport, and Clough took the wheel for the return journey to Hartlepool. Weeks later, Taylor's pal was unable to loan the coach, so Clough, Taylor and the Hartlepools, players travelled to their away game at Barnsley in cars.

George Best did some travelling in his time, particularly in 1977. On 1 October that year, George became the first player to play in all four home countries in the space of only ten days: for Northern Ireland v. Iceland (Belfast), for Fulham at Cardiff City (Division Two), for Fulham at St Mirren (Anglo-Scottish Cup), and for Fulham at Crystal Palace (Division Two).

Swansea City decided to travel the day before their Division Three match at Wigan on 29 December 1990 and stay at a hotel on the outskirts of the town. Though the hotel was only four miles from Central Park, on the day of the game the Swansea team bus was caught up in a horrendous traffic jam and they arrived at the ground just ten minutes prior to kick-off. Result: Wigan 2 Swansea 4.

On 15 March 1947, Kilmarnock were due to play Third Lanark at Third's temporary home Hampden Park. The Kilmarnock party endured a painfully fitful and slow train journey to Glasgow as a result of heavy snow. They eventually arrived at a snow-free Hampden 70 minutes after the designated kick-off time and were non-plussed to find the game taking place. To keep the crowd entertained, Third Lanark had hastily staged a match between their reserve team and Queen's Park.

On 13 November 1948, while playing for Millwall at Walsall, after only a matter of minutes goalkeeper Malcolm Finlayson sustained an injury and was taken to hospital. While he was off the field, Jim Constantine deputized in goal. Finlayson was discharged from hospital and returned to Fellows Park not long after the beginning of the second-half, only to find all doors and gates locked. Still wearing his kit and boots, Finlayson climbed over one of the exit gates, ran up on to the terraces, down on to the perimeter track and across to the dug-outs. He then took over in goal from Constantine. Millwall won 6-5.

In 1958, Port Vale embarked on a pre-season tour of Ireland. Unfortunately the club were so strapped financially they ran out of money and could no longer afford hotel bills. The team had flown out to Ireland, but having curtailed their tour they had to return to England by ferry.

On 25 October 1981, five Clydebank players found themselves marooned in trains on the line between Glasgow and Clydebank due to a signalling fault. Clydebank were playing Hamilton, and one player ran nigh on two miles from another station only to find a Clydebank team containing reserves getting changed. Two other players arrived at the ground at 2.55, and the other two turned up some 20 minutes into play. Despite assembling a team containing so many reserves, Clydebank beat Hamilton 2-1.

In his early days as a goalkeeper with Chesterfield, Gordon Banks and team-mates Paul Brown and Barry Hutchinson travelled from Sheffield to Chesterfield for matches together by train. On one occasion, on the advice of a porter at Sheffield Midland station, the trio boarded a train which failed to stop at Chesterfield. They eventually disembarked at Derby and, as there was no train from Derby to Chesterfield for an hour, hired a taxi to take them from Derby Midland station to Saltergate. Unfortunately they arrived too late for the match and had to watch the game from the stands. On Monday, when Banks, Brown and Hutchinson tendered their explanation to Chesterfield manager Duggie Livingstone, he insisted the trio accompany him to Sheffield station to find the porter who would verify their story. The porter was found and admitted he had made a mistake, but the three players were still docked their wages for having missed the match.

The wicker man gets his fingers burned. On 3 January 1969, Fulham left King's Cross station for a third round FA Cup tie against Sunderland the following day. Unfortunately the wicker skip containing the Fulham strip was left behind at Craven Cottage. Fulham had to borrow Sunderland's second strip of sky blue shirts, shorts and socks, which may have inspired them: Fulham won 4-1 at Roker Park. On their journey back to London, the train the Fulham party was travelling on was subjected to a two-hour delay south of York, and a further 40-minute delay outside Peterborough.

In 1978, a Barnet side that included Jimmy Greaves played a game at Bath City. On the journey home, the team coach stopped to allow players to buy a fish and chip supper, but the driver couldn't restart it. Two hours later a replacement coach arrived and the Barnet party set off for home. After 30 minutes, that bus broke down too. A second replacement bus was called for and it eventually arrived over three hours later. Having left Bath at 5.30 p.m., Barnet finally arrived back at Underhill at 2.30 a.m.

On 25 April 1981, three Stockport County players were stranded in a blizzard on their way to a Division Four match at Bury. Stockport played the first-half against Bury with only nine players. The three delayed players, who had been originally named on the team sheet, eventually arrived at half-time and took their place in the second-half with one of the original starting nine being substituted. Despite this setback, Stockport won 1-0 with a goal from Martin Fowler.

 People talk of players suffering from fatigue because they are playing too many games, particularly abroad in European competitions. It's not the actual games that tire players, it's the travel.
DON MACKAY

On 9 March 2007, three Sunderland players, Anthony Stokes, Tobias Hysen and Marton Fulop, were delayed on their way to meeting the team coach for a trip to Barnsley. The trio arrived some 20 minutes after the scheduled departure time only to find, on the orders of manager Roy Keane, that the team bus had left without them.

58 In January 1898, the match between Sheffield Wednesday and Aston Villa was abandoned with just ten minutes of the game remaining when Wednesday were leading 3-1. The Football League ordered that the final ten minutes should be completed on another date. In March 1899, 15 weeks later, Wednesday and Villa met again to play those remaining ten minutes. Wednesday won 4-1, but were relegated. Aston Villa won the championship.

Brentford won all 21 of their home League matches in Division Three (South) in 1929–30 – the only club to have won every home game in the course of a season.

In 1934–35, Harry Adamson finished the season as Bradford City's leading goalscorer in Division Three (North) with ten goals. He was also the leading goalscorer for the club's reserve team (Midland League), the youth team (Yorkshire League) and the 'A' team (Yorkshire Mid-Week League).

Raich Carter is the only player to have won FA Cup winners medals before and after World War Two. Carter was a member of the Sunderland team that triumphed in 1937, and of the successful Derby County team of 1946.

The only player to have picked up FA Cup losers medals before and after World War Two is Willie Fagan, who was in the Preston team that lost to Sunderland in 1937 and in the Liverpool side defeated by Arsenal in 1950.

The oldest player to have played in the Football League is Neil McBain, who was 52 years and four months old when he played for New Brighton against Hartlepools United (Division Three North) on 15 March 1947.

In the course of the 1946–47, Hull City called upon the services of 42 players in the Third Division (North) – the most players used by a club in a single post-war season.

In 1952–53, Huddersfield Town played the same defence throughout the entire season. Bill Wheeler, Ron Staniforth, Laurie Kelly, Bill McGarry, Don McEvoy and Bill Quested played together for 42 consecutive League matches, and in Huddersfield's two FA Cup matches. Outside-left Vic Metcalfe also played in every game.

On 9 January 1954, 15 of the 32 ties in the third round of the FA Cup were drawn – a record for the competition.

In 1954, Peter Dobing had the unique experience of being selected for two teams that were playing each other. Dobing had signed amateur forms for both Blackburn Rovers and Manchester United, and both clubs picked him for an 'A' team match between the two sides. Dobing solved the problem by diplomatically declining to play for either club. He eventually signed as a professional with Blackburn Rovers.

Arthur Perry is the only player to have spent nigh on ten years with a Football League club yet never make a first-team appearance. Perry signed for Hull City in 1947 but spent all that time playing for the reserves. He was transferred to Bradford Park Avenue in 1956 for a much-awaited League debut. It is interesting to note that had Perry remained at Hull for just a few more months he would have qualified for a testimonial, as players were then granted testimonials for ten years' service or more with a club. Imagine, Hull fans turning up at a testimonial match for a player they had never seen play!

In 1958–59, Lincoln City's centre-half was Ray Long who was six feet three inches tall, and their outside-left was Joe Short who was five feet two inches tall.

Jimmy Greaves was the first British player to score in two major European finals. In 1958, he netted for a London XI in the final of the Inter-Cities Fairs Cup (first leg) against Barcelona, and in 1963, he scored Tottenham's first goal when they beat Atlético Madrid 5-1 in Rotterdam to win the European Cup Winners' Cup.

On 12 October 1963, when Bradford Park Avenue played Bradford City in a Division Four match at Park Avenue, they became the first clubs from one city to play each other in all four divisions of the Football League. Bradford City won 3-1. Curiously, when Bradford Park Avenue played Oldham Athletic in 1958, they became the first two clubs to play each other in all four divisions of the Football League.

In February 1965, at the age of 50, Stanley Matthews became the oldest player to play in the First Division when he was selected for Stoke City against Fulham. The Fulham left-back marking Stan that day was Jimmy Langley, aged 36. Their combined age of 86 years is a record for two players facing each other in top-flight English football. Matthews retired from League football after this match, but Langley went on to join Queens Park Rangers and won a Football League Cup winners medal with Rangers at Wembley in 1967.

FOOTBALLER OF THE YEAR

1948-63
Stanley Matthews

Some people get all the breaks. During a 17-year career with Stoke City (1965–82), central defender Denis Smith suffered five broken legs, a broken nose on four occasions, a broken ankle and collar-bone, a chipped spine, nine fractures to fingers and a total of 102 facial stitches.

Neil Paterson played for Dundee United in the 1930s and 1940s while also working as a freelance writer. Paterson is the only British footballer to have won an Oscar, in 1959 for his screenplay for *Room at the Top*, based on the novel of the same name by John Braine.

The only Football League player to have a parent who is a Nobel Prize winner is Paul Williams (Preston, Sheffield United, Hartlepool United, Stockport County, West Bromwich Albion, Stockport County and Rochdale). He is the son of Betty Williams, who with Mairead Corrigan began the peace movement in Northern Ireland for which both were awarded the Nobel Prize for Peace.

In the 1960s, it was common during the close season for British teams to represent American cities in the USA United Soccer Association Championship. In July 1967, Wolves (representing Los Angeles) and Aberdeen (Washington) met in the USA Championship Final. The game was unique in that it lasted 133 minutes, as rules stipulated that should the scores be level after 90 minutes, teams would play on until a goal was scored. The game produced 11 goals, including four in three minutes, three penalties and one sending-off. Wolves won 6-5. The 'golden goal' was an own-goal by Aberdeen's Ally Shewin.

59 Football is played according to the laws of the game originally laid down by the English Football Association at a meeting on 1 December 1863. These were generally in line with those laid down at Cambridge University (The Cambridge Rules) in 1848, and later revised in 1856. By 1877, the laws of football were basically the same as they are today. There are 15 basic laws as designated by the International FA Board, encompassing the field of play, players' equipment, the referee, assistant referees, duration of play, start and restart of play, when the ball is in and out of play, awarding of goals, offside, fouls, free-kicks, penalty kicks, throw-ins, goal-kicks and corner-kicks. The laws apply to all member countries of FIFA, but ask any professional or semi-professional player or match official and the chances are they will tell you football is played only to a vague consensus.

 Every time a corner-kick is taken there is an offence committed in the penalty area, but if a referee blew up for every such offence, we'd have no game at all. You can't play the game strictly by the book.

TOMMY DOCHERTY

In addition to the official laws of the game, there are also the unwritten laws . . .

When two teams from the same division are drawn together in a cup competition, the team that wins both League matches will lose the cup match.

No matter how badly a player played for a club, and irrespective of how woeful he was in front of goal, once the player is transferred and returns to play against his old club he will score against them.

A team that couldn't put a win together to save their lives, once relegated, will start to win matches.

A team are on a fine run and playing really well. A regular supporter informs a friend, an irregular supporter, of this and encourages him/her to accompany him/her to the next home match. The team will play dreadfully and lose, prompting the irregular supporter to say something along the lines of, 'It's been two years since I've been here and it'll be another two years before I come back.'

When reading football news on Ceefax, the service will never give you enough time to read a page containing four items, yet will stop for an age on the final page containing a simple three-line item of news.

There will always be at least one TV commentator and one football journalist who will refer to the Community Shield as 'the traditional curtain raiser to the season'.

Wales has been adopted as the benchmark unit of measure for international football, as in, 'We're talking of a country about the size of Wales,' or, 'They do remarkably well for a country with a population similar to that of Wales.'

Just as it is impossible to look cool in a go-kart, it is impossible for even a top player to look cool when lying injured on a football pitch.

Once a manager has been sacked, the managerless team will win their next match.

Following the sacking of their manager, a team will suddenly pick up and record victories under a caretaker manager prompting the board of directors to appoint the caretaker on a full-time basis, from which point the team will start to lose regularly again.

Any World Cup or European Championship group that contains three decent teams will be referred to as 'The Group of Death'.

A goal will never come about as a result of a team taking a short corner.

Supporters will cheer and get excited when their team wins a corner, but invariably nothing will come of it.

The winning run of a team will come to an end when their manager is given the Manager of the Month award.

England will exit the finals of a major international competition in the most cruel and painful of circumstances.

A manager returning to a club for a second spell will never repeat the success enjoyed during his first spell at the club.

Should you support a Premiership club, but not one of the 'big four', following a defeat for Manchester United, your team will be playing United next. This law was applicable to Liverpool in the 1970s and 1980s. Often referred to as the 'game to write off law'.

When your team is enduring a wretched season, though it's against your nature, you want them to lose the next game in the hope the manager will be sacked and there will be a new start.

Every team will contain one player supporters don't like.

No matter how bad the traffic, there is no such thing as a long and tiresome journey home following an away win.

When your team is embroiled in a battle for promotion or against relegation, you will take an inordinate amount of interest in the exploits of other clubs that previously held no interest for you at all.

There is too much tension surrounding a derby match for supporters ever to enjoy the actual game.

Should a team from the north-east travel to play a team in the south-west they will always get at least a point. In the case of the team from the south-west visiting the north-east, the long-distance travellers will also avoid defeat.

A game at Manchester United is a good day out even though you know your team will not win, or be awarded a 'cert' penalty.

Everyone becomes a much better player once they have given up playing.

THE UNWRITTEN LAWS OF SUNDAY MORNING FOOTBALL

When the manager throws the kit-bag on the floor there will be a mad rush to grab one of the few decent pairs of socks and shorts. This will invariably result in the smallest player ending up with the largest pair of shorts and the biggest player with an indecently small pair – and an argument. It will also result in (a) one of the substitutes wearing a new sock on one leg and an old washed-out sock on the other leg, giving the impression he is wearing odd socks; (b) one of the substitutes wearing a sock with holes in it; and (c) one of the substitutes wearing a washed-out sock with holes in it.

One player will always complain that the shirt he is wearing is still damp from when it was washed. This cuts no ice with the manager, whose response is, 'It'll dry out quick once you start running about outside.'

As the players change, the manager/secretary will move among them with an old soap bag saying 'Any valuables?' As players deposit their valuables in the soap bag they feel compelled to tell the manager what they are putting in, as if he could ever remember.

The player who arrives late and rushes to get changed when his team-mates take to the pitch will be further delayed when a bootlace snaps. This never happens when a player has plenty of time in which to get changed.

There will be only one tracksuit, so other substitutes must suffer the indignity of standing on the line wearing their coats.

No substitute will ever volunteer to 'run the line' for the referee. He has to be press-ganged in to doing it.

The player with the most expensive boots will be the worst player in the team. This rule also applies to the player who turns up for training wearing an expensive and pristine tracksuit and training gear.

There will always be one player standing at a meeting point of an autumnal Sunday morning and wondering where everyone is, blissfully unaware that the clocks have gone back an hour. This same player will be the one who, in late March, rolls up when the match is in progress and asks, 'What's going on? It's only half nine.'

Should the pitch be frozen and the referee calls off the game, players from both sides will try to persuade him to play the match for no other reason than that they don't want to have got up early on a Sunday morning for nothing. The main argument of the players is that the rock-hard state of the pitch is no different to how it is at the end of the season after wind and sun have dried it out, and in such conditions matches are never postponed.

There will be only one ball available for the pre-match kick-in. It will be either the size and weight of a balloon or have the constitution of those large concrete balls one sees on the gateposts of stately homes.

At council-owned grounds where there are a number of pitches, there will come a point when the ball from the game on the neighbouring pitch encroaches on to yours. This will involve a player keeping his eye on his game while running across to kick the wayward ball back to the player from the other game who has been sent to retrieve it, this player invariably acknowledging the friendly gesture with a 'Cheers, mate'.

When the teams take to the pitch and see the goal nets billowing in the wind, it is the sure sign of an awful game to come. Following every wayward shot, the wind will blow the ball further and further from the pitch. Curiously, this results in the player sent to retrieve the ball having to continually stop and start, for just as he is about to collect the ball, another gust of wind will blow it further away.

In extremely bad weather, when the first-half ends both captains must readily agree to the referee's suggestion 'Straight round?', meaning no half-time interval.

No one celebrates a goal by running then belly-flopping across the grass for fear of what they might come into contact with.

There will always be one team that, having reached the semi-finals of a cup competition, suddenly fields a team comprising top local non-league players signed back in August for such an eventuality. This always causes grumbles among the players who have been regulars but now find themselves dropped – and the opposition.

An essential part of the kit of a Sunday morning referee is a handkerchief, a corner of which is used to prise grit out of eyes when a ball has been kicked on a heavy pitch and an oncoming player has been showered in the face with mud. Done with the stock advice, 'Look up!'

On the rare occasion of the taking of a team photograph, no substitute with a shred of self-esteem will pose wearing the tracksuit.

When signing players in August, the wily Sunday League manager will always register two fictitious players, thus enabling him to continue playing his best players under the fictitious names should they be suspended.

The aforementioned ruse is also used at the end of a season when Sunday teams catch up on postponed games by playing midweek, and players are unavailable due to work and unsigned players guest for the team. This will always result in the manager having to remind the unsigned player of his 'name' should he be booked or sent off.

Should a player have played on a muddy pitch on a Sunday and not have cleaned his boots for a midweek game, on removing his boots from his bag he will proudly display the young, new, tender grass shoots sprouting from the mud on the soles of his boots.

At the end of the game it is always the same players who try to slope off and avoid helping take the nets down.

As the players change out of muddy strips, the manager/secretary responsible for washing will plead, 'Socks and shorts the right way round, please.'

When everyone has collected their valuables there will always be one forgetful player who hasn't, resulting in the manager repeatedly calling out, 'Anyone hand in a watch and gold ring?'

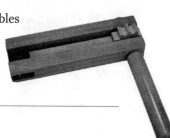

59

Professionalism was legalized in English football in 1885, primarily because it was common knowledge that many players were receiving payment for playing the game.

In 1893, professionalism was officially adopted in Scottish football.

In 1898, the Player's Union (now the PFA) was formed to look after the interests of players and to ensure they received an adequate wage for playing the game.

In 1901, the maximum wage was introduced to prevent clubs from luring players with the promise of higher wages. The maximum limit was set at £4 a week during the football season; players could receive a 'retainer' wage of a lesser sum during the close season.

In 1910, the maximum wage was raised to £5 a week. It was estimated at the time that only 10 per cent of professional players in England received it.

In 1920, the maximum wage was raised to £9.

In 1922, members of the Football League and FA met with club chairmen and the maximum wage was reduced from £9 to £8 a week. Players threatened strike action but nothing came of this and they reluctantly accepted the cut.

In 1928, the Football Associations of the four home nations (England, Scotland, Ireland and Wales) resigned from FIFA over disagreements about payments to amateur players. (They did not rejoin until 1947.)

One 'advantage' to the maximum wage was that it enabled provincial town clubs to retain the services of world-class players as the player could not earn more by moving to a big city club. Big clubs circumnavigated this problem by offering 'dolly' jobs to players to supplement their maximum wage. In 1929, Alex James moved to Arsenal from Preston North End for the same wage of £8 a week, but Arsenal provided James with a supplementary job as a 'sports demonstrator' at Selfridges for which he was paid £250 per annum.

In the 1930s, players could earn a maximum of £8 a week plus maximum bonuses of £2 for a win and £1 for a draw, and £6 per week in the summer close season.

In 1947, the maximum wage was raised to £12, but only for players who had been with their current club for five successive years. This, of course, excluded many players who had been in the armed services during the war, which was the vast majority.

Worth every penny? In 1947–48, according to club accounts, Derby County's part-time professional goalkeeper Alec Grant was on a weekly wage of 3d (1¼p).

Throughout the 1950s the maximum wage gradually rose, in 1953 from £12 to £14, in 1955 to £16, in 1957 to £18 and in 1959 to £20. With bonuses, players, particularly those with First and Second Division clubs, could earn more.

In 1959, many football club directors were alarmed that the maximum wage was £20 during the season and a maximum of £17 a week in the summer close season. Many chairmen believed this to be too much and were also of the mind that these sums did not tell the true story of how much players earned. The chairmen's stance was supported by Football League president Joe Richards and Arthur Drewry, the chairman of the Football Association. Richards and Drewry issued a joint press release on behalf of the Football League and FA entitled 'Wages and Entitlements of Professional Footballers'. Club chairmen repeated the contents in match programmes to inform supporters of what a footballer could really earn once the intricate bonus system was taken into account.

WAGES AND ENTITLEMENTS OF PROFESSIONAL FOOTBALLERS

Wages
Maximum £20 a week in the season, £17 a week in the summer.
Minimum (for a full-time player of 20 or over) £8 a week all year round.

Friendly match
£2 or £3 an appearance, plus £2 if the game is televised.

League bonuses
£4 a win, £2 a draw.

FA Cup bonuses
First round £4, second round £4, third round £5, fourth round £6, fifth round £8, sixth round £10, semi-final £20, final £25. Half these amounts are paid for drawn matches.

Talent money
League
First and Second Division Clubs
Champions £1,100, runners-up £880, third £660, fourth £440, fifth £220.
Third Division Clubs
Champions £550, runners-up £440, third £330, fourth £220.
Fourth Division Clubs
Champions £330, runners-up £220, third £110, fourth £55.

FA Cup
The winning club to receive £1,100.
Runners-up, £880.

Each defeated semi-finalist, £660.
Each defeated club in round six, £440.
Each defeated club in round five, £220.

European Cup
For each appearance in . . . first round £10, second round £20, third
round £30, fourth round £30, semi-final £40, final £50.

Benefits
£150 a year during the first five years at a club, and £200 a year for suc-
ceeding years of service with the same club.

On tour
£2 a day out-of-pocket expenses.

On transfer
Removal expenses and a sum of up to £300 if transferred at the club's
request and not that of the player.

Provident Fund
A sum equal to 8% of a player's total earnings is put aside each season
and is paid to him, free of Income Tax, on the 1 January following his
35th birthday or following his retirement from League football, whichever
is the later.

Vocational training
The Football League pays the whole or part of the expenses and fees for
players studying for another trade or occupation.

Coaching
The Football Association pay fees to over 200 players who have
qualified as coaches.

Representative matches
Fees are paid for appearances, up to a maximum of £50 for playing for
the full England team.

'Wages and Entitlements of Professional Footballers' was savaged by PFA chairman Jimmy Hill, PFA secretary Cliff Lloyd and many leading players including Spurs skipper Danny Blanchflower, Stanley Matthews (Blackpool), Tommy Banks (Bolton), Tommy Docherty (Arsenal), Norman Deeley (Wolves) and just about every player in the lower divisions. Blanchflower and Hill wrote articles in the press and appeared on both television and radio to refute the claims made in the document and to 'set the record straight'. In essence, they argued that few, if any, players earned anywhere near the sums they were entitled to earn as set out in what was described as being an 'inflammatory and misleading document'. Hill pointed out that only a minority of professional footballers received the maximum wage; many players were not paid for playing in friendly games; only one club out of the 92 in the Football League entered the European Cup; and so on. Hill stated that the average annual wage of a Third Division player was £420.

LIVERPOOL FC NET WAGES FOR WEEK ENDING 17 AUGUST 1959 (INCLUDING FRIENDLY V. NANTES)

A. A'Court	£28 10s 1d	J. Melia	£20 18s 3d
A. Banks	£10 10s 1d	R. Moran	£21 7s 1d
G. Byrne	£20 1s 1d	J. Morrisey	£15 15s 1d
I. Callaghan	£11 15s 1d	B. Slater	£19 3s 5d
R. Campbell	£12 13s 1d	F. Twist	£4 7s 0d
W. Carlin	£9 18s 1d		
D. Hickson	£19 4s 1d	**Staff**	
R. Hunt	£22 0s 1d	J. Fagan	£13 11s 11d
T. Lawrence	£10 16s 1d	B. Paisley	£19 6s 3d
W. Liddell	£16 2s 1d	R. Bennett	£16 17s 1d

The dispute raged for two years and came to a head in 1961, when the Football League offered to raise the maximum wage to £30 with freedom to negotiate contracts of up to three years (compared to the one-year contracts operating at the time). The package was rejected by PFA members as the 'deal' offered no change to the 'retain and transfer system' whereby players were subjected to contracts that bound them to a club for life – the so-called 'slavery contract'. The dispute was further fuelled by George Eastham, who was playing for Arsenal at the time but who had instigated legal proceedings against his former club Newcastle United on the grounds of 'restraint of trade' for having refused him a transfer.

The PFA held regional meetings. At a PFA North West meeting, among those who spoke out against the Football League's proposal and in favour of strike action were Stanley Matthews and Tommy Banks. All PFA members were balloted and voted to stage strike action on Saturday, 21 January 1961. The action, however, was called off on 18 January following a meeting between the League, FA and PFA presided over by John Hare MP, the government's Minister of Labour. During this meeting the Football League agreed to abolish contracts binding a player to a club for life, and also the maximum wage.

With the maximum wage abolished, clubs were free to pay players a sum in keeping with their worth. Players negotiated their contracts and wages with

the club manager or chairman. Players' wages rose over the years but nowhere near as quickly as they have since the formation of the Premiership.

Prior to the abolition of the maximum wage, Fulham chairman Tommy Trinder told Johnny Haynes (Fulham and England captain), 'You're such a marvellous player I would pay you a hundred quid a week because you're worth it, only the rules won't allow me.' Days after the maximum wage was abolished, Haynes asked for a meeting with Trinder and reminded the Fulham chairman of what he had said. Trinder couldn't go back on his word, so Johnny Haynes became English football's first £100-a-week player.

In the 1960s, Fulham were considered to be a club good enough to maintain First Division status but never to win trophies. When defender Bobby Keetch went to see Fulham manager Vic Buckingham to sign a new contract, Buckingham produced two contracts for Keetch to consider.

'This contract offers you a flat weekly wage of £40, win, lose or draw,' Buckingham informed Keetch. 'The other contract, however, pays a basic wage of only £25 a week, but has bonuses Spurs and Manchester United can't match. Should we finish in the top four you will receive a bonus of £1,000. If we are champions, you get £2,000. There is an extra £10 for a home draw, £20 for a home win, £30 bonus for an away draw, and £40 for an away win, which means you could earn £65 a week. If we reach the FA Cup Final you receive a £1,000 bonus. If we win the cup, your bonus is £2,500.'

'I'll take the forty quid,' said Keetch.

In 1961, when Stanley Matthews met with Stoke City manager Tony Waddington to discuss the terms of his return to Stoke from Blackpool, at one point Waddington informed Matthews that the club would pay him a bonus for every game he played of '£25 appearance money'.

'Forget the appearance bonus, it won't be necessary,' Matthews informed Waddington.

'Not necessary?' asked the bemused Stoke manager. 'Why?'

'What do you think I am going to do? Train all week then not turn up to play on a Saturday?' replied Stan.

The 'watershed' for players' wages was the formation of the Premiership and the influx of broadcasting money. In 1992–93, the inaugural season of the Premiership, the average annual salary of a Premiership player was £75,000.

In 1992, Eric Cantona's weekly wage at Leeds United was £4,000.

In 2000, Alen Boksic's weekly wage at Middlesbrough was £63,000.

Between 2001 and 2003, the aggregate salaries of Premiership players rose 26 per cent to £706 million. In 2001, an independent survey revealed that the average earnings of a Premiership footballer were £400,000 per annum.

In 2004, Deloitte reported that the average annual salary of a Premiership player was £676,000.

Premiership wages passed the £850 million mark for the first time in 2005–06 (they were were put at £854 million). Chelsea spent £114 million on wages, Manchester United £85 million, Arsenal £83 million and Liverpool £69 million.

In 2007, it was reported that the weekly wage of John Terry at Chelsea was £130,000.

In 2007, Deloitte predicted that the average salary of a Premiership player would rise to £1 million within a matter of a few years.

In 2007, FIFA president Sepp Blatter said he wanted to 'push football's social responsibility' and limit the 'pornographic greed in the game. A gulf is opening up in the distribution of finance. The rich are getting even richer.'

In 2007, Sepp Blatter's salary with FIFA was £500,000 per annum plus a £160,000 expenses allocation.

61

On 3 February 1940, England was gripped by snow, ice and freezing fog. All but one of the 56 wartime regional matches were postponed. The only game to survive was Plymouth Argyle's match against Bristol City. Plymouth won 10-3, and to compound the misery of the City players, on the journey home their train was held up in a blizzard north of Taunton, and then delayed for a further two hours due to snow and fog.

The longest extension to a season due to bad weather and the sheer number of postponements occurred in 1946–47. The final League matches were played on 7 June, six weeks after the FA Cup Final.

In January 1947, two feet and eight inches of snow was measured on Oldham's Boundary Park pitch.

Curiously, the following season, 1947–48, saw only six matches postponed due to bad weather – the lowest figure in any season of the Football League.

The pitch was frozen solid. It was so icy and slippery the teams couldn't turn round at half-time.

GORDON BANKS recalls his days in Sheffield junior football

In 1953, thick fog descended during a First Division match between Charlton Athletic and Chelsea. The Charlton goalkeeper, Sam Bartram, was peering through the pea-souper and was surprised to see a policeman approach him out of the gloom. The policeman was equally taken aback to see Bartram in his goal, as the game had been abandoned for 15 minutes.

A crowd of 63,840 turned up at St James' Park to watch Newcastle United's third round FA Cup tie against Swansea Town in 1953, but the game was abandoned after only eight minutes due to thick fog. Visibility was so bad, some 15 minutes after players and officials left the field, police entered the Leazes End terrace to disperse supporters unaware that the game was over.

The first England match to be abandoned took place on 17 May 1953 in Buenos Aires against Argentina. Incessant heavy rain and a waterlogged pitch greeted the players, and as England captain Billy Wright took to the centre-circle for the ritual spinning of a coin to choose which way to play, Nat Lofthouse quipped, 'If you win the toss, Billy, attack the deep end first-half.' The referee for this game was Englishman Arthur Ellis who, commenting on his decision to abandon the game after 23 minutes, told the press, 'If we had stayed out any longer we would have needed lifeboats.'

The only first-class match to be abandoned on the opening day of the season due to bad weather was the game between Tranmere Rovers and Workington Town at Prenton Park on 18 August 1956. The game kicked off in torrential rain which was followed by an extraordinary cloudburst. The pitch became waterlogged and the match was called off at half-time.

The severe winter of 1962–63, known as the 'Big Freeze', severely disrupted fixtures. Snow fell in northern parts of Britain prior to Christmas and continued to fall for weeks. Along with plummeting temperatures, this resulted in only three of the 32 third round FA Cup ties being played at the first attempt. In fact, the third round of 1962–63 is the longest-lasting round in the history of the FA Cup: it began on 5 January, was subjected to 261 postponements, and was not completed until 11 March. Fourteen ties were postponed ten or more times: Lincoln City v. Coventry City was postponed a record 15 times, and Birmingham City v. Bury suffered 14 postponements and one abandonment. When Birmingham and Bury eventually managed to play a full 90 minutes they drew 3-3, which necessitated a replay! After 17 attempts, Bury eventually triumphed 2-0. Blackburn Rovers and Middlesbrough were the last clubs to resolve their third round tie, on 11 March.

Following their victory over Spurs at Burnden Park on 8 December 1962, Bolton Wanderers did not play again until mid-March. Due to the sheer number of postponements the season was extended to late May, but the final fixture took place at Workington Town on 1 June.

The 'Big Freeze' of 1962–63 provided football with record days for numbers of postponements. On both 12 January and 2 February 1963 only four Football League matches were played in England. On 9 February only seven matches took place in England, but every game in Scotland was postponed. It was this season that led to the pools companies creating the pools panel which would determine the 'results' of matches not played due to inclement weather.

To combat the excessive heat during the 1970 World Cup in Mexico, England players wore a new type of shirt, the Aertex, which contained hundreds of small holes to enable air to reach and circulate around the body.

During the 1970 World Cup, Alf Ramsey was anxious England players should not suffer from sunburn. They were allowed to sunbathe for a maximum of 40 minutes each day. Trainer Harold Shepherdson watched over them and blew a whistle after 20 minutes to indicate that they should turn over.

On 29 October 1975, England's European Championship qualifying match against Czechoslovakia in Bratislava was abandoned after 17 minutes due to fog.

And what do you think of summer in England?

JIM ROSENTHAL, ITV

I think I missed it. I was in the dressing room getting changed.

RICARDO VILLA, Spurs

On 21 August 1976, the Football League season got underway during one of the hottest and driest summers on record. A temperature of 98 degrees was recorded on the pitch at Highbury prior to Arsenal's opener against Bristol City. The government appointed former Football League referee Denis Howell MP as the Minister for Drought. Three days after he took up his appointment, it rained.

Snow good. In January 1978, a battalion of Carlisle supporters worked from dawn to clear the Brunton Park pitch of snow, and finally succeeded at one p.m. Carlisle's game against Tranmere Rovers was still postponed, however, because the match officials' car got stuck in snow. At three p.m., it started snowing again in Carlisle. The teams met a week later, and the game ended in a 2-2 draw.

On 1 January 1979, 43 out of 46 Football League matches were postponed due to snow or ice.

The longest-running Scottish FA Cup tie is that between Inverness Thistle and Falkirk in 1978–79, which was postponed 29 times due to bad weather.

On 21 November 1979, thick fog forced the postponement of England's European Championship qualifying match against Bulgaria at Wembley – the only instance of an international match at Wembley being called off as a result of bad weather.

The latest the FA Cup Final has been played because of ties being postponed (and also the number of replays required) was in 1982. The FA Cup Final replay between Tottenham Hotspur and Queens Park Rangers that year took place at Wembley on 27 May.

During the World Cup Finals in Spain in 1982, England players were swathed in cold wet towels and given salt tablets at half-time during matches to combat water loss. During England's opening match against France, Bryan Robson lost seven pounds in weight.

On 17 January 1987, Rangers played one game but won two matches. Their Premier League fixture at Dundee was postponed due to a frozen pitch, so the club hastily rearranged a home fixture against Hamilton Academical. Rangers won 2-0 at Ibrox and the pools panel awarded them an 'away win' at Dundee.

On that January day in 1987, 37 of the 45 scheduled Football League matches were postponed due to snow. The Rangers v. Hamilton game was one of only two played in Scotland.

On 8 February 1991, only four Football League games took place due to snow and ice. Eleven matches in Scotland were also postponed.

On 27 January 1996, 44 FA Cup and League matches in England and Scotland were postponed due to frozen pitches or snow.

 If any non-football fans want guaranteed glorious sunshine for a day out in August, they should arrange their day out for the first day of the football season.

JOHN TURNOCK, former Nantwich Town player

The 2003–04 Football League season kicked off on 9 August amid a heatwave. A temperature of 102 degrees was recorded on the centre-circle at Kenilworth Road 15 minutes prior to the start of Luton Town's game against Rushden and Diamonds. A temperature of 101 degrees was recorded at Valley Parade prior to Bradford City's game against Norwich City. The following day, a temperature of 102 degrees was recorded at the Millennium Stadium prior to the 2003 Community Shield match between Arsenal and Manchester United.

62

It's a real grudge match – Pre-match media hype has worked on the players.

One of the game's few real characters – He wears an earring.

He did everything right but put the ball in the net – He can't finish.

We could do with another two players – We could do with at least another two players.

This is real cat-and-mouse stuff – Neither team has had a shot at goal.

I'm happy with the squad I've got – The board has told me I'm not getting another penny to spend on players.

A bit ring rusty – Couldn't get a place in the team, and now that he has been given a chance he is showing why the manager left him out in the first place.

Good footballing brain – Brain contains basically what you find inside a football.

Competitive player – Constantly hacking and committing fouls.

It would be unfair to single out one player – The rest are prima donnas and would sulk.

A very experienced player – Over the hill.

Great vision – Does not see a simple pass.

Loyal club player – Never had an offer from another club.

Creative player – Bit namby-pamby but can pass a ball.

As a manager, I felt I should demonstrate loyalty – The offer from the other club was nowhere near enough.

Not afraid to take people on – Blissfully unaware of team-mates screaming for him to pass the ball.

Makes a nuisance of himself in the box – Barges into opposing defenders, tramples on feet.

An individualist – Not popular with team-mates.

Workrate is excellent – Runs around the pitch like a madman but never gets the ball.

They have to squeeze the opposition, make more use of the channels, and stretch their back four – Producer doesn't know what I'm on about but thinks I do, so I may get more of this type of work.

We wouldn't mind getting Manchester United away – We want to make a lot of money.

We'll be looking to our supporters to lift us – We've got Manchester United at home.

That's the cup, the whole town is buzzing – The butcher has put a rosette in his window.

On the day it's 11 against 11 – I don't think we have a hope in hell.

We're just going out to enjoy ourselves – We all believe we haven't a hope in hell.

Anything can happen in the cup – Except us winning.

The cup is a great leveller – Wait till they see our pitch and the six-inch-deep mud down the middle.

This club is no stranger to giant-killing – Anyone remember 1932?

We'll settle for a replay – We need the money.

I wouldn't write them off, they're not relegated yet – They're dead and buried.

Did you see what happened there, Mark? – I wasn't watching.

He's happier when played as a striker – Midfield player who doesn't drop back and help out in defence.

He was on fire today – His contract's up for renegotiation.

Temperamental – Nutcase.

Looks to be struggling with his knee – Knows he's played rubbish and is about to be substituted.

I have the backing of the chairman – For the next three games.

He's still learning – He's rubbish, but he's young, so there's hope.

Shrewd – Devious.

Ambitious – Totally ruthless and will swat anybody who stands in his way.

Frank discussion – Raging argument.

Very frank discussion – Raging argument that ended with punches being exchanged.

There's more urgency to their play now – They're panicking like mad.

A prediction? – A guess?

He'll prove hard to replace – I can't believe I got rid of him at long last.

He's lost the dressing room – Manager is on to ringleader in dressing room.

An ambitious effort – Hopelessly wayward shot from 30 yards.

He got too much purchase on that – Open goal, leaned back, and blazed over.

I don't think we've seen the best of him yet – He's 28, he's never done a thing, but surely to God he must have one decent game in him.

They've left themselves with a mountain to climb – They're 4-0 down and haven't had a shot at goal yet.

You'd expect him to do better from there – He's missed from three yards.

It was a comfortable victory – San Marino really shouldn't be playing international football.

Which is why it's such a wonderful game – I'm wrong again.

He was given too much space – The marking was diabolical.

Genius! Absolute genius! – A decent goal scored by one of the leading lights of the Premiership.

He took that very well – Almost identical goal, if not a better one, scored by a lesser light of the Premiership or Championship

63

Even today's average Premiership player need not have to work once his playing days are over. The vast majority of players, however, do have to find alternative employment once they hang up their boots. Here's what some former heroes did for a living once they had retired from the game.

LEN ALLCHURCH (Swansea, Sheffield United) – ran own shoe and leather goods shop in Swansea.

WILLIE ANDERSON (Manchester United, Aston Villa) – emigrated to USA, executive for radio station in Oregon.

JOHN ASTON (Manchester United, Luton Town) – owns a pet shop in Cheshire.

GARY BAILEY (Manchester United) – presents South African equivalent of *Match of the Day*.

TUNJI BANJO (Orient) – London bus driver.

LES BARRETT (Fulham) – BT engineer, then garden centre, which he runs with his wife.

MICK BERNARD (Stoke City) – gardener in Wiltshire.

CLYDE BEST (West Ham United) – emigrated to USA, runs own dry cleaning business in Oregon.

ALAN BILEY (Cambridge, Derby, Everton, etc.) – owns a health and fitness club.

PETER BODAK (Coventry) – went to work for Press Association.

JOE BOLTON (Sunderland, Sheffield United) – lorry driver in Sheffield area.

BARRY BRIDGES (Chelsea, Birmingham, QPR) – had own milk round in Norfolk.

PETER BROADBENT (Wolves and England) – owned a babywear shop in Halesowen.

TOMMY BRYCELAND (St Mirren, Norwich City) – hotelier in Scotland.

JOHN BYRNE (QPR, Sunderland) – chiropodist.

NIGEL CALLAGHAN (Watford) – DJ in Greece, then returned to UK and became a coach.

WILLIE CARLIN (Liverpool, Carlisle, Derby, etc.) – owns a restaurant in Majorca.

MICK CHANNON (Southampton, Manchester City) – successful breeder and trainer of racehorses.

RALPH COATES (Burnley, Spurs) – owns a catering business in Hertfordshire.

JOHN CONNELLY (Blackburn, Manchester United) – ran two successful fish and chip shops in Lancashire.

PAUL COOPER (Ipswich Town) – runs South Tenerife Golf Services.

MICK CULLERTON (Hibernian, Port Vale, Derby County) – runs a business selling soccer ties to clubs, and works as a summarizer for BBC Radio Stoke.

JIM CUMBES (WBA, Aston Villa, etc.) – chief executive of Lancashire CCC.

DAI DAVIES (Everton, Swansea, Wrexham) – qualified as a teacher, now runs a natural healing centre in Llangollen.

MARK DENNIS (Birmingham City, Southampton, etc.) – became a sign-writer in Spain.

BRYAN DOUGLAS (Blackburn) – sales representative for paper manufacturing company.

HARRY DOWD (Manchester City, Stoke, Oldham) – became an area manager for brewers J. W. Lees.

MIKE DOYLE (Manchester City, Stoke, Bolton) – sales manager for Slazenger sportswear.

PAUL DYSON (Coventry City, Stoke, WBA) – joined the prison service.

STEVE EARLE (Fulham, Leicester City, Peterborough) – insurance sales executive in Tulsa, Arizona.

GEORGE EASTHAM (Newcastle, Arsenal, Stoke) – ran his own sportswear business in Johannesburg and became vice-president of the South African Arsenal Supporters Club.

KEITH EDWARDS (Sheffield United, Hull City, Leeds United, etc.) – lorry driver in Sheffield.

JOHN EVANSON (Oxford United, Blackpool, Fulham) – publican and restaurant owner in London.

DAVID FAIRCLOUGH (Liverpool) – qualified as a journalist, now works freelance.

JOHNNY FANTHAM (Sheffield Wednesday) – owns a metal company in Sheffield.

GEORGE FARM (Blackpool, Queen of the South) – lighthouse keeper.

MALCOLM FINLAYSON (Wolves) – ran a steel stockholding company in the West Midlands.

ALAN FOGGON (Middlesbrough, Newcastle, Sunderland, etc.) – security manager for a company on Tyneside.

DONALD FORD (Hearts) – accountant.

JIM FRYATT (Bradford, Southport, Blackburn, etc.) – croupier in Las Vegas casino.

TONY GALVIN (Spurs, Sheffield Wednesday, etc.) – college lecturer in the Midlands.

SIMON GARNER (Blackburn Rovers) – painter and decorator in Bucks.

ALAN GOWLING (Manchester United, Newcastle) – manager of a chemical company in Derbyshire.

TONY GREEN (Blackpool, Newcastle United) – school teacher in Blackpool.

GERRY GURR (Southampton, Aldershot) – moved to Stow-on-the-Wold and became an accomplished guitarist/singer and also a musical director for his wife, popular club, cabaret and theatre singer Lee Ann.

VIC HALOM (Sunderland) – PR executive with an Oldham plumbing company.

IAN 'CHICO' HAMILTON (Chelsea, Aston Villa, Sheffield United) – worked for Nike as a coach and as a play scheme organizer at Sheffield University.

DAVID HARVEY (Leeds United) – bought an old farmhouse in Orkney and runs his own farmstead.

TONY HATELEY (Chelsea, Liverpool, Coventry, etc.) – sales representative for Thwaites brewery.

JOHN HAWLEY (Hull, Leeds, Sunderland, etc.) – runs his own antiques business on Humberside.

DAVID HERD (Stockport, Arsenal, Manchester United, Stoke) – owned a successful garage business in Urmston, Manchester.

RAY HIRON (Portsmouth) – manager of a sports centre in Portsmouth.

DES HORNE (FA Cup winner with Wolves) – runs an air-conditioning business in South Africa.

ROGER HUNT (Liverpool) – runs his own haulage company.

TOMMY HUTCHISON (Manchester City, Coventry) – works for a PFA community scheme in Bristol.

BILLY INGHAM (Burnley, Bradford City) – bus driver in the Burnley area.

JOHN JACKSON (Crystal Palace, Orient, Millwall, etc.) – fitter of window blinds and a goalkeeping coach for Sussex School of Excellence.

GLYN JAMES (Blackpool) – owns a laundry and dry cleaning business.

SANDY JARDINE (Rangers) – works in the commercial department at Ibrox.

CLIFF JONES (Spurs) – teacher.

MICK JONES (Sheffield United, Leeds) – runs a market stall in Nottingham selling sportswear.

RAY KING (Newcastle, Port Vale) – became a qualified physiotherapist, writes books and for local Amble newspaper. Though in his eighties, still coaches on visits to Thailand.

JOE LAIDLAW (Middlesbrough, Carlisle, etc.) – roofer in Portsmouth.

JIMMY LANGLEY (Fulham) – steward of British Legion Club in Middlesex.

DAVE LATCHFORD (Birmingham City) – manager of Widney Manor Cemetery in Bentley Heath, Birmingham.

DUNCAN MCKENZIE (Everton, Leeds, etc.) – popular speaker on after-dinner circuit.

HUGHIE MCILMOYLE (Leicester, Carlisle, Wolves, etc.) – worked in storage/distribution for Walkers crisps.

TED MACDOUGALL (Bournemouth, Manchester United, West Ham, etc.) – emigrated to Canada and became a wealthy property developer.

JIMMY MACEWAN (Aston Villa, Walsall) – civil servant.

GARY MABBUTT (Spurs) – runs his own sports consultancy business.

PAUL MADELEY (Leeds United) – successfully underwent operation to remove brain tumour; he and his brothers sold their chain of 26 DIY stores for £27 million in 1987.

JOHN MARGERRISON (Spurs, Fulham, Leyton Orient) – telecoms engineer.

ERIC MARTIN (Southampton) – emigrated to USA to work for a mailing company in Washington DC.

DON MASSON (Notts County, QPR, Derby County, etc.) – owner of Gallery Hotel in Nottingham.

PETER MELLOR (Burnley, Fulham, etc.) – emigrated to USA, ran successful fireplace business, then a company maintaining swimming pools.

PAUL MILLER (Spurs) – worked for the sports sector of investment bank UBS Warburg.

WILLIE MORGAN (Manchester United) – owns a sports hospitality business in Cheshire.

ARNOLD MUHREN (Ipswich, Manchester United) – coach at Ajax academy.

SAMMY NELSON (Arsenal) – worked for Save & Prosper Insurance.

HENRY NEWTON (Nottingham Forest, Everton, Derby) – postmaster in Derbyshire.

KEITH NEWTON (Blackburn, Everton, Burnley) – ran a sports trophy business, then a newsagent's before working with a local motor dealer in Blackburn.

GORDON NISBET (WBA, Plymouth Argyle) – policeman in Devon.

PETER NOBLE (Swindon, Burnley, etc.) – runs a market stall in Burnley selling sports goods.

MAURICE NORMAN (Spurs) – landscape gardener in Suffolk.

TONY NORMAN (Hull City, Sunderland) – policeman in County Durham.

JOHN O'HARE (Sunderland, Derby, Nottingham Forest) – stock controller for a Derby motor dealership.

JESPER OLSEN (Manchester United) – owns a sports management and promotions company in Cheshire.

ROGER OSBORNE (Ipswich Town) – delivery driver for a wholesale fruit and vegetable business.

GARY OWEN (Manchester City, WBA, Sheffield Wednesday) – art dealer.

ROY PAUL (Manchester City, Swansea) – became a lorry driver.

BILL PERRY (Blackpool, Southport) – set up a successful manufacturing business producing promotional books of matches. So, every day's a match day for Bill.

FRED PICKERING (Blackburn Rovers, Everton) – fork lift truck driver.

JIM PLATT (Middlesbrough) – owns a rag trade business in Northern Ireland.

ALBERT QUIXALL (Sheffield Wednesday, Manchester United) – scrap metal dealer.

PAUL REANEY (Leeds United) – ran coaching courses and a partner in the Classic Portrait Company.

GEORGE REILLY (Watford, Cambridge United) – bricklayer.

TOM RITCHIE (Bristol City, Sunderland) – postman in Bristol area.

BRIAN ROBERTS (Coventry City) – a teacher.

DON ROGERS (Swindon Town, Crystal Palace, QPR) – owns a sports shop in Swindon.

ALAN ROSS (Carlisle United) – housing officer for Carlisle City Council.

DAVID SADLER (Manchester United, Preston) – branch manager for a building society, then owned a corporate hospitality business.

JON SAMMELS (Arsenal, Leicester City) – driving instructor.

LEE SANDFORD (Portsmouth, Stoke, Sheffield United) – gained a degree in Sports Science at Sheffield Hallam University, became a property developer, moved back to Hampshire.

STEVE SHERWOOD (Watford) – financial adviser.

BOBBY SHINTON (Wrexham, Manchester City, Newcastle United, etc.) – glazier.

TOMMY SMITH (Liverpool) – columnist for over 30 years for *Liverpool Echo* and one of the top names on the sports after-dinner circuit.

JIM SMITH (Aberdeen, Newcastle United) – taxi driver on Tyneside.

RON SPRINGETT (Sheffield Wednesday, QPR) – self-employed painter and decorator.

JIM STANDEN (Arsenal, Luton, West Ham United, etc.) – emigrated to California and worked for Honda Car Leasing; his own car bears the registration 'FA CUP 1964'.

COLIN STEIN (Hibernian, Rangers, Coventry City) – joiner in Linlithgow.

DENIS STEVENS (Bolton, Everton) – owned a menswear shop in Bolton.

KIRK STEVENS (Luton Town, Coventry City) – owner of a successful civil engineering business in the Midlands.

BARRY STOBART (Wolves, Manchester City) – ran a household domestic service company.

MIKE SUMMERBEE (Swindon, Manchester City) – runs his own bespoke shirt-making business and speaks on the sports after-dinner circuit.

DAVE SWINDLEHURST (Crystal Palace, Derby, Sunderland, Wimbledon, etc.) – works in IT installing computer systems.

ALAN TAYLOR (West Ham, Norwich, etc.) – milkman, then owned a newsagency in Norwich.

DEREK TEMPLE (Everton, Preston) – worked in the glass industry, then manager of Merseyside branch of a national industrial cleaning company.

DANNY THOMAS (Coventry City) – became a physiotherapist in Coventry.

MIKE TREBILCOCK (Everton, Portsmouth etc.) – emigrated to Australia, works as a storeman in Lake Macquarie, north of Sydney.

DENIS TUEART (Sunderland, Manchester City) – owns a highly successful corporate promotions company.

NORMAN UPRICHARD (Portsmouth, Swindon Town, etc.) – ran a bar at Queens University in Dublin for many years before returning to England and retiring in Sussex.

JOHN UZZELL (Plymouth Argyle, Torquay United) – postman in Devon.

KEN WAGSTAFF (Mansfield Town, Hull City) – ran a social club on Humberside, had a column with a local newspaper, and was hospitality host at Hull City.

COLIN WALDRON (Bury, Chelsea, Burnley, Manchester United, etc.) – manager of a bookmaker's in Nelson, Lancashire.

MARK WALLINGTON (Walsall, Leicester City, Derby County) – PE teacher in the Midlands.

TONY WANT (Leyton Orient, Charlton, Spurs, Birmingham City) – warehouse manager for a frozen food company in Birmingham.

DAVE WATSON (Sunderland, Manchester City, etc.) – owns a successful marketing and sponsorship company in Nottingham.

NEIL WHATMORE (Bolton Wanderers) – school caretaker in Notts.

NORMAN WHITESIDE (Manchester United, Everton) – studied podiatry at Salford University, now a chiropodist.

FRANK WIGNALL (Everton, Nottingham Forest, Wolves, Derby) – owner of a motor dealership in Nottingham.

OSHOR WILLIAMS (Manchester United, Southampton, Port Vale, etc.) – studied history and politics at Salford University, became a lecturer.

RAY WILSON (Huddersfield Town, Everton, etc.) – director of funeral business near Oldham.

TOMMY WILSON (Millwall, Hull City) – solicitor.

COLIN WITHERS (Birmingham City, Aston Villa) – hotelier in Blackpool, then in Bridgnorth.

TREVOR WOMBLE (Rotherham United, Crewe, etc.) – works in the catering trade in the Rotherham area.

GEORGE WOOD (Blackpool, Everton, Arsenal, Crystal Palace) – ornithologist with the Glamorgan Wildlife Trust.

TOMMY WRIGHT (Everton) – worked on the docks at Garston.

ALEX YOUNG (Hearts, Everton) – owns a wholesale business in Edinburgh.

GERRY YOUNG (Sheffield Wednesday) – went into the sportswear business in partnership with former team-mate John Quinn.

WILLIE YOUNG (Spurs, Arsenal, Nottingham Forest, etc.) – owner of Bramcote Manor pub/restaurant on outskirts of Nottingham.

Women's Football

64

The first official representative women's football match took place on 23 March 1895 at Crouch End FC in London. The North of England beat South of England 7-1.

From 1918 to 1922, women's football enjoyed great popularity in England. One of the most famous teams was Dick Kerr's Ladies (Preston), who on Boxing Day 1920 beat St Helen's Ladies 4-0 at Goodison Park, Everton, before a crowd of 53,000.

There were an estimated 150 women's football clubs in England in 1920.

In 1922, the FA banned women's teams from playing on any affiliated ground. The official FA order stated, 'The Council feel impelled to express their strong opinion that the game of football is quite unsuitable for females and ought not be encouraged.' Five days after the ban was imposed, 25 clubs met in Blackburn to form the English Ladies Football Association. Needless to say, it was not given FA blessing.

Women's football in England enjoyed a revival after World War Two. Dick Kerr's Ladies and Manchester Corinthians were the top two teams, but finding suitable grounds to stage matches was a problem. Many top games were played at rugby and cricket grounds.

The International Ladies Football Association was formed in 1957, and it organized a European Club Championship in the same year. Teams from England, Austria, West Germany, Holland and Luxembourg entered, and the winners were Manchester Corinthians.

The Women's Football Association was formed in 1969.

In January 1970, the FA finally lifted its ban on women's teams playing on affiliated grounds.

In 1970, an unofficial World Cup was launched — unofficial in that it was not recognized by FIFA or UEFA. The competition ran until 1988. England were the winners in 1985 and 1988.

In 1971, all international women's football associations came under the jurisdiction of FIFA/UEFA. Yet it was not until 1993 that the Football Association formed an FA Women's Committee and created the post of women's football co-ordinator.

The FA Women's Challenge Cup was launched in 1971.

The first official women's international match in the United Kingdom took place at Cappielow Park (Morton FC) in 1972–73. England beat Scotland 3-2.

The top English women's team in the 1970s was Southampton, who played in nine consecutive FA Cup finals (1971–79) and were winners on seven occasions.

In the 1980s, Doncaster Belles dominated English women's football, appearing in 11 cup finals and winning six.

The Women's National Football League began in 1991, with three divisions: a Premier League, and North and South.

In 1991, the FA repealed its rule that banned mixed football in schools for Under-11s.

The Women's National Football League came under the jurisdiction of the FA in 1994 and was renamed the FA Women's Premier League.

The England team came under FA control in 1993.

In 1989, there were 253 women's clubs registered with the FA. In 2007, the number is in excess of 1,000.

The European Championship for women began in 1982.

The first FIFA World Cup Finals for women were held in 1991. The winners were the USA, who beat Norway 2-1 at the Tianhe Stadium, Guangzhou, China, attendance 65,213.

The 1995 World Cup was won by Norway, who beat Germany 2-0 in the Rasunda Stadium, Stockholm, to become the first nation to play in two consecutive FIFA Women's World Cup Finals.

The 1999 Women's World Cup Final between the USA and China (the USA won 5-4 on penalties) attracted a crowd of 90,185 to Pasadena's Rose Bowl Stadium – the largest ever attendance at a women's football match and the largest at any sporting event involving only women.

England's best performance in the FIFA Women's World Cup is reaching the quarter-finals in 1995 and 2007.

England coach (since 1998) Hope Powell won 66 caps for England and scored 35 goals. She was awarded an OBE in 2002 for services to football and is the sister of ex-Libertines drummer Gary Powell.

Unfortunately, there was a familiar ring to 2002 for Doncaster Belles. They were the first team to be runners-up in a single season (2001–02) in both major women's competitions: to Arsenal in the League, and to Fulham (2-1) in the FA Women's Cup Final.

England's leading goalscorer is Karen Walker, who netted 40 times in her 83 games.

In the 2007 World Cup qualifiers, England conceded a goal to Austria in their opening match. They then scored 29 times before conceding their second goal, in the final qualifying match against France.

Angie Harriott holds the record for the fastest goal in English women's football. She got on the scoresheet after only seven seconds for Launton Ladies v. Thame United (Southern League Premier) in 1998–99.

Eniola Aluko made her debut for Birmingham City Ladies against Leeds at the age of 14 – and scored.

Kelly Smith was only 16 years old when she made her debut for England. She carved out a successful football career in the USA before returning home to play for Arsenal.

In 2006–07, Arsenal Ladies created football history by winning the quadruple of Premier League, FA Cup, Premier and UEFA Cups. They were the first English team to win the latter.

World Club Championship

65

The World Club Championship, as it is commonly known, has endured a chequered and fitful history, not least because the competition has been subjected to various changes of name and format (it was also, for instance, called the Inter-Continental Cup), occasionally it was not even held, and several clubs that qualified for participation have refused to take part. All of which has served to lessen its importance as far as supporters and some clubs in Europe are concerned.

The competition was the brainchild of UEFA general secretary Henri Delaunay, who first suggested the idea of having a cup contested by the champions of the two major football continents, Europe and South America, in 1958.

There was a problem from the start: South America did not have a competition for the league champions of each of its nations. But the various football federations soon put that right. The competition to provide a champion club of South America was named in honour of heroes of South American independence – the Copa Libertadores.

The first winners of the Copa Libertadores were Peñarol (Uruguay), who qualified to play the European Cup holders Real Madrid in the first World Club Championship, in 1960, to be played over two legs, home and away. The game in Uruguay ended goalless, but at the Bernabéu, Real won 5-1. This margin of victory was eclipsed by Peñarol the following year when they beat Benfica 5-0, having lost the first leg (0-1) in Portugal. Peñarol had to replay against Benfica in Montevideo and finally triumphed 2-1.

The first British club to play in the World Club Championship were Celtic, who in 1967 faced Racing Club of Argentina. Celtic won 1-0 at Hampden Park in the first leg, and Racing won the return 2-1 in Avellaneda (a suburb of Buenos Aires). FIFA rejected suggestions that the clubs should have the trophy for six months each as rules for the competition dictated the winner should be decided not by aggregate (2-2 in this case) but by games won. A play-off was organized in neutral Montevideo, Uruguay, a match that remains one of the most infamous in the history of football. The proceedings degenerated into a series of brawls before eventually chaos reigned, players of both sides exchanging punches. Four Celtic players and two from Racing were sent off. In the wake of the violence, Celtic fined each of their players £250. Racing Club, who won the game 1-0, gave each of their players a new car.

In 1968, Manchester United became the second British club to contest the World Club Championship. Their opponents were Estudiantes from Argentina, who won the first leg in Buenos Aires 1-0. The second leg at Old Trafford proved to be yet another highly volatile affair marred by fouls and assaults. Bobby Charlton was cynically hacked down and the resulting wound required several stitches. Nobby Stiles was headbutted and was later sent off for dissent. Denis Law left the field on a stretcher, and George Best, a marked man from the start, was also dismissed for retaliating when fouled. The perpetrator of the foul on Best, José Hugo Medina, was also sent from the field. The game ended 1-1, which meant that Estudiantes were world club champions by virtue of games won.

One of the fundamental reasons for the competition's history of violence was a clash of playing styles. In the days when few South American footballers plied their trade in European countries, South American teams saw the European style of football as overly physical and robust, whereas Europeans viewed the South American style of play as cynical. It was a volatile mix that prompted the *Daily Telegraph* to refer to the World Club Championship as 'an abomination of a competition'.

As far as European clubs were concerned, another problem with the World Club Championship was that it took place during the domestic season. The need to travel long-haul midweek prompted a number of European Cup winners in the 1970s to withdraw from the World Club Championship. In such instances FIFA offered their place to the beaten finalists in the European Cup, and sometimes these clubs too declined to play.

In 1978, Liverpool declined to enter the World Club Championship in which they were due to play Boca Juniors of Argentina. European Cup runners-up Borussia Moenchengladbach also said no, so the competition was not held in that year.

In 1979, European Cup holders Nottingham Forest declined to play against Olimpia of Asunción in Paraguay. Their place, however, was taken by European Cup runners-up Malmö of Sweden.

FIFA was aware the competition was not held in high regard and re-launched it in 1980. The final was to be played as a one-off match in Tokyo, Japan, as the competition now had its first sponsor, Toyota. There was also now a considerable financial advantage to participation, which led to Nottingham Forest contesting the 'Toyota Cup' in 1980. They lost 1-0 to Nacional of Uruguay.

That match between Forest and Nacional was played on a Wednesday. Forest were due to play a Division One game against Bristol City on the Saturday, so in an effort to minimize the effects of jet lag, Forest manager Brian Clough instructed his players not to reset their watches when in Tokyo. While in Japan, the Forest team adhered to Greenwich Mean Time. They trained at night, slept during the day, and breakfasted when other hotel guests were taking dinner.

The financial incentives for playing in what was now the Toyota Cup were such that no club has declined an invitation to enter since the re-launch of the competition in 1980.

Finals involving British clubs from 1981 to 1999: Liverpool 0 Flamengo (Brazil) 3 in 1981; Peñarol (Uruguay) 2 Aston Villa 0 in 1982; Independiente (Argentina) 1 Liverpool 0 in 1984; and Manchester United 1 Palmeiras (Brazil) 0 in 1999. United remain the only British club to have won the competition.

In 2000, the competition having been overhauled yet again, Manchester United represented Europe. As the Club World Cup took place mid-season, United had to withdraw from the FA Cup. This was a highly controversial decision. The consensus of opinion was that United were pressured into participating in the Club World Cup as their presence in the tournament would aid England's bid to stage the World Cup. The 2000 Club World Cup in Brazil was not a success, the final excepted. Attendances were poor and it was generally felt that the participating clubs were not fully committed to the competition. The 2001 Club World Cup, due to be staged in Spain, was cancelled.

In 2005, FIFA re-launched the competition yet again in association with Toyota, and the venue was switched back to Japan. Liverpool featured in the final that year, losing 1-0 to São Paulo of Brazil.

The current participants in the FIFA Club World Cup comprise the champions from all six FIFA continental federations plus the champions of the host nation (Japan), though the champions of Oceania must play a qualifying play-off tie against the champions of the host nation.

The Club World Cup is scheduled to take place in Japan on an annual basis until at least 2009, when FIFA will invite bids from nations to stage the competition in much the same way as countries bid to stage the European Championship and World Cup.

Origins

FIFA president Jules Rimet and secretary Henri Delaunay (both French) put
forward the idea for a World Cup at FIFA's Annual Congress in Antwerp in
1920. FIFA delegates warmed to the idea but decided the suggestion should be
debated. It must have been some debate: the first World Cup tournament took
place in Uruguay in 1930.

Uruguay was chosen as host nation as they were Olympic football
champions. One can be sure their selection had nothing to do with the fact
that they informed FIFA that should they be chosen they would pay all the
expenses incurred by visiting teams and officials.

The World Cup (also known as the Coupe du Monde) was 35cm high and
weighed 3.8kg. It was made of silver but gold plated and set on a base of lapis
lazuli. It was the work of French sculptor Abel Lafleur, and it depicted the
goddess of victory holding aloft an eight-sided chalice.

1930

The teams that contested the first World Cup were Argentina, Belgium, Bolivia, Brazil, Chile, France, Mexico, Paraguay, Peru, Romania, United States, Uruguay and Yugoslavia. England, Scotland, Wales and Northern Ireland declined to take part due to a row with FIFA over 'sham-amateurism' (payment to players registered as amateurs) in other member countries.

The first matches, taking place simultaneously, were between France and Mexico, and Belgium and the USA. The first player to score in the World Cup was Lucien Laurent, who scored for France in the 19th minute. France went on to win their opening match 4-1.

The USA, whose team contained six British-born players, reached the semi-finals, beating Belgium and Paraguay without conceding a goal.

The France captain, Alex Villaplane, was 'executed' by the French Resistance in 1944 for having collaborated with the Nazis.

The Romanian FA was ordered by their government to play their king, King Carol, who also got to pick the Romanian team. King Carol is the only reigning monarch to have played in the finals of a World Cup.

Host nation Uruguay won the first World Cup, beating Argentina 4-2 after trailing 2-1 at half-time. The first player to score in a World Cup Final was Pablo Dorado (Uruguay), after 12 minutes.

The referee was Jan Langenus (Belgium), whose name you can now mention when asked to name some famous Belgians.

Hector Castro, who scored Uruguay's fourth goal in the final, had no right hand; it was lost as the result of an accident in childhood. During the match Castro sprained his left wrist, which must mean he is the only player ever to accept a winners medal without shaking someone's hand.

1934

FIFA somewhat reluctantly chose Italy as the venue for the 1934 World Cup. They were not keen on staging the tournament in a country ruled by a fascist dictator, concerned as they were that Mussolini might hijack the tournament for political gain. But Il Duce played the 'Uruguay card', in addition agreeing to fund the entire tournament. That swung it.

Uruguay were unable to defend their title as their players were on strike in a dispute over club wages. It remains the only time the holders have not defended their title.

Thirty-two countries entered the 1934 World Cup, which necessitated the first ever qualifying stage. Even host nation Italy were asked to qualify. They were drawn in a group with Greece and . . . er, that was it, just Greece.

Again the home nations declined to enter, but the Irish Republic, then known as Irish Free State, entered a team. The Irish were drawn in a qualifying group which included Holland and Belgium. Holland, along with Belgium, qualified for the finals.

The only player to be sent off during the tournament was Imre Markos of Hungary, in the quarter-final against Austria – the first dismissal in World Cup Finals.

The final was held on 10 June in Rome; Italy beat Czechoslovakia 2-1 (after extra-time). Both teams were captained by goalkeepers, Combi (Italy) and Planicka (Czechoslovakia) – the only instance of this happening in a World Cup Final.

1938

The World Cup's coming home . . . the host nation was France.

Spain did not enter because the country was racked by civil war. Austria qualified for the finals but withdrew due to invasion by Hitler's Nazis. Only one South American team competed – Brazil. Uruguay again didn't enter, and Argentina withdrew over the selection of France as host nation, because they believed the finals should have been awarded to a South American country (e.g. Argentina) as the previous competition was held in Europe. The home nations did not enter as they had resigned from FIFA. FIFA offered Austria's place in the finals to England, but the FA declined. The Irish Republic, now known as Eire, was eliminated in the qualifying stage.

Four Austrian players did in fact compete though their country had withdrawn: they were 'invited' to play for Germany by Hitler. One of them, Hans Pesser, had been very reluctant to do so. Curiously, for a player who had never previously been booked in his career, Pesser was sent off in the early stages of the first match for continually fouling Switzerland's Minelli.

Leonidas da Silva (Brazil) became the first player to claim four goals in a match in the World Cup Finals, against Poland (6-5), though later FIFA records credited him with only three.

The first triple sending-off in a World Cup match occurred in the second round game between Brazil and Czechoslovakia (1-1) – Zeze Procopio and Machado (Brazil), and Riha (Czechoslovakia). Brazil won the replay 2-1. Procopio was so distraught after being dismissed that for a while he sat on the Brazil bench with the trainer's bucket over his head. (Who wouldn't have paid good money to see that?)

The final took place at the Stade Colombes in Paris on 19 June. Italy became the first nation to retain the World Cup by beating Hungary 4-2.

Giuseppe Meazza and Giovanni Ferrari were the only survivors of the Italy team that won in 1934. Thus, they became the first players to win successive World Cup winners medals.

The World Cup and official international football was then suspended for the duration of World War Two. Italy retained the cup during that time. The president of the Italian FA kept the trophy in a shoe box under his bed for fear it would fall into the hands of the occupying Nazis.

1950

With the home nations having rejoined FIFA (1946), they were offered two places in the 1950 World Cup Finals in Brazil. FIFA decreed that the Home International Championship would be accepted as a World Cup qualifying group, the winners and runners-up qualifying for the finals. The Scottish FA stated that Scotland would only participate in the World Cup if they won the Home International Championship, which in the end came down to the final match, at Hampden, between Scotland and England. Roy Bentley (Chelsea), on his England debut, scored the only goal of the game. The Scottish FA obstinately stuck to their guns and remained at home.

England's first World Cup match (qualifier) was against Wales on 15 October 1949 at Ninian Park, Cardiff. England won 4-1, and Jackie Milburn (Newcastle United) scored a hat-trick.

England's first home World Cup match took place not at Wembley, but at Maine Road – the venue for England's 9-2 demolition of Northern Ireland (16 November 1949). Jack Rowley (Manchester United) scored four. Cricketer Willie Watson became the first man to play in a cricket Test match and football World Cup match for England.

As hosts, Brazil became the only country to have competed in all four World Cups. In fact, Brazil have competed in the finals of every World Cup there has ever been.

FIFA did not invite Germany or Japan to participate.

England were drawn in Group 2 along with Spain, Chile and the USA. They made an unconvincing start, though they beat a Chile team that included George Robledo (Newcastle United) 2-0 in Rio de Janeiro. But their next match in Belo Horizonte is arguably England's most humiliating defeat of all time. Playing against a USA team comprising part-time professionals and amateurs, an England side containing Alf Ramsey, Billy Wright, Tom Finney, Wilf Mannion and Stan Mortensen lost 1-0. England hit the woodwork three times, but the only goal of the game was the one scored by the USA's Joe Gaetjens, in the 37th minute.

The USA captain was Eddie McIlvenny, a Scot who had played for Wrexham. The USA coach was also Scottish – Bill Jeffrey. Joe Gaetjens was originally from Haiti, and later died in a Haitian jail for helping organize a guerrilla revolt against the island's notorious dictator Papa Doc Duvalier.

When the result – USA 1 England 0 – was relayed on the wires to Britain, one London news agency thought it was a misprint and released the news that England had won 10-1.

It was during this World Cup that Stan Matthews noticed the lightweight boots worn by the South American players. He bought four pairs from a Rio de Janeiro sports shop and wore them on his return to England when playing for Blackpool. Stan was so impressed with the boots he engaged a company in Yorkshire to make him bespoke pairs. The boots were so light and flexible they could be folded and put into a jacket pocket.

Following England's 1-0 defeat by Spain and subsequent elimination, Stan Matthews and Tom Finney asked the FA for permission to stay on in Brazil so they could study the tactics and technique of the South American players, who had impressed them so much. Their request was denied and they were ordered to travel home with the rest of the England party.

Following England's elimination, not one member of the English press stayed on to report on the World Cup. All were ordered home by their respective editors.

Uruguay won the competition, beating Brazil 2-1 in the last match of the final group (16 July) in Rio de Janeiro. The game marked the first appearance of an Englishman in a World Cup Final – referee George Reader.

Not one player was sent off during the tournament.

1954
Switzerland were awarded the World Cup to mark FIFA's 50th anniversary. Their headquarters were in Zurich.

FIFA again allowed the Home International Championship to serve as a qualifying group, with the winners and the runners-up qualifying for the finals. This time the Scottish FA did not insist on winning the group – just as well: Scotland were runners-up again to England.

Turkey's qualification is the most bizarre of any team to have made it to the finals of a World Cup. They were drawn in a group that comprised only themselves and Spain, and lost 4-1 in Madrid but won 1-0 in Istanbul. Goal difference did not apply so the teams met in a play-off in neutral Rome which ended 2-2 (aet). In their wisdom, FIFA decided the winners should be decided by the drawing of straws by a blind Italian boy. Turkey 'won'.

The Scottish players were offered the choice of receiving a £15 fee for matches or retaining their shirts as keepsakes. Every player opted to keep the shirts.

Unbelievably, the Scotland squad comprised only 13 players, one of them a goalkeeper. The Scottish FA party numbered 23 officials.

Scotland produced a spirited performance in their first match but lost 1-0 to a much-fancied Austria. After the game the Scotland manager, Andy Beattie, resigned in frustration at 'too much interference from Scottish FA officials'. He remains the only manager ever to have resigned during the finals of a World Cup when his team was still in with a chance of progressing further in the tournament.

On a day of blistering sunshine with temperatures in the nineties, in their second match a managerless Scotland were outclassed by Uruguay, losing 7-0. Scotland left-back Willie Cunningham (Preston) was given the run-around by winger Borges, prompting Tommy Docherty to remark, 'Willie is the only player I have seen come off a pitch with a sunburned tongue.'

Hungary (Olympic champions) emerged from the group stage as favourites after beating Korea 9-0 and West Germany 8-3, though the West Germany manager, Sepp Herberger, fielded a team mostly of reserves. The ploy nearly backfired when West Germany finished level on points with Turkey. The two teams met in a play-off which the Germans won 7-2.

The quarter-final between Brazil and Hungary in Berne is one of the most infamous of all World Cup matches. With Hungary (minus the injured Puskás) leading 2-0, Brazil resorted to rough-house play that at times was simply violent. Hungary retaliated, and the game degenerated into a series of brawls. Hungary won 4-2, and both teams finished with only nine players (three had been dismissed, the fourth had left the field due to injury). When the final whistle went, both sets of players set about one another, and spectators also began fighting. The match ended in a riot and was dubbed 'The Battle of Berne'.

In another quarter-final, Austria beat Switzerland 7-5 – the most goals (12) scored in a single World Cup Finals match!

The semi-finals were also high-scoring games: West Germany 6 Austria 1; Hungary 4 Uruguay 2.

The final took place in Berne on 4 July. Hungary raced into a 2-0 lead but, sensationally, West Germany came back to win 3-2.

The attendance for the final was 60,000, half of whom had travelled from West Germany. (Those were the days, when genuine supporters were able to get tickets to see their team in a World Cup Final!)

For a second successive World Cup Final, the referee was English – Bill Ling.

The 1954 World Cup was the first to be televised, though only a handful of matches were broadcast.

1958
The 1958 World Cup in Sweden is the only occasion on which all four home nations have qualified for the finals. Northern Ireland qualified from their group at the expense of Italy and Portugal.

The first player to score a hat-trick in a World Cup match for Scotland was Jackie Mudie (Blackpool) in the qualifying group game against Spain on 8 May 1957. Result: 4-2.

This was the first World Cup Finals to be broadcast worldwide on television, though not all matches were shown.

Prior to the competition few, if any, people had heard of Brazil's 17-year-old forward Pelé. His genius became apparent in this tournament when he scored a hat-trick in the semi-final against France and two goals in the final.

Northern Ireland had the most hectic schedule: they had to play five matches in 12 days.

The assistant England manager was Spurs manager Bill Nicholson, who came up with the idea of playing a defensive formation against Brazil. The match ended goalless. This was the first time Brazil had failed to score in a World Cup match since the competition began in 1930.

The USSR were without star centre-forward Edouard Streltsov, who prior to the tournament was sentenced to 12 years in a Siberian labour camp for assault.

At their first attempt, Wales and Northern Ireland reached the quarter-finals. England failed to get that far, beaten by the USSR in a Group 4 play-off.

France beat West Germany 6-3 to clinch third place.

Just Fontaine scored 13 goals in the tournament for France, which is still the record for an individual.

Brazil beat Sweden 5-2 in the final and became the first country to win the World Cup when playing on a continent other than their own.

George Raynor became the first Englishman to manage a team in a World Cup Final (Sweden).

1962

Chile was chosen as host nation. Prior to the tournament, the country was devastated by an earthquake.

The only home nation to qualify were England.

Bobby Moore, winning only his second cap, made his World Cup debut in England's opening match against Hungary.

Mazola, who played for Brazil in the 1958 World Cup, had since acquired Italian citizenship and this time played for Italy under his new name, José Altafini. Altafini is one of four players to have played for two different countries in the finals of two World Cups: the others are Luis Monti (Argentina 1930 and Italy 1934), Ferenc Puskás (Hungary 1954 and Spain 1962) and José Santamaria (Uruguay 1954 and Spain 1962).

Yugoslav full-back Mujic was ordered back to Yugoslavia by the country's leader, Marshal Tito, following a horrendous tackle on the USSR's Dubinski which resulted in the Russian suffering a broken leg.

The Chile v. Italy game was a violent encounter peppered with brawls. Italy's Mario David was knocked out following one punch from Chile's Lionel Sanchez. The referee was Ken Aston (Birmingham), who later remarked, 'Chile won 2-0 . . . and on points.'

This was the lowest attended of any World Cup Finals. England's three matches attracted a total of only 23,432 spectators. The reason cited was 'high admission prices Chilean football supporters could not afford'. The average attendance was 24,250.

The attendance for the semi-final between Brazil and Chile was 76,594 – nearly 8,000 more than the figure for the final between Brazil and Czechoslovakia (68,679). Brazil won 3-1.

Brazil used only 12 players throughout the tournament – still a record for the World Cup. The only change was Amarildo for the injured Pelé.

1966

England was chosen as host nation. The venues were Wembley, White City Stadium, Villa Park, Hillsborough, Old Trafford, Goodison Park, Roker Park and Ayresome Park.

To comply with FIFA rules regarding the minimum amount of seating, some grounds (for example, Roker Park and Ayresome Park) erected temporary seats on terracing.

Panic gripped the nation on 20 March when the World Cup was stolen while on display at a stamp exhibition in Central Hall, Westminster. Given that the police and the FA were in a right pickle, it was ironic that the trophy was eventually found by a dog named Pickles, in the garden of a house in south London. The dog's owner was David Corbett.

The 1966 World Cup was the first to be commercially exploited on a large scale. Perhaps the most bizarre piece of World Cup merchandise was the glass Wellington boot bearing the tournament logo, which the manufacturers described as 'an ideal ornament and memento of the World Cup for your mantelpiece'. There was also the first World Cup song – 'World Cup Willie' by Lonnie Donegan. Named after the England mascot (a lion, by the way, just in case you thought . . .), the song was a radio hit but not a chart hit. (Can't think why.)

The FA adopted the Union Jack as part of the branding of the World Cup in England, not the flag of St George.

England played every one of their games at Wembley, though had they finished runners-up in their group, they would have played their quarter-final at Hillsborough.

England drew the opening match, against Uruguay, 0-0. It was the first time England had failed to score at Wembley.

The Bulgaria manager was Rudolf Vytlacil, who became the first man to manage two different teams in World Cup Finals. He had been manager of Czechoslovakia in 1962.

The shock result of the tournament was North Korea 1 Italy 0. When the Italian players returned home via Genoa airport they were pelted with tomatoes.

Jimmy Greaves was injured during England's 2-0 victory over France. His replacement was Geoff Hurst, who scored England's winner in the quarter-final against Argentina (1-0), a match that was held up for seven minutes when the Argentina captain Antonio Rattin refused to leave the pitch after being sent off by referee Rudolf Kreitlin (West Germany).

Alf Ramsey never referred to the Argentinian players as 'animals.' When asked to comment on the tournament thus far, what he actually said was, 'The behaviour of some players in the competition reminds me of animals.' This was widely misquoted and erroneously attached to Argentina, which subsequently caused Ramsey and England much grief, particularly when visiting South American countries.

Alf Ramsey threatened to resign as England manager prior to that quarter-final against Argentina following pressure from the FA to omit Nobby Stiles from the team. Ramsey told the FA, 'If Stiles has to go, then so do I.'

On 30 July, England beat West Germany 4-2 (after extra-time) to win the World Cup. Geoff Hurst scored a hat-trick, the only player ever to have done so in a World Cup Final.

The England team received a total bonus of £22,000 for winning the World Cup. They shared the money equally among the 22-man squad, so after tax, each England player received £600. Over the years, TV commentator Kenneth Wolstenholme, who uttered the immortal line 'Some people are on the pitch, they think it's all over . . . it is now!', earned more in royalties from that than the England players did for winning the World Cup.

That was a goal good enough to win the League, the FA Cup, the World Cup and the Grand National.

KENNETH WOLSTENHOLME gets overly excited on BBC TV at the sight of Bobby Charlton's goal for England v. Mexico, 1966 World Cup

In addition to being presented with the World Cup, in the evening Jack Charlton was presented with the Jimmy Riddle Cup. The 1966 World Cup was the first tournament in which drug tests were conducted following every game. One player per team was chosen at random to give a sample of his water; coincidentally, Jack Charlton was selected for testing after every England match. To mark this, FIFA doctors had a specially inscribed cup made and presented it to Jack after the final.

The 1966 World Cup was the first tournament in which every match was broadcast on television, though due to the fact that some games (e.g. quarter-finals) took place at the same time, some matches were shown only in the form of highlights.

England's success and the elimination of Brazil prevented the World Cup from being renamed the Winston Churchill Trophy. Prior to the tournament, FIFA announced that should Brazil win the World Cup for a record third time they would retain the trophy, and a new cup would be commissioned and named in honour of Sir Winston Churchill, who died the previous year. FIFA, it seemed, had forgotten about the Churchill idea by 1970, when Brazil won that third title.

1970

Mexico was host nation. The only home nation to qualify was England, as holders.

In their qualifying group, the matches between Honduras and El Salvador were so bitterly contested they sparked a war between the two countries.

Prior to the tournament, in Bogotá, Colombia, England captain Bobby Moore was arrested and imprisoned on suspicion of stealing a bracelet from a jeweller's shop. The shop assistant who falsely accused him later fled to the USA.

In the opening match between Mexico and the USSR the temperature on the pitch was recorded at 108 degrees. The USSR sent out a team of reserves to stand in the sun for the presentation to officials and the playing of the national anthems. This done, the selected USSR team took to the pitch.

The referee began the second-half of the game between Morocco and West Germany while some Morocco players were still taking to the pitch. Morocco's goalkeeper Allal Benvassou had to sprint down the pitch, arriving in his penalty area just in time to save a goal-bound shot from Uwe Seeler.

Following Gordon Banks's incredible save from Pelé's downward header in the England v. Brazil group match in Guadalajara, Bobby Moore turned to Banks and quipped, 'You're getting old, Banksy . . . you used to hold those.'

When England were 2-0 up against West Germany in the quarter-final, Alf Ramsey replaced Bobby Charlton with Colin Bell. The Germans came back to win 3-2. Gordon Banks was suffering from a stomach upset and watched the game on TV in his hotel bedroom. The match was broadcast on Mexican TV an hour behind real time, so when the England players returned to the hotel to visit Banks, the broadcast had only reached half-time, with England leading 2-0. Banks at first didn't believe his team-mates when they told him they had lost.

Jairzinho created a World Cup record by scoring in every round.

In arguably the greatest World Cup Final of all time, Brazil beat Italy 4-1. Pelé became the second player to score in two World Cup Finals (1958 and 1970), after another Brazilian, Vava (1958 and 1962).

1974
Host nation was West Germany.

The teams competed for a new trophy. Following Brazil's victory in 1970, to mark their third World Cup success, FIFA awarded them the Jules Rimet trophy for posterity. In 1983, the trophy was stolen in Rio de Janeiro and never recovered.

The new (and current) trophy was designed and created by Italian sculptor Silvio Gazzaniga. It stands 36cm high and is made from solid gold with a base of malachite.

The only home nation to qualify was Scotland. They remained unbeaten, winning one and drawing two of their group matches (including a goalless encounter with Brazil) but failed to qualify from their group on goal difference. Scotland were the only unbeaten team in the competition.

In the group stages, West Germany played East Germany for the first time. East Germany won 1-0.

West Germany beat Holland 2-1 in the final. The referee was Jack Taylor (Wolverhampton), who awarded a penalty to Holland in the very first minute of the match; it was converted by Johan Neeskens. When the penalty was awarded, not one West German player had yet touched the ball.

1978
A record number of 107 countries entered the World Cup. The host nation was Argentina.

Once again, the only home nation to qualify was Scotland. Such was the hyperbole surrounding manager Ally McLeod's team that over 30,000 fans turned up at Hampden Park to wave goodbye to the Scottish squad even though no game was taking place!

For the fourth successive finals the opening match (Poland v. West Germany) was a goalless draw.

Following Scotland's 3-1 defeat against Peru, winger Willie Johnson failed a drugs test and was sent home by the Scottish FA, who banned him from international football for life.

Due to the time difference, some matches broadcast live on British television started at 10.30 p.m.

Prior to the final, the Argentines kept the match officials and the Dutch team waiting on the pitch for six minutes before they eventually emerged. The start of the match was further delayed when Argentinian players complained to referee Sergio Gonella about the protection wrapped around René van der Kerkhof's injured arm.

Argentina defeated Holland 3-1, after extra-time. It was their first World Cup success.

1982

The 1982 World Cup in Spain was extended to include 24 teams, but the idea of having two group qualification stages prior to the semi-finals rather than a straight knockout round was not well received – by anybody.

England, Scotland and Northern Ireland qualified for the finals.

Hungary created a record score in the finals of a World Cup, beating El Salvador 10-1.

England qualified from the initial group stage. In the second group phase, they remained unbeaten and did not concede a goal. They didn't score one either, and failed to progress, finishing a point behind group winners West Germany.

Northern Ireland also failed to progress past the second group stage.

Kenny Dalglish and Joe Jordan (the only Scot to score in three World Cups) created a record by playing in their third World Cup Finals for Scotland.

In a thrilling semi-final between West Germany and France (3-2 aet), German goalkeeper Harald Schumacher floored France's Patrick Battiston without playing the ball after racing to the edge of his penalty area as the French substitute bore down on goal. Battiston was knocked unconscious, lost three teeth, and was stretchered from the field. Amazingly, Schumacher stayed on.

Italy beat West Germany 3-1 in the final. The Italian hero was Paolo Rossi, who finished as the tournament's leading goalscorer with six goals. Previously he had been banned in Italy for his alleged involvement in a football bribe scandal.

At 40, Italy goalkeeper Dino Zoff became the oldest captain of a World Cup-winning team.

Arnaldo Cesar Coelho (Brazil) created World Cup history by becoming the first South American to referee a World Cup Final.

1986

Mexico became the first nation to stage two World Cups. FIFA's original choice as host nation was Colombia, but the Colombians did not have the necessary finance, facilities or infrastructure to stage the tournament. Perhaps what also did not help their cause were reports alleging that two members of the Colombian FA had been involved in a gun battle in a district of Bogotá.

The Scotland manager was Alex Ferguson (also manager of Aberdeen). Ferguson took over as manager following the tragic death of Jock Stein during Scotland's final qualifying match against Wales.

In addition to Scotland, England and Northern Ireland also qualified for the competition.

In England's group match against Morocco, Ray Wilkins (Manchester United) was dismissed after advancing towards the referee and throwing the ball at the official in frustration at a decision. (Cynics were given to remark that it was the only time Wilkins played the ball forward.)

The South Korea goalkeeper was called Oh, prompting one TV commentator to say, 'Oh dear!' when he conceded a soft goal against Argentina.

Morocco became the first African nation to progress beyond the first round of a World Cup Finals.

England's hero and the tournament's leading goalscorer was Gary Lineker with six goals – the only British player to finish as the leading marksman in the finals of a World Cup.

England lost 2-1 to Argentina in the quarter-finals. Argentina's first goal was Maradona's infamous 'Hand of God' effort. The Argentinians went on to beat West Germany 3-2 in the final.

The aggregate attendance for the finals was 2.4 million at an average of 46,000 per match – at the time a record for the finals of a World Cup.

1990
Italy was host nation.

England, Scotland and, for the first time, the Republic of Ireland qualified. Italia 90 was Scotland's fifth successive World Cup.

The Scotland manager, Andy Roxburgh, had been a team-mate of Alex Ferguson at Falkirk.

The opening match saw Cameroon beat Argentina 1-0 (Omam Biyik) despite having two players sent off.

England won Group F. Though the group comprised four teams (six matches) it produced only one win: England 1 Egypt 0.

Italy goalkeeper Walter Zenga created a new record for World Cup Finals by not conceding a goal for 517 minutes (five matches) until Claudio Caniggia of Argentina put one past him in the semi-finals.

The TV audience for England's semi-final against West Germany (1-1 and 3-4 on penalties) on 4 July 1990 was recorded as 25.6 million – a record viewing figure for British television.

Bobby Robson became the first manager to lead England to the semi-finals of a World Cup on foreign soil.

Following England's semi-final defeat to West Germany, Paul Gascoigne cried uncontrollably and won the hearts of the nation. Peter Shilton later commented in his autobiography, 'Gazza went on to make more money out of tears than Ken Dodd.'

The England players who scored in the penalty shoot-out against West Germany were Gary Lineker, Peter Beardsley and David Platt. Those who failed were Stuart Pearce and Chris Waddle.

The Final between West Germany and Argentina (1-0) created unwanted World Cup history. It was the first World Cup Final in which a player was sent off – Pedro Monzon, who was later followed by Gustavo Dezotti (both Argentina).

Franz Beckenbauer is the only man to have won the World Cup both as a player and as manager (1974 and 1990) – and as a bidder for 2006!

Argentina had a total of three players dismissed and received 21 bookings – a record for a team in the finals of a World Cup.

The 52 matches produced 115 goals at an average of 2.2 per game – the lowest of any World Cup Finals.

1994
The USA was host nation.

For the first time since 1950, when they first participated in a World Cup, none of the Home Nations qualified, though the Republic of Ireland did.

FIFA introduced a new rule: the mandatory stretchering-off of any injured player. This led to numerous instances of stretcher-bearers appearing on a pitch only to return empty-handed when a supposedly injured player quickly took to his feet. In the match between Belgium and Morocco, the bearers ventured on to the pitch to attend to an injured player only to return immediately as they had forgotten the stretcher.

Swiss referee Leo Roethlisberger became the first match official to be sent home during the finals of a World Cup. He was adjudged to have missed a blatant penalty offence committed by Germany's Thomas Helmer in the game against Belgium. The consensus of opinion was that FIFA had treated Mr Roethlisberger 'too harshly'.

Rigobert Song, aged 17, became the youngest player to be sent off in a World Cup Finals match when playing for Cameroon against Brazil.

Bora Milutinovic created World Cup history by becoming the first man to manage three different countries in three consecutive World Cup Finals: Mexico (1986), Costa Rica (1990) and USA (1994).

The match between Bulgaria and Mexico was held up for 16 minutes after the crossbar collapsed, broke, and had to be replaced.

The final between Italy and Brazil was the first not to produce a goal, even after extra-time had been played. Brazil won 3-2 on penalties.

The USA tournament produced 141 goals – 26 more than in Italia 90 and nine more than Mexico 86.

1998
France was host nation.

From the first qualifying match between Dominica and Antigua (10 March 1996) to the final (12 July 1998), this was the longest World Cup in duration, at 28 months.

A record 174 countries participated, 160 more than in the first World Cup (1930).

Australia's coach in the qualifying stages was Terry Venables.

Following England's qualifying match against Moldova, the England players donated their match fees totalling £30,000 to the Princess Diana Memorial Fund.

Of the home nations and Ireland, only England and Scotland qualified.

Bora Milutinovic made it four World Cup Finals teams managed: he was now in charge of Nigeria.

England manager Glenn Hoddle went on record as saying that David Beckham was 'not concentrating on the tournament'. Hoddle did not include Beckham in the starting line-up for England's first two matches, against Tunisia and Romania, though he did appear as a substitute for the injured Paul Ince in the latter.

For their final group match against Tunisia, the Romanian players dyed their hair yellow.

Cameroon defender Rigobert Song became the first player to be sent off in the finals of two World Cups when he was dismissed against Chile.

David Beckham was recalled for England's third group game, against Colombia, and characteristically scored with a 25-yard free-kick. It was his first goal for England.

Michael Owen scored his first World Cup goal in the 2-2 draw with Argentina in the second round. His first and only other goal for England came in the warm-up friendly against Morocco on 27 May 1998.

It was against Argentina that David Beckham was sent off for the first time when playing for England, for retaliation after being fouled by Diego Simeone.

England lost to Argentina on penalties (after 2-2); the England players who failed to convert their spot-kicks were David Batty and Paul Ince. For a second successive time England were eliminated from a World Cup on penalties (1990 and 1998, having not qualified in 1994).

Lothar Matthäus created an all-time record when he played his 22nd match in a finals tournament. He ended France 98 with 25 appearances in World Cup Finals to his name over five competitions.

The final between France and Brazil was the first between host and holders. France won 3-0.

When the Brazil team sheet for the final was handed in to the match officials, it did not contain the name of star player Ronaldo. Brazil subsequently handed a second team sheet to the officials that did include Ronaldo, and as it was submitted before the deadline this was quite within the rules. Rumours abounded as to why Ronaldo had originally been omitted from the line-up, the most common being that he had suffered a breakdown due to mental exhaustion.

The tournament produced another new unwanted record: 22 red and 254 yellow cards.

2002
For the first time in the history of the competition, the finals were hosted by two countries, Japan and South Korea. It was also the first time the World Cup was held in Asia.

Managed by Sven-Göran Eriksson, in the qualifying stages England beat Germany 5-1 in Munich. This was England's record margin of victory against Germany (home or away) but not their record score, which remains 6-3 (Berlin, 1938).

England and the Republic of Ireland qualified.

On the eve of the finals, Republic of Ireland captain Roy Keane was sent home following a row with manager Mick McCarthy.

Thierry Henry was sent off for the first time when playing for France against Uruguay.

For the first time in the history of the World Cup, the holders (France) were eliminated without having won a match or scored a goal.

When Germany beat Saudi Arabia 8-0, Miroslav Klose became the first player to score a World Cup Finals hat-trick with his head.

Having recovered from a broken bone in his left foot, David Beckham captained England for the first time in the finals of a World Cup.

England reached the quarter-finals and were beaten 2-1 by Brazil, this after having taken a first-half lead through Michael Owen. Brazil's winning goal was (depending on your viewpoint) (i) a spectacular free-kick from 35 yards by Ronaldinho so precisely struck that it beat David Seaman, who had taken up an excellent position, and went into the net, or, (ii) a speculative lob by Ronaldinho from 35 yards that caught David Seaman, not for the first time in his career, in no-man's land before, to the amazement of the Brazilian and everyone watching, the ball dropped into the net.

As he waited to take a corner-kick during the match between Brazil and Turkey, Rivaldo was hit on the legs by the ball which had been kicked towards him by Turkey's Hakan Unsal. The Brazilian fell to the ground clutching his head. Unsal received a second yellow card which resulted in his dismissal. Rivaldo was subsequently fined by FIFA for 'ungentlemanly conduct'.

Seventeen players were red-carded, among them Claudio Caniggia of Argentina, who became the first player to be sent off in the finals of a World Cup while not actually being on the field of play. He was on the bench as a substitute.

Bora Milutinovic continued to break his own record for having managed the most teams at World Cup Finals. He made it five with China.

A record aggregate worldwide TV audience of 45 billion watched the finals.

Brazil regained their world crown, beating Germany 2-0 in the final. Prior to that Germany had conceded only one goal in the competition, in a group match against Ireland (1-1).

A record nine managers lost their jobs as a result of their respective teams' performances in the finals: Jerzy Engel (Poland), Srecko Katanec (Slovenia), Roger Lemerre (France), Bora Milutinovic (China), Cesar Maldini (Paraguay), Victor Pua (Uruguay), Oleg Romantsev (Russia), Winifried Schafer (Cameroon) and Jomo Sono (South Africa).

2006

The host nation was Germany.

All but one of the previous winners of the World Cup qualified: Argentina, Brazil (holders), England, France, Germany (hosts) and Italy. The odd one out was Uruguay.

FIFA granted German evangelical churches the rights to broadcast matches free of charge.

In a repetition of David Beckham's situation prior to the 2002 finals, Wayne Rooney suffered a broken metatarsal prior to the 2006 finals. He made a remarkable recovery from his injury and appeared in his first World Cup Finals as a substitute against Trinidad and Tobago.

Rooney continued to mirror Beckham's 2002 experience when he was red-carded during England's quarter-final with Portugal for stamping on Ricardo Carvalho.

England exited the finals of a World Cup for a third time on a penalty shoot-out, losing 3-1 to Portugal (0-0 aet). The only England player to successfully convert a penalty was Owen Hargreaves; those who failed were Frank Lampard, Steven Gerrard and Jamie Carragher.

Only five teams scored more than one goal in the knockout stages: Germany, Argentina, Italy, Brazil and France.

This was the only World Cup when the first and last goals of the competition were scored by defenders: Philipp Lahm (opening match, Germany v. Costa Rica) and Marco Materazzi (Italy v. France, the final).

Italy won the World Cup, beating France 5-3 on penalties (after 1-1), and created a new goalscoring record for the tournament: no one player scored more than two goals, but ten different Italian players scored in the competition.

 Owen Hargreaves was far and away England's best player in the finals. That says it all for me.
JIMMY GREAVES

2010

Perhaps the most amazing and, arguably, spookiest World Cup fact . . .

Brazil won the World Cup in 2002 and also won it in 1962. Add 1962 to 2002 and it comes to 3,964.

Brazil won the World Cup in 1994 and had previously won it in 1970. Add 1970 to 1994 and it comes to 3,964.

Argentina won the World Cup in 1986 and had previously won it in 1978. Add 1978 to 1986 and it comes to 3,964.

West Germany won the World Cup in 1990 and had previously won it in 1974. Add 1974 to 1990 and it comes to 3,964.

Deduct 2010 from 3,964 and it comes to 1954. The winners of the 1954 World Cup were West Germany, so if you fancy a bet on who will win the 2010 World Cup in South Africa, get your money on Germany!